28May'80

11.75

B+T

THE
CHRISTIAN DOCTRINE OF MAN

THE
CHRISTIAN DOCTRINE
OF MAN

BY

H. WHEELER ROBINSON, M.A., D.D.

LATE PRINCIPAL OF REGENT'S PARK COLLEGE, LONDON

THIRD EDITION

(WITH AN APPENDIX, "RECENT THOUGHT ON THE DOCTRINE OF SIN")

EDINBURGH : T. & T. CLARK, 38 GEORGE STREET

Printed in Great Britain by
Lewis Reprints Ltd.,
member of Brown, Knight & Truscott group
London and Tonbridge

for

T. & T. CLARK, EDINBURGH

ISBN 0 567 22219 5

First Edition .   .   . *April 1911*
Second Edition .   . *May 1913*
Third Edition   . *December 1926*
Fourth Edition .   *October 1958*
Reprinted   .   .   . *April 1974*

PREFACE TO FIRST EDITION

———◆———

A GENERAL introduction to a great subject can be useful by giving a concise outline of its contents or by arousing independent thought on its problems. I have tried to make this volume useful in both ways to the student and to the general reader. It brings together much historical and exegetical detail not elsewhere accessible in a single volume written from a modern standpoint; it frequently emphasizes rather than attempts to reconcile the antitheses from which the problems of this subject spring. This will be apparent from the "Table of Contents", which the reader is advised to study before turning to the text. In particular, I have presented the psychology of the Old Testament (on which that of the New rests), of the Patristic writers, and of the modern period with more detail than the general reader may desire or the general scale of the book may seem to warrant. I have done this in the conviction that the psychology of any age must profoundly affect its interpretation of Christian anthropology. The key to the Pelagian Controversy, for example, lies in the difference between the conceptions of personality entertained by the opponents. My initial approach to the whole subject was through a study of the Hebrew psychological terms; this has probably affected the treatment and emphasis throughout.

In this connection, I am indebted to Messrs. Hodder & Stoughton for permission to reproduce several paragraphs from my contribution to the volume called *Mansfield College Essays*, under the title " Hebrew Psychology in Relation to Pauline Anthropology."

It is hardly necessary to remind the reader that almost every section and subsection of this book touches controversial points, and that no two writers will agree on every detail of such a subject as this. I have spared no pains to secure accuracy of fact, but am very conscious, in other respects, of the limitations of this volume; some of these are due to the necessary limits of space, though far more to the demands the subject makes on both theological learning and Christian experience.

The book (though not the subject) was undertaken at the suggestion of Dr. Hastings. In addition to my obligations to the general literature of the subject indicated in the notes, I am indebted to several friends for helpful criticisms and suggestions. My former tutors, Drs. Buchanan Gray and Vernon Bartlet, have read in manuscript Chapters I. and III. respectively; Principal R. S. Franks, M.A., B.Litt., Chapter II.; the Revs. D. Stewart, M.A., and H. C. Rowse, M.A., Chapters IV. and V., and the entire proof. In particular, I am indebted to Mr. Stewart for constant and unwearied assistance throughout the preparation of the whole book; those who may find it of use will be under a much greater obligation than they will realize to his keen insight into philosophical and social problems.

H. W. R.

RAWDON, *March* 1911.

PREFACE TO SECOND EDITION

———◆———

It is gratifying to learn, from the comparatively early
need for a second edition of this book, that it appears
to be answering the purpose for which it was written.
No changes have been made in this edition, beyond a
few trifling corrections. I am grateful for the generous
welcome given to the book by its critics, and especially
for the fact that so many who have differed from its
standpoint or conclusions have found it worthy of their
approval as a contribution to the subject. Amongst
suggestions for its improvement, two in particular deserve
mention—a fuller treatment of the doctrine of the Spirit
in the New Testament, and a wider review of the
mediæval influences (such as monasticism, the penitential
system, and sacramental piety) which modified the
conception of human nature within the Catholic Church.
In both cases, the omissions are chiefly due to considerations of space; the usefulness of such a book as this
largely depends on its brevity. But to the former topic
I hope eventually to return, in a review of the history
of the doctrine of the Holy Spirit, on lines similar to
those of the present volume.

H. W. R.

May 1913.

PREFACE TO THIRD EDITION

—◆—

I AM indebted to the Editor of *The Expository Times* for permission to reprint the article which forms the Appendix to this edition. The text of the book is virtually unchanged; but a few references to recent literature have been added in the footnotes.

H. W. R.

REGENT'S PARK COLLEGE,
LONDON, N.W. 8,
November 1926.

CONTENTS

——◆——

INTRODUCTION.

PAGE

The unity of human nature ; its progressive interpretation through the development of Christian doctrine ; the relation of this doctrine to modern thought 1

CHAPTER I.

THE OLD TESTAMENT DOCTRINE OF MAN.

1. INTRODUCTION.
    (a) The Old Testament in relation to anthropology . . 4
    (b) The characteristics of primitive psychology . . . 6
    (c) Hebrew ideas of man contrasted with those of some other ancient or primitive peoples 8
2. THE EVOLUTION OF THE PSYCHOLOGICAL TERMS.
    (a) The physiology of the Hebrews 11
    (b) The principles of life (breath and blood) . . . 14
    (c) The physical organs to which psychical functions are ascribed 20
    (d) Inter-relation of the resultant terminology . . . 26
3. THE RELIGIOUS VALUE OF THE INDIVIDUAL.
    (a) Corporate personality 27
    (b) The development of individualism 30
    (c) The problem of individual retribution . . . 34
    (d) The eschatology of the individual 39
4. THE CONCEPTION OF SIN.
    (a) Terminology 42
    (b) Earlier limitations of morality 45
    (c) The prophetic union of morality and religion . . 49
    (d) Post-exilic developments 52
    (e) Relation to later dogmatic theories 55

5. THE RELATION OF MAN TO NATURE AND GOD. PAGE
    (*a*) Creation and the natural order of the world .   .   . 61
    (*b*) Providence and the Spirit of God   63
    (*c*) The fellowship of man and God   65

CHAPTER II.

THE NEW TESTAMENT DOCTRINE OF MAN.

1. INTRODUCTION.
    (*a*) The Old Testament foundation   68
    (*b*) Anthropology of the later Judaism   70
    (*c*) The chief New Testament conceptions   .   .   . 75
2. THE SYNOPTIC TEACHING OF JESUS.
    (*a*) The historic setting   76
    (*b*) The supreme value of man as the child of God   .   . 80
    (*c*) The duty of man as the child of God 83
    (*d*) The brotherhood of man   87
    (*e*) The broken sonship and the unbroken Fatherhood   .   . 91
    (*f*) Life beyond death   99
3. THE PAULINE ANTHROPOLOGY.
    (*a*) Psychology   104
    (*b*) The sovereignty of sin and death   .   .   . 112
    (*c*) Deliverance by the Spirit   122
    (*d*) Freedom and the absoluteness of grace   .   . 131
    (*e*) The social relationships of man   .   .   . 134
4. THE JOHANNINE ANTHROPOLOGY.
    (*a*) God and the world   136
    (*b*) The darkness of the world   138
    (*c*) Faith in Christ; the new birth   .   .   . 140
    (*d*) Eternal life   144
5. DATA AND PROBLEMS FOR THE CHURCH .   .   . 148

CHAPTER III.

DOGMATIC ANTHROPOLOGY.

1. INTRODUCTION.
    The contrast and conflict between Hebrew and Greek ideas of
        human nature   151
2. PATRISTIC THEORIES OF HUMAN NATURE.
    (*a*) Psychology   156
    (*b*) The origin of the soul   161
    (*c*) Original and fallen state of man   .   .   . 163
    (*d*) Immortality and resurrection 169

3. THE CONFLICT WITH DUALISM. PAGE
    (*a*) The problem of Sin 171
    (*b*) The Gnostic dualism 172
    (*c*) The Manichæan dualism 174
    (*d*) The privative theory of evil 175
    (*e*) The will as the cause of sin 177
4. THE PELAGIAN CONTROVERSY AND ITS SEQUEL.
    (*a*) The opposed interests : freedom and grace . . . 178
    (*b*) The history of the controversy 183
    (*c*) The anthropology of Augustine 187
    (*d*) The sequel in "Semi-Pelagianism" . . . 191
5. MEDIAEVAL AND SCHOLASTIC ANTHROPOLOGY.
    (*a*) The Mediaeval Church and the institution of Penance . 195
    (*b*) Mediaeval Augustinianism 197
    (*c*) Merit and grace in Scholasticism 201
    (*d*) The anthropology of Aquinas 204
    (*e*) The anthropology of Duns Scotus 207
6 TRIDENTINE ANTHROPOLOGY AND THE AUGUSTINIAN REACTION.
    (*a*) Original Sin and Justification at the Council of Trent . 209
    (*b*) Jansenism 213
7. THE REFORMATION.
    (*a*) The preparation in mediaeval religion . . . 215
    (*b*) The central principle—Justification by Faith . . . 217
    (*c*) The formulation of Protestant anthropology . . . 221
    (*d*) The doctrine of Predestination, and the Arminian reaction . 223

CHAPTER IV.

THE CONTRIBUTIONS OF POST-REFORMATION SCIENCE AND THOUGHT.

1. THE LARGER HORIZON 229
2 THE SCIENTIFIC CONTRIBUTION.
    (*a*) The birth of modern science 231
    (*b*) The founders of modern science 231
    (*c*) Resultant conceptions 233
    (*d*) Evolution in relation to Christian anthropology . . 242
3. THE PHILOSOPHIC CONTRIBUTION.
    (*a*) Influence of the old Scholasticism and the new Science . 245
    (*b*) The metaphysical reality of spirit 246
    (*c*) The individuality of spiritual life 250
    (*d*) The values of personality 253
    (*e*) The philosophic recognition of Christian data . . 256

4. THE SOCIOLOGICAL CONTRIBUTION.   PAGE
    (*a*) The transition from an individual to a social emphasis . 257
    (*b*) Some typical theories of society   259
    (*c*) The rise of social democracy 264
    (*d*) The socialization of Christian anthropology .   . . 265

CHAPTER V.

THE CHRISTIAN DOCTRINE OF MAN IN RELATION TO CURRENT THOUGHT.

1. INTRODUCTION.
    (*a*) Relation of historical to systematic statement   . . 268
    (*b*) The Biblical data of Christian experience   .   . . 270
    (*c*) The ecclesiastical development of the problems   . . 272
    (*d*) Lines of modern approach   273
2. HUMAN PERSONALITY.
    (*a*) Personality and evolution   275
    (*b*) Human nature as interpreted by Christ's Person   . . 278
    (*c*) The eternal values and their independence of death . . 282
3. FREEDOM AND MORAL EVIL.
    (*a*) The reality and problems of freedom 288
    (*b*) Moral evil in relation to freedom   294
4 SIN AND SALVATION.
    (*a*) Man's worth to God 300
    (*b*) The nature and universality of sin   301
    (*c*) The consequences of sin   307
    (*d*) The cosmic significance of sin   313
    (*e*) Grace as cosmic atonement   315
    (*f*) The Spirit of God in the Christian life   .   . . 321
    (*g*) The relation of the human will to the divine .   . . 333
5. MAN IN SOCIETY.
    (*a*) Individual development socially conditioned .   . . 338
    (*b*) The basis of Christian brotherhood 341
    (*c*) The inter-relation of human and divine fellowship   . . 343
6 CONCLUSION.
    (*a*) Historical continuity of the Christian idea of man   . . 344
    (*b*) Some rival conceptions of human nature   .   . . 346
    (*c*) The adequacy of the Christian idea of man .   . . 350

APPENDIX. RECENT THOUGHT ON THE DOCTRINE OF SIN . 353
GENERAL INDEX 368
INDEX OF TEXTS 373

THE CHRISTIAN DOCTRINE
OF MAN

———◆———

INTRODUCTION.

THE Christian doctrine of man is in historical influence
the greatest, as in its intrinsic claim the noblest, of all
attempts to interpret human life. Beneath the boundless
wealth of individual variety which characterizes that life
there lies the ultimate unity which any reference to
"human nature" must imply. The plays of Shakespeare
illustrate the immense variety of human character, but
they are not less impressive as to its unity. The varieties
of religious experience have perhaps never been presented
so fully as in *The Pilgrim's Progress*; but behind the
various types of the long procession on the road to Zion
there is the individual experience of *Grace Abounding*,
revealing Bunyan himself as passing through almost all
the conditions he depicts. The variety in unity of his
own life enabled him to recognize and portray the unity
in variety of the lives around him; but that was only
possible on the assumption of a common human
nature in which he and they shared. What all great
literature or art implies, theology may fairly claim; the

I

postulate of the unity of the human race is not an arbitrary dogmatic claim, but an inevitable assumption made by every serious interpretation of life.

But can the ultimate unity which constitutes human nature be stated adequately for all the generations in terms drawn from any one of them? If there is progress of the race, must there not be progress in the interpretation of its nature? The Christian doctrine of man begins historically with the life and teaching of Jesus Christ. He gathered round Him a group of men who, to some degree, were trained to share His attitude towards man. But this attitude is genetically related to that of the highest religion of Israel, whilst the literature of the Old Testament carries us still further back for its own elucidation to the dim beginnings of primitive life and civilization. Again, from that group of disciples there has come the Church of many lands and many centuries. The earlier conceptions, transplanted into new environments, have been transformed in many ways. Yet they have not lost their vital continuity with Him who is their source; their history is the record of the germination and growth of the seed sown by Jesus Christ. Its inherent vitality is the more evident through this continued power of assimilation. We shall best come to know this doctrine by tracing the history of it; its statement in terms of to-day can be no more than a cross-section of this continuous development. The toil of historical detail is indispensable; in this way alone we recover something of the living individuality of growth; it is this which makes the unity of the doctrine as of the race more than a colourless and abstract generalization. Historical details are to doctrine what the individual features are to noble portraiture; they are the medium through which we catch a glimpse of the eternal and abiding realities.

In any attempt to understand the Christian doctrine of man, we ought to remember two things. On the one hand, it has so passed into the common stock of our higher Western thought as to be the chief formative influence in our conception of personality. Our familiarity with it, our unconscious dependence upon it, may result in the failure to do justice to it. Men unfamiliar with the history of modern thought are often apt to despise the "dogmas" which have mediated to us some of our highest conceptions. On the other hand, in the natural eagerness of the Christian to defend those dogmas from such injustice, he must not forget that every generation has its part to play in the unceasing evolution of Christian doctrine, and that our part to-day is a somewhat stirring one. The primitive conceptions of Hebrew cosmology are replaced in the modern mind by the evolutionary view of man; the wider horizon of nature and history involves many changes in earlier conclusions. Some problems fall into the background, others emerge for the first time, others again reveal their depth and difficulty by their presence in the wider as in the narrower horizon. We cannot evade them, except by being false to our stewardship of a great inheritance. The Christian doctrine of man is not to be secluded from the thought of the age in timorous unbelief; it is to be employed amid the common wealth of the world so that it may be worthily developed by us. as it was by those who went before us.

CHAPTER I.

THE OLD TESTAMENT DOCTRINE OF MAN.

1. INTRODUCTION.

(*a*) *The Old Testament in relation to anthropology.*— The object of this chapter is to collect and interpret the evidence afforded by the Old Testament as to the ideas of human personality current amongst the Hebrew (or Jewish) people. It is customary to refer to the result as "The Old Testament Doctrine of Man", and the custom is here retained for the sake of convenience; but it must not be supposed that any formal statement of belief on these matters is contained in the literature itself, much less that the title is intended to suggest that the results of our inquiry are necessarily binding for Christian faith. The precise degree of the authority of Scripture is a question for subsequent consideration, when the actual contents of Scripture have first been studied and understood. He who believes that there is a unique activity of divine purpose in Hebrew and Jewish life and thought, which culminates providentially in the Christian revelation, can be quite content to study both Testaments on the plane of "natural" development; the more faithfully he interprets the historical record, the more clearly will the "supernatural" ultimately prove its presence. Consequently, the Bible is here studied simply as ancient literature, and

interpreted simply in the light of ancient thought, however
remote from modern that may prove to be. If we find in
the Old Testament some idea concerning man resembling
that suggested by an ancient place of burial or a modern
camp of Bedouins, we may assume, failing evidence to the
contrary, that both are natural phenomena and that one may
throw light on the other. Sometimes the primitive character of such an idea is sufficiently obvious from the Old
Testament itself; more often, its original meaning must
be patiently elicited as a half-hidden survival from earlier
times, which has become the vehicle of higher ideas. It
will often involve a distinct effort to put aside the interpretation natural to an Augustine or a Calvin, with which
we have been familiarized, and to read the Old Testament
in its original sense; yet this original sense is often the
key to historic problems of exegesis. Indeed, it is best to
assume, as a working hypothesis, that the meaning we
ourselves are inclined to give to the words of Scripture
will in no case be quite that of the original writer; we
may repeat the same words, but we cannot easily recall
the same attitude in saying them, and it is attitude that
says the last word as to meaning. The application of
this method of study to the Old Testament may sometimes reveal crude and primitive ideas that repel us;
indeed, some are ready to assert that their presence is
incredible in a divine revelation. But just as we rightly
trace the highest prophetic ideas of the Old Testament
onwards to their perfect expression in Christ, so we may
follow back the lower anthropological conceptions to their
origin in primitive belief and practice; the higher is no
more degraded by the presence of the lower amid which
it finds expression than a mother's love by the ignorance

and rags through which it shines, or a doctor's skill by the loathsome disease it cures.

(*b*) *The characteristics of primitive psychology.*—Amid the mass of anthropological detail, there are certain broad principles of distinction between ancient (including Old Testament) psychology and modern; but it should be noted at the outset that the use of the term "psychology" itself does not remain quite the same when we attach to it the adjective "ancient" or "modern." In regard to the ancient world, and primitive thought in general, the study of psychology must ignore the boundaries drawn by the modern mind between anthropology, theology, physiology, and philosophy; facts must be drawn from all these and other sources, if we are to reconstruct ancient ideas of personality. Moreover, the term "psychology" must not be taken to imply amongst the ancients the scientific study and systematic statement of states of consciousness; this hardly begins anywhere before Aristotle, and is, in large measure, a quite modern development. The points to be emphasized as in general distinguishing ancient from modern ideas about man are chiefly these three. (1) The idea of the soul is not that of a metaphysical entity, or even of an x in the equation of life; it is that of a quasi-physical *something*, frequently identified (as, for example, by the Hebrews) with the breath. But the body inhabited by this breath-soul is not a mere machine; because it is alive, every part of it may have psychical as well as physiological functions; to the primitive mind, indeed, that distinction does not exist. "The savage", as Frazer says (*The Golden Bough*, ii. p. 353), "commonly believes that by eating the flesh of an animal or man he acquires not only the physical, but even the moral and intellectual qualities which were characteristic of that animal or man." To quote this is not to imply that the Hebrews passed through a cannibal stage; but it is intended to imply that the psychological standpoint of the early Hebrew, as we can gather it from the Old Testament, is genetically connected with that which underlies such practices. This will be seen when we come to the study of the Hebrew psychological terms. It is important to notice that, as will be illustrated from Hebrew physiology, ancient ignorance of the nervous system and of the circulation of the blood caused the physical organs to be regarded as detached and self-contained. *We* find it easy to leave them their physiological activity, whilst transferring the psychical and moral aspects of their use to brain and " conscience "; but we stand on the physiological labours of centuries, on results necessarily unknown to the ancient world. (2) Another important point of difference lies in the ancient conception of the accessibility of personality to all manner of external influences, not exercised through the natural sense-organs. The modern man, like Bunyan, thinks of Man-soul as having simply Eye-gate, Ear-gate, Nose-gate, etc., whilst extra-sensuous influence, if admitted at all by his range of thought, is spiritualized and confined to his relations with God. But, to get the ancient point of view, we have to think of telepathic powers, now ascribed to a few, as possessed by many and experienced by all; we must think of the phenomena of fetishism and totemism, demonology and witchcraft, of a vast world of possible outside influences extending (for the Hebrew) right up to the Spirit of God. Once more, let it be said, such a grouping by no means minimizes the worth or the reality of divine influences on man; all that here concerns us is to notice the manner in which this influence is conceived to act, and the parallels to such belief afforded in our own days by village ignorance, revivalistic excitement, or spiritualistic ideas of "possession." (3) Finally, throughout ancient thought in general, we find what Mozley has called "the defective sense of individuality" (*Ruling Ideas in Early Ages*, p. 87), but what is better described positively as "the idea of corporate personality." We find men dealt with, in primitive legislation and religion, not on the basis of the single life which consciousness binds together for each of us, but as members of a tribe, a clan, or a family; hence the familiar practice of blood-revenge, or the idea that the sin of one (*e.g.* Achan) can properly be visited on the group to which he belongs, and into which his own personality, so to speak, extends.

(*c*) *Hebrew ideas of man contrasted with those of some other ancient or primitive peoples.*—The ideas just indicated are common to all ancient or primitive thought, but its types naturally vary, according as the emphasis falls on one or other of these, or on other differences that might be named. Some of these types may be briefly noticed, both to illustrate what has been said, and to bring out the characteristic features of that Hebrew development with which we are specially concerned. One of the lowest types is the aboriginal life and thought of Australia, as described in the elaborate volumes of Spencer, Gillen, and Howitt. The two most strongly marked features of this type, group relationship and totemism, both illustrate what has been said of "corporate personality." In regard to the former, "Strictly speaking, in our sense of the word, they have no individual terms of relationship, but every person has certain groups of men and women who stand in a definite relationship to him, and he to them" (Spencer & Gillen, *The Northern Tribes of Central Australia*, p. 95). Formerly, though this is now exceptional, this group relationship extended to what is for the modern civilized man the most individualistic of relationships, namely, marriage. Parallel with this social feature, and equally based on the idea of corporate personality, is the religious, namely, totemism, of which the central characteristic is "that the members of the totemic group are regarded as responsible for the increase of the animal or plant which gives its name to the group" (*op. cit.* p. xi). A second type—afforded by various tribes on the West African coast, described in the works of Ellis, Kingsley, and Nassau—is fetishistic, and illustrates the belief in external spirit-influences. The fetish is some material object which has mediated supra-natural activities and has thus become the local channel of their action, which is controlled through it. As Nassau points out (*Fetichism in West Africa*, p. 76), the African does not worship these material objects, but his theory of them constitutes his philosophy and dominates his life. A third type may be seen in the religion of the ancient Egyptians, characterized in historic times by the practice of embalming the dead. The continuance of life beyond death is intimately connected with the preservation of the corpse; in Budge's words (*The Book of the Dead*, i. p. lviii, ed. 1901), "All the available evidence shows that the Egyptians of dynastic times mummified the dead body because they believed that a spiritual body would 'germinate' or develop itself in it." A mummy consists of little more than the skeleton, covered by the skin, the fat being destroyed by chemical agents, and the intestines being preserved in jars with the mummy. These details are to the point, because it was precisely through the preservation of the body and its principal parts that the personality became immortal; missing members, indeed, were sometimes replaced by artificial (such as a bronze ear or a leather great-toe, as may be seen in the collection of the British Museum). All this is but an impressive example of the ideas as to the body indicated above; the body, down to its very details, has a psychical as well as a physical significance. The importance of this ancient conception for the psychology of the Old Testament, and even for the New, as will be seen, is often overlooked. Other types may be seen in the striking development of ancestor-worship, central and fundamental amongst Mongolian races; in the idea of the transmigration of the soul into other bodies for subsequent lives, with the complementary theory of *karma*, or moral continuity, which characterizes the vast expanse of Indian thought; and in the beginning of the more scientific study of personality amongst the Greeks, especially by Aristotle. But over against these various types of totemistic, fetishistic, physiological, ancestral, metaphysical and psychological emphasis there is the peculiar contribution to ancient thought made along the Semitic line of development and culminating amongst the Hebrews. A dominating belief amongst the pre-Islamic Arabs, and to a considerable extent within the Assyrio-Babylonian civilization, is that of the spirit-control of human personality from without (*supra*, p. 7). But, in the Old Testament, this belief in the accessibility of man to the will of demons and spirits, good or evil, is concentrated into belief in accessibility to the Spirit of Yahweh, and is deepened by the moral consciousness and by progressive conceptions of both God and man till it becomes spiritual in the fuller sense of the word. The conception of man developed in close relation with this belief may be traced through the literature of the Old Testament along two principal lines. From the emphasis on corporate personality we move forwards to the recognition of moral individuality; from cruder physiological ideas there is developed a more spiritual conception of human personality, of which the finer shades of meaning are understood only in the light of what may seem to many readers much unnecessary detail. We may speak, then, of moral and spiritual individualism, in close dependence on God, as the specific contribution of the Old Testament, as compared with other ancient types of the interpretation of human personality. Its sharpest antithesis is perhaps found in Buddha's doctrine of salvation by the rejection of individuality; its fullest development in the Christian faith. For, in Vinet's words [1] with reference to individuality, "the glory of the Gospel lies in strengthening it in a few, in awakening it in the majority, in purifying it in all."

2. THE EVOLUTION OF THE PSYCHOLOGICAL TERMS. [2]

(a) *The physiology of the Hebrews.*—In view of what has been said (1 (b)), the reader will be prepared for an approach to the psychology of the Hebrews

---

[1] Quoted by Schaumann in the *Theologische Studien und Kritiken* (1902), p. 67.

[2] The general conclusions of this section will be found under (d) by readers who find its necessary detail tedious.

through their physiology. The body, not the soul, is
the characteristic element of Hebrew personality; and
Hebrew thought, working by a primitive and instinctive
logic, has developed from the functions of the physical
organs a somewhat complex psychical usage. About
eighty different parts of the body are named in the Old
Testament. No doubt other terms were in use which do
not happen to occur in the extant Hebrew literature; but
in regard to certain points, the omissions from this list
are highly significant. The most remarkable omission,
from our modern standpoint, is that of the brain. The
physical substance of the brain was perhaps known in
Hebrew, as it actually is in Syriac, as "the marrow of the
head." Similarly, there is no distinct term for "nerve";
if any nerve (*e.g.* the *nervus ischiadicus*) was conspicuous
enough to be noticed, it was classed with the sinews and
tendons, in accordance with the general opinion of the
ancient world. These omissions justify us in saying that,
for the Hebrew, the centre of consciousness did not lie in
the head, and that the peripheral sense-organs must have
been conceived very differently from our own, since to the
Hebrew they would seem to be self-contained, without
connection with the central organs. Further, we find no
terms for the diaphragm and lungs, to which important
psychical functions are allotted by Greek psychology.
Apparently, the Hebrews did not sharply distinguish the
thoracic and abdominal viscera, nor understand the method,
to say nothing of the purpose, of respiration. The visible
movement of the abdomen in respiration would naturally
suggest that the breath came from it (cf. "the breath of
my belly," Job xxxii. 18). Further, there is no term for
the blood-vessels, though blood plays so large a part in

Hebrew thought and life.[1] This omission suggests the ancient ignorance of the circulation of the blood, which lasted until A.D. 1628. This must not be taken to mean that the Hebrew saw no connection at all between the heart and the blood; on the contrary, the clotted blood on and in the heart of every sacrificial victim would suggest by its quantity that the heart was in some mysterious way a centre of the blood-life, and consequently an important psychical organ. But want of knowledge of the circulation of the blood, as of the nervous system, would render the idea of physiological and psychical unity (in our sense) much more difficult to attain. In addition to these negative inferences, there are three primary passages to which we may turn for positive information as to Hebrew ideas of physiology. One is the account of Ezekiel's vision of the valley of dry bones (ch. xxxvii.). They were very dry, *i.e.* their quasi-vitality had gone and they were now lifeless. The stages of their restoration to life are as follows: each bone falls into its proper place and relation; sinews and tendons are put on them, and with them form the framework of the body; over these, flesh (*i.e.* muscular tissue) is brought up; the outer skin is then drawn over above this flesh; life-energy, still wanting to the otherwise complete bodies, is supplied by the wind that blows and fills the dead bodies with breath, so that they rise and stand on their feet. The correct anatomy of this description agrees with that of the two principal references to the evolution of the human embryo, a proverbial (Prov. xxx. 19; Eccles. xi. 5) mystery among the Hebrews—

---

[1] See the article " Blood ", by the present writer, in Hastings' *Encyclopædia of Religion and Ethics.*

"Didst thou not pour me out like milk, and curdle me like cheese? With skin and flesh thou didst clothe me, and with bones and sinews thou didst weave me together" (Job x. 10 11).

> "For thou didst create my kidneys,
> Thou didst weave me together in my mother's belly.
>
> .   .   .   .
>
> Not hidden was my bony frame from thee
> When I was made in secret ;
> I was embroidered in the lowest parts of the earth,
> My unformed mass thine eyes saw" (Ps. cxxxix. 13, 15, 16).

Whatever the obscure reference to "the lowest parts of the earth" may mean, it must not be taken to imply Hebrew belief in the pre-existence of the soul (contrast Wisd. viii. 19). God gives or withholds "the fruit of the belly" (Gen. xxx. 2) and fashions all in the womb (Job xxxi. 15; Ps. cxix. 73); but there is no Hebrew belief in a pre-existent spirit which inhabits a body prepared for it. The only stages preparatory to life are the three named in Hos. ix. 11, namely, conception, pregnancy, and delivery. When Yahweh says to Jeremiah, "Before I formed thee in the belly I knew thee" (Jer. i. 5), the reference is to predestination, not pre-existence.

(*b*) *The principles of life* (*breath and blood*).—We have already seen, from the passage in Ezekiel, that the physical organism, or rather group of organs, was conceived as drawing its life-energies from the breath within it ; the same idea underlies Gen. ii. 7 : "And Yahweh shaped man from dust out of the ground, and blew into his nostrils breath of life, so that man became a living soul." [1]

---

[1] The Hebrew phrase is exactly the same as that rendered "living creature" by AV. and RV. in ver. 19 ; in itself it in no way distinguishes man from the animal world ; so far as such distinction is implied, it must be found in the special " inbreathing " of Yahweh in man's case.

It is the common idea of the breath-soul, which is so frequent in animistic thought, and indeed provides a name for animism (Latin, *anima*). The reader unfamiliar with such thought must beware of treating it simply as a metaphor; the breath *is* the life, which finds expression in so many different ways, physical or psychical; the Hebrew did not start with the idea of physical "breath" and then extend it to "life" and "soul", but he employed a term which might denote any of the various activities of life, physical or psychical. His justification was that "breath" was the constant accompaniment of conscious life, yet was absent in death, and, apparently, in unconsciousness. He found a parallel idea in "blood", whose shedding was accompanied by growing weakness, and possibly by death; the blood also was the "life", though it did not lend itself so easily to the idea of psychical activity. The next step was to correlate "breath" and "blood" by the idea that the breath-soul is in (Lev. xvii. 11) or is somehow identical with the blood (Gen. ix. 4; Deut. xii. 23; Lev. xvii. 14), an idea which may have been suggested, as Stade says, by the visible reek of shed blood. The psychical ideas attaching to blood (Heb. *dām*) are, however, of importance for the theory of sacrifice, rather than for our present study, and we may confine our attention to the three Hebrew terms employed to denote the "breath-soul," namely, *neshāmāh*, *nephesh*,[1] and *ruach*. The first of these occurs twenty-four times, in nine of which it denotes the breath-soul as the principle of physical life, or, as we should say, the actual breath; thus,

---

[1] The term *nephesh* does not appear to denote breath in the purely physical reference within the O.T.; see the *Journal of Biblical Literature* (1897), p. 30.

in the case of the son of the widow of Zarephath, his
sickness was so severe that "there was no *neshāmāh*
left in him" (1 Kings xvii. 17); Job describes the
continuance of his life by saying "all my *neshāmāh*
is still in me" (Job xxvii. 3). In three cases, the term
denotes the breath-soul as the principle of the moral and
spiritual life, as when it is said that man's discernment
is due to God's *neshāmāh* within him (Job xxxii. 8;
cf. xxvi. 4 and Prov. xx. 27). The other instances are
those in which the term is applied to the wind as God's
breath (2 Sam. xxii. 16; Ps. xviii. 16; Job iv. 9, xxxvii. 10;
Isa. xxx. 33), or those in which it has come to mean man
as an individual "person," a breathing creature (*e.g.* Josh.
xi. 11, shewing also similar use of *nephesh*; in both cases, this
usage does not appear before the Deuteronomistic school
of writers). Much more important are the two other terms,
namely, *nephesh* and *ruach*. *Nephesh* occurs 754 times, and
its usages may be classified as (A) Principle of Life (282);
(B) Psychical (249); (C) Personal (223). As a typical
example of the first class may be taken Elijah's complaint,
"they seek my *nephesh* to take it away" (1 Kings xix.
10). (It should be noted by the reader of the English Bible
that this word is often translated "soul", when all that
it means in our usage is "life"; this is notably the case
in the Book of Psalms (AV. and RV.), where a false
"spiritual" connotation is, in consequence, often suggested; thus, in Ps. xxxv. 4, where the same phrase
occurs as that last quoted, it is rendered "that seek after
my *soul*", as though spiritual, not physical, peril were in
question.) The psychical usage of *nephesh* is very varied,
and covers all kinds of states of consciousness, even
volitional (Gen. xxiii. 8) and intellectual (Prov. ii. 10),

though the emotional (*e.g.* Gen. xlii. 21) strongly predominate, especially in the particular sense of appetite (Num. xxi. 5) or desire (Deut. xxi. 14: "whither she will"). The term may also denote the whole inner life of thought and feeling, as when the law is said to restore the *nephesh* (Ps. xix. 7). The third class of usages, called above "personal," includes the use of the term as a pathetic personal pronoun (Ezek. iv. 14) or as a reflexive (Lev. xi. 43, where "yourselves" is in Hebrew expressed through *nephesh*), and also the use for "individual person" (Gen. xii. 5) already noticed in the case of *neshāmāh*. A somewhat curious extension of meaning, by which the principle of life comes to denote a dead body, seems to belong here (cf. Num. v. 2, where "unclean by the dead" is literally "unclean in respect of a *nephesh*"); it is best explained through the idea of the body, dead or alive, as the "person," somewhat as the Syriac cognate has come to mean "tombstone," the visible representative of the dead. Apart from this somewhat debatable case, it will be seen that the whole range of usage of the term *nephesh* is perfectly natural, given the animistic starting-point; the actual principle of life is credited with its (chiefly) emotional manifestations, and at the same time may denote their subject or agent. At death, the *nephesh* "goes out" (Gen. xxxv. 18), as it may do in a swoon (Song of Songs v. 6); in the case of the widow's son, his recovery consists in the "return" of his *nephesh* (1 Kings xvii. 21); the *nephesh* may be said to die (Judg. xvi. 30), but is never used of the spirit of the dead.[1]

The remaining term, *ruach*, covers a wider range of

[1] Cf. Moore, *Judges*, p. 362 : "There is nowhere a suggestion that the soul survives the man whose life it was ; the inhabitants of the nether world

usage, in a development less easy to trace. It occurs
378 times, denoting (A) wind, natural or figurative (131);
(B) supernatural influences acting on man, rarely on inanimate objects (134); (C) the principle of life (like *nephesh*)
or of its energies (39); (D) the resultant psychical life (74).
The classification itself, with the proportion of usage,
shews that we have to do with something more than
a mere synonym of *nephesh*, and this is corroborated by
certain details of the process of its development. *Ruach*
is not used of the breath-soul in man in any pre-exilic
document, though it occurs in the sense of " life-energy "
in some early passages (Gen. xlv. 27 (JE); Judg. xv. 19;
1 Sam. xxx. 12; 1 Kings x. 5). *Ruach* is not used with
psychical predicates[1] in any pre-exilic passage, though
from the exile onwards this usage becomes frequent,
whilst in Psalms and Proverbs *ruach* is practically a
synonym of both *nephesh* and "heart," denoting the inner
life in general. Further, we find a marked use of *ruach*
to denote the stronger emotions of passion (Judg. viii. 3),
grief (Gen. xxvi. 35), zeal (Hag. i. 14); thus *ruach* in
the sense of " breath " is specially connected with the
nostrils (2 Sam. xxii. 16; Ps. xviii. 16; Ex. xv. 8;
Job iv. 9, xxvii. 3; Lam. iv. 20; Gen. vii. 22); the
word for " nostril " in Hebrew is frequently used in
the sense "anger," *e.g.* Gen. xxvii. 45. Both in the

(*sheol*) are not *souls* but shades (*refaïm*, εἴδωλα)." On the subsequent eschatological extension of " soul " and " spirit," see § 3 (*d*) and Chap. II. § 1 (*b*).

[1] *E.g.* as in Gen. xxvi. 35 (P), " bitterness of *ruach.*" The only apparent
exceptions are Gen. xli. 8 (= Dan. ii. 3), where the phrase, as a whole, is possibly
late; and Mic. ii. 7 (of Yahweh), where the immediate context is admittedly
in disorder. It is conceivable that the term *ruach* was applied to both the
" breath " and the " spirit " of Yahweh earlier than to those of man (cf. Ex.
xv. 8; Isa. xxx. 28), though similar *ideas* (expressed through *nephesh*) must, of
course, have existed already in regard to human psychology.

cognate languages and in Hebrew itself the term for "smell" is closely connected with *ruach*. From these facts, it is natural to infer that the term was originally applied both to the "blowing" of the wind and to the "blowing" or panting of men and animals in distress or excitement. This inference would explain the actual use of *ruach* in the pre-exilic period for the wind, caused by God (Ex. x. 13), for the passion of anger, etc., in man (Judg. viii. 3), or the stronger energies of life (Gen. xlv. 27; Judg. xv. 19; I Sam. xxx. 12; I Kings x. 5), and for the external influence (ascribed to Yahweh) causing the abnormal actions of men (insanity, I Sam. xvi. 14; prophesying, x. 5, 6; extraordinary strength, Judg. xiv. 6, etc.). In this earlier period, *ruach* is confined to the stormier breathing of excited feeling, and the accompanying physical or mental condition; the contemporary term for the normal breathing of life is *neshāmāh* (as in the passage quoted from Gen. ii. 7 above). The wind may have been already conceived in poetry as the strong "breath" of God (2 Sam. xxii. 16; Ps. xviii. 16; Ex. xv. 8, if these are pre-exilic; cf. the post-exilic passages, Isa. xxx. 28, lix. 19; Job iv. 9); but, by the time of Ezekiel, we find that *ruach* has come to denote *the normal breath-soul as the principle of life in man* (Ezek. xxxvii. 5, 6, 8),[1] which is directly derived from the wind at the bidding of God (cf. Isa. xlii. 5; Zech. xii. 1; Job xxvii. 3; Ps. civ. 29; Eccles. xii. 7); and from this point onwards we find *ruach* following a line of development somewhat similar to that of *nephesh*, with which it

---

[1] It is possible that the "supernaturalism" exemplified in Ezekiel may have contributed to this development; a higher anthropology might naturally conceive man's breath-soul to be the very *ruach* of God (Job xxvii. 3).

may occur in parallelism; cf. Isa. xxvi. 9 (post-exilic).
"With my *nephesh* I desired thee in the night, yea, with
my *ruach* within me, I sought longingly for thee." But
whilst *ruach* is thus used in the later literature of Israel
of the inner life in general, like "heart," two points should
be noticed, namely, that the earlier emotional use for strong
passion (anger, zeal, impatience) is still represented (Job
xv. 13; Eccles. x. 4), whilst the higher associations of the
ruach of God, developing with the conception of God
Himself, serve, on the whole, to keep the use of the term
for human psychology at a higher plane of meaning
than that of *nephesh*. These higher associations will be discussed at a later stage (§ 5 (*b*)); the point for present notice
is the development of the two terms, *nephesh* and *ruach*,
to denote lower and higher aspects of man's psychical
nature, not sharply or systematically defined and distinguished, but with a sufficiently clear distinction of emphasis,
in view of the history of their respective developments.

(*c*) *The physical organs to which psychical functions are
ascribed.*—When we pass from the psychical ideas connected with the breath-soul to those connected with the
physical organs, any thought of an original dualism of
soul and body must be rejected; all that we have is a
parallel theory of the conscious life of man, based on the
primitive ideas of his body already indicated (1 (*b*)). It
is very important that the independence of this parallel
development should be realized, because it explains much
of the subsequent overlapping of terms,[1] inexplicable on

---

[1] A striking example of such syncretism is afforded by the complex
Egyptian psychology, with at least nine elements, drawn from more or less
independent lines of animistic thought (dream-soul, shadow-soul, bird-soul.
name, etc.).

the theory of a systematic division. The whole conscious life might have found its explanation along the line of either soul or body; had this contrast been realized dualistically, we should have expected at least that the higher attributes would be assigned to the soul and the lower to the body. But this is distinctly not the case in Hebrew psychology, which can assign the highest intellectual or spiritual activities to the working of a physical organ, and the sensations of animal hunger or sexual passion to the "soul." No clearer proof could be given that the term "dualism" is inappropriate and misleading in relation to Hebrew psychology; what we actually find is the explanation of the unity of personality along two parallel lines of primitive thought, according as the (supposed) immediate organ or the more ultimate and mysterious breath might be made the starting-point. At a later stage, no doubt, the establishment of usage, and in some cases the development of thought, led to a rough working classification, with elements drawn from both lines of development; but to understand such a working psychology, as we find it in the post-exilic period of Israel's literature, we must remember the independent sources from which it is derived. A point of equal importance to remember in what follows is the fact that the distinction between science and imagination, fact and metaphor, is a comparatively modern one. We still use the term "heart", for example, in a popular psychical sense, but every educated man knows that he is using it metaphorically. What the educated man frequently does not know, or, at any rate, forgets, is the fact that such a usage is *not* metaphor in the Bible, but represents the extent of current scientific

knowledge. This non-metaphorical point of view underlies the use of every physiological term for psychical
activities, including the peripheral sense-organs (eye, ear,
etc.). Even though we grant that the psychical activity,
not the physical organ, is primarily in view in most
cases, the source of the terminology and the implicit
standpoint involved will remain; together they contribute an important element in the peculiar and characteristic atmosphere of such ancient literature as the
Old Testament.

The physical organs (parts of the body) which concern
us may be grouped in three classes, according as they
are central, peripheral, or general. Of the central organs,
four (heart, liver, kidneys, bowels) have acquired a
psychical use in Hebrew. The terms for "heart" (*lēb,
lēbāb*) occur 851 times, and may be grouped in five
classes: (A) physical or figurative ("midst"; 29); (B)
personality, inner life, or character in general (257: *e.g.*
Ex. ix. 14; 1 Sam. xvi. 7; Gen. xx. 5); (C) emotional
states of consciousness, found in widest range (166: in-
toxication, 1 Sam. xxv. 36; joy or sorrow, Judg. xviii. 20,
1 Sam. i. 8; anxiety, 1 Sam. iv. 13; courage and fear, Gen.
xlii. 28; love, 2 Sam. xiv. 1); (D) intellectual activities
(204: attention, Ex. vii. 23; reflection, Deut. vii. 17; memory,
Deut. iv. 9; understanding, 1 Kings iii. 9; technical skill,
Ex. xxviii. 3); (E) volition or purpose (195: 1 Sam. ii. 35),
this being one of the most characteristic usages of the
term in the O.T. The psychical range of "heart" is
therefore quite general, as its central physiological
position might naturally suggest; any specialization of
its meaning would be likely to come negatively, by the
appropriation of particular ranges of its usage to other

terms, such as *nephesh*.[1] The other central organs are
of less importance. "Liver" (*kābēd*), so frequent an
Assyrian parallel to "heart," is used psychically twice
only, as a general life-centre of consciousness (Lam. ii. 11;
Prov. vii. 23), though it should probably be read by re-
punctuation of the Hebrew in some other cases (for
"glory" in Gen. xlix. 6; Ps. vii. 6, xvi. 9). "Kidneys"
(*kelāyōth*) are named as an emotional centre in ten cases,
e.g. of joy (Prov. xxiii. 16), discontent (Ps. lxxiii. 21),
impulse to right action (Ps. xvi. 7), desire (Job xix. 27).
"Bowels" (*mē'im*) occur with psychical reference in nine
cases, namely, to sexual love (Song v. 4), religious affection
(Ps. xl. 9), compassion and pity (Isa. xvi. 11, lxiii. 15; Jer.
xxxi. 20), distress (Lam. i. 20, ii. 11; Jer. iv. 19, *bis*). In
the case of the four central terms named, the psychical
usage is probably derived from real or supposed connection
with the blood and from the central position (heart, liver),
or from the physiological accompaniments of emotion.
The Hebrew usage (except of "heart") is sufficiently
remote from our own to attract our attention and compel
us to assume something of the primitive standpoint. This
is not the case with the peripheral organs, of which we
could use most of the Hebrew language ourselves, in a
consciously metaphorical sense. Yet, in view of what has
been said, it ought to be admitted that the Hebrew meant
something other than we do when he spoke of the eye
as unsatisfied (Prov. xxvii. 20), expectant (Ps. cxlv. 15),
asking (Eccles. ii. 10), desiring (Ezek. xxiv. 16), pleasurably
beholding vengeance (Mic. iv. 11), mocking (Prov. xxx. 17),
testifying (Job xxix. 11), covenanting (Job xxxi. 1), proud

---

[1] Thus, in the New Testament, part of the connotation of *lēb* is appropriated
by *nous*; see Chap. II. § 3 (*a*).

(Ps. cxxxi. 1), humble (Job xxii. 29), pure (Hab. i. 13), pitiless (Isa. xiii. 18), and evil (Prov. xxiii. 6, xxviii. 22 ; cf. Deut. xv. 9, xxviii. 54, 56). It was for the Hebrew an element of personality, with psychical and moral life of its own, not a mere condition of sensation and instrument of perception, as with us. How real this localization of function was, might be shown from many parallels amongst primitive peoples; [1] within the Old Testament itself, it is significant that Elisha, when restoring the dead child to life (2 Kings iv. 34), places his mouth on the child's mouth, his eyes on the child's eyes, his hands on the child's hands, in accordance with the belief that the life of the separate organs was imparted by this local contact.   A similar line of argument can be traced by the reader, with the help of a concordance, for "ear", "tongue", "hand", etc., as for "eye"; he will be impressed by the increased vividness of many references. But the argument has a greater significance for us here; it extends to more general terms, *i.e.* "flesh" and "bones", and affords a natural line of explanation of the ethical development of "flesh" in the Pauline epistles, without resort to any dualistic theory.

"Flesh" (*bāsār*) is used with a more or less psychical shade of meaning in about 45 cases (out of 266 in all), including 14 in which it is used of kinship (Gen. ii. 23, 24). The flesh is contrasted with stone (Ezek. xi. 19, xxxvi. 26) or bronze (Job vi. 12) as being sensitive (Job ii. 5) and warm with life (2 Kings iv. 34); it suffers (Eccles. xi. 10)

---

[1] *E.g.* an enemy's eyes are eaten by savages to obtain their qualities of vision (Spencer, *Sociology*, i. p. 116 ; cf. Frazer, *The Golden Bough*, ii. p. 360).   In West Africa, graves are rifled to obtain human eyeballs, especially those of white men, for charms (Kingsley, *Travels*, p. 449).   Cf. Ezekiel's wheels "full of eyes" (i. 18).

like the heart, shudders in fear (Ps. cxix. 120; Job iv. 15; cf. xxi. 6), is weary (Eccles. xii. 12), abides in confidence (Ps. xvi. 9), longs (Ps. lxiii. 2), enjoys wine (Eccles. ii. 3), rejoices (Ps. lxxxiv. 3), sins (Eccles. v. 5), is influenced by mental state (Prov. xiv. 30), and retains a certain sensitiveness, even after death (Job xiv. 22). The corruption and dissolution of the body after death suggests the idea of Gen. iii. 19: "Dust thou art, and unto dust shalt thou return." In an important group of cases, "flesh" is used of man, or man's essential nature, in contrast with God, or with "Spirit", to emphasize man's frailty, dependence, or incapacity (Isa. xxxi. 3, xl. 6; Ps. lvi. 5, lxxviii. 39; Job x. 4, xxxiv. 15; Jer. xvii. 5: cf. Ps. ciii. 14; Job iv. 17, xxv. 4 f.). The contrast does not occur before Isa. xxxi. 3, and must not be read into the earlier Hebrew thought; its importance consists in its being the point of departure for the development of the Pauline doctrine of "flesh", with distinct ethical reference. In some cases in the Old Testament (*e.g.* Job iv. 17–19, xxv. 5, 6) physical frailty is used to explain or to exculpate ethical imperfection, which would be inconsistent if "flesh" were supposed to be essentially evil. *Ethical dualism of soul and body is remote from Hebrew thought.*

Another general term is that for the "bones." They have so much life inherent in them that some of it remains even after death, as is seen from the story of the dead man revived by contact with the bones of Elisha (2 Kings xiii. 21). They shake in fear (Job iv. 14; Jer. xxiii. 9) and acknowledge God's power (Ps. xxxv. 10); they are pierced with pain (Job xxx. 17) as well as burned by the heat of disease (Job xxx. 30; Ps. cii. 4; Lam. i. 13). "Bone and flesh" together (or separately) serve to express

kinship (Gen. xxix. 14; cf. ii. 23), or the general idea
of "body" for which Hebrew has no proper term; the
latter fact is very significant in view of what has been
said as to the absence of dualism from Hebrew thought.
Another term employed to express "body" is that denoting
"belly" (*beṭen*) (Ps. xxxi. 10, xliv. 26; Hab. iii. 16; Prov.
xx. 27, 30). The term is naturally employed with reference to physical appetite (Prov. xviii. 8, xxvi. 22) and to
greed (Job xx. 15, 20, 23), which prepares for the use of
koilia in the New Testament.

   (*d*) *Inter-relation of the resultant terminology.* — The
parallel development of the breath-soul and the physical
organs, briefly outlined above, issues in four terms of
primary importance, namely, "heart," *nephesh*, *ruach*, and
"flesh." But, in the latter half of the period covered by
the Old Testament literature, they have ceased to be
independent, and are brought, in actual usage, into some
sort of inter-relation. It is not possible to give any exact
differentiation of the provinces covered by "heart", *nephesh*,
and *ruach*, for the simple reason that such exact differentiation was never made, and alternatives of expression for
the same state of consciousness could be employed until
the close of the Old Testament. But, by that time, a
sufficiently recognized usage of the terms in inter-relation had been established to make some indication of it
possible. We may say, then, that the unity of personality,
as conceived by the Hebrew, found its emotional expression chiefly under the name of the *nephesh*, whilst
intellectual and volitional activity centred in the heart
as its organ; consciousness, therefore, finds its complete
expression in the well-known phrase of Deut. vi. 5 : "Thou
shalt love Yahweh thy God with all thy heart and with
all thy *nephesh*, and with all thy might." On the other

hand, the much less frequent psychical term *ruach* still carried with it some suggestion of its earlier usage, for the more noticeable energies of life in their ebb and flow, on the one hand, and, on the other, for the divine influences affecting man from without, either physically or psychically ; it can, however, be used as a synonym of *nephesh* (Isa. xxvi. 9 ; Ps. lxxvii. 4 : cf. *nephesh* in Jonah ii. 8) or, more usually, of "heart" (Ex. xxxv. 21 : cf. xxv. 2, "heart"; Deut. ii. 30; Isa. xxix. 24 : cf. Ps. xcv. 10, " heart"; Isa. lvii. 15, and about sixteen other cases). Its chief importance for the doctrine of man lies, however, in the higher association of the term with the "Spirit" of God ; the similarity of terminology kept open a heavenward door, so to speak, in human nature, and no more striking case could be found of the influence of language on the thought it shapes, even whilst it serves. The final emphasis must fall on the fact that the four terms (including that for "flesh") simply present different aspects of the unity of personality. The Hebrew idea of personality is that of an animated body, not (like the Greek) that of an incarnated soul.

3. THE RELIGIOUS VALUE OF THE INDIVIDUAL.

(*a*) *Corporate personality.*—This term has already been employed (1 (*b*)) to denote a characteristic of primitive thought in general ; we have now to trace its special form amongst the Hebrews before the rise of moral individualism. For ourselves, it has become instinctive to assume the individual rights of man in society and his individual value for God in religion ; but it was not so for pre-exilic Hebrew thought. Whether in relation to man or to God, the individual person was conceived and treated as merged in the larger group of family or clan or nation. This does not, of course, mean that the ultimate

values of life for each were not those of individual consciousness; since man has been man, he has lived his own life,
his heart knowing its own bitterness, and a stranger inter-
meddling not with its joy.   But it does mean that these
individualistic values were modified in important ways, by
the unquestioned acceptance of certain social customs and
religious ideas which to us are immoral, because based on
the discredited idea of corporate personality.   One of the
best-known examples of such social customs is that of
blood-revenge, the primitive justice by which a near
kinsman of the slain man avenges his death.   Here we
find not only the corporate infliction of vengeance (2 Sam.
xiv. 7 : "Deliver him that smote his brother, that we may
kill him for the life of his brother whom he slew") but, in the
earlier forms of the practice (*e.g.* as found amongst the
pre-Islamic Arabs), the corporate suffering of vengeance,
since any member of the group to which the slayer
belongs may be slain in his stead.   A striking instance
of this is found in the narrative of 2 Sam. xxi. 1–14: a
continued famine is traced to the unavenged slaughter of
the Gibeonites by Saul; it is brought to an end when the
two sons of Saul by Rizpah and five of his grandsons are
killed and publicly exposed by the Gibeonites with the con-
sent of David.   Here Yahweh is represented as enforcing
the social morality of the age, just as He is introduced
in 1 Sam. xv. 3 as commanding Saul through Samuel:
"Now go and smite Amalek, and devote all that they
have, and spare them not; but slay both man and woman,
infant and suckling, ox and sheep, camel and ass."   This
is a case of the "ban"[1] so frequently put into practice on

---

[1] See the note by the present writer in the *Century Bible*, "Deuteronomy
and Joshua", p. 158.

the corporate unity of a tribe or group in the Old Testament; the individual rights of the innocent, to our ideas so cruelly wronged, simply did not exist for Hebrew thought. Other customs, also, alien to our thought and practice, draw part at least of their explanation from the same absence of individualism, *e.g.* the practice of Levirate marriage (Deut. xxv. 5), in which a man is regarded as identical with his dead brother, or that of the absolute disposal of a child by the father, seen in Abraham's proposed sacrifice of his son (Gen. xxii.), or Jephthah's accomplished sacrifice of his daughter (Judg. xi. 29 f.), or Reuben's offer of his two sons as hostages to be slain if Benjamin is not brought back safely (Gen. xlii. 37). In such cases of paternal absolutism, it is the negative side of corporate personality that is in view; but the positive side in the same relationship appears when Yahweh is represented as "visiting the iniquity of the fathers upon the children, upon the third and upon the fourth generation of them that hate me" (Ex. xx. 5); or as avenging Ahab's crime against Naboth on Ahab's son, Jehoram, when the latter was killed by Jehu (2 Kings ix. 26). The underlying conception which makes such statements possible is precisely the same as that which meets us in the legislation of the Code of Hammurabi. If a man has caused a woman's death in a certain way, his own daughter is killed (§ 210). If a builder has built a house so badly that it falls and causes the death of the owner's son, the builder's son is to be killed (§ 230). One of the most instructive cases of corporate responsibility in the Old Testament is that of Achan (Josh. vii. 24–26). It illustrates the close bond uniting the individual on the one hand to the larger group of the society in which he lives, on the other to the smaller group of his own family. Achan's theft, serious because a breach of the taboo, first affects the fortunes of all Israel, and then involves the destruction of himself and all his family. It is, indeed, chiefly through the national fortunes that the individual person comes into relation with Yahweh, who is concerned at this period with Israel rather than with individual Israelites. Yahweh is the war-god of Israel; the nation is a unity,[1] chosen by His favour (Amos iii. 2, ix. 7); to leave Israel's land is to leave Yahweh's protection (1 Sam. xxvi. 19). Robertson Smith's words *(Religion of the Semites,* pp. 258, 259), written of ancient religion in general, are true in large measure of the phase of Israel's religion we are considering: "It was not the business of the gods of heathenism to watch, by a series of special providences, over the welfare of every individual. . . . The god was the god of the nation or of the tribe, and he knew and cared for the individual only as a member of the community."[2]

(*b*) *The development of individualism.*—It is clear that primitive morality and religious conceptions, based on the idea of corporate personality, were seriously limited by the absence of a fuller recognition of individual rights and needs. The development of Israel's morality and religion involved, as one of its aspects, a new emphasis on the individual person; consequently, a full account of the rise of individualism would be the history of the prophetic reformation. It would be necessary to begin with Elijah in the ninth century. His protests against Ahab's intro-duction of foreign worship and against his immoral

---

[1] Note here the significance of the collective "I" of national speech, on which see Gray, *The Divine Discipline of Israel,* pp. 79, 80, or *Numbers,* p. 265 f.

[2] See, further, *The Cross of the Servant* (1927), by H. Wheeler Robinson, pp. 32–36.

acquisition of Naboth's vineyard already shew the double line of advance in religion and morality. These protests were continued by the great prophetic group of the eighth century, Amos, Hosea, Isaiah, and Micah. These prophets, it is true, address Israel as a nation; but their insistence on moral righteousness as the true bond of connection between man and God already contains the implicit individualistic principle which finds explicit statement in the prophetic law-book of the seventh century: "The fathers shall not be put to death for the children, neither shall the children be put to death for the fathers : every man shall be put to death for his own sin" (Deut. xxiv. 16). What served, however, to bring out the latent individualism of prophetic teaching, and to impress it on the common consciousness of men, was the pressure of foreign foes on Israel, threatening and at last destroying the national unity. Indeed, the political history of Israel, from the eighth century to the sixth, is the explanation, so far as any external factor ever can be, of her religious history as a whole. This becomes clear, in regard to the particular element of religious development at present before us, when we turn to the teaching of the three great prophets, Isaiah, Jeremiah, and Ezekiel.

Isaiah, interpreting the advance of Assyria as the beginning of Yahweh's discipline of His people, sees, as the principal result of that discipline, the survival of a "righteous remnant" which shall be the nucleus of a holy nation (Isa. i. 24–31 ; cf. the later passages, x. 20, xxviii. 5). This characteristic doctrine of his finds expression in the narrative of his call, where Israel is compared to "the terebinth and the oak, of which, when they are felled, a stock remaineth" (vi. 13); again in the reference to the band of trusted disciples (viii. 16); in the symbolic name of his son, " Remnant shall return" (to Yahweh; vii. 3); and in the later conception of a register of survivors: " He who is left in Zion, and he who remains in Jerusalem— 'holy' shall he be named, every one written down for life in Jerusalem " (iv. 3). This has well been called "the first conception in history of the Church within the Church."[1] In the result, the emphasis still falls on the purged *nation*; but the process of purging is individualistic,[2] because moral.

Jeremiah has no doctrine of this kind; he declares, indeed, that the purging is vain, for the wicked are not plucked away (vi. 29); nor does he contemplate a separate community of the true Israel. His contribution to individualism consists of the truths brought home to him through the isolation of his prophetic work (xv. 17) and through the experiences of a highly wrought nature taught to be dependent on God for its only strength (i. 4–10). The man who trusts God is a tree planted by the waters (xvii. 8) in vitality, and a wall of bronze (xv. 20) in strength. The significance of such statements lies in the man who makes them; we have to think of the whole inner story of Jeremiah's life, its dramatic alternation of hope and fear, submissive obedience and wild complaint, in order to realize the wealth of individuality which this prophet poured into the treasury of revelation. The positive expression of this experience is found in the prophecy of the " new covenant " (xxxi. 31 f.): " I will put my law in their inward parts, and in their heart will I write it; and I will be their God, and they shall be My people: and they shall teach no more every man his neighbour, and every man his

---

[1] G. A. Smith, in Hastings' *Dictionary of the Bible*, ii. p. 490.
[2] Cf. Köberle, *Sünde und Gnade*, p. 165.

brother, saying, Know the Lord: for they shall all know
Me, from the least of them unto the greatest of them."
Jeremiah hopes for the renewal of the whole house of
Judah and of Israel (ver. 31) through the grace of God, not,
like Isaiah, for the survival of a remnant of the nation, purged
through the judgment of God; but Jeremiah's conception
springs from a personal and individualistic consciousness
of religion to which the earlier prophet had not attained.

The most explicit, though not the deepest, conception of individuality is found in Ezekiel. He does
not simply proclaim the selection of those who are to
be kept alive, with the mark on their foreheads (ix. 4),
and the purging of the wilderness journey (xx. 38);
he also lays the greatest emphasis on the doctrine of
individual retribution (xviii.; cf. xxxiii. 12 f.). He finds
his point of departure in the current proverb (already,
perhaps, rejected by Jeremiah; see Jer. xxxi. 29, 30),
"The fathers have eaten sour grapes, and the children's
teeth are set on edge" (xviii. 2). The application of the
proverb in the mouth of the people seems to have been
primarily to the troubles of the exile, if we may judge
from the parallel and contemporary complaint, "Our
fathers sinned and are not, and we have borne their
iniquities" (Lam. v. 7). Ezekiel meets the proverb,
which faithfully expresses the earlier doctrine of corporate personality, with a blank denial of its truth. A
man is not punished for the sins of his fathers (nor even
for the sins of his own past, if he repents, xviii. 21):
God's principle is, "all souls are Mine; as the soul of
the father, so also the soul of the son is Mine: the soul
that sinneth, *it* shall die" (xviii. 4). The good man
finds his present reward, the bad man his present

3

punishment, in accordance with the strictest individual equity, and quite unaffected by the solidarity of the family or race, and even by the continuity of personality itself. Such a theory may be a logical deduction from belief in the moral government of the visible world. but it is untrue to the facts of life, as subsequent thinkers of Israel discovered; moreover, its view of repentance, logically pressed, would lead to results as immoral as were reached along the line of corporate personality Indeed, the two theories must in some form be combined, to answer to the truth of life; part of the value of Israel's religious history is the emergence of both in so clear a manner. Even Ezekiel looks forward to a restored nation, reconstituted from the individuals rewarded with life. The spiritual influence of the exile on Israel's religious life can hardly be overrated; the essentials of religion were seen to stand, in contrast with the things that could be shaken and overthrown; the nation was resolved into the units of which it was composed. Yet this resolution was not ultimate and sufficient in itself; it was but the necessary stage towards the constitution of a spiritual Israel. The individualism of the Old Testament is usually, if not always, conceived as realized in and through the society which is based upon it. It is no small contribution to the Christian doctrine of man that the individualism through which the Gospel makes its appeal was penetrated through and through with the sense of social relationship; that contribution was essentially made by the Old Testament, even though the horizon of relationship was still limited.

(*c*) *The problem of individual retribution.*—The doctrine of individual retribution, asserted by Ezekiel, dominates most of the subsequent religious thought of Israel, as exhibited in the Old Testament. It forms the basis of practical appeal in the Book of Proverbs; it constitutes, with few exceptions, the unbroken faith of the Psalmists; it becomes a philosophy of history in the hands of the compilers of ancient documents. These compilers seem to have felt that where the piety of the past was recorded, its historic reward could be inferred, and where its sin alone was remembered, the due punishment could not have been wanting.[1] Yet what is easy to the optimism of moral exhortation, or to the intensity of religious devotion, or to the historian deciphering the dim page of the past by the lamp of current thought, was not so easy for men face to face with the actual facts of individual experience. It would have been strange had not the doctrine of individualism, in the form given it by Ezekiel, been challenged by some of Israel's deeper thinkers. As a matter of fact, side by side with the unquestioning acceptance of the doctrine, we may see various attempts to solve the problem created by this clash of life with theory. The wonderful catholicity of the Old Testament has kept for us not only the mystic vision of the Psalmist (Ps. lxxiii. 23 f.), penetrating into a life untouched by decay and above all the perplexities of experience, but the figure of Job, flinging down his challenge of faith, even where the problem is to him insoluble, and the doubts of the Preacher, sceptical as to the very existence of a moral order at all. These three attitudes may be taken as typical in regard to the problem

---

[1] The remark is due to Marti, *Geschichte der israelitischen Religion*[3], p. 251. He gives as an example the contrast between 1 Kings xxii. 49 and 2 Chron. xx. 35-37.

before us. It is convenient to take the second and third here, and to reserve the first until we consider the eschatology of the individual (*infra*, (*d*)). The Book of the Preacher (Ecclesiastes) is one of the latest within the Old Testament, and the inconsistencies of its present form would make it one of the most difficult, if we could think this form was original. There are concessions to the orthodox doctrine of individual retribution (iii. 17, viii. 12, 13, xii. 14), but they are probably to be regarded as later corrections of the scepticism and fatalism which in any case supply the general atmosphere of the book. In the Preacher's experience, righteousness is not rewarded with long life, and wickedness with early death, as ought to be the case on the conventional theory (vii. 15), nor are the general fortunes of each proportionate to his deserts (viii. 14); moreover, even after death, he saw the wicked honoured, and the righteous forgotten (viii. 10). The conclusion he draws is that life does *not* receive exact moral retribution: " the race is not to the swift, nor the battle to the strong, neither yet bread to the wise, nor yet riches to men of understanding, nor yet favour to men of skill; but time and chance happeneth to them all " (ix. 11). He chants his mournful and pessimistic refrain, " one event unto all ", over the fortunes of the wise and the foolish (ii. 14), the good and the evil (ix. 2). He points his moral, that there is no adequate moral retribution in the course of life, by the story of a great city saved, and a great king defeated, by the wisdom of a poor and forgotten deliverer (ix. 13 ff.). The solution of the problem reached by the Preacher is, therefore, to deny the principle of moral government from which it sprang, though the cost of this solution is to leave life itself more insoluble than ever.

The Book of Job shows no less close observation of life and reflection on it, and rejects no less emphatically the theory of individual retribution as the complete explanation of the facts of experience. It offers another explanation of those facts, in which faith concerning the moral government of God can still live and move. The problem presented is that of Job as an innocent man, who is yet a sufferer. The first stage of its solution is the rejection of the theory of the three friends, Eliphaz the mystic, Bildad the thinker, Zophar the dogmatist, who apply the philosophy of history described above, and argue from the visible suffering of Job to the denial of his self-asserted innocence. The rejection of this conventional view is to be found in the arguments of Job himself, on which, so far as this point goes, the seal of divine approval is set (xlii. 7). He can reject it because he is conscious of practical innocence, and has lived up to the best moral standards of his age (xxxi.). This rejection carries with it logically the rejection of the additional (and later) contribution made by Elihu, who appears to urge in particular the view of suffering as *discipline* (xxxiii. 8–12, 17, 26, 27, xxxiv. 31–33, xxxv. 11, xxxvi. 16, 22) to be received in humility, though he reasserts the general theory of the three friends (xxxiv. 11). The second stage of the solution is found in the progress of Job's own thought up to its final challenge of God, and God's acceptance of this challenge, with emphasis on the truth that His ways cannot be wholly understood by man. If the chapters in which Job speaks are read consecutively, they will be found to start from the fact of suffering (iii.), to move downwards through the sense of loneliness (vi.), bitterness (vii.), helplessness and injustice (ix.), then upwards in appeal to God (x.), followed by the explicit rejection of the conventional theory (xii., xiii.). From various hopes and fears (xiv.), Job sinks to the thought that God is his enemy (xvi.), and thus to despair (xvii.), from which he springs to his highest point in the conviction, " My Redeemer liveth " (xix.). He drops from this once more to the vision of an immoral universe (xxi.),[1] but begins to climb again through the thought of the mysteries of providence (xxiii., xxiv.), the greatness of God (xxvi.), the doom of evil (xxvii.), the contrast between divine and human wisdom (xxviii.). After an interlude of memories (xxix.) and humiliation (xxx.), Job steps forward with his final challenge (xxxi.), which shows a deeper faith in God than any of his doubts can touch. This development of thought can only be intended to show that the problem as presented to man's reason is not soluble, yet that faith in a divine moral purpose for the individual ought to be maintained. This view is confirmed by the answer of God, who rebukes Job's expectation that he could understand all, yet establishes his position, as against the theory of the friends, by word and by work (Epilogue). The third stage of the solution of the problem, deliberately hidden from the sufferer himself, is that of the Prologue. Here God is represented as answering the challenge of the Adversary by allowing the unconscious Job to suffer; thus Job proves that religion and morality are not bound up with the experience of visible retribution, but have a positive and independent worth and vitality of their own; Job still serves God for nought, and becomes His trusted

---

[1] Incidentally (vers. 19, 20) Job here reasserts Ezekiel's claim for individual retribution, as against the theory that a father can be punished in his children (cf. Ecclus. xi. 28); but Job, unlike Ezekiel, does not find the claim fulfilled in actual life.

representative and witness. This view of the religious
value of the individual has far-reaching issues for the
doctrine of Atonement; it connects not only with the
sufferings of Jeremiah for the word of God, or those of
the "Servant" for the people of God, but with those of
Christ and His servants (Col. i. 24).

(*d*) *The eschatology of the individual.*—To ourselves, the
simplest solution of the problem of individual retribution
lies in the doctrine of a future life, where the residue of
reward or punishment due to the individual will be given.
But the thought of Israel, within the limits set by the
Old Testament literature, had not reached any conception
of the future likely to be of much service in this connection. The need for such a conception was more or less
consciously realized through the pressure of the problem
just outlined. The view found in the Old Testament
of what lies beyond death seems to have affinities
with what we find amongst other peoples (*e.g.* the
Mongolian races) as "ancestor-worship";[1] the dead man
went to his fathers (Gen. xv. 15) when buried in the
family grave (2 Sam. xix. 37); from the idea of the
collected graves of a social group grew that of "Sheol"
(Ezek. xxxii. 22 f.), the dim region beneath the earth in
which are gathered the "shades" (*rephāīm*) of the dead,
still retaining their familiar appearance (1 Sam. xxviii. 14),
though they have neither souls nor bodies; they meet the
newcomer with the cry, "Art thou also become weak as
we? art thou become like unto us?" (Isa. xiv. 10). The
shadowy life of this realm lies outside the jurisdiction or
interest of Yahweh (Ps. lxxxviii. 5), and is without moral

[1] For the proof of this statement, the reader may refer to the article on
"Eschatology," by Charles, in the *Encyclopædia Biblica*, cc. 1335 f.

distinctions; it is simply "the house of meeting for all living" (Job xxx. 23).[1] Such a conception, which prevailed into the times in which the problem of individual retribution was acutely felt, could add little to its solution; it was a survival from the past, a blind alley along which thought and faith could make no progress. Even when genuine faith in immortality was coming to be maintained, the Preacher definitely rejected it; man and beast are resolved alike into their elements at death (iii. 19–21); "a living dog is better than a dead lion. The living know that they shall die: but the dead know not anything" (ix. 4). On the other hand, the author of the Book of Job would probably have accepted this faith, had he lived and written somewhat later; as it is, we can hardly say more than that he throws out the suggestion of some future beyond death in connection with his problem, yet turns from it to the stern realities of present life. He, for a moment, imagines himself hidden away in the gloom of Sheol, and awaiting that day when the deeper gloom of God's wrath should have passed away. Then Yahweh would think of his faithful and neglected servant, and cry aloud his name, and from the cavernous depths of Sheol would Job's answering cry of joy be heard (xiv. 13–15). This is a splendid venture of faith; but it is not a doctrine of future life. Nor does the better-known passage (xix. 25–27), "I know that my Redeemer liveth", take us beyond the idea of a special and extraordinary vindication of a wronged man, by a divine act in which the hidden God shall reveal Himself to Job. There is no assertion here of immortal life. On the other hand, it

---

[1] Other passages, *e.g.* Ps. cxxxix. 7, 8, illustrate the (later) extension of Yahweh's rule into Sheol; cf. Charles, *op. cit.* 1339.

is fair to say that the faith behind such statements involves a transcendence of death which is of the highest significance for the future. This sense of a personal relationship to God, which underlies all Job's hopes and fears, becomes most explicit in Ps. lxxiii. The writer is here struggling with the same problem of individual retribution—"the prosperity of the wicked " (ver. 3). Only in the temple could he recover his faith that retribution was delayed, not escaped. For himself, his thought ascends through the sense of personal fellowship with God till he reaches one of the highest levels of Old Testament religion (verses 23–26). It is doubtful whether this recognition of the divine presence, support and guidance, this utterance of devoted and exclusive attachment, this faith in divine power, ought to be directly related to more than a present deliverance; still, as in the case of Job, such a personal relation to God implicitly demands more, and can only be satisfied with a doctrine of personal immortality.[1] Indeed, we ought to group together, as chief factors in the development of that doctrine, both the need for a solution of the problem of individual retribution, and the claims of spiritual experience entering a realm where it knew itself to be above death.[2]

From what has been said, the doctrine of a *resurrection* exhibited in Isa. xxvi. and in Dan. xii. should be carefully distinguished.[3] This belongs to the circle of Messianic ideas, rather than to anticipations of personal immortality.

[1] On the much-disputed question as to the doctrine of future life in the Psalter, see the Commentaries on Pss. 16, 17, 49, and 73.

[2] Cf. the connection of Greek ideas of immortality with the experience of mystical fellowship, discussed in Rohde's *Psyche*, ii. pp. 1–37.

[3] Cf. Charles, *op. cit.* 1354 f., for further details of what is here summarily stated.

In the former passage, certainly post-exilic, and possibly of the fourth century, the righteous nation to be re-established is not drawn from the living only ; with it are incorporated the righteous dead: "Thy dead shall live; my dead bodies shall arise. Awake and sing, ye that dwell in the dust: for thy dew is as the dew of herbs, and the earth shall cast forth the dead" (ver. 19). In the latter passage (Dan. xii. 2), belonging to the second century B.C., and also in connection with the Messianic deliverance, it is said: "And many of them that sleep in the dust of the earth shall awake, some to everlasting life, and some to shame and everlasting contempt." This is notable as the first reference to the resurrection of the wicked, and consequently to moral distinctions in the life beyond death.[1]

4. THE CONCEPTION OF SIN.

(*a*) *Terminology.*—The account already given of the development of individualism has itself involved the frequent recognition of a growing consciousness of sin amongst the religious thinkers of Israel. This fact is full of meaning for our subject ; we shall find the most characteristic features of the doctrine of man at every period brought to light through the study of the doctrine of sin, just as the central and characteristic element in the doctrine of God will always be the doctrine of grace. Both sin and grace require a survey of the whole history of religion in any given period for their adequate doctrinal statement ; in regard to religious experience they are complementary factors, so that in any detailed examination they

---

[1] The reference, however, is to a resurrection, not of all, but only of those Jews who are conspicuous for righteousness and for wickedness (*op. cit.* c. 1358). Later developments are noted below, pp. 71, 72. See "The Old Testament Approach to Life after Death," by H. Wheeler Robinson, in *The Congregational Quarterly*, April 1925.

would throw most light on each other by being studied together. It must be sufficient for the present purpose to glance at the chief successive phases of the conception of sin in the Old Testament. The most natural beginning is to attempt some classification of the terms for sin, in which the Hebrew vocabulary is so rich. But the value of such a classification is chiefly that it affords an introduction to the subject in its salient features; the revelation of the Old Testament is not philological, but historical; the mere term is a locked drawer until we have opened it with the key of history.

The principal terms employed in the Old Testament with reference to sin may be grouped in four classes, according as they denote (1) deviation from the right way;[1] (2) the changed status (guilt) of the agent;[2] (3) rebellion against a superior, or unfaithfulness to an agreement;[3] (4) some characterization of the quality of the act itself.[4] In the first class, the most important term is the verb *ḥāṭā̔* (with derivative nouns and adjectives), occurring 238 times, whilst the chief nominal form (*ḥaṭṭā'th*) is found 295 times. The original meaning of this root is that of "*missing*" some goal or path; thus, amongst the warriors of Benjamin, there were seven hundred men who were left-handed, "slinging with stones at a hair, and would not miss" (Judg. xx. 16; cf. Prov. xix. 2). The term tells us nothing that is definite about sin; it is the failure to do something or other, in relation (as the usage shows)

---

[1] ‏חטא‏, ‏עון‏, ‏עיל (עולה)‏, ‏שנה‏, ‏סור‏, ‏שטה‏.

[2] ‏אשם‏, ‏רשע‏.

[3] ‏פשע‏, ‏מרד‏, ‏מרה‏, ‏סרר‏, ‏מעל‏, ‏בגד‏, ‏רמיה (מרמה)‏.

[4] ‏רעה‏, ‏חמס‏, ‏שחת‏, ‏חבל‏, ‏און‏, ‏שוא‏, ‏הבל‏, ‏בליעל‏, ‏זלל‏, ‏סכל‏, ‏נבלה‏, ‏תועבה‏.

The terms are discussed in greater detail by Schultz, *Old Test. Theology* (E.T.), ii. pp. 281–291.

either to man or God (1 Sam. ii. 25). The similar idea of *going astray* underlies the use of '*āwōn*, usually rendered "iniquity", in regard to man (1 Sam. xx. 1) or God (Job xiii. 23), or of *shāgāh* (Ezek. xxxiv. 6; 1 Sam. xxvi. 21; Lev. iv. 13); and that of *turning aside* is equally capable of an ethical or religious (Ex. xxxii. 8) as of a physical (1 Sam. vi. 12) connotation. The second class of terms includes one (*rāshā'*) of which the derivation is obscure, though the usage suggests that the verb was primarily employed in a forensic sense, *i.e.* to pronounce guilty (Ex. xxii. 8), whilst the corresponding adjective is used of the guilty as opposed to the innocent (Deut. xxv. 2). Another term specially used to imply guilt is *āshām* (Gen. xxvi. 10; Prov. xiv. 9; Jer. li. 5; for the verb, Num. v. 7 and Ezek. xxv. 12, towards man; Lev. v. 19, towards God); the original suggestion may be that of the compensation paid for the wrong done (1 Sam. vi. 3, 4, 8, 17). But it should be noted that other terms (*e.g. āwōn* Ps. lix. 5, and *hāṭā'*, Gen. xliii. 9) easily pass over to denote the guilt of sin. The third class is the most important, because it yields a positive idea of sin, that of *rebellion*, and because this idea conducts us along the line of the religious history of Israel to the specific sense of sin in relation to God. The most important term here (*pāsha'*) is illustrated in its primary meaning by the words, " Israel rebelled against the house of David " (1 Kings xii. 19; cf. 2 Kings i. 1, iii. 5, 7, viii. 20, 22), and in its religious application by Isa. xliii. 27 : " Thy first father sinned, and thy ambassadors have rebelled against me "; the corresponding noun (inadequately rendered " trespass " or " transgression ") is found in Gen. xxxi. 36, l. 17 (against man), and Isa. lviii. 1 (against God). The intensity of meaning in this term is well illustrated by Job xxxiv 37 : " He addeth rebellion (*pesha'*) unto his sin (*ḥaṭṭā'th*) " ; the forceful suggestiveness of the term, in the prophetic literature where it is first employed, is best seen in Isa. i. 2 : "Sons I have brought up and reared, and *they* have rebelled against me," cries Yahweh, though the very ox and ass acknowledge their master. The word, as Davidson says (*Theology of the O.T.* p. 210), " describes sin as a personal, voluntary act. It also implies something rebelled against, something which is of the nature of a superior or an authority. . . . The word could not be used of the withdrawal of an equal from co-operation with another equal." The same idea of rebellion is implied in the terms *mārad* (2 Kings xviii. 7, against a human king ; Num. xiv. 9, against God), *mārāh* (Deut. xxi. 18, 20, against a father ; Num. xx. 10, against God), and *sārar* (Deut. xxi. 18, against a father ; Isa. lxv. 2, against God). With these it is natural to group such terms as denote treachery or infidelity, such as *mā'al* (Num. v. 12, 27, of wife against husband, v. 6, against God) and *bāgad* (1 Sam. xiv. 33). The fourth class is very wide in range, and hardly calls for detailed illustration ; some salient aspect of sin or its consequences is brought to view, namely, its badness, violence, destructiveness, trouble, worthlessness, vanity, folly, senselessness ; the most general of these terms (*rā'āh*) covers all kinds of evil (1 Sam. xii. 17).

(*b*) *Earlier limitations of morality.*—Whenever we study the moral ideas of a primitive or ancient people, what is apt to strike us most is their negative aspect, their marked limitations in contrast with our own more developed ideas. The truth of this general impression must not, however, blind us to the positive element in such ideas, often the germ of truer conceptions for ourselves. One of these positive elements we have already seen to be the sense of corporate responsibility, revealed to us on its negative side as "the defective sense of individuality." It is but an extension of the same circle of ideas when we find the fundamental notions of morality in Israel conditioned by emphasis on the nation as a group, not by reference to the individual Israelite, much less to man as man. The direct result of this emphasis is seen, for example, in the Song of Deborah (Judg. v.), where the highest praise is given to the warrior's patriotism that has saved the nation, and the deepest blame is cast on those who hung back from the battlefield ; Jael is exalted because she did not shrink from striking down Sisera, Israel's foe, whilst he drank from the bowl she had given him. We are apt to forget that Samuel's word, "to obey is better than sacrifice" (1 Sam. xv. 22), relates to the complete extermination of the Amalekites (with their possessions), who have been put under the ban as Israel's enemies by Samuel, "both man and woman, infant and suckling, ox and sheep, camel and ass" (ver. 3). The actual inhumanity of such conduct is not present to Israel's consciousness at all, but simply the supreme virtue of fidelity to national interests, and the expressed will of Yahweh. It is to be noted that the same attitude is retained, at least in theory, in the Book of Deuteronomy, though that book is characterized by its spirit of humanity ; this is because so definite a circle is drawn, within which humanity is obligatory. The "stranger", or settled foreigner (*gēr*), is indeed recognized and protected (i. 16, x. 19, xiv. 21, xxiv. 17, xxvii. 19), but this is because he has identified himself with Israel, becoming ultimately amenable to the same law (Ex. xii. 49, P) and the historical ancestor of the "proselyte." The exclusiveness of Israel is, no doubt, one of the secrets of her vitality; but it must also be recognized as a limitation of her morality, whatever its historical justification. This particular limitation is not only early but late, for it continues through the Judaism of the New Testament (Luke x. 29) into modern history, though, of course, with very different forms of expression.

A second line of limitation, belonging to early morality in general, and exhibited by Israel, lies in the close relation or dentification of custom and morality, and in the resultant externalism of morality. Whatever inferences are to be drawn for ethical theory, there is a very close relation between the recognized customs of a social group and its sense of obligation, especially at the stage with which we are concerned. "The rule of custom is conceived of as a moral rule, which decides what is right and wrong."[1] We find custom named as the explicit standard of appeal against an immoral act, when Tamar says to Amnon: "Nay, my brother, do not humble me; for no such thing ought to be done in Israel" (2 Sam. xiii. 12; cf. Gen. xxxiv. 7); whilst men express their horror of the outrage at Gibeah by saying, "There was no such deed done nor seen from the day that the children of Israel came up out of the land of Egypt unto this day" (Judg. xix. 30). Nabal's refusal to pay the customary levy to David and his band is characterized as evil-doing, rightly deserving the

---

[1] Westermarck, *The Origin and Development of the Moral Ideas,* i. p. 118; the subject is discussed and illustrated fully, pp. 158 f. (ch. vii. "Customs and Laws as Expressions of Moral Ideas"). For the earlier stages of Hebrew legislation, see "Deuteronomy and Joshua" (*Century Bible*), pp. 18 f.

sudden death which punished it (1 Sam. xxv. 39). We
see another side of the same phase of thought when the
punishment is itself inflicted by the social group whose
customs have been broken (Deut. xxii. 21), or when
neglect of such a custom as that of Levirate marriage is
threatened with social disgrace and an opprobrious name
(Deut. xxv. 8–10). Such "custom" practically becomes
"law" when administered by the elders, and "religion"
when interpreted by priests and prophets; there is no
clear differentiation at this stage. It is significant that the
words which subsequently became usual for "righteousness" and "wickedness" are those used at an earlier
period in a forensic sense: they are employed, *e.g.*, in
Deut. xxv. 1–3 (where the translation "righteous" and
"wicked" obscures the fact that we are concerned with
what we should now call the purely legal contrast of
"innocent" and "guilty"). This development at once
suggests the limitation of morality when linked to the
idea of "custom", whether vindicated or not by the
representatives of the society. The stress must inevitably
fall at this stage on the external act; the customs of a
society cannot be infringed by the thoughts and motives
of an individual until the latter find social expression,
and admit of being dealt with on the testimony of
witnesses. How serious the resultant limitation can be,
we may learn by contrasting this attitude with that of an
honourable man to-day, who is controlled by a sense of duty
clearly distinguished from, and often opposed to, public
opinion, and moving in a realm untouched by any law-
court. The limitation in the case of Israel can be seen
when a mere innovation, like David's census (2 Sam. xxiv.),
is condemned as sinful, because it is a breach of custom;

or when a case of pure ignorance, like that of Jonathan's eating honey in spite of his father's taboo (1 Sam. xiv. 24–27, 37 f.), is a sin to be punished ordinarily with death. "The greatest defect in ancient Israel's idea of sin is the fact that there is throughout no distinction between the conscious act of a free man against the will of God, failure through weakness, the unconscious deviation from a moral command, and the chance infringements of God's holiness through want of care or through ignorance."[1]

A third limitation, closely connected with the last, is that due to the incomplete moralization of the idea of Yahweh. This is involved in what has been said as to customary morality ; for Yahweh is conceived to be the enforcer of the social custom, just because the society itself is inseparably linked to Him. But this limitation will become more apparent if we turn to the process of its removal through the prophetic reformation of the religion of Israel.

(c) *The prophetic union of morality and religion.*—In the period of the great literary prophets of Israel, from Amos in the eighth century to the second Isaiah (Isa. xl.–lv.) in the sixth, there is a profound change in the conception of sin. It is lifted to the level of moral judgment; immorality is condemned as sin by reference to a new

---

[1] Stade, *Geschichte des Volkes Israel*, i. p. 512 ; cf. his *Biblische Theologie*, § 101. The externalism of customary morality is analysed by Robertson Smith as follows : "In two respects, then, the Hebrew idea of sin, in its earlier stages, is quite distinct from that which we attach to the word. In the first place, it is not necessarily thought of as offence against God, but includes any act that puts a man in the wrong with those who have power to make him rue it. . . . In the second place, the notion of sin has no necessary reference to the conscience of the sinner ; it does not necessarily involve moral guilt, but only, so to speak, forensic liability " (*Prophets of Israel*[2], pp. 102, 103).

4

conception of Yahweh; the true product of religious motive is declared to be moral conduct. The whole change may be most briefly described as the union of morality and religion, and three principal factors may be seen to have contributed to it. First and foremost, we have the personalities and activities of these great prophets themselves. No doubt they are in one sense simply the channels through which the deeper undercurrent of the national consciousness flows into daylight ; it would be foolish to contrast them too sharply with the prophets of the preceding period, when it contains such a narrative as that of the rebuke of David by Nathan—"unsurpassed in the moral literature of the world."[1] But Israel's literary records point to Amos, Hosea, Isaiah, and Micah, as of primary importance. Through their moral consciousness issued the principles rightly regarded by them as a divine revelation to their generation. The second principal factor is the Book of Deuteronomy, which is the expression of these prophetic ideals. Through it they found a permanent sanction and an enduring place in the life of Israel, and morality wedded to religion gave birth to the law, the written declaration of the will of Yahweh. The third factor was the exile, which did a work for the conceptions of sin and of righteousness similar to that done for the conception of individualism. Israel, separated from the temple, the land, and the law, which it had regarded as essential to religion, was made to realize that there is also an inner sanctuary which may be consecrated or defiled, an inner realm that belongs to its King, an inner law which expresses His will. The exile completed the work of the prophets, demonstrating their theorems and

[1] Gray, *The Divine Discipline of Israel*, p. 94.

partly solving their problems. The legalism of the Priestly Code must not hide from us the intense, if imperfect, sense of morality which created it.

The central feature in the teaching of the prophets is their insistence on the union of morality and religion. This, in itself, removed the principal earlier limitations of morality. In regard to individualism, the effect of their work has already been traced ; in regard to the social outlook, patriotism itself found a new and nobler purpose in the conception of Israel as the Servant of Yahweh, serving Him by its very sorrows. As against the earlier blending of custom with morality, the prophets who addressed the moral consciousness of Israel (*e.g.* as in the first chapter of Isaiah) were appealing from prevalent custom to an inner tribunal by which they declared it to be condemned. They were faced by the immoral worship of the Canaanites ; they asserted that this dishonoured Yahweh, who, indeed, desires mercy, not sacrifice (Hos. vi. 6), and requires nothing but justice, mercy, and humility from man (Mic. vi. 8). But the greatest step taken by the prophets in this respect was to declare that Yahweh was concerned rather with right-eousness than with Israel ; that He Himself acted as He required of men ; that He stood in relation with all men, though His special relation with Israel involved for the nation a higher and more searching test, and not mere favouritism (Amos iii. 2).

In the light of this development we can see the deeper meaning of the conception of sin as rebellion against the will of Yahweh (see § 4 (*a*), p. 44) with which the book of Isaiah's prophecies opens. It is no longer the breach of Israel's custom, nor is it even the defiance of an arbitrary ruler whose anger may be avoided or appeased. All that conscience condemns in social injustice, personal selfishness, or sensuality, the God who is Himself pure and upright condemns and will surely punish ; this is the lesson taught by past and present experience (Hos. xi. 1 f.; Amos iv. 6 f.). He seeks, moreover, for that intimate relation between His true worshippers and Himself called the " knowledge of God " (Hos. vi. 6) ; want of faith in Him becomes itself a sin (Isa. vii. 9).

(*d*) *Post-exilic developments.*—The Old Testament literature subsequent to the exile shows three lines along which the conception of sin was modified or developed, namely, the ritualism of the Law, the utilitarianism of Proverbs, and the piety of the Psalter. These terms must, of course, be taken simply as indicating a tendency, and not as a sufficient characterization; the Law, in its primary conception and national recognition, is the work of prophetic piety, whilst there are psalms that exalt the Law, and proverbs that confess sin. Along all three lines the influence of the prophets is to be seen, however far the result from their own position. The first national law-book, Deuteronomy, is the product of prophetic principles ; out of the lion of prophecy (Amos iii. 8) came forth the honey of the Law (Ps. xix. 10). As the clear declaration of the will of Yahweh, the written law may be regarded as the representative of the living voice of His messengers. But the Law contains, even in its later strata, many traditional elements (*e.g.* the distinction of clean and unclean) which are survivals from pre-prophetic days ; insistence on the observance of such rules, side by side with those of morality proper, could hardly fail to obscure the prophetic emphasis in the conception of sin. Ezekiel already includes a purely physical element in his description of the good man's conduct (xviii. 6: withdrawal from a woman in her separation). Further, the standard of morality can never be transferred from the inner voice to the outer code without externalizing the conception of righteousness and sin. Sin thus became violation of an external law [1] rather than the expression of a spiritual attitude. The limited standard of " righteousness " encouraged the idea of merit to be acquired, and " good works " to be done, by a conceivably complete obedience. On the other hand, we must not lose sight of the growing intensity of the sense of sin, as expressed in the ritual of sacrifice. In the first legislative code of the Old Testament, the Book of the Covenant (Ex. xx. 22–xxiii. 19), the only sacrifices are the burnt-offering and the peace-offering (Ex. xx. 24), to which the Deuteronomic Code, a century or two later, adds the heave-offering (Deut. xii. 6, 17). But more specific connection of sin with sacrifice meets us in the post-exilic legislation. Here we have the guilt-offering (Lev. v. 14–16) closely connected with the idea of compensation for wrongful appropriation, though extended to other cases, such as ceremonial uncleanness; also, the sin-offering (Lev. iv. 1 f.) available for the removal of ceremonial uncleanness, such as that of the leper (Lev. xiv. 19), or in cases of unintentional disobedience to the law (Num. xv. 27), and central in the ceremonies of the Day of Atonement (Lev. xvi. 3). It should be clearly noted that the Law makes no provision for the forgiveness

---

[1] This is seen, *e.g.*, in the fact that guilt is not affected by ignorance of the law that has been broken (Lev. v. 17), any more than by ignorance of the "customs" of Israel. In fact, the old externalism is renewed in part through the new influences, though Christian scholars probably tend to over-emphasize the darker side of legalism.

or atonement of intentional sin, as the last-named context shows ; sin committed, not "in error", but "with a high hand", involves the death of the sinner, and this is illustrated by an alleged case in which the penalty of death was inflicted for breach of the Sabbath law (Num. xv. 32-36). Similarly, the Psalmist speaks only of sins of inadvertence or error (Ps. xix. 12), and does not contemplate the case of wilful disobedience to the law.

The "utilitarianism" of the Book of Proverbs lies in its thorough-going application of the theory of moral retribution, noticed above, to the circumstances of individual life. On the basis of practical experience, its authors claim to construct a manual of practical ethics ; the motive to which they appeal is primarily the desire for personal happiness. The keynote is given by the belief that "righteousness delivereth from death" (xi. 4), where death must be taken in a purely natural sense. The book assumes that virtue, if not itself knowledge, is largely the product of knowledge ; the prudent man, knowing the practical value of righteousness, is expected to act rightly, *i.e.* in accordance with the rules of conscience, as universally recognized. Thus we gain a new terminology for right and wrong, ideas which now become interchangeable with "wisdom" and "folly"; "folly" is represented in various grades, from that of the mere simpleton to that of the scorner.[1] The limitations of such a conception of sin are sufficiently obvious; but the truth that the sinner sets himself against the morally directed forces of the universe must not be overlooked, since it is a valuable product of the prophetic teaching.

The piety of the Psalter rests, for the most part, on the same basis ; but its special significance for the conception

[1] Cf. Davidson, *op. cit.* pp. 209, 210.

of sin belongs to the religious atmosphere of its higher levels, so different from that of the confined valley in which the wise men move. The religion of the Psalms directly continues that of the prophets, as when God is said to desire not sacrifice, but obedience (xl. 6–8; cf. lxix. 30, 31), and when morality is made essential to worship (xv., xxiv.; cf. lxvi. 18, 19, l. 16). In regard to the consciousness of sin, there is a remarkable blending of the sense of Israel's superiority as a nation with that of individual sin.[1] This will not be affected by the question as to how far a particular psalm is individual or national; whatever the temple use of the Psalter, its confessions of sin and convictions of forgiveness (li., xxxii.) ultimately spring from the experience of individual hearts. Sin cannot be hidden from God (lxix. 5), and none can stand (cxxx. 3) or be justified (cxliii. 2) in His sight; it is God who must purge away the sin of man (lxv. 3). No doubt, it is misfortune or suffering which brings men to think of God, as in the series of pictures of the traveller, the prisoner, the sick man, and the sailor of Ps. cvii.; "forgiveness" is largely the removal of external trouble, such as serious illness (Ps. xxxii. 4, 5). It is easy to read into such words as those of Ps. li. a spirituality of meaning beyond what is present. But that psalm lays at least the foundation for the Christian conception of sin by its recognition of sin as an inner reality (6, 10) wrought against God (4), which God only can forgive (7) when He sees true repentance (16, 17).

(*e*) *Relation to later dogmatic theories.*—The above outline of the development of the conception of sin in the Old Testament includes no reference to certain points which

---

[1] Cf. Montefiore, *Hibbert Lectures*, pp. 514 f.

dogmatic theory subsequently made prominent, namely, (1) the absolute universality of sin; (2) the idea of inborn sinfulness; (3) the origin of sin, with its consequences for human nature. The silence has been intentional, not only because of the undogmatic character of the Old Testament in general, but because incidental discussion of these points would have blurred the historical perspective of the development. It remains, however, to state briefly the extent to which the Old Testament is in harmony on these points with later ecclesiastical doctrine.

(1) The universality of sin is both presupposed and explicitly stated from the prophetic period onwards. But the presupposition and the statement indicate a fact of general experience, not an absolute dogma. This will be seen by reference to the contexts of the "proof passages" usually given (*e.g.* by Müller, *The Christian Doctrine of Sin* (E.T.), ii. p. 256). "There is no man that sinneth not" (1 Kings viii. 46; cf. 2 Chron. vi. 36) is a parenthetic statement in a prayer that God may hear the penitent and forgive. "No living man is acquitted before thee" (Ps. cxliii. 2) is also part of a prayer, which seeks deliverance from enemies through the loving-kindness of God, and asks not to be treated on purely forensic terms. The couplet of Prov. xx. 9, "Who can say, I have made my heart clean, I am pure from my sin?" is counter-balanced by the previous verse but one, "A just man that walketh in his integrity, blessed are his children after him", showing the relativity of both statements. The remark of Eccles. vii. 20, "Surely there is not a righteous man upon earth, that doeth good and sinneth not", may itself be a later corrective of the statement in ver. 15, "There is a righteous man that perisheth in his righteousness." No

doubt, as a fact of experience, the practical universality of sinfulness raises important problems; but no solution of them is forthcoming in the Old Testament.

(2) A possible explanation of the universality of sin might have been found in the theory that sin, as an active principle, was inborn in each man; and it has often been held that this theory is represented in the Old Testament. Some of the passages usually cited in proof of this (*e.g.* Job. xiv. 4; Gen. viii. 21) imply no more than the actual universality of sin; that which Müller regards as "most conclusive" is found in Ps. li. 5: "Behold, in iniquity was I brought forth, and in sin my mother conceived me." Such words are interpreted according to the line of approach of the reader; an ascetic might see in them a clear statement that sexual relations are essentially evil, just as a student of Augustine might think of the *peccatum originale*, the sin of Adam, with its consequences transmitted through the parents to the child.[1] But if we come to them from the standpoint of the Old Testament itself, we can hardly see more in them than the pointed and realistic declaration that the speaker belongs to a sinful race, and that those before him were sinners as well as himself. For the peculiar form of the statement we may compare Ps. lviii. 3, "Estranged are the wicked from the womb; they have gone astray from birth, speaking lies"; or Isa. xlviii. 8, "Rebellious from birth art thou called."[2] The speaker urges the fact that he started life, as we should say, in a sinful environment, as one element in his prayer for forgiveness; similarly, Yahweh is elsewhere presented as abstaining from a second destruction of

---

[1] This theory is, of course, to be distinguished from the idea of simply inborn sin, without reference to Adam.   [2] Cf. also Job xxxi. 18.

mankind, because He now recognizes that "the imagination of man's heart is evil from his youth" (Gen. viii. 21); cf. the various references to man's sinfulness in the Book of Job, *e.g.* "How shall man be acquitted with God, and how shall the offspring of woman be pure?" (xxv. 4). To speak of inherited sinfulness in the case of any of these passages, including Ps. li. 5, is not justified by historical exegesis; probably no more is intended than what Isaiah says (vi. 5): "I am a man of unclean lips, and I dwell in the midst of a people of unclean lips", though it is expressed with the Hebrew love of the concrete and vivid statement, equally shewn in Pss. xxii. 10 and lxxi. 6.

(3) Prior to the modern historical study of the Old Testament, it was generally assumed that the third chapter of Genesis was intended to supply both an explanation of the origin of sin and a statement of its consequences for the whole race, which included mortality and a corrupted nature. This view is no longer possible to the modern student who studies the narrative in its historic setting. It would have been strange that such a doctrine, if really found in Gen. iii. by its earliest readers, had left no definite trace on the rest of the Old Testament; yet there is none. The silence of the Old Testament might, to some extent, be explained by tracing this and the kindred narratives to similar stories found amongst other peoples, notably amongst the Babylonians; borrowed legends as to the origins of mankind and civilization would be likely to exert little influence on the development of native Israelite thought. But it is not necessary to depend on this explanation; Gen. iii. really raises no problem as to the silence of the rest of the Old Testament about "original sin", for this conception is absent from

that passage. In itself, the narrative is one of a cycle of stories tracing the progress of civilization in prehistoric days, but with especial interest in its moral and religious aspects. The centre of the narrative, in its present form,[1] is the tree of the knowledge of good and evil. The words "good" and "evil" suggest distinct ethical issues to the modern reader; but to Hebrew thought they are of broader significance, and cover what is useful or advantageous on the one hand, and what is harmful on the other, *i.e.* the knowledge implied is that of civilization, culture, progress. This is sufficiently shewn by Hebrew parallels: thus, Barzillai says to David, "I am this day fourscore years old; can I discern between good and bad? can thy servant taste what I eat or what I drink? can I hear any more the voice of singing men and singing women?" (2 Sam. xix. 35), and the same non-moral meaning is probable in Isa. vii. 15, 16. That there is a deep ethical meaning in the narrative of Gen. iii. is clear, but it lies in man's disobedience of a divine command through his desire for what God sees fit to withhold from him. Man gains what he desires, and passes from the naked innocence of the child to the knowledge and powers of maturity; but the price he has paid makes his civilization accursed, since progress in civilization proves to be progress also in evil. This seems to be the original thought of the narrative, in which the more ethical elements may represent the working of Israel's own thought (on the material of Semitic legend) in the ninth and eighth centuries. The act of disobedience is done by one in a state of moral freedom, according to

[1] The subject is discussed in detail by Tennant, *The Sources of the Doctrines of the Fall and Original Sin*, pp. 1–88; the point of view taken above is, broadly, that of Smend, Marti, and Wellhausen; the important point as to the significance of the tree is due to the last named.

the general view of the Old Testament; the fact that temptation is mediated through the woman is a natural trait, especially to the Oriental; that the suggestion springs from the wise serpent (not to be identified with the much later Satan) may be due chiefly to the original machinery of the story, according to widespread ethnic ideas about this particular animal. In regard to the consequences of the act of disobedience, the threat of ii. 17 [1] is in any case unfulfilled, so that we are not entitled to infer from it that man's mortality is here traced directly to his sin; on the other hand, we read in iii. 22 f. that man is removed from Eden in order that he may not eat of the tree of life, and live for ever, the inference being that without it he is naturally mortal. This is the view elsewhere found in the Old Testament; we are not justified, therefore, in saying more than that man is left to his natural mortality because of his sin, whilst the woman's travail and the man's toil are its direct punishments. There is no suggestion in the narrative that man's nature is changed by his act of disobedience; still less, that he handed on a corrupted nature to his children, which placed them in an ethical position essentially different from his own; in fact, Cain, when his turn comes, is bidden by Yahweh to master the sin that crouches at his door (iv. 7). The obscure and probably fragmentary narrative in vi. 1–4 is apparently used in its present context to explain the wickedness prior to the Flood, by reference to the cohabitation of supernatural beings with women of the earth; but, in itself, the passage simply describes the rise of a race of prehistoric giants from this union.[2]

---

[1] "In the day that thou eatest thereof, thou shalt surely die."

[2] Cf. Skinner, *Genesis*, p. 145, for meaning of verse 3.

5. The Relation of Man to Nature and God.

(*a*) *Creation and the natural order of the world.*—The aspects of the Old Testament doctrine of man already considered are those of his personality, of his relation to the society in which he lives, and of the most characteristic fact of his moral nature, namely, sin. To complete our survey it is necessary to give a brief account of man's place in the Hebrew conception of the universe—a conception which necessarily involves the idea of the general relation of man to God. The Old Testament begins with two narratives of man's creation, that of Gen. i.–ii. 4*a* being post-exilic (P), and that of Gen. ii. 4*b* f. being pre-exilic (J) and dating in its literary form from the ninth century. It is probable that we have not the whole of the earlier account (J); but, in its present form, it describes how the dry earth was fertilized by a recurrent mist, how man was shaped by Yahweh and animated by His breath, how trees were made to grow and animals to live for the sake of man, for whose companionship, finally, woman was created. It is clear that man constitutes the central interest in this narrative, and all else becomes little more than scenic background. This central emphasis on man continues throughout the Old Testament, and is characteristic of Hebrew thought. The principle remains when we pass to the prophets; from Amos (*e.g.* iv. 13) to the second Isaiah (*e.g.* xlii. 5) we find, indeed, a growing conception of the creative activity of Yahweh, but this only serves to exalt His power as ruler of the world of men. Similarly, in the post-exilic creation narrative (P), the orderly process traced to the personal will of God culmin-

ates in the creation of man, made in the image of God
(Gen. i. 26, 27), to have dominion over every living thing.
We may trace the same idea of man's unique position
through the well-known nature-psalms. They assert the
absolute power of God over Nature, only to give man more
confidence in Him. God has raised man far above the
world (viii. 5 f.); whilst the heavens declare His glory
(xix. 1), the earth brings forth its fruits for man (civ. 14 f.,
lxv. 9 f.), and the sea fulfils God's educative purpose
(cvii. 25; cf. Jonah i. 9 f.). In the nature-poems of the
Book of Job the mystery and majesty of Nature are chiefly
emphasized as beyond man's comprehension (*e.g.* xxxviii.
4 f.); whilst in Prov. viii. 22–31 Nature is viewed as the
product of divine Wisdom, whose delight is with the sons
of men. Through the influence of the great prophets,
the Hebrew learnt to approach Nature from the standpoint of religion,[1] and saw it primarily as the framework
for human life—a framework which often thrills in sympathy with the living drama which it subserves (Isa. xxxv.).
On the other hand, man is himself part of the Nature over
which he rules, helpless like it before God; he passes away
like the grass (Ps. ciii. 15; cf. xc. 5; Isa. xl. 6), his life is but a
breath in his nostrils (Isa. ii. 22), dependent on God's favour
(Ps. civ. 29), and his flesh is of no more permanence than the
passing wind (Ps. lxxviii. 39). But this serves only to make
God's favour and providence more wonderful (Ps. viii. 3 f.)
In the conception of this providence, the thought of the
direct presence and activity of Yahweh in Nature is never

[1] The earlier conception of Yahweh as a tribal deity, worshipped at
"holy places", makes Him but one element, however important, in the
whole environment. Köberle (*Natur und Geist*, p. 261) points out how
reaction from the nature-worship of Canaanite sanctuaries would influence
the higher thought of Israel; no room was left within Hebrew theism for the
quasi-independence of Nature.

lost when once (in the prophets) attained ; nightly does He bring out the stars (Isa. xl. 26); winds are His messengers, and fire and flame His ministers (Ps. civ. 4). A miracle is no mere entrance of Yahweh into the arena of Nature, for He was already there. Though He works regularly, there is no conception of a " law of Nature " in the Old Testament to make His access to man less conceivable. " This opposition between a divine will, which has stamped itself on the natural order, and another, better divine will, which shews itself in the violation of this natural order, could not arise at all for the Hebrew " (Marti, *Gesch. d. isr. Religion*, p. 144). Yet in some natural effects He is felt to be nearer than in others; because Palestine is watered chiefly by infrequent rains, and Egypt by the more constant Nile, the former is specially dependent on Yahweh, and a peculiar object of His care (Deut. xi. 10–12).

(*b*) *Providence and the Spirit of God.*—The unbroken control exercised by God over the outer world of man's life extends into the inner also; Hebrew thought is as emphatic on this point as on the equally maintained truth of moral freedom. " Man's are the heart's plans ; but from Yahweh the tongue's answer " (Prov. xvi. 1); whilst the Psalmist's conviction is that Yahweh knows the unspoken word, and shuts man in to His will (Ps. cxxxix. 4, 5). The divine control of human life in the whole of its activities is, indeed, one of the profoundest conceptions of Old Testament religion, and one which penetrates every aspect of its doctrine of man. It receives most striking expression in the figure of the potter and the clay (Jer. xviii. 6); the destinies of Israel, as of all the nations, are absolutely in Yahweh's hands. Yet the absoluteness of divine power is conceived by the prophets as conditioned in two fundamental ways. It is power animated by a gracious, because a righteous, purpose, in which Israel occupies a central and covenanted place; and that purpose is so far conditioned by the recognition of human freedom that, in the very passage indicated above, a change of character in man is answered by a change of attitude in God (Jer. xviii. 7 f.). The philosophical problems that occur to ourselves in this connection lay beyond the horizon of Israel; in particular, Hebrew thought does not face the implicates of its conviction that all has a purpose and even the wicked is made for the day of evil (Prov. xvi. 4). It was enough for Hebrew faith that Nature and history alike are at God's disposal, and for Hebrew experience that man is able to rebel against God, though he cannot escape from God. The conception of the Spirit of God initiates a deeper conception of the relation of man to Him. The term "spirit" (*ruach*; *supra*, 2 (*b*)) occurs about 134 times in the Old Testament in regard to supernatural influences, acting on man in almost every case; it is rarely used, as in Gen. i. 2, of influence on inanimate objects. The idea of the specific iufluence develops with the idea of God Himself. In its personal use we may trace at least five stages, according to the effect produced, the classification being broadly chronological as well as conceptual. (1) In the earliest literature such phenomena as madness (1 Sam. xvi. 14), ecstatic prophesying (xix. 20 f.), or superhuman strength (Judg. xiv. 6), are ascribed to divine influence. (2) This is also seen in remarkable events (Judg. vi. 34) or lives (Gen. xli. 38). (3) To the *ruach* of God is ascribed the prophetic consciousness (Num. xxiv. 2; Ezek. ii. 2), though the prophets of the eighth century avoid a term probably discredited by some of its alleged manifestations. Later on, however, revelation in general is thought to be mediated by the *ruach* of God (Zech. vii. 12; Neh. ix. 30). (4) To the same source are ascribed technical skill (Ex. xxviii. 3) and practical ability (Deut. xxxiv. 9), when exhibited in some marked degree. (5) Finally, we reach a group of cases in which the effect of the *ruach* of God is seen in more general conduct and character, as when the Psalmist prays, " Take not thy holy *ruach* from me " (li. 11) ; or the *ruach* of Yahweh is said to be on one who gives himself to the proclamation of the Old Testament gospel (Isa. lxi. 1 f.). In this group we reach a direct point of contact with the New Testament doctrine of the Spirit of God ; the out-pouring of the Spirit on all flesh declared by Joel (ii. 28 f.; cf. Isa. xxxii. 15, xliv. 3, lix. 21 ; Zech. xii. 10) is said by Peter to be fulfilled in the era inaugurated by Pentecost (Acts ii. 16). The connection in this case is more than verbal ; the Old Testament doctrine of the Spirit of God is in closest genetic relation to the New Testament doctrine of man's renewal by the Spirit of Christ, and divine providence fitly culminates in the experience of Christian salvation.

(c) *The fellowship of man and God.*—The Spirit of God, however, always in the Old Testament retains the sense of a specially given energy, an *ad hoc* influence. It is clear that some more permanent and abiding relationship between man and God must underlie the products and records of Old Testament religion. The history of that relationship would become a history of the religion; but its chief features come sufficiently into view through the two ideas of it which underlie Semitic religion in general : " The two leading conceptions of the relation of the god to his people are those of fatherhood and of kingship . . . the

5

clan and the state are both represented in religion: as
father the god belongs to the family or clan, as king he
belongs to the state."[1]   What has been said (p. 27 f.) as to
the incorporation of the individual in the social group
must of course be remembered here; in the Old Testament
Yahweh is the father of Israel rather than of the Israelite
(Deut.xxxii.6)—"our father", not "my father" (Isa.lxiii.16).
He calls His son Israel from Egypt, teaching His people
to walk as a father teaches a little child, carrying it when
tired (Hos. xi. 1–3).   God is called the father of individuals
in the special case of David's descendants alone, as actual
(2 Sam. vii. 14) or as ideal (Ps. ii. 7, lxxxix. 27) kings of
Israel.   But though God's fatherly pity of "those who
fear Him" (Ps. ciii. 13), and His fatherly protection of the
orphans (lxviii. 5), may not be unduly pressed in the
direction of individualism, yet something at least of their
individual bearing must have been felt by those who sang
of them together in the "great congregation." The
idea of Yahweh's kingship, on the other hand, suggests
social rather than individualistic development.   Yahweh
is King of Israel (1 Sam. xii. 12), or "a great king over all
the earth" (Ps. xlvii. 2), "whose name is terrible among
the Gentiles" (Mal. i. 14).   The social development of the
important conception of the kingdom of God characterizes
the New Testament, not less than that of His Fatherhood.
The demand of both is for individual loyalty.   Around
the two conceptions of kingship and fatherhood were
destined to gather two primary principles of the Christian
relation to God—the duty of absolute obedience, and the
privilege of absolute trust.

It is fitting that our survey of the Old Testament

---

[1] Robertson Smith, *Religion of the Semites*, p. 40.

doctrine of man should close with these cardinal conceptions. But we must not forget that the relationship of Israel and the Israelite to God found expression, as the hymn-book of the Temple still shews us, in many ways—in the outlook on Nature, or the memory of history, or the reunion for some festival in the Temple itself. It came in solitude through the devout study of the law; it came amid the throng when the smoke of sacrifice curled up. But whatever the external channel, and however limited, from a later standpoint, were the ideas reached, the whole history of Israel, and the tenacity of its grasp on its religion, shew how real the fellowship of man and God must have been. Its fruit was the knowledge of God, and "what Scripture means by knowledge of God is an ethical relation to Him; and, on the other side, when it says that God knows man, it means He has sympathy and fellowship with him."[1] In the Psalter there are two powers able to break that fellowship, sin and death. We have seen that the power of death was practically absolute for the Hebrew, though his spiritual vision might sometimes lift him beyond it; but the power of sin could be cancelled by the simple grace of God, in forgiving love and cleansing pardon for the penitent heart. It was not yet that a Hebrew of the Hebrews should be taught to cry, in face of death, "Thanks be to God who giveth us the victory", and in face of sin, "I thank God through Jesus Christ our Lord."[2]

---

[1] Davidson, *Theology of the Old Testament*, p. 78.

[2] The general results of this chapter are summed up at the beginning of the next. For a more recent discussion see Burton's *Spirit, Soul, and Flesh* (1918), and H. Wheeler Robinson's "Hebrew Psychology" in *The People and the Book* (1925; ed. by Peake).

CHAPTER II.

THE NEW TESTAMENT DOCTRINE OF MAN.

1. INTRODUCTION.

(*a*) *The Old Testament foundation.*—Even had there been no New Testament, the conception of man found amongst the most profoundly religious people of antiquity would possess peculiar interest for the historical student. That interest, however, is raised to a higher plane when it is recognized that the New Testament pre-supposes the Old, and that the idea of human person-ality which characterizes the Christian revelation would be unintelligible to us, at least in its finer ramifications of meaning, if we were not able to trace its roots in Hebrew soil. The result of our previous study of the Old Testament doctrine of man has been to bring out three conceptions of primary importance. In the first place, we have seen the high place and dignity of man postulated by the moral and religious experience of the Hebrew. Man is the centre of the created world, with little less than angelic rank; man is endowed with the power to rebel even against the will of God, though he cannot ultimately defeat that will. But the submission of Job is as typical for Hebrew, as the defiance of Prometheus is for Greek, thought. The characteristic Hebrew emphasis on the

need for penitence and humility before God, the consciousness of man's littleness over against God's greatness, the
religious sense of dependence on God, are all of them
indirect testimonies to, not contradictions of, the Hebrew
sense of man's worth. The close relation of man to God
marks him off from the rest of Nature, and elevates him
above it ; the moral demands upon him witness to the
deep meaning of human life ; the sense of sin is the
shadow cast by a religious experience that lifts man,
at its highest moments, into fellowship with his Maker.
Clearly we have here a presupposition of the greatest
significance for the comprehension of the Gospel of Jesus
Christ; humility and dignity are here met together. In
the second place, the Hebrew conception of personality on
its psychological side is distinctly that of a unity, not of a
dualistic union of soul (or spirit) and body. It is true
that we have two principal terms (*nephesh* and *ruach*)
to denote the lower and higher levels of the inner life
respectively, whilst various physical organs, together with
a psychical conception of " flesh ", denote by their usage
the more outward and visible aspects of human personality. But our study of these terms has shewn the
impossibility of dissecting the conception into " soul "
(or " spirit ") and " body." Man is what he is by the
union of certain quasi-physical principles of life with
certain physical organs, psychically conceived ; separate
them, and you are left not with either soul or body in our
sense, but with impersonal energies on the one hand, and
with *disjecta membra* on the other.[1] Two important

---

[1] It will be remembered that the outlook is confined to this world ; the
dissolution of this personal unity is the end of any real personal existence for
Hebrew thought.

results follow from this conception; on the one hand, moral evil is not explained dualistically by the opposition of soul and body, though the weakness of the flesh against temptation is admitted; on the other, the higher side of human personality (expressed by *ruach*) is conceived to be accessible to God to a much greater degree than our present ideas of personality would usually suggest to us. In these two results we have the prolegomena to the Christian doctrines of sin and grace, in their New Testament, and, to some extent, in their ecclesiastical, form. Then, in the third place, the Old Testament presents us with the social conception of man, his religion being intimately bound up with the relationship to God of the whole group to which he belongs. It is out of this social background that individualism with its many problems emerges; the result is that the individualism brings with it a rich colouring of social life, which is reflected in the New Testament conception of the kingdom of God. Amongst the problems of this individualism a foremost place belongs to the question of the future of the individual after death. Here we come to the most marked limitation of the Old Testament doctrine of man; little more than the tendency towards the doctrine of a future life can be found in its pages. But even this tendency would justify us in expecting that the development will be towards a larger idea of social life, both on earth and in heaven, by the path of a more spiritual individualism. What the Old Testament failed to reach in eschatological result can be studied in the literature of the period lying between it and the New Testament.

(*b*) *Anthropology of the later Judaism.*—The literature

of Judaism lying between the Old and New Testaments is so varied in type, and raises so many complex critical problems, that brief generalization is difficult, even if not misleading. It would, however, be more misleading to leave the gulf unbridged, when the historic continuity is so real as it is between the two collections of canonical literature. It is possible at least to indicate the main lines of anthropological development which have contributed to make the New Testament a different book from the Old. This development centres primarily in the extension of eschatological outlook. The tendency to this extension has been pointed out in the Old Testament itself; but the new projection of man's destiny into the unseen world is so important, both in itself and in its reaction on the general conception of human personality, that it may be called the chief contribution of later Judaism to our subject.[1] The old conception of Sheol, as the land of shades, but not of real personal existence, is transformed. The bones of men may remain in the earth, but their spirits continue to live (Jubilees xxiii. 31). The non-moral realm of Sheol is differentiated on ethical lines (Enoch xxii.). The old problems of nationalism and individualism are transplanted into this new realm, and the political subjection of Judaism in the present is avenged in the panorama of the future. Two principal lines of Judaistic thought can be traced, namely, the Hellenistic, shewing the clear influence of Greek ideas, and the Palestinian, that of Judaism proper. In the

---

[1] Details will be found in the article on " Eschatology ', by Charles, in the *Encyclopædia Biblica*, cc. 1335 f. The general anthropology of the period is discussed by Bousset, *Die Religion des Judentums im neutest. Zeitalter*[2], and in Fairweather's article, " Development of Doctrine in the Apocryphal Period " (Hastings' *Dictionary of the Bible*, vol. v.).

former, represented by the Book of Wisdom and culminating in Philo, the main principle is that of immortality
(*e.g.* Wisd. ii. 23, iii. 1), and we even find the conception of
the pre-existence of souls (Wisd. viii. 19, 20), an idea quite
foreign to the thought of the Old Testament. Retribution
is expected immediately after death (Wisd. iv. 7 f.). Palestinian Judaism, on the other hand, emphasizes the necessity
for the final resurrection of the body, but so far unites
this idea with the doctrine of immediate retribution as to
conceive an intermediate state, a partial and temporary
differentiation of the good and the evil, pending the final
day of judgment.[1] The importance of these conceptions
for the study of the New Testament may be illustrated
from the Apocalypse of Baruch (cc. xlix.–li.), which teaches
that, though the dead will be raised with the actual bodies
of earth, these will be transformed into more suitable
bodies for their new existence—an interesting parallel, as
Charles has pointed out (*loc. cit.* 1369), to the Pauline doctrine
of the pneumatic body.

Such conceptions as these could not but transfer the
centre of gravity of the general anthropology from this
age to the next; the Old Testament ideas of man continue,
but with important changes of emphasis. Two of these
can be seen to prepare directly for the New Testament
point of view. The first is the accentuation of individualism.
The gateway into the other world is passed by men one
by one. Here was an obvious refuge for those who saw
their national religious hopes baffled. The inner life of
the individual thus secured increasing recognition, for
along this line the future lay. That future might or
might not secure the establishment of the kingdom of

---

[1] Cf. Bousset, *op. cit.* pp. 339 f., and the references there.

God as a divine society ;[1] but, in either case, eschatology resulted in a deepened individual emphasis, and in the consequent elaboration of religious psychology,[2] which will receive a sufficient illustration in the thought of Paul. In close relation with this, as a second result of the new outlook, we may trace a fuller and clearer recognition of the ethical problems. The narrative of Genesis is enlisted into dogmatic service, though we must beware of attributing Augustinian anthropology to Judaistic thinkers. The actual existence of evil is connected historically with the beginning of the human race: "From a woman was the beginning of sin, and because of her we all die" (Ecclus. xxv. 24); "By the envy of the devil death entered into the world" (Wisd. ii. 24). We shall see, however, in the Pauline reproduction of Jewish ideas on this point, that the connection of the entrance of death with the first historical sin does not necessarily involve the doctrine of original sin. We come somewhat nearer to this doctrine, it is true, in the late work known as 4 Ezra, where it is taught that there is a principle of evil in Adam and all his descendants, explaining his and their sin.[3] But we also meet with the clear assertion that Adam is the arbiter of his own soul's destiny, and that "every one of us has been the Adam of his own soul" (Apoc. Baruch liv. 19). This assertion of human freedom runs all through the period (as, indeed, through both the Old Testament and the New); we meet it in Sirach (Ecclus. xv. 11) at the

For the variety of view on this point, see Charles, *loc. cit.* 1366.

[2] Bousset, *op. cit.* pp. 345, 346.

[3] It is doubtful whether the Apocryphal literature contains anything that ought to be called a doctrine of original sin. The appeal of Tennant (*The Fall and Original Sin*, pp. 217, 228) to Apoc. Baruch xlviii. 42, 43 and 4 Ezra vii. 118, 119 does not carry us far, as he himself points out.

beginning,and at the end in the Mishnah(*Pirqe Aboth*, iii. 24), where, however, it is combined with the antithetic assertion of foreknowledge, in characteristic Jewish fashion : " Everything is foreseen, and free will is given. And the world is judged by grace ; and everything is according to work." It is recognized that man's freedom is modified by a tendency to evil, but this must neither be pressed into determinism nor conceived dualistically.[1] The dualistic interpretation of the relation of body and soul (or spirit) is found in the Hellenistic line of Judaism (Wisd. ix. 15); but it is alien to the Palestinian line, which directly links the thought of the Old Testament with that of much of the New.

Over against the eschatological development, which forms the chief contribution of later Judaistic theology to the Christian doctrine of man, we may notice the chief lacuna in the religious experience generated by Judaism. This lacuna is the absence of any adequate development of the Old Testament idea of the Spirit of God. The Canon came to be in large measure the sepulchre of that idea, however true it be that the Messiah was anticipated as both possessing and distributing the gift of the Spirit (*e.g.* Test. Levi xviii.). The attitude of the record of Maccabean history (1 Macc. iv. 46) is typical of much in the period ; the consciousness of the immediate inspiration and presence of God, which the doctrine of the Spirit implies, had passed into more or less hopeful expectancy of some return of the heroic age. Christian faith saw that expectation realized in Christ ; its experience

---

[1] Weber's well-known discussion of the " evil impulse " (*Jüdische Theologie*, pp. 209 f.) is to be corrected by Porter's later examination of the facts in his essay on " The Yeçer Hara " (*Yale Bicentennial Publications*, 1901).

was of the present possession of the outpoured Spirit
(Acts ii. 16 f.), given through the Lord the Spirit
(2 Cor. iii. 18).

(c) *The chief New Testament conceptions.*—In the New
Testament we do not find dogmatic discussions of human
nature and its problems, any more than in the Old ; nor
ought we to expect the unity and consistency rightly
demanded of a formal system. What we do find is a new
centre, around which the ideas of the Old Testament, as
modified by the later Judaism, can arrange themselves in
all their fluidity, the time of dogmatic crystallization not
yet having come. This new centre is the personality of
Jesus, around whom all the problems of God and man
ultimately gather. In the New Testament, however, these
problems are hardly as yet felt ; the experiences generated
by the presence of Jesus Christ are sufficient to engross its
pages. This concentration of interest is the more clearly
marked, because the thousand years of Old Testament
literature here shrink into a mere half-century. Even
within this short span there are the varieties of interpretation which belong to every living experience; but underneath these varieties there is a real unity—the unity of
the new character created by the new relation to an historic
Person.

Three principal types of the interpretation of this
relation will concern us, types which also mark stages of
development, namely, the Synoptic, the Pauline, and the
Johannine. In the Synoptic Gospels we seem to be
brought nearest to the historic teaching and life of Jesus ;
according to that teaching and example, man is objectively
presented to us as the child of God, obedient or disobedient, the child God seeks to save. In the Pauline

Epistles Christian experience itself becomes the datum, and man is primarily conceived as the organ of the Spirit, mediated through the risen Christ. In the Johannine writings we return to the realm of history, but of history so presented as to reveal some of its ultimate meanings; the world is interpreted and judged by the manifestation of Christ, and human nature is estimated according to its belief or disbelief in Him. Besides these principal conceptions, there are anthropological references in the rest of the New Testament literature of great interest and raising great issues, but too isolated in their setting to have had much historical influence. Such, for example, are Jas. i. 13–15 (sin does not originate in God, but in a man's own evil desires, and it issues in death); Heb. vi. 4–6 (the limits of possible penitence); Heb. ii. 14, 15 (the fear of death); 1 Pet. iii. 19, 20 (the salvation of those who have died before Christ's coming). The three interpretations to be studied have had, and will always have, a peculiar and authoritative position from their historical place and intrinsic character; the consciousness of the Church has been abundantly justified in making them primary data for her further investigations.

2. The Synoptic Teaching of Jesus.

(a) *The historic setting.*—The contemporary verdict of the multitude on Jesus is recorded for us in the words, "This is the prophet, Jesus, from Nazareth of Galilee" (Matt. xxi. 11). The justice of that impression, so far as it went, is confirmed as we study the Synoptic Gospels. The faith of disciples, indeed, recognized the presence of the anointed and kingly Son of God (Matt. xvi. 16) as the culmination of the prophetic line (Heb. i. 1, 2); His disciples were brought to see in His death the priestly act of covenant sacrifice (Matt. xxvi. 28; cf. Heb. ix. 11, 12); but the primary and fundamental aspect of His life and teaching to His own age was that of the prophet. Nor is the relationship one of simple resemblance to the prophet of the Old Testament, unconsciously produced by the unchanging background of the Jewish land and life; the teaching of Jesus follows on that of the prophets before Him, in avowed dependence and direct development. " The doctrine of Jesus is the ethical monotheism of Israelitish religion elevated, enriched, and purified. There is nothing in His doctrine for which the Old Testament does not supply a beginning and a basis." [1] The appeal to the Old Testament for justification, made by Jesus at the crises of His career, is characteristic of His essential relationship to the prophetic line ; in the desert of temptation He takes His stand on the prophetic law-book (Matt. iv. 4, 7, 10; cf. Deut. viii. 3, vi. 16 and 13 respectively); in the synagogue of Nazareth He claims to realize the hopes of the prophet of the exile (Luke iv. 17–19; cf. Isa. lxi. 1, 2); challenged for His rejection of social and religious conventions, He turns to the prophet who best knew the divine compassion towards the degraded and sinful (Matt. ix. 13, xii. 7 ; cf. Hos. vi. 6); and on the cross His depth of agony and height of trust are expressed in the language of prophetic hymns (Matt. xxvii. 46; Luke xxiii. 46; cf. Ps. xxii. 1, xxxi. 5). Through the hidden years of preparation the Old Testament prophets stand revealed as His spiritual sustenance; we need not wonder, therefore, that His teaching about man's nature and God's

[1] Stevens, *The Theology of the New Testament*[2], p. 65.

dealings with him are the natural sequence of what we have already studied in the Old Testament.[1]

The new features in the teaching of Jesus, as has often been pointed out, are due rather to a redistribution of emphasis than to a change of content. We have seen (Chap. I. § 5 (c)) that the fellowship of God and man in the Old Testament rested on the dual conception of the divine kingship and the divine fatherhood; Jesus brings the conception of fatherhood into the forefront and emphasizes the family relationship amongst men, whilst retaining the absolute duty of loyal obedience. The whole idea of the family — fatherhood, sonship, brotherhood —is the unifying conception in His doctrine of human

---

[1] This practical continuance of the Old Testament into the Synoptic Gospels may be further illustrated from their psychology—always a delicate and reliable test of " atmosphere." Certain features of this will be indicated in what follows ; here we may note that the connotation of the Hebrew terms is simply transferred, for the most part, to the Greek equivalents. The three fundamental Hebrew terms, namely, *nephesh, ruach*, and *lēb*, are represented by *psuche, pneuma*, and *kardia* respectively. *Psuche* occurs thirty-seven times, of which sixteen cases denote physical life (Matt. ii. 20), six denote emotional states (Mark xiv. 34), and four occur in quotations from the O.T. The one new feature here is supplied by the eleven cases denoting the continuance of life after death (p. 100), to which nothing corresponds in the usage of *nephesh* —one of the important Jewish eschatological developments after the O.T. *Pneuma* occurs in seventy-eight cases, of which thirty-four denote some aspect of the Holy Spirit, and thirty-two refer to demonic influences, whilst there are three cases of *pneuma* to denote the principle of life (Matt. xxvii. 50 ; Luke viii. 55, xxiii. 46 ; cf. the later use of *ruach*), seven to denote psychical life proper (Matt. v. 3, xxvi. 41 ; Mark ii. 8, viii. 12, xiv. 38 ; Luke i. 47, 80), and two cases in quotation. A somewhat higher aspect of conscious life is denoted by *pneuma* in comparison with *psuche*, just as was the case with the Hebrew terms. *Kardia* occurs forty-nine times, namely, once figuratively (Matt. xii. 40) ; in eighteen cases it is used of personality, inner life, and character (*e.g.* Mark vii. 21), in two cases of emotional (Luke xxiv. 32), in twelve of intellectual (Mark ii. 6), in nine of volitional (Matt. v. 28) life, whilst the term also occurs in seven quotations from the O.T. There is no new feature whatever in this group of usages ; the prevailing usage of "heart", to denote the inner as opposed to the outer life, is a natural consequence of Christ's emphasis on the inwardness of character.

nature; we do well to classify and test all our results by it, including our whole idea of the kingdom of God.[1] This is the more necessary, because of the peculiar difficulty attaching to any formal presentation of the teaching of Jesus. It is as unsystematic as the many-sided life with which it deals; it is incidental and occasional in form; its animating aim is concrete truth rather than intellectual consistency. The real unity beneath this variety is one of spiritual attitude; no words will ever carry us nearer to that attitude than the consecrated metaphors of fatherhood and sonship.

It is necessary to distinguish the permanent and universal elements in the teaching of Jesus (with which alone we are here concerned) from those transitory and more external features which are the necessary accompaniment of the Incarnation. Every reader of the Gospels consciously allows for these, so far as the material features are concerned—the realm of bird and tree and flower, of personal dress and social custom, even of sects and parties. So familiar have such Eastern accessories become to us, that we are quick to mark the anachronism in any painting of the Lord's Supper which shews us the disciples sitting, instead of reclining, at table. But this local and temporal element in the Gospels has deeper results. Not only did the Light of the World shine first on Semitic faces, and flash its glory to us from the jewels of Oriental parable and paradox, but, in the humility of the Incarnation, the divine Thought was moulded to the pattern of Jewish conceptions. In particular, the eschatology of the Gospels

[1] "The family is by nature the social unit, and Jesus makes its terms dominate the whole series of his conceptions. . . . His ideal is not a republic like Plato's, but the family extended to all mankind" (Knox, *The Gospel of Jesus*, pp. 76, 83).

is distinctively Jewish, and its influence on Christian thought has been out of all proportion to the worth of its forms. Scientific conceptions of the world and of the limits of its material destiny have replaced the panorama of Jewish apocalypse in the modern man's imaginative forecasts; the ultimate questions lie beyond both modern and ancient forms. The omission of eschatological detail (cf. *infra*, p. 100) would be unjustifiable in a study of our Lord's teaching as a whole. As Charles has said, "It must be abundantly clear from the evidence that the expectation of the nearness of the end formed a real factor in Jesus' views of the future" (*Ency. Bib.* c. 1374). It is to this expectation that we must in part ascribe the marked absence of "social legislation" from the teaching of Jesus.[1] Yet it is plain that the real interest of Jesus lies in that moral and spiritual realm which gathers round the filial relation of man to God. We are therefore justified in comparative neglect of the eschatological element in the original teaching of Jesus, in order to attend the more closely to what has been and is of permanent significance.

(*b*) *The supreme value of man as the child of God.*— The first logical consequence which Jesus draws from this relation is the unique and priceless worth of human life in the eyes of God. This conception underlies the activity as well as the teaching of Jesus, and is seen particularly in His work amongst the poor and degraded classes of the society of His day; not only do the externals of life count for nothing, but no depth even of moral degradation, such as prostitution, can hide from the eyes of Jesus the golden possibilities of a child of God. Three comparisons made by Jesus will illustrate the infinite value of man in

[1] Cf. Pfleiderer, *Das Urchristentum*, i. p. 653.

His eyes. He contrasts man with cherished institutions, and asserts, without qualification, that no institution has the worth of the human lives for which it was instituted : "The sabbath was made for man, and not man for the sabbath" (Mark ii. 27). He contrasts men with the other tenants of the world, and says, "Ye are of more value than many sparrows. . . . How much is a man of more value than a sheep!" (Matt. x. 31 ; Luke xii. 7 ; Matt. xii. 12). Finally, the spiritual possibilities of one man's life are said to be worth more than the actual possession of the whole material world (Mark viii. 36, 37). He makes clear that this supreme value lies in the distinctive attributes of human nature, its spiritual and moral interests. A maimed body is better than a lost life (Mark ix. 43–47); the one thing needful is spiritual life (Luke x. 38–42); the leaven of the Pharisees is more perilous than it is to have but one loaf in the boat (Mark viii. 14 f.). In all this there is no trace of the dualism of body and soul, matter and spirit, which we associate with Greek thought. The psychology implied in the teaching of Jesus is that of the Old Testament; the flesh is not the spirit's enemy, but the spirit's weakness, the gate of the city through which the peril may easily come (Mark xiv. 38). Jesus addresses Himself to the inner life, not because its outer present conditions are necessarily evil (cf. the noticeable absence of asceticism from His theory and practice, Matt. xi. 19), but because the inner life is the peculiar and initial realm of the divine sovereignty: "The kingdom of God is within you" (Luke xvii. 21).[1] The only defilement to be feared is

[1] Cf. Dalman, *The Words of Jesus* (E.T.), p. 146: "What Jesus had in view in this utterance was the unseen genesis of the theocracy caused by the 'Word', and its effectual working, as the latter is set forth in the Parables of the Sower (Luke viii. 4 f.), the Grain of Mustard Seed, and the

6

that from within (Mark vii. 14–23); it is this inner, spiritual life of man which gives him his infinite potentiality and consequent worth in the eyes of God. This emphasis on the inwardness of man's true nature is seen most clearly in the "Sermon on the Mount", of which the text is the inwardness of true religion. It is to the unrealized possibilities of human personality that Jesus appeals in seeking the "lost"; the parables which portray this search (Luke xv.) emphasize at once the attitude of the Father, the mission of Jesus, and the value to both of what is "lost."

In using the phrase "possibilities of human personality", we have already answered by anticipation the only problem likely to arise in this connection—that of the "Universal Fatherhood." That God is the Father of all men is not explicitly declared, though there can be little doubt that it is implied; but that every man is a son of God is only true when we think of what each may become (Luke vi. 35; Matt. v. 9, 45). In our modern terminology, there is a real universal Fatherhood and an ideal universal sonship; in other words, the sonship is less a natural than a spiritual fact,[1] which agrees with what has been said about the inwardness of man's true nature. Because the relationship is moral, and morality is essentially universal, the relationship itself must be conceived as ideally universal. The very name "Father" is sufficient to imply this: "It is not the will of your Father which is in heaven that one of these little ones should perish" (Matt. xviii. 14). This, then, is the first consequence of the idea of divine Fatherhood in the teaching of Jesus—to warn us against

Leaven (Luke xiii. 18 f.). Such an inner advent of the sovereignty of God realized itself in all those to whom the teaching of Jesus had access."

[1] *i.e.* not kinship with God as the basis of our existence, but likeness to God as the pattern of our character (Pfleiderer, *Das Urchristentum*, i. p. 642).

despising one of these little ones (*ibid.* ver. 10). We may justly claim that this doctrine of the supreme value of human nature is characteristic of Christianity. " The absence of any certainty that life has a permanent value is the canker at the heart of heathenism." [1] " First through Jesus Christ has the value of every single human soul become manifest." [2]

(*c*) *The duty of man as the child of God.*—This is the second logical consequence drawn from the relation of God and man as father and child; we see man no longer passive, but active, free to obey God. The ideal son of God is characterized by the spirit of trustful obedience. Here we see that the conception of divine Fatherhood held by Jesus has assimilated to itself the parallel conception of divine kingship; the *patria potestas* of the Roman father,[3] which corresponds in some respects to Semitic kingship, is added to the looser legal relation of father and child in the social life of Israel.[4] It is the assertion of this divine sovereignty which underlies the familiar and frequent use of the phrase "the kingdom" (of God or heaven), which ought to be rendered, at least in thought, "kingly rule." [5] The modern extensive associations of the phrase "kingdom of God" have not only made more plausible the misguided attempts to represent Jesus chiefly as legislator for the Christian

---

[1] Glover, *Life and Letters in the Fourth Century*, p. 303.

[2] Harnack, *Das Wesen des Christentums*, p. 44.

[3] Maine, *Ancient Law* (ed. 14), pp. 135 f.

[4] S A. Cook, *The Laws of Moses and the Code of Ḥammurabi*, p. 128.

[5] Dalman, *The Words of Jesus* (E.T.), p. 94: "No doubt can be entertained that both in the Old Testament and in Jewish literature מַלְכוּת, when applied to God, means always the 'kingly rule', never the 'kingdom', as if it were meant to suggest the territory governed by Him." Cf. Pfleiderer, *op. cit.* i. p. 615.

society, but have helped to obscure His emphasis on direct individual obedience (Matt. vii. 21 f.).

This kingly Fatherhood of God claims both trust and obedience on man's part. Just as man can depend absolutely on God, so God should be able to depend absolutely on man. The temptation of Jesus in the desert is to abandon the spirit of absolute dependence; the achievement of Jesus in Gethsemane is to manifest the spirit of absolute obedience. The material needs of man are as much more the care of the Father than those of bird and flower as man is worth more to Him than they (Matt. vi. 25 f.); "the very hairs of your head are all numbered" (Matt. x. 30; Luke xii. 7); the divine Father will supply the needs of His children more certainly than any human father, in proportion as He is morally higher than they (Matt. vii. 7–11). The divine provision applies equally to spiritual need (Mark xiii. 11; Matt. x. 16 f.; Luke xii. 11, 12, xxi. 14 f.). The human correlative of this divine care is faith, on which Jesus so constantly insists (*e.g.* Mark ix. 23; Luke xvii. 6). The full significance of the demand made by Jesus for absolute obedience to the will of God is seen only against this cease-less background of divine providence. Christian ethics makes demands that seem impossible without Christian faith. "Consciousness of the ground of an authority is trust."[1] It is this conception of the Person to whom obedience is due that gives its characteristic tone to the emphasis of Jesus on duty, and distinguishes this from the Pharisaic "righteousness." We put the same thing in

---

[1] Herrmann, *Ethik*, p. 31. Cf. George Eliot, *Romola*, p. 434: "That supremely hallowed motive which men call duty, but which can have no inward constraining existence save through some form of believing love."

other words when we speak of the inwardness of morality
for Jesus, and set the Beatitudes over against tithe of
mint and anise and cummin ; the trustful love of the child
towards the father is a flowing tide across the deep, not
the ripple on the little pools along the seashore. There
can be no place, as there is no need, for either bargains
or "merit." The kingly rule of the Father inspires the
surrender of all, as did the unique pearl or the hidden
treasure. All these thoughts are gathered up in the
saying, "Seek ye first the establishment of His kingly
rule and His righteousness ; and all these things shall be
added unto you" (Matt. vi. 33).

No single incident in the Gospels throws clearer light
on the central place of duty in the teaching of Jesus than
that which contrasts spiritual with natural obligations
(Mark iii. 31-35 ; cf. ver. 21). The "friends" of Jesus are
anxious to lay hold on Him, saying, "He is beside Himself." His mother and brethren come to call Him away
from what seems to them the madness of His career.
This mistaken interference explains the apparent harsh-
ness of His attitude. He sternly rejects their claim to
annul the greater claim of the will of God ; He goes
further and substitutes a still higher family relation than
that which rests on ties of blood ; His truest kin are His
disciples. "For whosoever shall do the will of God, the
same is my brother, and sister, and mother" (cf. Matt. x.
37 f.; Luke xiv. 26). In the Lord's Prayer, it is the doing
the will of God which forms the chief constitutive feature
of heaven ; it is equally the characteristic feature of the
family of God on earth. Jesus rebuked the religionists
of His day for the substitution of a ritual obligation for
that of the child towards his parents (Mark vii. 9-13);

but this did not prevent Him from recognizing an obligation higher than both, and a spiritual relationship holier and more blessed than any of the ties of nature (Luke xi. 27, 28). It follows from this that Jesus did not hesitate to ask from the inner ring of disciples, and from those who were ambitious to enter it, the "heroic" attitude to life. Let them count the cost (Luke xiv. 27 f.), for "whosoever he be of you that renounceth not all that he hath, he cannot be my disciple." This may mean, on occasion, the literal abandonment of all possessions (Mark x. 17 f.; Matt. xix. 16 f.; Luke xviii. 18 f.), the sacrifice of all "assured prospects" (Matt. viii. 19, 20; Luke ix. 57, 58), the neglect of common obligations and even civilities (Matt. viii. 21, 22; Luke ix. 59–62). What, then, is the standard of appeal, the authoritative code of this regal "will of God", which requires such absolute obedience? The answer confirms what has been already said, that it is emphasis and attitude, rather than actual content, which chiefly distinguish the teaching of Jesus from that of His contemporaries. A "lawyer" can quote the written commandment of love to God and to man as the one duty, and Jesus can accept this statement of what He means by the "will of God" (Luke x. 25 f.; cf. Mark xii. 28 f.; Matt. xxii. 34 f.).[1] But Jesus does not accept this simply or chiefly as written in the ancient law, which He did not scruple to set aside when it conflicted with the claims of an enlightened conscience (*e.g.* Matt. v. 38, 39); He accepted it because it could

---

[1] According to the version of this incident in Matthew and Mark, the combination is due to Jesus, and Wendt (*Die Lehre Jesu* (1901), p. 381 *n.*) argues strongly for this. In any case, the two statements taken separately were familiar enough in Jewish teaching, which is all that the above argument requires (cf. Bousset, *Die Religion des Judentums* (1906), p. 159).

express the living reality of trustful obedience, the personal response to the concrete claims of life. That response never can be codified, because it grows with life itself and is as varied in its detail as the human lives it concerns. It is something incommunicable by any external authority or printed page ; we cannot come nearer to its definition than to relate it to its source—the free activity of a child of God in whom is the spirit of Jesus.

(*d*) *The brotherhood of man.*—The third logical consequence from the Fatherhood of God is the brotherhood of man. This is universal, because, and in the same sense as, the Fatherhood is universal. All men are potentially sons of God ; therefore, all men are potentially brothers of one another. The family arms may be a cross, but the legend is "never despairing" (Luke vi. 35). The father's passion through which God seeks the "lost" will be reflected in every son of His as brotherly affection (cf. Luke xv. 32 : "This thy brother"; Matt. vi. 15). So far as the actual term "brother" goes, no example can be cited in which it is used in this universalistic sense by Jesus. In each of the twenty-six cases of its spiritual usage it is applied to the group of those who are realizing their sonship through discipleship to Jesus : "One is your teacher, and all ye are brethren. . . . One is your Father, which is in heaven" (Matt. xxiii. 8, 9). Jesus expressly designates as His brethren those who do the Father's will (Matt. xii. 49, 50; Mark iii. 34, 35 ; Luke viii. 21). The limited extension is best seen in the words, " If ye salute your brethren only, what do ye more than others ? " (Matt. v. 47). Yet the context of this very passage shews that the principle, if not the actual name of brotherhood, is made universal by Jesus, and this on the basis of the universal Fatherhood of God : " Love your enemies, and pray for them that persecute you ; that ye may be sons of your Father which is in heaven : for He maketh His sun to rise on the evil and the good, and sendeth rain on the just and the unjust " (v. 44, 45).[1] In this passage, also, the term " neighbour " (v. 43) appears as a synonym of " brother " ; the extension of the former term by Jesus in the Parable of the Good Samaritan is one of the most familiar of New Testament principles. The combination of love to God and love to man as the essentials of religion (*supra*, p. 86) at least implies that there is some vital connection between them, *i.e.* that the spirit of brotherhood towards man constitutes the only right relation to the Father.[2]   From what is here implicit, there results the explicit assertion that service to man is the true service to God, and that such moral service is far superior to ceremonial worship as an offering to Him (Mark xii. 33, 34).   The ethical emphasis of the prophets of the Old Testament is continued in the declarations that the weightier matters of the law are justice, mercy, and fidelity (Matt. xxiii. 23 ; cf. Mic. vi. 8) ; that God desires mercy and not sacrifice (Matt. xii. 7 ; cf. Hos. vi. 6)—a correction of the rigour of Sabbath observance ; and that the altar-offering is valueless whilst the moral relation to the " brother " is at fault (Matt. v. 23, 24). The effective recognition of this brotherhood belongs to the simple level of daily life and its material conditions,

---

[1] The other passages are Matt. v. 22–24, vii. 3–5 (Luke vi. 41, 42), xviii. 15, 21, 35 (Luke xvii. 3) ; Luke xxii. 32 ; Matt. xxv. 40, xxviii. 10 ; Mark x. 30.

[2] Cf. Charles (*Ency. Bib.* c. 1372) on the Messianic Kingdom of the New Testament : "So closely is the individual life bound to that of the brethren that no soul can reach its consummation apart."

as in the cup of water offered to the thirsty, or the meal to the hungry (Matt. x. 42; Luke xiv. 12–14). Such helpful service, done apparently to man, is really an offering to the Messianic King Himself (Matt. xxv. 40).

The new feature in this moral exhortation is not simply or chiefly the extension in the range of its application,[1] but the spontaneity of brotherliness and the infinite degree of obligation which result from the conception of the family relationship amongst men, under the common Fatherhood of God. When Jesus says to His disciples, " Ye therefore shall be perfect, as your heavenly Father is perfect ", the context (Matt. v. 43–48) shews that perfection in the spirit of love and forgiveness is meant; the godlikeness lies in the spontaneous and unrequited output of affection, and it knows no limit. The spirit of brotherliness cannot tabulate its exercise in statistical form (Matt. xviii. 21, 22); the only measure of man's duty is God's mercy (*ibid.* verses 23–35). The "golden rule" is significantly positive in form (Matt. vii. 12); its positive spirit is a necessary consequence of its dependence on the brotherhood of man and the Fatherhood of God. This interpenetration of morality by religion, of social duty by personal faith, is a central element in the teaching of Jesus, both in the present and future (eschatological) aspects of His conception of the kingdom of God. As to the various organized spheres of brotherhood, He has comparatively little to say. In regard to the natural family, He asserts the duty of the child to its parents (Mark vii. 10–13) and of the husband to the wife (Mark x. 2–12), in both cases against the

[1] Cf. Wendt, *op. cit.* p. 386.

evasive subtleties of an externalized religion. Of the
Church, His only direct mention is in Matt. xvi. 18, as
established on the believing Peter;[1] but the gathering
of the "brethren" around Himself in discipleship is,
of course, the substance, if not the form, of Church
fellowship.[2] As for the State, the only element of direct
teaching is the "Render unto Cæsar the things that are
Cæsar's, and unto God the things that are God's" (Mark
xii. 17). This makes a clear distinction between religion
and politics; in presence of the party that identified them,
Jesus refuses to make the payment of this tax a religious
question. It is possible that Jesus has in view the
political spirit in religion when He warns the disciples
against "the leaven of the Pharisees and the leaven of
Herod" (Mark viii. 15); the political interest was, as
Wendt remarks (*op. cit.* p. 264 *n.*), the common ground of
the two parties. The general absence of interest in
"social questions" displayed by Jesus[3] may be explained
on several grounds, such as His eschatological outlook, or
the political status of the Jewish people, so widely
different from that of a modern democracy; in any case,
we must not overlook the primary emphasis on the
religion of the individual as the condition of the "kingly

---

[1] The term *ecclesia* also occurs in Matt. xviii. 17, but appears to denote
there the local Jewish community (cf. Hort, *The Christian Ecclesia*,
p. 10).

[2] The Ecclesia is not to be confused with the "Kingdom." Cf. Hort,
op. cit. p. 19 : "We may speak of the Ecclesia as the visible representative
of the Kingdom of God, or as the primary instrument of its sway, or under
other analogous forms of language. But we are not justified in identifying
the one with the other, so as to be able to apply directly to the Ecclesia
whatever is said in the Gospels about the Kingdom of Heaven or of
God."

[3] Cf. Holtzmann, *Lehrbuch der neutestamentlichen Theologie*, i. p. 180 ;
also above, § 2 (*a*).

rule" of God on earth. "The tendency of Christ's
doctrine of man to make for social improvement is apt
to be overlooked because of the indirectness of its method
of working. . . . To ardent reformers the method may
appear slow, and those who use it chargeable with
apathy. On this very account the Baptist doubted the
Messiahship of Jesus."[1]

(*e*) *The broken sonship and the unbroken Fatherhood* (*Sin
and Grace*).—The above consequences from the doctrine
of divine Fatherhood for the doctrine of man—man's
worth, his trustful obedience to God, his brotherly spirit
—have chiefly moved in the realm of *ideal* sonship.
They present the goal of development rather than the
point of departure of the human nature we know; to
find these ideals fully actualized, we have to turn to
Jesus Himself. Just because His consciousness of sonship
was unbroken,[2] His vision of God and man in their true
relation was what it was, and His authority is intrinsically
unique: "All things", He says, "have been delivered unto
me of my Father: and no one knoweth the Son, save the
Father; neither doth any know the Father, save the Son,
and he to whomsoever the Son willeth to reveal Him"
(Matt. xi. 27 ; Luke x. 22). But even more than a Revealer,
Jesus was a Saviour; He could not remain within the
realm of ideal teaching about human nature, whilst all
actual sonship but His own was broken by sinfulness.
We have, then, to ask how Jesus viewed the actual

---

[1] Bruce, *The Kingdom of God* (1889), pp. 132, 133.

[2] Cf. Drummond, *Studies in Christian Doctrine*, p. 314: "There is in
Christ's history no trace of any experience of conversion. Teaching a religion
which more than any other has awakened the sense of sin, He seems quite
unconscious of it Himself. He lives serenely in a Divine atmosphere, with
no confessions and no repentances."

condition of the human nature He found about Him, and what was His attitude to the fact of sin.

To say that the subject of sin formed but a small element in the thought of Jesus is at least misleading.[1] He began His public teaching with the call to men, "Repent" (Mark i. 15); He bade His disciples pray for forgiveness as regularly as for the daily bread (Matt. vi. 12) He pictures the true relation of man to God in the humble prayer of one who said, "God, be merciful to me a sinner" (Luke xviii. 13); He offers the forgiveness of sins as a greater boon than the healing of the body (Mark ii. 6 f.); He declares that the penitence of one sinner is re-echoed amongst heaven's very angels in a chorus of triumphant joy (Luke xv. 10); He comes to call sinners (Mark ii. 17), whilst His severest condemnation falls on those who account themselves righteous (Matt. xxiii.). None could have spoken more emphatically than He has done of the actual sin of His betrayer (Mark xiv. 21; Matt. xxvi. 24), or of the state of those who do not love the highest when they see it (Mark iii. 29). What it *is* true to say, is that His absorbing practical interest, His sympathetic insight into the uniqueness of each individual case, His constant vision of the eternal possibilities of the lowest life, have prevented Him from giving us either such generalizations as are familiar and necessary in dogmatic theology or a pessimistic emphasis on the actual to the exclusion of the ideal. But there can be no doubt that He holds sin to be universally present in the actual world.

---

[1] A fair statement is given by Beyschlag, *New Testament Theology* (E.T.), i. p. 90: "Jesus . . . has spoken little of sin in general, and has proposed no doctrine of it, least of all a doctrine of its origin; He presupposed it as a fact, and showed its evil nature by the penalties He attached to it."

Some of the passages to which reference is made above are sufficient to imply this, *e.g.* the call to repentance addressed to men in general, simply as men; with this may be compared the remark concerning the slaughter of the Galileans: "Except ye repent, ye shall all in like manner perish" (Luke xiii. 3). The Parable of the Unmerciful Servant (Matt. xviii. 21–35) owes its point to the supposition that all men are in God's debt. Earthly fathers are classed as "evil" in comparison with the heavenly Father, even though they are discharging the ordinary duties of their fatherhood (Matt. vii. 11). The man who sees his brother's fault but not his own is sternly dealt with as a hypocrite by Jesus (Matt. vii. 3–5). From the standpoint of these sayings, we can see that the reference to the "righteous" (Mark ii. 17; cf. Luke xv. 7) simply takes a certain class of people, for the time being, at their own estimate, and forms no real exception to the truth that Jesus treats all men as in some sense sinful. On the other hand, the attitude of Jesus towards human nature is by no means expressed by the ecclesiastical doctrine of "total depravity." There is an optimistic note in His outlook on the multitude, of which "the harvest truly is plenteous" (Matt. ix. 37; Luke x. 2); the positive righteousness of the Samaritan springs from his natural humanity, lying beyond the boundaries of "religion" (Luke x. 30 f.); the fact that little children are made the type of believers points to a deep sympathy with human life in its natural relationships rather than to its condemnation (Matt. xviii. 2 f., xix. 13, 14; Mark ix. 36, 37, x. 14, 15; Luke ix. 46 f., xviii. 16, 17). The sinfulness of man is conceived dynamically rather than statically, and as an intermittent, if universal, element in human life

The sonship of man is broken by wilful disobedience; Jesus has no concern in tracing sin back beyond the will of the individual, but short of this He will in no case stop. He follows a prophetic model (Isa. i. 5 f.) in comparing the results of sin with those of disease (Mark ii. 17), and the obligation incurred by sin is described under the figure of a "debt" (Matt. vi. 12 : cf. xviii. 23 f.; Luke vii. 41 f.); but the central conception of sin keeps close to the conception of divine Fatherhood which animates the whole teaching of Jesus. Sin is the "lawlessness" (Matt. vii. 23, xiii. 41, xxiii. 28, xxiv. 12) of the disobedient son (Matt. xxi. 28–32). In the Parable of the Two Sons just cited, which presents this idea most definitely, we are further taught the distinction between the intermittent act of disobedience and the final and persistent attitude of "lawlessness." We are, moreover, carried back past the external act to the inward disposition. This is one of the most strongly marked features in the teaching of Jesus about sin. The outer acts are but the fruits by which the inward spirit is to be judged (Matt. vii. 16), or the "things" brought out from the storehouse of the inner life, which may be taken as samples of its general contents and character (xii. 35). In the "Sermon on the Mount", three of the most important realms of legislative morality—murder, adultery, and perjury—are extended to include respectively the angry word, the lustful look, the evasive formula (Matt. v. 21–37); or, rather, Jesus maintains that the sin lies expressly in the act of will behind these indications of it, and is independent of the accident of its external fulfilment or non-fulfilment. The only defilement comes from the heart (xv. 19, 20); this is the laboratory in which the poison of life is distilled by each for himself. The inside of the cup and the platter calls for the first cleansing (xxiii. 25, 26). One consequence of this absolute emphasis on the inner life is the recognition of many shades in the darkness of sin, many gradations of sinfulness and responsibility. Legislation and jurisprudence necessarily deal with the overt act, however far questions of motive may enter into particular cases; and the overt act does admit of rough classification and adjudication. But the attitude of the will, which Jesus has always in view, evades our judgment not only because it is itself hidden,[1] but also because of its practically infinite variety, as great as that of life itself This variety Jesus fully recognizes, as far as such recognition can be given through the conceptions of popular eschatology. "That servant, which knew his lord's will, and made not ready, nor did according to his will, shall be beaten with many stripes; but he that knew not, and did things worthy of stripes, shall be beaten with few stripes" (Luke xii. 47, 48). Similarly, the level of judgment for Tyre and Sidon is not that of Chorazin and Bethsaida (Matt. xi. 20–24). Another aspect of the emphasis on the inner life is the absence from the teaching of Jesus of any theory as to the origin of sin. Certain accompaniments or occasions of human sin are incidentally indicated, but never so as to raise any doubt as to the responsibility of the disobedient. In one passage, creaturely weakness is named as the gate by which evil enters, quite after the manner of the Old

---

[1] In this connection we may notice that Jesus expressly refuses to allow any inference to be drawn from a calamity to the guilt of the sufferer; the reverse inference alone is legitimate (Luke xiii. 1–5; cf. Holtzmann, *ad loc.*). On the other hand, the connection of the cure of the palsied man (Mark ii. 1 f.) with the forgiveness of his sins seems to accept the popular inference from suffering to guilt.

Testament : " The spirit indeed is willing, but the flesh is weak " (Mark xiv. 38). There is clearly no support here for the assertion of a dualistic theory of evil. Another passage speaks of the responsibility of those who lead others astray : " Woe unto the world because of occasions of stumbling ! for it must needs be that the occasions come ; but woe to that man through whom the occasion cometh ! (Matt. xviii. 7) ; but, even so, there remains the responsibility for " little ones " misled into disobedience ; they may perish, though not by their Father's will (ver. 14). There is also Satan the tempter (Matt. iv. 1) at the head of the kingdom of evil (Luke xi. 18), who snatches away the good seed when it is sown (Matt. xiii. 19) and plants tares (ver. 39), themselves " the sons of the evil one " (ver. 38), and sifts Peter (Luke xxii. 31) ; but this personage inherited from Jewish thought is simply an enemy to be overcome by God and man, not the final explanation of sin. The last word of Jesus concerning man's sin and its origin remains that uttered over Jerusalem : " Ye would not ! " (Matt. xxiii. 37).

Face to face with this broken sonship of man, Jesus presents the gospel of the unbroken Fatherhood of God. Whatever eschatological element was involved in the declaration that " the kingly rule of God is at hand " (Mark i. 15),[1] it is clear that the central feature of the declaration was " to proclaim the acceptable year of the Lord " (Luke iv. 19). The effective significance of the declaration lay in the person of the Proclaimer. He made the gospel of the unbroken Fatherhood credible to men by His own

---

[1] The reader may be reminded again that the discussion of this eschatological element (probably great) in the original teaching of Jesus is here deliberately put aside. However marked was His emphasis on the

unbroken brotherhood with them. The simplest manifestation of this gospel of grace is seen in such cases as
that of Zaccheus (Luke xix. 1 f.), whose heart is opened by
the unwonted friendliness of the prophet willing to become
his guest, or that of the sinful woman in Simon's house,
who is drawn to the "prophet", just as the Pharisee is repelled, by the graciousness of His welcome to her (vii. 36 f.).
These cases are instructive because they shew that the
gospel of grace is not dependent on words ; any act or
attitude that demonstrates the unbroken Fatherhood of
God becomes its sufficient sacrament. This silent attitude
of Jesus becomes explicit when He gives the Parable of
the Forgiving Father (Luke xv. 11–32) to justify His
own attitude to the "lost" (cf. xix. 10) as founded on
God's ; or when He authoritatively declares the divine
forgiveness (Mark ii. 6, 10 ; Luke vii. 47, xxiii. 43); or,
most of all, in the cardinal passage, Matt. xi. 27–30,
where, after the statement, " All things have been delivered
unto me of my Father ", Jesus proceeds to one of the most
familiar expressions of the gospel of grace—" Come unto
me, all ye that labour and are heavy laden." It is this
identity of attitude of the Father and the Son that explains
—within the limits of the Synoptic teaching—why man's
relation to Jesus is of crucial importance for his destiny.
To reject the grace of the Son is to reject the grace of the
Father (cf. Matt. x. 32, 33).

It will be seen that this gospel of the unbroken
Fatherhood, taken in its Synoptic simplicity, at once
clears the ground for the discussion of what " repentance "
is or involves. Jesus brings the Father and the son face

immediate future, it has ceased to be of practical importance to Christian
anthropology.

7

to face, and lifts the whole relation of the two wills into the spiritual realm. From the standpoint of the kingly Fatherhood there is nothing that man can do, nothing that he needs to do, to win back the divine grace.[1] All doctrines of "merit", Pharisaic or ecclesiastical, are *ipso facto* excluded. The one vital fact for the Father is the change of attitude in the will of the son, from the spirit of disobedience to that of trustful obedience. No period of "hired service" lies between the "I will arise" and the coming forth of the Father in welcome. The peculiar Parable of the Labourers in the Vineyard (Matt. xx. 1–16), even whilst it uses the almost inevitable figure of "pay", excludes every thought of an earned reward and teaches that all is of grace.[2] "Repentance" stands in the closest relation to "the remission of sins" (Luke xxiv. 47), and, for once, we are safe in defining a term by its etymology, and in making "change of mind" (μετάνοια) the meaning of "repentance." The "confession" of that change may be as simple as that of the publican praying in the temple (Luke xviii. 13); the conviction of sin is simply the retrospective effect of the change. There is too little analytic psychology in the teaching of Jesus to throw any light on the theological problem of the work of grace in the conviction of sin, or that of the general relation of the human to the divine will; but the broad statement is true that the effective presentation of the divine Fatherhood

---

[1] There is no explicit doctrine of the divine grace operating in conversion ; Jesus simply assumes that, whatever the sin, men are able to repent and do righteousness. This is, of course, neither "Pelagianism" nor "Augustinianism" ; the source of the ability is not discussed.

[2] In the same spirit we must interpret occasional references to "reward", *e.g.* Matt. v. 12 ; Luke vi. 23 ; cf. xvi. 9. Some of these (*e.g.* Matt. xix. 29) by their very terms, warn us not to insist on the mere figure.

alone reveals disobedience in its true light. Indeed, the distinction of "before" and "after" in regard to the work of grace is here meaningless; the new relation is the beginning of a moral and spiritual unity, of which the consciousness of Jesus Himself is the complete expression. The judgment of the King forms the dark but necessary background of the Father's grace; but the new consciousness is essentially that of a little child (Mark x. 15)—a consciousness in which perfect love casts out fear. Fellowship of the child with the Father constitutes Christian life, and it may extend from the simplest and most rudimentary obedience up to the heroism of utter self-sacrifice (Mark x. 17–22). The "laws" of this life are outlined in the Beatitudes, with which we do well, as Harnack has said,[1] to saturate ourselves whenever we are threatened with doubt as to the meaning of Jesus. The welcome of the Father is into just as much of this fellowship as the child is *willing* to receive. Yet, that men might not forget the sterner side of grace, Jesus spoke of the "unpardonable sin" (Mark iii. 28–30; Matt. xii. 31, 32; Luke xii. 10). "The man who was capable of calling good evil, of painting the Source of holiness in the colours of Hell, was beyond repentance and therefore beyond forgiveness; his sin must pass with him unremitted into the next æon, to which the earthly mission of the Saviour did not extend."[2]

(*f*) *Life beyond death.*—The reality of the present moral issues is enforced by the eschatological background of human destiny. "Man in Christ's teaching is so great a being that he inevitably projects himself into

---

[1] *Das Wesen des Christentums*, p. 47.
[2] Swete, *The Holy Spirit in the New Testament*, p. 117.

eternity. The present world cannot hold him."[1]   The
assertion of life beyond death, though new as compared
with the teaching of the Old Testament, is made, as we
have seen, in common with the general anthropology of the
later Judaism.[2]   The difference between the Old Testament
and the New is well brought home to us by a comparison
of the range of meaning of the Hebrew *nephesh* with the
equivalent word for " soul " in the Synoptic Gospels, namely,
psuche (see footnote, p. 78).   No examples of the former,
but almost one-third of the usages of the latter, refer to
the continuance of life beyond death.[3]   This continuance
reminds us of a cardinal fact in the Synoptic eschacology,
namely, the combination of the present with the future in
the conception of the "kingdom" of God (cf. *e.g.* Matt. vi. 10
and xii. 28).[4]   Its future coming, as an external event, lies
beyond the doctrine of human nature, with which we are
here concerned ; nor need we try to reconcile the distinct
conceptions of the parousia of Christ as within His own
generation (Matt. xxiv. 34) and as preceded by the
evangelization of the world (Mark xiii. 10; cf. the parables
of Mark iv. 26–32).   The point of interest for our present
purpose is that whenever and however the kingly rule of
the Father be established in its fulness, the future belongs
to that " little flock " which Jesus has gathered around
Him (Luke xii. 32).   The stage may be Jerusalem, and
the scenery that elaborated in Jewish prophetic and
apocalyptic literature ; the permanent truth is that the
chief human actors in that moving drama already know
their part, the triumphant victory of the sons of God.

[1] Bruce, *op. cit.* p. 131.
[2] Bousset, *op. cit.* p. 461 ; see also above, Introduction (*b*), pp. 71 f.
[3] Matt. x. 28, 39, xvi. 25, 26 ; Mark viii. 35, 36, 37 ; Luke ix. 24, xxi. 19 (?)
[4] Charles, art. " Eschatology " in *Ency. Bib.* c. 1373.

They are called as individuals into the new society; its racial solidarity will then be demonstrated.[1]

The salient feature of this life beyond death is the judgment to be administered by the Messiah Himself (Matt. xxv. 32), and the consequent separation of the good from the evil, the true sons of God from those unworthy of the name (Matt. vii. 21 f.). The certainty of this judgment, underlying the whole teaching of Jesus, emerges in His most solemn warnings; its moral principles provide the ultimate test that the confession of penitent sonship has been genuine. Such glimpses of the other world as are given us shew that the vital test of sonship is brotherliness: those who are condemned are the rich man who daily swept past his brother Lazarus crouching at the gate (Luke xvi. 19 f.), and the indifferent who failed to recognize Christ in the disguise of the prisoner, the stranger, the sick man, the hungry, the thirsty, the naked (Matt. xxv. 31 f.). If the material here is scanty, yet it has a stern simplicity which cannot be mistaken. The essence of sin is depicted as the unbrotherly spirit of selfishness. The former picture represents judgment as immediately following death (cf. Luke xii. 20); the latter agrees with the prevailing conception in connecting it with the parousia (Matt. xxv. 31). It has been a matter of considerable debate whether Jesus teaches in the Synoptic Gospels a universal resurrection of the dead for this judgment,[2] or whether the resurrection is of the righteous only.[3] In support of the former view may be cited the belief

---

[1] Charles, *loc. cit.* c. 1372 : "The teaching of Christ and of Christianity at last furnished a synthesis of the eschatologies of the race and the individual."

[2] Salmond, *The Christian Doctrine of Immortality* (ed. 5), p. 270.

[3] Charles, *loc. cit.* c. 1375 ; more fully in *A Critical History of the Doctrine of a Future Life* (1899), pp. 340 f.

that God "is able to destroy both soul and body in Gehenna" (Matt. x. 28) and the unqualified statement, "As touching the dead, that they are raised" (Mark xii. 26), besides our general expectation from the fact of a judgment at all; whilst, for the latter view, there are the inference from the comparison of the risen life with that of angels in heaven (in the last-named context), and the more explicit statement, "They that are accounted worthy to attain to that world, and the resurrection from the dead, . . . are equal to the angels, and are sons of God, being sons of the resurrection" (Luke xx. 35, 36; cf. the more debatable phrase, "the resurrection of the just", in xiv. 14). But, as Charles points out,[1] on the evidence of contemporary eschatological literature, "the final judgment and the resurrection have no necessary connection." The positive conception of "eternal life" (Mark x. 30), or "life" simply (ix. 43, 45), is represented as the eschatological reward of true sonship, the spiritual enlargement, "as angels in heaven" (Mark xii. 25), of the present life of fellowship with the Father. Resurrection is conceived to be necessary to this life just because the Greek doctrine of the immortality of the soul never found a home in the thought of the Jew, who continued to require the body also, in some sense or other, for his idea of a full personality. The life of those who could be thought of as condemned to Gehenna[2] is really a no-life

[1] *Ency. Bib.* c. 1375.

[2] "Though in conformity with Jewish tradition the punishment is generally conceived as everlasting in the Gospels, yet there are not wanting passages which appear to fix a finite and limited punishment for certain offenders, and hence recognize the possibility of moral change in the inter-mediate state" (Charles, *Doctrine of a Future Life,* p. 343; cf. Luke xii. 47, 48 ; Matt. v. 26, xii. 32).

of outer darkness (Matt. viii. 12), the more to be dreaded because of its disembodied state, like that of tormented spirits (Matt. viii. 29). The references to the body in Gehenna (Matt. v. 29, 30, x. 28; Mark ix. 43, 45) seem rather to continue the Old Testament conception of entrance immediately after death into the under-world (though now with ethical differentiation) than to define man's constitutive elements there; at any rate, they can hardly be applied to the resurrection body without further evidence. It is worth notice, as shewing the primitive atmosphere of much of the detail in these realms, that the shadowy personality in this pre-resurrection state of the good, and resurrectionless state of the bad, is conceived as still maimed or whole, according to its physical condition at death. But such details are of historic interest only; the essential fact is the contrast, so far as the look of Jesus travels, between life and death—a contrast begun in this world and continued into the next.[1] All the passion and power of His teaching and example find expression in the words, " Whosoever would save his life shall lose it; and whosoever shall lose his life for My sake and the Gospel's shall save it " (Mark viii. 35). The life of the true child of God is that which mounts on the stepping-stone of its dead self to higher things; the sacrificial life of heroic venture is already in some sense that which it would be—the life with God that cannot end (cf. Ps. lxxiii. 25, 26).

---

[1] Cf. Dalman, *op. cit.* p. 161 : "With Jesus 'eternal life' and 'life' form the correlative idea to expressions which denote eternal perdition. . . . Both 'eternal life' and 'Gehenna' have as necessary presupposition a judgment which awaits all men, in which the fate of men is for ever decided. . . . Hence, 'eternal life' radically means participation in the 'theocracy'; and it is substantially the same thing whether it be the entrance into the theocracy or into eternal life that is spoken of."

3. THE PAULINE ANTHROPOLOGY.

(*a*) *Psychology.*—The psychological vocabulary of Paul is the most elaborate in the New Testament; this is the result of his characteristic emphasis on personal experience. In regard to details the problems are many, and the controversy has been great; but, for our present purpose, the main lines are sufficiently clear. The Pauline psychological vocabulary, in most of its elements, is drawn from that of the Old Testament (mediated by the usage of the Septuagint); but it has been much discussed whether the change from Hebrew into Greek corresponds with deeper changes of attitude in the use of these terms, and, in particular, whether Paul's conception of the flesh as the seat and immediate source of sin points to the influence of " Hellenistic dualism." The view here maintained is that Paul, in spite of the use of some Greek terms ("inner man", "mind", "conscience"), remains psychologically what he calls himself, a Hebrew of the Hebrews; the advances he makes on the conceptions of the Old Testament are a natural Jewish development, whilst their originality can be shewn as compared with Palestinian Judaism, as well as with the Hellenistic thought of Alexandria; his modifications of current Jewish thought are primarily due to his personal experience, and such Hellenistic influences as were inevitable in his period were unconsciously imbibed by Paul and subordinated or assimilated to his Jewish Psychology.[1]

We have already seen that the psychological vocabu-

---

[1] This thesis is argued by the present writer in *Mansfield College Essays*, pp. 267–286: "Hebrew Psychology in relation to Pauline Anthropology." For the whole section see Peake's excellent article, " The Quintessence of Paulinism " in *Bulletin of the John Rylands Library, Manchester*, iv. 2, pp. 285 f. (1918).

lary of the Old Testament came into existence along more or less independent and parallel lines, a fact which explains its evident want of system. By the close of the Old Testament period, however, this development had resulted in four principal terms, namely, "heart", *nephesh*, and *ruach*, to denote different aspects of the inner life, and "flesh", to denote man's visible personality. These four terms, in their Greek equivalents, form the basis of Paul's vocabulary, namely, *kardia, psuche, pneuma*, and *sarx*. But the tendency already seen in the Old Testament to make *nephesh* predominantly emotional is carried further by Paul, who connects *psuche* and its adjective *psuchikos* specially with the life of the flesh, in contrast with *pneuma* and its adjective *pneumatikos* used of the "spiritual" and higher life (*infra*, p. 109). This contrast, which is of fundamental importance for Pauline thought in general, is further emphasized by the introduction of the antithetical terms, the "inner" and "outer" man, whilst a general term occurs for "body" (*soma*), for which, also, there is no Old Testament equivalent. These developments, it will be seen, are closely connected with the idea of a spiritual life after death, and a consequent separation of the "spirit" from its present body of flesh, an idea which was not reached in the Old Testament. On the other hand, Paul's detailed references to the present inner life called for something more exact than the general and inclusive term "heart", which was sufficient for the Old Testament; consequently, we find him using two other Greek terms, *nous* and *suneidesis* ("mind" and "conscience"), to denote special groups of psychical phenomena which, amongst others, the Old Testament ascribes to "heart." [1]

[1] Paul's use of *splanchna*, "bowels" (Philem. 7 ; 2 Cor. vi. 12), continues

In the detailed examination of the usages of the terms named, the reader should compare each of those having Old Testament equivalents with the discussion of the latter in Chapter I. § 2 ; the principles of classification adopted are the same. The essential proof of the view given above lies in the relationship of the Pauline psychology with the Hebrew in their total contents; the mere equivalence of particular terms would prove little. We may begin with the general and central term "heart", which Paul uses in 52 instances. (1) He makes no use of "heart" in a purely physical or simply figurative reference. (2) In 15 cases, "heart" denotes personality, character, or the inner life in general; *e.g.* 1 Cor. xiv. 25 : "The secrets of his heart are made manifest." (3) In 13 cases, it is the seat of emotional states of consciousness ; *e.g.* Rom. ix. 2 : " I have great sorrow and unceasing pain in my heart." (4) In 11 cases, it is the seat of intellectual activities ; *e.g.* Rom. i. 21 : " They were made foolish in their reasonings and their stupid *kardia* was darkened." (5) In 13 cases, it is the seat of volition ; *e.g.* Rom. ii. 5 : "According to thy stubbornness and impenitent *kardia* thou art storing up for thyself anger against the day of anger." These usages present no difficulty to one familiar with those found in the Old Testament ; the only differences are some increase (proportionately) in the volitional use, and some decrease in the intellectual use. The latter difference is, however, explained when we turn to the new terms *nous* and *suneidesis*, which represent sections cut out of the usage of *lēb* and made prominent by a special terminology.

---

that of the Hebrew *mē'im* ; his use of *koilia*, " belly " (Phil. iii. 19), that of the Hebrew *beṭen.*

The term *nous* (occurring 21 times) denotes the intellectual faculty of the natural man (1 Cor. xiv. 14; Phil. iv. 7), and is also applied to the "mind" of God or Christ (Rom. xi. 34; 1 Cor. ii. 16). This faculty is employed in theistic argument from nature (Rom. i. 20, verb corresponding to *nous*) or in practical moral judgment (Rom. xiv. 5). In a particular individual, its moral quality may be good or bad; the *nous* of Paul comprehends or contains that law of God in which he delights, and of which he approves (Rom. vii. 23, 25); on the other hand, the *nous* may be immoral, vain, fleshly, corrupt, defiled (Rom. i. 28; Eph. iv. 17; Col. ii. 18; 1 Tim. vi. 5; 2 Tim. iii. 8; Tit. i. 15); in the Christian, its renewal works the transformation of the life (Rom. xii. 2). The Greek term for "conscience" (*suneidesis*) is used 20 times by Paul, and its use covers the consciousness of rectitude within one's own heart (Rom. ii. 15), the appeal to similar moral judgment in the consciousness of others (2 Cor. iv. 2; cf. 1 Cor. x. 23 f.), and the characterization of this faculty for moral judgment as either "defiled" (1 Cor. viii. 7) or "pure" (1 Tim. iii. 9). It will be noticed that the term is not used by Paul, any more than by the Greeks, to denote the *source* of ethical knowledge, but, in a sense near to "consciousness", of judgment upon the moral quality of an action.[1] The moral law itself is "the law of the *nous*" (Rom. vii. 23), or is "written in the heart" (Rom. ii. 15). It was to the "heart" that the Old Testament ascribed the phenomena of the *suneidesis*; *e.g.* "David's heart smote

---

[1] "Conscience, with the ancients, was the faculty which passed judgment upon actions *after they were done.* . . . It is one of the few technical terms in St. Paul which seem to have Greek rather than Jewish affinities" (Sanday and Headlam, *Romans*[4], p. 61). Cf. Wisdom, xvii. 11.

him, because he had cut off Saul's skirt" (1 Sam. xxiv. 5 : cf. xxv. 31 ; 2 Sam. xxiv. 10 ; Job xxvii. 6).

The most significant point in regard to *psuche* is Paul's very limited use of the term, which occurs only 13 times. In 6 cases, it denotes "life", without psychological content; thus, Epaphroditus "for the work of Christ came nigh unto death, hazarding his *life*" (Phil. ii. 30; cf. Rom. xvi. 4; 2 Cor. i. 23; 1 Thess. ii. 8; in quotation from the Old Testament, Rom. xi. 3; 1 Cor. xv. 45). In 3 cases, *psuche* denotes "individual" (*pasa psuche=kol nephesh*, Rom. ii. 9, xiii. 1) or the strong personal pronoun (2 Cor. xii. 15) exactly like *nephesh*. In 3 psychical cases, the special Old Testament sense of "desire" reappears (Eph. vi. 6, RV. marg.; Phil. i. 27; Col. iii. 23, RV. marg.). There is left one case only on which to rear the stately and wholly artificial structure of Pauline "trichotomy", namely, the well-known passage, 1 Thess. v. 23 : "And the God of peace Himself sanctify you wholly : and may your spirit (*pneuma*) and soul (*psuche*) and body (*soma*) be preserved entire, without blame at the coming of our Lord Jesus Christ." But this is not a systematic dissection of the distinct elements of personality; its true analogy is such an Old Testament sentence as Deut. vi. 5, where a somewhat similar enumeration emphasizes the totality of the personality : "Thou shalt love the Lord thy God with all thine heart (*lēb*), and with all thy soul (*nephesh*), and with all thy might." In both cases, the inner life is viewed under the two aspects of intellect (with volition) and emotion ; *psuche*, like *nephesh*, marks the emotional side of consciousness. In this connection must be noticed Paul's use of the adjective *psuchikos*, occurring 4 times in two contexts. In 1 Cor. ii. 14, 15, the "psychic" man is contrasted with the "pneumatic", as being without knowledge of what belongs to the divine *pneuma*; in 1 Cor. xv. 44–46, the present "psychic" body of man is contrasted with the future "pneumatic" body of the resurrection. The common element in these two contrasts is the present body of flesh, which is animated by the *psuche* as the principle of its life and the basis of its emotional aspect. The Old Testament usage had evolved a psychological term, *ruach*, with higher associations, and was tending to confine the originally general term *nephesh* to the lower aspects of consciousness; hence the developed Pauline contrast of the corresponding Greek adjectives. The contrast implicit in the Hebrew terms is accentuated and made explicit in their Greek equivalents, largely through the Pauline doctrine of the flesh as animated by the *psuche*. This connection with the flesh helps to explain the limited and largely conventional Pauline use of *psuche*; it belongs to the present fleshly manner of existence, which will eventually be superseded.[1]

It is far otherwise with *pneuma*, the most important word in Paul's psychological vocabulary, perhaps in his vocabulary as a whole. It occurs 146 times, and its usages are here classified on the same lines as those of *ruach*, which it continues and develops. (1) In the natural sense of "wind", it is not used by Paul, who employs *anemos* in this sense (Eph. iv. 14). (2) Most of the cases (116) fall into the second class, namely, "super-

---

[1] The prayer that the *psuche* may be preserved at the *parousia* (1 Thess. v. 23) need occasion no difficulty in regard to the pneumatic or resurrection body, for in this epistle Paul is expecting the *parousia* of Christ during the lifetime of his readers. His pneumatic doctrine of the resurrection body probably belongs to a later stage of his development.

natural influences", and will be discussed at a later stage (*infra*, p. 125). (3) The use of *ruach* to denote the principle of life, or breath (in man), is hardly represented amongst the usages of *pneuma*.[1] This connotation, like that of "wind", has been displaced by the higher associations of the term. (4) There remain 30 cases of the psychical use of *pneuma* in the narrower sense, of which 14 refer to the higher nature of a Christian man, and are hardly to be distinguished from the result of the divine *pneuma*, whilst 16 denote a normal element in human nature. The former may be illustrated by Rom. i. 9: "God is my witness, whom I worship with my *pneuma* in the Gospel of His Son"; the latter by Rom. viii. 16: "The Spirit Himself bears witness along with our spirit that we are God's children." Such a passage as this last, in which the human *pneuma*, as original, is distinguished from the divine indwelling *pneuma*, ought to be conclusive against those who deny that Paul conceived the presence of *pneuma* in any but "pneumatic" men; the inference is confirmed by 2 Cor. vii. 1: "Let us cleanse ourselves from all defilement of flesh and *pneuma*", and many other passages (*e.g.* vii. 13; 1 Cor. ii. 11; Rom. viii. 10; 1 Cor. v. 5). It is evident that the use of such an important term, in regard to the "psychic" as well as to the "pneumatic" man, is a source of obscurity and ambiguity; no thinker, formulating his vocabulary on systematic lines, would be guilty of such confusion. But the very fact of its presence shews that we are on the right track in claiming a central place for Hebrew psychology in the interpretation of Paul's thought; the same ambiguity already exists in the Old Testament,

---

[1] 2 Thess. ii. 8 (cf. Isa. xi. 4) belongs to the second group.

in the double use of *ruach* (after the exile) to denote both a supernatural influence and a natural element in human nature. To Paul, doubtless, this double use did not appear as a confusion at all ; it supplied a point of contact in human nature for the regenerative action of the Spirit of God.

The usage of the important Pauline term *sarx* (flesh) will be considered in the next subsection. But before we approach this much-discussed topic, the reader should ask himself how far a distinctly Greek element has been found in the other terms. The one marked advance on Old Testament psychology lies in the contrast of the inner and the outer man. That this approximates to Greek usage is evident ; but the approximation does not prove that Greek thought is needed to explain it. Given, on the one hand, the doctrine of a future life (developed on Jewish soil), and the acute experience of moral conflict on the other (an experience so characteristic of Paul), it was almost inevitable that the unity of personality in the Old Testament should be developed into the contrast of inner and outer life. A further stage of equally natural development is afforded by the Pauline doctrine of flesh ; for, in any moral conflict, the lower element will tend to be identified, in whole or in part, with physical impulses ; these, sooner or later, supply the energy of the spiritual foes of the higher life in man.[1]

---

[1] It is important to notice that the physical organs, together with the "flesh", are already psychical in the Old Testament, and that to some of them ethical qualities (good or evil) are ascribed (see Chap. I. § 2 (*c*)). It was not, therefore, so marked a change as it might seem, when Paul taught that one amongst the psychical elements of man's nature became the means of his general corruption. This resulted from the weakness of the "flesh", and demanded radical reconstitution, or transformation, into a "pneumatic" body.

(*b*) *The sovereignty of sin and death.*—It is not necessary to trace the elaborate argument by which Paul, in the opening chapters of the Epistle to the Romans, proves that it may be laid to the charge of both Gentiles and Jews "that they are all under sin" (iii. 9); the actual universality of sin is the necessary presupposition of Pauline doctrine as a whole: "God hath shut up all unto disobedience, that He might have mercy upon all" (xi. 32). In this result, the Jewish law, itself holy, righteous, and good (vii. 12), has been a factor of supreme importance. It was added to constitute transgressions (Gal. iii. 19), because, where there is no law, *i.e.* no knowledge of what God requires, there can be no transgression, no stepping aside from His will, in the full sense of sin (Rom. iv. 15); thus it is that through the law comes the knowledge of sin (Rom. iii. 20). This applies primarily to the Jews, with their privilege of a divine revelation ; but there is a parallel, if less complete, revelation of God's will among the Gentiles, for "they shew the work of the law written in their hearts, their conscience bearing witness therewith, and their thoughts one with another accusing or else excusing them" (Rom. ii. 15). In the case of every man, therefore, God's wrath against sin is justified (iii. 19); and "the wages of sin is death" (vi. 23). By "death" Paul means the actual physical death which comes to each man visibly, whatever else this may carry with it. Thus, he does not hesitate to prove the universality of sin by the indisputable universality of death (Rom. v. 14). The sovereignty, therefore, both of sin and of death (as its fitting reward), is universal.

What explanation has Paul to offer of these admitted facts? Why is sin universal, and why is death its penalty? These are the problems which at once challenge the attention of a modern theologian. They did not, however, so present themselves to Paul; the reason is that his aims were practical rather than theoretical. As an ambassador of Christ, he brought to men the divine message of reconciliation (2 Cor. v. 19, 20); the problems of thought touched him only as they affected his life-task. Consequently, we have to gather his attitude to these problems from indirect references, of which the meaning is often obscure and open to dispute. Moreover, it must not be assumed that Paul attained or even sought systematic consistency of statement. The Hebrew mind often rested in an antithesis, if not a paradox;[1] this is notably the case in Paul's attitude to freedom and divine control. The modern mind must therefore be prepared for references to sin and death which to it are unreconciled statements, but to Paul may have seemed complementary aspects of a mysterious truth. Thus, if it be asked what reason Paul could give for the universality of sin, he is found, in one of the two cardinal passages (Rom. vii. 7–25), apparently offering the fleshly nature of man as the immediate source of sin, so that the predisposition to sinful acts is, in some sense, in every man, apart from Adam; in the other passage (Rom. v. 12 f.), however, he has been held to assert that Adam's act, by which sin entered the world, somehow involved the sinfulness of his descendants.

To understand the former explanation, it is necessary to consider Paul's ethical use of the term *sarx* (flesh). The term occurs 91 times, and its usages may be classified under five heads, namely: (1) physical structure; (2) kinship;

---

[1] Cf. the famous saying of Rabbi Akibah, quoted above, § 1 (*b*), p. 74.

8

(3) sphere of present existence; (4) fleshly weakness; (5) ethical experience.[1] There are 35 cases in which there is a more or less distinct ethical reference, implying (*a*) a general relation of "flesh" and sin, or (*b*) that the flesh is, in some sense, active in the production of evil. Under (*a*) there are 15 cases supplied by the phrases "in the flesh" (Rom. vii. 5, viii. 8, 9), "walk, live, be, be born, after the flesh" (2 Cor. x. 2; Rom. viii. 4, 5, 12, 13; Gal. iv. 29), "mind" or "mind of" the flesh (Rom. viii. 5, 6, 7), together with references to spiritual uncircumcision (Col. ii. 11, 13) and defilement (2 Cor. vii. 1). It should be noted here that, though to the Romans the mind of the flesh is declared to be "enmity against God", the Corinthian Christians are exhorted to make holiness perfect by cleansing the flesh as well as the spirit from all defilement; the latter reference[2] must hinder us from

---

[1] The reference is (1) primarily physical in 12 cases, mention being made of circumcision (Rom. ii. 28; Eph. ii. 11), the Apostle's infirmity (2 Cor. xii. 7; Gal. iv.13, 14), the suffering body of Christ (Eph. ii. 15; Col. i. 22), the flesh of man or other creatures (Eph. v. 29; 1 Cor. xv. 39, *quater*). (2) "Flesh" implies simply kinship in 11 cases (Rom. i. 3, iv. 1, ix. 3, 5, 8, xi. 14; 1 Cor. x. 18; Gal. iv. 23; Eph. ii. 11; Gen. ii. 24 is quoted in 1 Cor. vi. 16 and Eph. v. 31). (3) "Flesh" denotes the sphere or condition of present existence in 14 cases; in the flesh man lives (2 Cor. x. 3; Gal. ii. 20; Phil. i. 22, 24; 1 Tim. iii. 16), is present or absent (Col. ii. 1, 5), enters into social relations, etc. (Philem. 16; Eph. vi. 5; Col. iii. 22; 2 Cor. v. 16, *bis*), and suffers (1 Cor. vii. 28; Col. i. 24). (4) "Flesh" carries with it (in light of context) the implication of (*a*) physical or (*b*) intellectual weakness, or (*c*) limitation in value, in 19 cases, without any assertion that the usually implied contrast turns on ethical considerations, namely : (*a*) 2 Cor. vii. 5, x. 3; Eph. vi. 12; 2 Cor. iv. 11 (mortal); 1 Cor. xv. 50 (corruptible). (*b*) Rom vi. 19; Gal. i. 16; Col. ii. 18 (*nous* of flesh). (*c*) Phil. iii. 3, 4 (*bis*); 2 Cor. xi. 18; Gal. vi. 12, 13 (confidence or glory in the temporary and external); Rom. iii. 20; Gal. ii. 16, iii. 3; 1 Cor. i. 29; cf. ver. 26 : "Not many wise, mighty, noble, after the flesh."

[2] Even if 2 Cor. vi. 14-vii. 1 were held to be a fragment of a lost epistle (Moffatt), it would not necessarily be of other than Pauline authorship; the argument of Schmiedel (*Comm.* p. 252 f.) is by no means convincing.

regarding the flesh as essentially evil in the case of the former ; for how could that which is essentially evil ever be cleansed from all defilement? Under the other class (*b*) there are 20 cases, of which 10 refer to the desires of the flesh ("lusts") as evil (Rom. xiii. 14; Gal. v. 16, 24; Eph. ii. 3, *bis*), to its claims, its want of restraint, and its satisfaction (Rom. viii. 12; Gal. v. 13; Col. ii. 23), and to its evil "works" (Gal. v. 19; cf. 2 Cor. i. 17, the latter of designing self-interest). The general principle underlying these cases is explicitly stated in Gal. v. 16 f.: "The flesh lusteth against the Spirit and the Spirit against the flesh; for these are contrary the one to the other." It is clear that Paul finds in man's physical nature the *immediate* foe of the higher principle, though this does not, of course, prove that the flesh is the *ultimate* enemy, as is implied when "Hellenistic dualism" is ascribed to Paul. In the actual list given of "the works of the flesh" (Gal. v. 19–21), only 5 out of the 15 examples can be ascribed directly to physical appetites; but it is clear that Paul conceives the fleshly opposition to the Spirit to extend throughout the whole personality, as when he speaks of one falsely exalted by "the *nous* of his flesh" (Col. ii. 18; cf. Rom. i. 28 f.), which must mean the *nous* under the influence of the flesh. Finally, we have the most important passage of all, Rom. vii. 7–25. Here Paul is giving his personal experience of moral conflict (prior to the Christian sense of salvation), but he does this in general terms applicable to the normal man; his argument obviously requires that all men are sooner or later thus brought into captivity to sin, from which there is no deliverance save through the power of the Spirit, as the following chapter shews. He makes no direct reference

to the fall of Adam, though his use of the phrase "sin
    deceived me" (ver. 11.), in the light of his parallel
phrase "the serpent deceived Eve" (2 Cor. xi. 3), has been
taken to imply some conscious reference to Gen. iii. 13.
In any case, however, Paul does no more than draw a
parallel between Adam's fall and that of each man, as
was done by current Jewish theology.[1] The account he
here gives of the origin of sin is that it springs into
conscious life and being through the clash of "the law of
sin" in the flesh, or members of the body (verses 23, 25),
with the law of God accepted by the inner man or the
nous as its own (verses 22, 23). The whole conflict is
focused in ver. 14: "We know that the law is spiritual
(*pneumatikos*), but I am made of flesh (*sarkinos*), sold (to
be) under sin." Here we find exactly the same opposition
of flesh and Spirit in the legal as in the Gospel stage of
morality (Gal. v. 17), though the spiritual energy of the
law can do no more than make a man fight bravely a
losing battle, whilst that which flows through Christ can
overwhelm its foe and issue in the exultant cry of victory
(ver. 25). But Paul's statement in Rom. vii. 14 takes us
a step further in his philosophy of sin than Gal. v. 17.
Because I am made of flesh, and am therefore weak (see
p. 114 *n.* for this fourth usage of "flesh", continuing
that of the Old Testament), I have passed into slavery
to sin. This figure of an external power, obtaining or
usurping authority over man[2] (through the weakness of
the flesh), is paralleled in other contexts; Paul's whole
conception of *hamartia* (sin) is dominated by it, as

---

[1] Cf. Apoc. Baruch liv. 19: "Every one of us has been the Adam of his
own soul"; also refer to § 1 (*b*) of this chapter, p. 73.

[2] Cf. the striking figure of Gen. iv. 7 (Sin crouching like a wild beast at
the door), and that of Zech. v. 8, where Sin is an external entity.

appears when we collect some of the more striking
references. Sin, finding its base of attack in the law that
limits the uncontrolled impulses of the flesh (Rom. vii.
8, 11), comes to living activity (verses 8, 9) and works death
in man (ver. 13). It is now established in the flesh (verses
17,18), from which acquired territory it wages war against
the higher life of the inner man (ver. 23). In this war it is
so victorious that man (as a whole) has become its captive
slave (Rom. vi. 6, 17) and prisoner (vii. 23 ; cf. Gal. iii. 22) ;
the very members of man's body now become weapons
in the hand of Sin (Rom. vi. 13), until man is set free by
another power (vi. 18, 22, viii. 2). Thus Sin becomes king
and lord over man (v. 21, vi. 12, 14), until he gives his
slaves death as their pay (vi. 23), the poisoned death of
the slavery of Sin (1 Cor. xv. 56). In view of this vivid
conception, which is something more than mere " personification ", we are entitled to say that the ultimate enemy of
the Spirit of God is not flesh, but the Sin of which the
flesh has become the weak and corrupted instrument.
This energy of Sin is connected, though not identified, with
Satan, who controls " the spirit that now works in the sons
of disobedience " (Eph. ii. 2). The human struggle against
Sin thus gains cosmic significance : " Our wrestling is not
against flesh and blood, but against the principalities,
against the powers, against the rulers of the darkness of
this world, against the spiritual hosts of wickedness in the
heavenly places " (Eph. vi. 12). This is, of course, a very
marked advance on the doctrine of the Old Testament ;
but Paul's use of the Old Testament conception of the
flesh as weak and frail, and at the same time as a
psychical factor in man's nature (*supra*, p. 111, footnote),
prepares for this further conception of the flesh as invaded

by the enemies of God. Paul offers no explanation of the origin of these evil spirits; it is enough for him that their existence helps to explain man's present state, and that Christ "must reign, till He hath put all His enemies under His feet" (1 Cor. xv. 25).[1]

It will be seen that this doctrine of the fall of each man through the weakness of his physical nature, which is of primary importance in Pauline theology, takes no account of the pseudo-historic Adam other than is implied in the fact that he was the first to fall in this way. But another passage remains, on which the traditional doctrine of the Fall has been based, namely, Rom. v. 12 f. (cf. 1 Cor. xv. 21 f.). The difficulties of this famous passage are great, and the opinions of exegetes are very varied. But a contrast is drawn between Adam and Christ in their relation to mankind, which implies that Adam's transgression affected the race in a manner at least comparable with the redemptive act of Christ: "As through the one man's disobedience the many were made sinners, even so through the obedience of the One shall the many be made righteous" (ver. 19). A connection of this kind between Adam and the race had become a commonplace of contemporary Jewish theology; it is sufficient to

---

[1] Paul's angelology and demonology is, in general, that of contemporary Judaism, though he makes much less use of it. Satan is supreme over the realm of evil spirits (2 Thess. ii. 9; Eph. ii. 2), and to him may be traced both physical (1 Cor. v. 5; 2 Cor. xii. 7) and moral (1 Cor. vii. 5; 2 Cor. xi. 3) evil. But he is not conceived dualistically over against God, and he can be overcome by Christians now (Eph. vi. 16), as he will finally be brought into subjection by Christ (1 Cor. xv. 25; cf. Col. ii. 15). Thus he is simply the greatest superhuman energy on the side of evil, and his existence leaves the problem of evil where it was (cf. Whitehouse, in *Dict. of the Bible*, iv. 410 f.), though extending the range of its activity. Paul has no theory of the ultimate origin of evil other than what may be deduced from the psychology of Rom. vii., *i.e.* the freedom of personal volition.

quote 4 Ezra vii. 118 : " O thou Adam, what hast thou done ?
for though it was thou that sinned, the evil is not fallen
on thee alone, but upon all of us that come of thee." To
the question what that evil precisely was, the most definite answer of the writer is the same as that of Paul in the
present passage : " Unto him Thou gavest Thy one commandment, which he transgressed, and immediately Thou
appointedst death for him and in his generations " (iii. 7).
What Paul adds to this is the contrast with Him who
mediates the gift of life. But did Paul also maintain that
the universal sin of mankind, which he elsewhere asserts
as a fact of experience, was itself a consequence of Adam's
transgression ? The present passage certainly supplies no
clear proof that he did, or exegetes would not be so
divided as they are on this crucial point of exegesis. The
contrast of Adam and Christ would find sufficient
explanation if the first were regarded simply as the
bringer of death to all, and the second as the bringer of
life to all (potentially ; actually to those alone made one
with Him by faith). It must be admitted, however, that
this contrast would be strengthened if the sin of the race
sprang from Adam as the righteousness of the new race
springs from Christ. But historical exegesis must beware
of the assumption that every issue which centuries of theological debate have brought home to us was present to
Paul. It has been frequently supposed that Paul thought
of the transmission of an evil bias by natural heredity, as
a consequence of Adam's transgression.[1] If this had been
prominent in his mind, we should have expected him to

[1] Eph. ii. 3 must not be cited in this connection. True exegesis shews
" (1) that '*children of wrath*' is a Hebraism for 'objects of wrath', and (2)
that '*by nature*' means simply 'in ourselves', as apart from the Divine
purpose of mercy" (J. Armitage Robinson, *Comm. ad loc.*).

refer to it; but as a matter of fact there is the same generality of (possible) reference to the connection of Adam's sin with that of the race, in the passage before us, as in similar passages of contemporary Judaism (cf. 4 Ezra vii. 116–118; Apoc. Baruch xlviii. 42, 43). The one positive contribution which the theology of Judaism may be held to make, towards filling up the lacuna in Paul's statements, is the doctrine of the *yeẓer hara*, the evil impulse common to the race with Adam. But this was held to have been in Adam prior to his fall. "The evil heart explains Adam's sin, but is not explained by it. Men continued to do even as Adam did, because they also had the wicked heart"[1] (cf. 4 Ezra iii. 26). Paul does not anywhere reproduce this doctrine, but he has his own characteristic equivalent for it in the psychology of Rom. vii., which would apply to Adam as well as to the apostle himself.[2] In the light of this latter passage, which makes every man the Adam of his own soul, without reference to any corrupting influence within man's nature other than his fleshly weakness, we do not seem to be justified in ascribing to Paul in Rom. v. 12–21 any further idea of the direct influence of Adam's act upon racial sin than belongs externally to the example and unique place in history of that act. The fountain of the ever-deepening stream of actual evil within human nature is the corruptibility (rather than the corruption) of the flesh—a corruptibility which we share with Adam by nature (cf. 1 Cor. xv. 45), quite apart from the historic act which first revealed it. Such thoughts as these may well

[1] Porter, *op. cit.* p. 147.

[2] Holtzmann (*Lehrbuch der neutest. Theologie*, ii. p. 42) regards "sin deceived me" (ver. 11) as a conscious reference to the Fall story, in view of 2 Cor. xi. 3: "The serpent deceived Eve."

have lain in the background of Paul's mind. In the foreground, we have here the other and distinct thought of Adam as the " corporate personality "[1] of the race, over against Christ as the corporate personality of His body, the Church. God dealt with the race in Adam, because, in a real sense for ancient thought, he was the race ; because of Adam's sin, God passes sentence of death on the race. That sentence is a just one, because " all sinned " (ver. 12) as a matter of experience; but Paul has not connected this fact causally with his conception of the race as (corporately) constituted sinners through Adam's transgression (ver. 19).[2]

The prominence of death (rather than sin) in the passage last discussed, and its contrast with life through Christ, find a more explicit parallel in 1 Cor. xv. 20 f., though there is an important difference in the way in which death is related to man. Adam stands here as the source of death, as before (verses 21, 22). But the contrast between him and Christ is further developed into one between the " psychic " and the " pneumatic " (ver. 45). Adam is *psuche* (*nephesh*); Christ is *pneuma* (*ruach*). The first man, being " earthy ", is not able, as " flesh and blood ", to inherit the kingdom of heaven ; man, by his nature, is corruptible and mortal. This agrees with the general doctrine of Paul as to the work of the Spirit in bestowing immortality, as we shall see; but how does it agree with the statement of Rom. v. 12 that death was the result of sin, not of man's physical nature ? The simplest recon-

---

[1] For the explanation of this term (not to be confused with later theories of imputation or representation or physical inclusion), see Chap. I. 1 (*b*) and 3 (*a*), pp. 8, 30.

[2] A fuller discussion of the passage, with somewhat similar conclusions, will be found in Tennant's *The Fall and Original Sin*, ch. xi.

ciliation would be to suppose that Paul conceived man to be mortal by his original nature, but with the prospect of immortality; this, however, he forfeited when he was driven forth from Eden, and therefore from the tree of life, which would have nourished immortality in him; thus came death through sin. But Paul does not give any explicit data for such a conjecture, except that his general teaching gives no ground for the opposite conjecture that he held the corruption of an originally immortal nature through Adam's sin. It is not, therefore, justifiable to unite what may have seemed complementary truths to Paul, namely, the actual mortality of man on the one hand, and the justice of that mortality as a penalty for man's actual sin. The difficulty is similar to that noticed above, in regard to the relation between the sin of Adam and the sin of the race; the two statements are not co-ordinated. A consistent system should not be expected where there was no attempt to frame one.

(*c*) *Deliverance by the Spirit.*—Pauline anthropology raises many theoretical problems, but (as the foregoing pages shew) Paul himself had little interest in them. His real interest lies in the practical problem of man's salvation from the sovereignty of sin and death. This has for Paul a double aspect. To use terms which have become technical in theology, salvation from the guilt of sin, or justification, and salvation from the power of sin, or sanctification, are alike beyond man's own reach. To bring them within it, the work of Christ was necessary in both aspects. The Godward aspect of the atoning work of Christ cannot here be discussed. "To Paul's mind there is, in the nature of God, an obstacle to forgiveness which can never be overcome until sin has

been virtually punished. . . . It would not misrepresent
Paul's thought to say that he regarded Christ's sufferings
as representatively penal, or as involving penal consequences."[1] It is better, however, to avoid the term
"penal" (because of its later associations), and to say that
Paul regarded Christ's death as an expiatory sacrifice
(Rom. iii. 25). This objective work of Christ for man is
essential to Pauline soteriology; yet to separate it from
the subjective side, the work of Christ in man, would be
utterly to misread the true significance of the doctrine.
Luther is true to the heart of Pauline thought when he
says: "If then in the matter of justification thou separate
the person of Christ from thy person, then art thou in
the law, thou abidest in the law, thou livest in the law,
and not in Christ, and so thou art condemned of the law
and dead before God."[2] The work of Christ for us and
in us is a unity, which can be distinguished as subjective
and objective only by abstract thought, but was hardly so
distinguished by Paul. When He died and rose from
death, He not only brought men who were spiritually
united to Him into a new sacrificial relation to God,
but brought into operation spiritual forces effective
in the believer through Christ's indwelling presence:
"Where the Spirit of the Lord is, there is liberty"
(2 Cor. iii. 17). It is with these energies that we are
here concerned. But what first calls for notice is the
means by which contact is established between the
Christian and Christ, so that the current of new power
may flow into the life of the former. We find two means
of contact named, namely, faith and baptism; the problem

---

[1] Stevens, *The Christian Doctrine of Salvation*, pp. 64, 65.
[2] Commentary on Gal. ii. 20 (E.T. of 1575, fol. 79).

of their inter-relation did not arise for Paul, since he was not faced by the anomaly of an unbaptized believer. It is by faith that the Christian has obtained access into his present condition of grace (Rom. v. 2) as a son of God (Gal. iii. 26); it is by faith that the loving self-surrender of Christ is individually appropriated (ii. 20). This faith is primarily an attitude of trust and assured confidence,[1] such as was exemplified by Abraham (Rom. iv. 20); in the Christian it is directed towards Christ (iii. 22), especially towards His death and resurrection (iv. 24, 25). Such faith, existent in the heart (the centre of personality), carries with it the open confession of the mouth (x. 9), and follows on the preacher's testimony (x. 14); thus, through faith, Christ dwells in the heart (Eph. iii. 17), and the union of personality is so intimate and real that the consequent life is Christ's rather than the believer's (Gal. ii. 20). Thus faith becomes the essential energy of the Christian life (v. 5, 6). But Paul clearly conceives this faith to be accompanied always by baptism, so that he can pass in thought without break from one to the other: "Ye are all sons of God, through faith, in Christ Jesus. For as many of you as were baptized into Christ did put on Christ" (iii. 26, 27). Baptism, therefore, becomes the cardinal ceremony of union with Christ, the objective aspect of what is subjectively faith. This is impressively shewn in Rom. vi. 1–11, which must imply a realistic, and not a merely symbolic, union. The death of Christ is brought into relation with the death of the believer (in the body of sin) by the believer's burial-like entrance into

---

[1] "It is not merely assent or adhesion, but *enthusiastic* adhesion, personal adhesion; the highest and most effective motive-power of which human character is capable" (Sanday and Headlam, *Romans*, p. 34).

the waters of baptism; on the basis of this fact of experience, Paul argues that the new man is bound over to the risen Christ, in the vital relation of his new life, by his emergence from those same waters of baptism; this new life of union with Christ implies not only present sanctification, but also future life. This emphasis on the rite of baptism (cf. 1 Cor. vi. 11; Tit. iii. 5, 6) is not to be explained as merely illustrative symbolism; here, as when Paul insists on "one Lord, one faith, one baptism" (Eph. iv. 5) as the basis of the unity of the Spirit in the body of Christ, he cannot be thought to co-ordinate a mere symbol with "the Lord the Spirit" (2 Cor. iii. 18) and with the faith by which the Spirit is received (Gal. iii. 2, 14). By baptism, as well as by faith, Christians have been "saturated" with one Spirit (1 Cor. xii. 13). But that which baptism is conceived to mediate sacramentally can be forfeited, as in the case of the Israelites, who "were all baptized unto Moses in the cloud and in the sea" (x. 2), yet fell.

Paul's doctrine of the Spirit, as active in the regeneration and sanctification of the believer united with Christ through faith and baptism, is his most important and characteristic contribution to Christian anthropology. But this contribution, it should be noticed, is the direct continuation and development of lines of thought already opened up in the Old Testament. The relation of man to God was there conceived (Chap. I. § 5 (*b, c*)) along two principal lines, namely, that of the Spirit of God as acting more or less intermittently and externally upon man, and that of spiritual fellowship with God, which sought realization in many ways. As religious conceptions each of these lacked something; the doctrine of the Spirit was not brought into sufficiently close relation with the daily life of men, and the experience of fellowship with God, however vital and exalted in the nobler men of Israel, required some more definite revelation of His personality to vitalize it for the average man's thought. Paul came to his epoch-making vision of the risen Christ along these distinct lines of Jewish thought; his originality lies in combining them and realizing them through the Person of Christ. The result is that the Spirit of God becomes the Spirit of Christ: "God sent forth the Spirit of His Son into our hearts, crying, Abba, Father" (Gal. iv. 6; cf. Phil. i. 19); similarly, the phrase "the Spirit of God" is seen to be interchangeable with "the Spirit of Christ" in Rom. viii. 9, 10. The conception of the Spirit, as mediated by the human life and historic work of Christ, becomes more personal and ethical; the Spirit of God is so identified with Christ in Paul's thought that he says, "The Lord is the Spirit" (2 Cor. iii. 17; cf. ver. 18), and calls the "last Adam" "life-giving Spirit" (1 Cor. xv. 45). On the other hand, the Old Testament idea of fellowship with God, which had been realized by the first disciples so vividly through their companionship with Jesus, is retained and enriched by Paul's doctrine of fellowship with the risen Christ. Thus the Spirit of God comes to be for Paul the dynamic energy of God (Rom. xv. 13; cf. i. 16), supremely mediated through Christ's life and resurrection, and available for all who are His in abiding fellowship. With this great conception, Paul comes to the help of the man whom the facts of moral experience have compelled to cry, "Who will deliver me from the body of this death?" Man's need for that deliverance is due, as we have seen, to the invasion of his

physical nature by the external power of Sin, from which
his higher and inner nature has the desire (but not the
energy) to escape, so far as it is not already corrupted by
the proximity of the invader. The deliverance must come
from another " invasion ", in the interests of that higher
nature itself. The *Pneuma* of God, whose presence in and
through the Law the inner man had welcomed, yet
without power to admit this ally into effective occupation,
now comes through Christ into the inner man and
entrenches itself there against the power of Sin, already
established in the outer man, the *sarx*.[1] This *Pneuma*
is not powerless, like the spiritual but ineffective Law, to
accomplish its will, but writes its effectual record on " tables
that are hearts of flesh " (2 Cor. iii. 3: cf. verses 6, 8;
Rom. ii. 29, vii. 6; Gal. iii. 3, 5). The cardinal passage
(Rom. viii. 1–14), in which life after the Spirit is contrasted
with life after the flesh, issues in the definite assertion that
sonship to God is essentially marked by the controlling
influence of the Spirit of God (ver. 14); this results in a
fulfilment of the law hitherto impossible (ver. 4). A parallel
contrast is drawn between the ethical products of the two
lives in Gal. v. 16–25; the immoral " works " of the flesh
are opposed to the " love, joy, peace, long-suffering,
kindness, goodness, faithfulness, meekness, temperance "
which are the " fruit " of the Spirit. This enumeration is
paralleled or enlarged by scattered references (Rom. xiv.
17, xv. 13, 30; 1 Thess. i. 6; Col. i. 8), which help to shew
that all Christian conduct is ascribed to the strengthening
power of the Spirit in the inner man (Eph. iii. 16). It is

---

[1] Here we see Paul passing beyond " the Jewish conception of the Law as
the divinely given remedy for the evil nature of man, the power before
which it must yield " (Porter, *op. cit.* p. 135).

in such "sanctification of the Spirit" that present
salvation consists. (2 Thess. ii. 13); the indwelling Spirit
demands a holy temple (1 Cor. iii. 16, vi. 19). The
influence of the Spirit is not less visible in the Christian
consciousness of God's Fatherhood (Gal. iv. 6; Rom. viii.
15, 16) and His love (Rom. v. 5), and in the characteristic
activities of that consciousness, namely, worship (Phil. iii. 3),
prayer (Rom. viii. 26, 27; cf. Eph. vi. 18), praise (Eph. v. 18 f.),
preaching (1 Thess. i. 5; 1 Cor. ii. 4), as well as in the
special "gifts" (1 Cor. xii. 4–11; cf. xiv. 2, 12; Rom. xv. 19),
amongst which spiritual "knowledge" must be reckoned
(1 Cor. ii. 10–16, vii. 40; Eph. i. 17, iii. 5; 2 Thess. ii. 2).
It is through the Spirit that Christian life has its beginning
(1 Cor. vi. 11; Eph. i. 13, iv. 30; 2 Cor. i. 22, v. 5), since
both the initial renewal (Tit. iii. 5) and the utterance of
faith itself (1 Cor. xii. 3; cf 2 Cor. iv. 13) are ascribed to
the Spirit.   So also it is in the Spirit that Jew and Gentile
alike have access to the Father (Eph. ii. 18), and that all
Christians participate and have fellowship one with another
(2 Cor. xiii. 14; Phil. ii. 1; cf. Eph. iv. 3, 4).

The deliverance of the inner man from the power of
sin established in the flesh is, therefore, one to be actually
accomplished during the present life; salvation, in one
sense, is by "works", for by "works" shall every man be
judged (Rom. ii. 5–11) when he appears before the judgment-
seat of God (Rom. xiv. 10) or of Christ (2 Cor. v. 10). But
these works, as we have seen, are really the "fruit" of the
indwelling Spirit, in those who are obedient unto righteousness (Rom. vi. 16–19). Paul is not conscious of any
contradiction to the doctrine of justification by faith when
he contemplates his own rejection, should he relax his
discipline of the body (1 Cor. ix. 27), or when he makes

his attainment of resurrection to depend on present strenuous effort (Phil. iii. 8–14). Here, as elsewhere, Paul states a double truth, without any apparent consciousness of inconsistency. Ethics and religion both underlie Eph. ii. 10: "For His making are we, shaped in Christ Jesus unto good works." But the completeness of such ethical salvation is clearly an ideal in man's present life. Ideally, he has bound himself to put to death the (evil) doings of the body (Rom. viii. 13), by virtue of that spiritual union with Christ, in which the old man is crucified with Him (vi. 6) ; but really, as the very context of such passages shews (Rom. viii. 12 f., vi. 12 f.), Paul's readers still require the exhortation to make their members instruments of righteousness and to be willing to suffer with Christ. Through the power of the Spirit, what was before impossible is now possible ; but the actuality is still conditioned by the degree of "the obedience of faith" (Rom. i. 5). It follows that even those who have the first-fruits of the Spirit are waiting for the full harvest in the redemption of the body, *i.e.* its deliverance from the present condition of fleshly weakness, to which was due its previous captivity and its continued accessibility to Sin

The redemption of the body is a central feature in the later eschatology of Paul. In the earlier stage of his thought, represented by the Epistles to the Thessalonians, we move in the circles of current apocalyptic imagination ; with dramatic accompaniments, the Lord will descend from heaven in the immediate future, the Christian dead will be raised and, together with living Christians, be with Him for ever (1 Thess. iv. 16, 17). But the failure of this expectation led to the more spiritual development of Paul's thought. The physical corruption visible in death

9

raised doubts as to the reality of life beyond it ; for how could there be life without a body? Paul's answer (1 Cor. xv. 35–58) implies the important distinction between the idea of the body and that of the flesh. Expressed in modern terminology, the distinction is that between organic form and substance or material ; the body may be constituted of differing material, for "all flesh is not the same flesh " (ver. 39).   God gives a body of what material He pleases (ver. 38) ; we have at present a fleshly, corruptible, " psychic " body (see p. 109).   But, in the resurrection - life, the Christian will obtain an incorruptible, "pneumatic" body through his relation to Christ.   At this stage of his thought, Paul still dwells simply on the early return of Christ, for he says: " We shall not all sleep, but we shall all be changed " (ver. 51). But, a little later (cf. 2 Cor. v. 1–8), Paul's thought includes also what happens at death,[1] when he conceives the heavenly body to become our immediate possession. Here, as already in the First Epistle to the Corinthians,[2] the heavenly body is conceived to be the outcome of the spiritual life " sown " in the corruption, dishonour, and weakness of man's present life (1 Cor. xv. 42, 43 ; 2 Cor. v. 1–5 ; cf. Gal. vi. 7, 8); it is the result of the gradual transformation of the Christian into the image of " the

---

[1] Holtzmann (*op. cit.* ii. p. 193) suggests that the change is due to the peril of death encountered by Paul in the interval between the two epistles (2 Cor. i. 9 ; cf. iv. 10, 11).

[2] The reasons are given by Charles, *Doctrine of a Future Life*, p. 392 f., or *Ency. Bib.* c. 1384.   In this connection, it should be noticed that there is no resurrection of the wicked in the anthropology of Paul's Epistles, for the righteous alone are developing a resurrection body : " Since the faithless lose their psychical body at death, and can never, *so long as they are such*, possess a spiritual body, they are necessarily conceived as 'naked ', that is, disembodied beings " (*op. cit.* p. 394).   Charles thinks that the Pauline eschatology points to the destruction of the finally impenitent (*op. cit.* p. 405).

Lord the Spirit " (2 Cor. iii. 18). The resurrection body is
definitely ascribed to the indwelling Spirit in Rom. viii. 11 :
" If the Spirit of Him who raised Jesus from the dead
dwells in you, He who raised from the dead Christ Jesus
shall make your mortal bodies to live through the Spirit
dwelling in you." The hidden life of the believer has yet
to find its worthy manifestation (Col. iii. 4): " Christ shall
transform the body of our humiliation (to make it)
conformable to the body of His glory " (Phil. iii. 21).
This is the last stage in the deliverance by the Spirit; the
flesh, already condemned by Him who came in the
likeness of sinful flesh (Rom. viii. 3), though Himself
without sin (2 Cor. v. 21), is abandoned to the death
which claims it, both by its nature and by the desert of
its sin, whilst the spiritual nature of the believer emerges
from its chrysalis stage in the glory (*doxa*) of a spiritual
body. Here we see most clearly Paul's characteristic differences from both Greek and Jewish thought : a true Jew,
he shrinks from the idea of a disembodied spirit; yet, as a
Christian Jew, he looks forward to a new body, no longer of
flesh, and no longer, therefore, open to the invasion of Sin.

(*d*) *Freedom and the absoluteness of grace.*—It is
significant of Paul's emphasis that the salient facts of
the Christian consciousness, as he interprets them, can be
fairly included under "Deliverance by the Spirit." The
energies of that Spirit are liberated for the believer by the
justifying death of Christ, and mediated to the believer by
the present life of "the Lord the Spirit" (2 Cor. iii. 17), to
whom the believer is joined to form "one Spirit" (1 Cor.
vi. 17). Thus viewed, the Christian life is essentially the
product of the new conditions, the spiritual atmosphere
into which the believer has been transferred. The

reference already made to the absence of any explicit formulation of the relation of "works" and justification has already indicated how little Paul's interest lay in pure speculation. This is seen also in the connected problem of the relation of the Spirit of God and freedom. To the modern mind, taught by the interminable debates of ecclesiastical history how difficult it is to state the inter-relation of grace and freedom without doing violence to one or both, it is apt to seem incredible that Paul should have failed to relate his theory of the supernatural life of the Christian to the practical freedom of the hearer to accept or reject his Gospel. Yet historic exegesis must simply record the fact, without any attempt to force Paul's ample recognition of the double truth into any of the later moulds of reconciliation. Behind Paul's conceptions of justification by grace[1] on the one hand, and of sanctification by the Spirit on the other (the two conceptions emphasized as "grace" by Luther and by Augustine respectively), there is found the recognition of both justification and sanctification as rooted and grounded in the divine purpose. The cardinal passages for the Pauline doctrine of election are, in the first place, the lengthy discussion in Rom. ix.-xi. of the apparent rejection of Israel in favour of the Gentiles, and, in the second, the survey of divine agency from the call to the final glory of the redeemed (Rom. viii. 28 f.), immediately preceding this passage. Of the former, it is sufficient to say that the direct application is national rather than individual, and relates to present conditions rather than

---

[1] The dominant Pauline conception of "grace" relates to the free favour of God manifested in justification; it should be distinguished from the Augustinian use of *gratia*, though Paul includes that in his conception of the work of the Spirit.

to final issues. Yet it is to be admitted that the figure of the potter and the clay (ix. 21 f.) implies the omnipotence of God in regard to individual destiny, to a degree not apparently reconcilable with the reality of man's free acceptance or refusal of the Gospel. On the other hand, this reality underlies Paul's missionary enthusiasm, and is reflected in his personal attitude to the peril of being himself rejected (1 Cor. ix. 27). The second passage (Rom. viii. 28 f.) has clearly in view the individual believer; it represents the divine grace as absolute and unconditioned in its operation, from the beginning to the end of the Christian life. Link follows link in unbroken succession; nor could it be otherwise for one whose Christian consciousness began, as Paul's did, with the overwhelming sense of a divine revelation (Gal. i. 15, 16), and was continued with so intense a realization of divine control. We have here the Old Testament national consciousness emerging in that of a new and spiritual, individually gathered, Israel.[1] To this is added the conception of the Gospel of absolute grace, in reaction from the conception of the Law as conditional reward. If we wished to do what Paul himself has nowhere done — to relate the deep-rooted religious instinct which carries eternal values up to the eternal purposes of God to the ethical basis of moral responsibility in human freedom — we might say that Paul's varied teaching would logically issue in metaphysical absolutism and psychological freedom. But such a contrast is really foreign to the thought of Paul, and does him injustice. His clearest statement of individual election and predestination shews its essentially practical character; the

---

[1] Cf. Holtzmann, *op. cit.* ii. p. 169.

passage in question (Rom. viii. 28 f.) is intended to give
confidence in the final issue to those who are proved to
be sons of God by the operative influence of His Spirit.
Paul has simply thrown into the form natural to Hebrew
monotheism the conviction, elsewhere expressed by him,
that the elements of spiritual life—faith, hope, love—
are permanent, because they are the gifts of God.   The
problem of their relation to a life in time is a very real
one; in the particular form of the rival interests of freedom
and grace, the human and the divine factors in salvation,
it is *the* problem of anthropology during the dogmatic
period; but, as a problem, it did not exist for Paul, perhaps
because his religion was so intensely ethical and his ethics
so permeated with religion.

   (*e*) *The social relationships of man.*—Paul is so dominated by the consciousness that "the fashion of this
world passeth away" (1 Cor. vii. 31) that we cannot
expect to find in his letters any elaborate discussion
of the transient forms of social life.   This does not
mean that he takes up any attitude of rebellion against
them; his sane and practical outlook on human life
leads him to rebuke those whose eschatological hopes
have resulted in present idleness (2 Thess. iii. 7–12).   His
general principle is the acceptance of the existing forms
of society in such ways as may best promote the spiritual
interests of the individuals constituting it.   The life of
the individual Christian, as he conceives it, necessarily
expands into social relationships; the resultant obligations can be adequately discharged only in the spirit of
love prompting mutual service.   The particular problems
of duty are to be solved by the principle that spiritual
interests are supreme, and that the heart of those interests

is the attitude of love to all men, though specially to the
Christian society. This general principle may be traced
in particular application to such relationships as the
circumstances of his time and the accidents of his corre-
spondence have preserved to us. For instance, Paul sees
nothing wrong in slavery; he is simply anxious that the
strained relationship of a Philemon and an Onesimus
shall be transformed by the Christian atmosphere of
mutual helpfulness. In regard to the question of marriage
(1 Cor. vii.), Paul prefers celibacy, not on grounds of
asceticism—a view which has no basis in his psychology
or explicit teaching—but as expedient (*ibid.* ver. 28)
in view of the immediate future, unless a more pressing
expediency makes marriage advisable (verses 1–6).[1] It is of
little consequence to him whether a man be bond or free,
married or unmarried; the essential thing is that there
be Christian companionship with God in each and every
one of these transient relationships (ver. 24). Behind the
temporal powers of the State, Paul sees not only the over-
ruling hand of God, but the delegated ministry of public
law (Rom. xiii. 1–7), so that the payment of tribute itself
becomes a conscientious obligation. It is, however, in
regard to the social group constituting the Church that
these principles find clearest statement. The Church is,
indeed, more than one of the transient forms of society;
it is the body of Christ (1 Cor. xii. 27). As such, it
represents the new humanity, which Christ has quickened
into life (1 Cor. xv. 22). The ideal relationships within
this new humanity, in its present forms, are sufficiently

---

[1] It must, however, be admitted that his resultant attitude, as distinct
from its source, affords some apparent justification to the Catholic preference
for celibacy.

indicated by the metaphor of the body, worked out in detail (1 Cor. xii. 12 f.).   The social solidarity of the race, naturally established in Adam along the lines of " corporate personality ", is spiritually re-established in Christ, and the Church becomes the organic expression of Him, just so far as its constituent members have yielded themselves to the one Spirit, their ultimate unity (*ibid.* ver. 4).   For here, in the social sphere, just as in the experience of the individual, character lies behind conduct, and the Spirit is immanent in every Christian character.   In every relationship, love is the fulfilling of the law, and love is the first of the Spirit's fruits (Gal. v. 22 ; cf. 1 Cor. xiii. 13).

4. THE JOHANNINE ANTHROPOLOGY.

(*a*) *God and the world.*—The third principal type of New Testament anthropology is supplied by the Gospel and First Epistle of John.   In regard to the teaching of Jesus as recorded in this Gospel, it is here assumed that " we must . . . attribute the language, the colour, and the form of these Johannine discourses to the evangelist."[1] This justifies the present classification, whilst it leaves open the question as to the degree to which the contents of these discourses may be traced back to Jesus.   The point of view from which we can most naturally approach the Johannine doctrine of man is that of the present contrast between God and the world,[2] the most general and inclusive of the Johannine antitheses.[3]   In some cases the

---

[1] Stevens, *Theol. of the N.T.* p. 172.

[2] So Pfleiderer, *op. cit.* vol. ii. p. 451, in regard to the Johannine theology in general, in which he marks the three stages of the pre-existent Logos, the manifestation of the historical Christ, and the representative work of the Spirit.   The contrast is due to the sin of man, which has marred the creative work of the Logos.

[3] A list of these is given by Holtzmann, *op. cit.* vol. ii. pp. 466, 467.

contrast is made explicitly: "They are of the world . . . we are of God" (1 John iv. 5, 6); "If any man love the world, the love of the Father is not in him" (1 John ii. 15); "Ye are of this world; I am not of this world" (viii. 23). In other cases the same contrast is implied in those of light and darkness, spirit and flesh, life and death, truth and untruth, righteousness and sin. In each case it is characteristic of the writer to shew the lower in the light of the higher, and to interpret time from the standpoint of eternity. The presence of Christ in the world makes this possible, for Christ is to him the search-light of eternity flashing over the dark fields and cities of time (viii. 12, ix. 5, xii. 46). The presence of Christ in this dark world is due to the only motive that could bridge the gulf between man and God—the passion of divine love which sent the only-begotten Son to be the bringer of life to a world of death (iii. 16; 1 John iv. 9; cf. x. 36, xvii. 18). To the historic manifestation of this life it is the writer's chief aim to testify: "We have seen, and bear witness, and declare unto you the life, the eternal life, which was with the Father, and was manifested unto us" (1 John i. 2). The period of that historic manifestation was, indeed, limited: "A little while", said Christ, "and the world beholdeth Me no more" (xiv. 19; cf. xii. 35). But the historic work of Christ is still continued by the presence of the Spirit of God in the world, sent expressly to continue the mission of Christ (xiv. 26); "He shall take of Mine and declare unto you" (xvi. 14). "The life and teaching of Jesus supplies, as it were, the materials, in forms which men can apprehend, upon which the Spirit works."[1] It is from the viewpoint of this character-

[1] Stevens, *op. cit.* p. 220.

istic Johannine contrast of God and the world that we collect what the writer has to tell of human nature—its darkness without Christ, and the issues of life and death which His coming reveals and makes acute.

(*b*) *The darkness of the world.*—The frequent use of the term "world" is a marked feature of these writings;[1] it points to a unifying conception of human life, which is seen most clearly when the evil aspect of human nature, its darkness, is emphasized. The transience of the world in itself, with all the desires that attach to it, is contrasted with the permanence of the life that consists in moral obedience to God (1 John ii. 16, 17). The world is ignorant of God (xvii. 25); but a moral element is involved in this blind ignorance which makes it sin: "If ye were blind, ye would have no sin : but now ye say, We see; your sin remaineth" (ix. 41). The love of the world, then, which is contrasted with the love of the Father (1 John ii. 15), is not due simply to the limitation of the creature over against the Creator; it is something positive —a love of darkness for its own sake (iii. 19), a hatred for the light (iii. 20) and for those who belong to it (xv. 19; 1 John iii. 13). The works of the world are evil (vii. 7); the sin of the world calls for a Saviour (i. 29). But His very coming, by its brightness, accentuates the darkness of sin ; sin is brought to a focus in the rejection of Him (v. 40), the refusal to believe on Him (xvi. 9). Sin implies the absence of any true vision or knowledge of God (1 John iii. 6); but it is the offer of that vision and knowledge in Christ which now makes sin what it is :

---

[1] The term κόσμος is found 77 times in the Gospel and 24 times in the Epp., *i.e.* a total greater than that of all its occurrences in the rest of the N.T. (83).

"If I had not come and spoken unto them, they had not had sin, but now they have no excuse for their sin" (xv. 22). This essentially moral element in the evil of the world[1] is expressly designated by a Pauline term, when sin is defined as "lawlessness" (1 John iii. 4). The primary Johannine type of sin is hatred of one's brother (1 John ii. 9–11); he who hates is still in the realm of darkness. Thus, when "truth" replaces "light" as the description of Christ's realm (xviii. 37), we are saved from any intellectualist misinterpretation by the correlation of truth with practical liberation from the bondage of sin (viii. 32). A distinction is made between sin as a fixed attitude of character (ver. 34: "Every one that doeth sin is the slave of sin"; cf. 1 John iii. 4, 8) and sin as a single act, found even in the Christian life, which needs and can obtain forgiveness (1 John i. 9). It is in the first sense only that it is true to say that "every one who is begotten of God sinneth not" (1 John v. 18; *ibid.* iii. 6); on the other hand, even the "Christian" brother may be found to have sinned sin unto death (1 John v. 16), *i.e.* sin which reveals the ultimately unchristian character.[2] For the outcome of sin is death (viii. 23, 24; cf. pp. 146 f.). The judgment of sin[3] is involved in the very presence of Christ in the

---

[1] Cf. Westcott, *The Epistles of John* (ed. 3), p. 40: "The relation of good to evil is not one which exists of necessity in the nature of things. The difference is not metaphysical, inherent in being, so that the existence of evil is involved in the existence of good; nor physical, as if there were an essential antagonism between matter and spirit; but moral, that is, recognized in the actual course of life, so that evil when present is known to be opposed to good."

[2] Westcott, *op. cit.* p. 210: "We are not to think of specific acts, defined absolutely, but of acts as the revelation of moral life."

[3] It should be noted that Christ explicitly rejects the view that present suffering is necessarily the punishment of sin (ix. 2, 3).

world's darkness: "This is the judgment, that the light is come into the world, and men loved the darkness rather than the light" (iii. 19); "Now is the judgment of this world" (xii. 31); "The Father hath given all judgment unto the Son" (v. 22). The underlying assumption in all these references to sin is that it is of universal occurrence; standing behind this universality, with more prominence than is found in the Synoptics, is the figure of the devil. "The whole world lieth in (the realm of) the evil one" (1 John v. 19); "He that doeth sin is of the devil; for the devil sinneth from the beginning" (*ibid.* iii. 8); so that we may speak of "the children of the devil" as well as of "the children of God" (*ibid.* ver. 10). It is he who inspires the treachery of Judas (xiii. 2) and is active in Christ's death (xiv. 30). The most detailed reference to him is in viii. 44. Christ is denying the claim of the Jews, whom He is addressing, to spiritual kinship with either Abraham or God. They are of their father the devil, and will to do his desires. He is characterized as a murderer and a liar, with reference, apparently, to his part in the deception and death of Adam and Eve; he stands not in the truth,[1] *i.e.* is outside its realm, and is the father of the liar. This implies that the devil has both a real existence and an active share in the production of evil, though the concurrent will of man is necessary. As prince of this world, he is judged (xii. 31, xvi. 11) and overcome by a greater (1 John iii. 8, iv. 4; cf. *ibid.* ii. 13, 14). For the world has been overcome by Christ (xvi. 33), and, therefore, by all the children of God, for "this is the victory that hath overcome the world, even our faith" (1 John v. 4).

(c) *Faith in Christ; the new birth.*—"Believe on the

---

[1] Reading ἕστηκεν, with Holtzmann and others, against RV.

light", says Christ, "that ye may become sons of light" (xii. 36). This belief is characterized as the reception of Christ: "As many as received Him, He gave to them the right to become children of God, to those believing on His name" (i. 12; cf. v. 43, xiii. 20). Belief on Christ is belief on God (xii. 44) and on the divine mission of Christ (xvii. 21). It is in full accordance with the more developed theology of the Fourth Gospel that knowledge should become a more explicit element in the content of faith, *i.e.* the knowledge that Christ is what He represents Himself to be (xvii. 3). Such faith is the condition of vision (xi. 40) and of life itself (viii. 24, etc.), and continues to be required, under new conditions, after the earthly life of Christ is completed (xx. 29). The Holy Spirit will convict men of sin, says Christ, "because they believe not on Me" (xvi. 9). In other words, want of faith in Christ will reveal the sinful love of the world's darkness and the wilful rejection of His light. The close connection between character and faith is emphasized from both sides. On the one hand, moral obedience is the condition of that "knowledge" which lies at the heart of faith: "If any man wills to do God's will, he shall know of the teaching, whether it be of God, or whether I speak from Myself" (vii. 17). On the other hand, the hope of future likeness to Christ that springs from Christian faith carries with it the necessary moral volition on the Christian's part: "Every one that hath this hope (set) on Him purifieth himself, even as He is pure" (1 John iii. 3; *ibid.* ii. 3, etc.). It is this essential moral quality of faith that makes it an adequate test of character—a test that runs through the Fourth Gospel and forms the correlate to the manifestation of the glory of God in Christ: "The light shineth in the darkness, and the darkness apprehended it not" (i. 5) ; "We beheld His glory, glory as of the only-begotten from the Father" (i. 14). "Mine own know Me", says Christ, as the Good Shepherd (x. 15); "My sheep hear My voice, and I know them, and they follow Me" (x. 27); "If God were your Father, ye would love Me" (viii. 42); "Every one that is of the truth heareth My voice" (xviii. 37). "Thine they were, and thou gavest them to Me", says Christ of His disciples (xvii. 6); He came "that He might also gather together into one the children of God that are scattered abroad" (xi. 52). In such response of men to Christ, there is a divine as well as a human factor: "No man can come unto Me, except the Father which sent Me draw him" (vi. 44). This divine factor is brought out most forcibly under the figure of birth : "Except a man be born anew,[1] he cannot see the kingdom of God" (iii. 3). Emphasis is laid on the distinct source of this new life : "Every one that is begotten of God doeth no sin, because His seed abideth in Him" (1 John iii. 9); "Everything begotten of God conquers the world" (*ibid.* v. 4). The most emphatic expression of this truth is found in the prologue to the Gospel, a passage which also brings together the two factors of conversion, human and divine, and shews that, for the writer at least,[2] there was no inconsistency in asserting them side by side : "As many as received Him, He gave to them the right to become children of God, to those believing on His name, who were born, not of blood, nor of the will of the flesh, nor of the will of man, but of God" (i. 12, 13). What is

---

[1] If the rendering "from above" be preferred, this will further emphasize the supernatural source of the new life.

[2] Holtzmann (*op. cit.* vol. ii. p. 493) seems to over-emphasize the irreconcilability of these factors. Cf. Wendt, *op. cit.* p. 304.

in view here is the double aspect of the new life; seen from the standpoint of human consciousness, it begins in an act of faith; but the life expressed in this act is seen to be a new principle, only to be explained from its divine source. No doubt there is a problem here, which we shall see emerging into fuller consciousness in the Pelagian Controversy; but, at present, these are regarded as complementary truths. None can make himself a child of God; but none is a child of God without personal faith in Christ. We do not, therefore, need to ask which of the two factors is initial or fundamental; it is sufficient to say, with this writer, "Every one that believeth that Jesus is the Christ is begotten of God" (1 John v. 1). At the same time, we recognize in this emphasis on the divine factor a new element; "in the Synoptics God is Father, because the children are bound to become what He is Himself; in John, because He begets them; Paul deals with the rights, John with the nature of the child. . . . The 'seed of God' is the germ of divine life which descends into the world of men and develops into likeness of nature."[1] The distinction of "flesh" and "spirit" in this connection is important, but must not be pressed into a metaphysical dualism, as is done by the writer just quoted. The term for "flesh" (*sarx*) occurs 12 times[2] in the Gospel and twice in the First Epistle of John. In 8 of these instances, it refers to Christ, either as having come in the flesh (i. 14; 1 John iv. 2) or as mystically giving His flesh for food (*infra*, p. 145); in

[1] Holtzmann, *op. cit.* pp. 470, 471. Note the significance of the Johannine use of τέκνον instead of υἱός to denote the relation of Christians to God. "He regards their position not as the result of an 'adoption' (υἱοθεσία), but as the result of a new life which advances from the vital germ to full maturity" (Westcott, *Epp. of St. John*, p. 124). [2] Or 13, counting twice in iii. 6.

one case, we meet with "all flesh" in a recognized Old Testament usage (xvii. 2); in the remaining 5 cases, "flesh" is contrasted with "spirit" or with God, who is "Spirit" (iv. 24). In two of these cases, natural birth is contrasted with spiritual, without any shadow of suggestion that natural birth is an evil thing (i. 13, iii. 6). In a more general sense, the natural and spiritual orders are contrasted in vi. 63 : "It is the spirit that quickeneth; the flesh profiteth nothing"; a similar expression of the limitation of the lower sphere is found in the words, "Ye judge after the flesh" (viii. 15), *i.e.*, as we should say, "by appearances." The nearest approach to the ascription of a moral signification to the term "flesh" is supplied by 1 John ii. 16: "The desire of the flesh . . . is not of the Father, but is of the world." But we have already seen, in the case of the Pauline use of this very phrase, that it can be a natural development from Hebrew psychology, without any need for appeal to Hellenistic dualism.

(*d*) *Eternal life.*—The spiritual birth of the believer implies that a principle of new life is imparted to him; the term "life" or "eternal life" is another characteristic Johannine expression.[1] This life is God's gift to man through His Son (1 John v. 11), who is the life (xi. 25, xiv. 6) which He comes to impart (x. 10), so that "he that hath the Son hath life" (1 John v. 12). The Petrine confession in the Fourth Gospel emphasizes this life, as the point of attachment of the twelve to Christ: "Thou hast the words of eternal life" (vi. 68). The condition of this life is that mystical fellowship of the believer with

---

[1] The term "life" ($\zeta\omega\acute{\eta}$) occurs 36 times in the Gospel and 13 times in the First Epistle of John; in the first three Gospels together, it is used only 16 times.

Christ which forms the keynote of the discourses in the Upper Room and is pictured in the Parable of the Vine, whose fruitful branches are nourished by the life of the parent stock. The same thought underlies the metaphors of food and drink by which Christ describes His own relation to the believer: "I am the bread of life" (vi. 48); "If any man thirst, let him come unto Me and drink" (vii. 37). It is clear that "life" in so deep a meaning as this does not admit of definition by any concise statement; the nearest approach to this is given in xvii. 3: "This is life eternal, that they should know Thee the only true God, and Him whom thou didst send, even Jesus Christ" (cf. xii. 50; 1 John v. 20). But the "knowledge" here in view is as much emotional and volitional as intellectual;[1] this life springing from the spiritual birth is love: "Every one that loveth is begotten of God, and knoweth God" (1 John iv. 7); moral obedience is itself the condition of "knowledge", since conviction of the truth of Christ's teaching is promised to those who will to do God's will (vii. 17). The practical test of the presence of this life is found in no intellectual statement of its nature, but in the exhibition of its inherent vitality through love to the fellow-members of the community: "We know that we have passed out of death into life, because we love the brethren" (1 John iii. 14; *ibid.* iv. 20; cf. xiii. 35, xv. 12).

The Johannine conception of "life", itself the development of Synoptic teaching (Matt. vii. 14; Mark ix. 43; Luke xii. 15, etc.), really corresponds to the Synoptic

[1] Cf. the well-known usage of the corresponding Hebrew verb (ידע) to denote moral as well as intellectual relationship; thus the sons of Eli "knew not Yahweh" (1 Sam. ii. 12); "I will even betroth thee unto Me in faithfulness, and thou shalt know Yahweh" (Hos. ii. 20).

conception of the "kingdom", a term which occurs in two contexts only in the Fourth Gospel. The spiritual birth is explicitly made the condition of seeing or entering into the kingdom of God (iii. 3, 5; cf. xviii. 36). Here, as in the Pauline teaching, the emphasis falls on the *present* aspect of "life"; future "life" is represented as the development of what is begun here and now. In the Fourth Gospel, indeed, eschatology proper falls into the background; the interest of the writer does not lie there, and it is of little use to ask him for details of the topography of "life" and "death." The believer is already begotten a child of God; changed external conditions will only serve to bring the fulfilment of that status or relationship (1 John iii. 2). This timeless or "eternal" life already belongs to a plane to which the mere event of physical death cannot reach: "If any man keep my word", says Christ, "he shall never see death" (viii. 51). The explanation of the words is suggested by their opposite: "He that disobeyeth the Son shall not see life" (iii. 36). In both cases, the physical condition of life or death is the mere circumstance of a spiritual reality. Life that is life is contrasted with an existence that is death. This death is the forfeiture of the child's destiny; instead of fellowship with the Father in the Son, "the wrath of God abideth on him" (iii. 36). The exact relation of "resurrection" to "life" is made clear only on the positive side. Of the believer, Christ says, "I will raise him up at the last day" (vi. 40; cf. 51); but the context shews that this resurrection is but the sequence and issue of the life already possessed. In the conversation between Christ and Martha, He contrasts belief in a future resurrection only, which Martha professes,

with that deeper view which regards the resurrection as
but the manifestation of Christian life, which passes
through physical death untouched : " I am the resurrection
and the life : he that believeth on Me, even if he die, yet
shall he live ; and every one that liveth and believeth on
Me shall never die" (xi. 25, 26). On the positive side,
then, the resurrection will simply be the completion of
personality necessary for the full realization of life. On
the negative side, the natural inference would be that the
" dead " have no resurrection, because its very principle
is not in them. In one passage (v. 28, 29), however, a
general resurrection of both good and evil men is proclaimed : " The hour cometh in which all that are in the
tombs shall hear His voice, and shall come forth ; they
that have done good, unto the resurrection of life ; and
they that have done ill, unto the resurrection of judgment."
This passage is so inconsistent with the general tenor
of Johannine teaching on this point that some [1] have
supposed it to be an interpolation ; but possibly the
conventional phrase, "the resurrection of judgment", has
lost its precise meaning and does not imply full
resumption of personality.[2] The future judgment itself
must necessarily be the manifestation and ratification of
that judgment which is virtually contained in man's
acceptance or rejection of Christ ; He is the rock set in
mid-current, at which men divide to the right and to
the left.[3] The time of the parousia is near at hand ;
it is the last hour (1 John ii. 18 ; cf. xxi. 22) ; we

---

[1] Wendt, *op. cit.* p. 554, *note* ; Charles, *Doctrine of a Future Life*,
p. 371.
[2] Cf. Stevens, *op. cit.* p. 241 : " It must have a widely different meaning
from that which is associated with the realization of eternal life."
[3] The figure is Holtzmann's (*op. cit.* ii. p. 514).

must apparently refer to this coming of Christ the words of xiv. 3 : " I come again and will receive you unto Myself."[1] Then will be completed the work of the Son of God, who, as the divine Logos, has been immanent in human life throughout its whole course (i. 9, 10).

5. DATA AND PROBLEMS FOR THE CHURCH.

Behind all great movements lie great ideas; yet the ideas become explicit only as the movement works itself out in history, and human thought never wholly exhausts the content of the movement, because personality is more than intellect. The New Testament is the partly conscious record of a great movement; the wealth of Christian experience it reflects has supplied data for many centuries of thought. Many problems have arisen and will arise that find no explicit solution in those data; it is the duty of historical exegesis to go no further in definition (*qua* exegesis) than the Christian thought of the first century had actually gone. Our study of the New Testament has sufficiently shewn the clear continuance in its pages of the Hebrew conception of human nature. Throughout the three principal types examined, there is obvious concentration on the moral and spiritual values of human personality; the æsthetic and intellectual are almost severely neglected. There is the creation of a new society through a new individualism, and the growing sense of a new solidarity within this society, which is ideally and potentially universal. Fundamental to all else is the deep sense of dependence on God, as the

[1] So Charles, *op. cit.* p. 363.

condition of all that is best in human life. More
particularly, we have seen in the Synoptic teaching of
Jesus an unmistakable emphasis on man's worth to God;
his salvation lies in fellowship with the Father, his ruin
in admitting to his heart the intruder, sin. We have
seen that Paul conceives human life as the arena of
vast and far-extending energies of good and evil; the
fundamental facts for the individual and for society
are sin and grace; human personality is ruined by sin,
as it is saved by grace, though man's freedom is of
decisive significance for his destiny. We have seen,
further, how the Johannine writings centre in the
consciousness of the absolute worth of the new life in
Christ; from this standpoint they judge all life in the
spirit of Hebrew prophecy, without resort to Judaistic
eschatology. These are the principal data, in regard to
the nature of man, for the further thought of the Church.
Great problems obviously remain. The Synoptic emphasis on the value of man can be to-day justified only
by an adequate philosophy of personality, over against
all naturalistic tendencies. Paul gives us no explanation
of the relation of human freedom to divine purpose;
we have still to ask how evil can find a place within
Christian theism; his contrast of flesh and spirit,
though not dualistic, might seem to point towards that
dualistic interpretation of the world which the Church
had to meet and overcome; his conception of grace was
a more or less undifferentiated complex of justification
and sanctification, each with its own difficulties. John
projects time into eternity, and brings eternity down
into time; he leaves us with the ultimate problems of
human character and destiny on the one hand, and with

those of divine immanence on the other. In him we are already brought into partial relation with the non-Hebraic thought of the age—the Greek philosophy in the light of which the Church began to work out the problems of its experience.

CHAPTER III.

DOGMATIC ANTHROPOLOGY.

I. INTRODUCTION.

The contrast and conflict between Hebrew and Greek ideas of human nature.—The Christian consciousness revealed in the pages of the New Testament is fundamentally, as we have seen, the development and modification of Hebrew religion;[1] but it flowed from its native hills, with this unbroken continuity, to satisfy the thirst of a world essentially Greek in its thought. There was much, naturally, in the Greek world of the Roman Empire which directly prepared for and reinforced the Christian consciousness; for example, the Stoic cosmopolitanism and the Platonic spirituality of outlook. It has been fairly said of Greek philosophy that it "recognized the kinship of the human soul to God, established regard for human life, proclaimed the inner freedom of personality from the outer course of events, was conscious of the truth that all men are one in a moral fellowship higher than all natural limitations, and derived from this truth, at least in theory, the duty of humanity towards all, including the weak and the wretched."[2] In order, how-

[1] What Hebrew religion was destined to become when its fundamental presuppositions were not only interpreted but largely replaced by Greek thought, we may learn from Philo.

[2] Pfleiderer, *Vorbereitung des Christentums in der griechischen Philosophie*, p. 74.

ever, to understand the history of anthropological dogma (*i.e.* of doctrine recognized as authoritative by the Christian Church), it is of more importance to notice the points of contrast and conflict, than those of harmony and co-operation, between the Hebrew and Greek conceptions of human nature. Christian doctrine in the earlier centuries is the product of a religious experience ultimately Hebrew, interpreted in terms of Greek thought ; but every experience carries with it its own implicates, as every system of living thought springs from a characteristic experience. Here, then, lay the possibility, or rather the inevitability, of collision between the two primary factors of Christian doctrine; the salient features in its development in large measure find their explanation through the initial contrast of the two factors.

From a comparatively early period,[1] certain characteristic differences are visible ; and the following are of most importance for our particular purpose. (*a*) The Hebrew interest in human nature is concrete, synthetic, and religious ; the Greek is abstract, analytic, and philosophical. When the Greek speculations as to nature first arise (sixth century B.C.), the Hebrew is beginning to elaborate his ritual duties under the Levitical law ; the dialogues of Plato must be set against the exhortations of Deuteronomy, and the thought of Aristotle against the faith of Isaiah, when we measure the respective literary products and their tendencies ; and if the Stoicism of the Greeks can become religious, and the Pharisaism of the

---

[1] It must be remembered that the ideas of man found amongst both peoples have their roots in a common Animism, and that there is consequently much in common between the psychology of the Homeric world and that of the roughly corresponding period (Judges and the JE narratives) amongst the Hebrews.

Hebrews sophistical, this does not invalidate the truth of the general contrast. (*b*) Greek metaphysic is chiefly dualistic, contrasting spirit and matter; Hebrew is theistic, contrasting God the Creator and man the created, and deriving soul and body from a single source. The dualism of Greek thought emerges in Anaxagoras, and the place he gives to *nous* as primal intelligence marks an epoch, in spite of its quasi-materialism, over against his predecessors. The psychology of Plato makes the body the prison of the soul, whilst his metaphysic posits the material element without deriving it from the ideal world. The psychology of Aristotle does not correlate the "active" and the "passive" *nous*, whilst his metaphysic is bound up with the contrast of form and matter.[1] Finally, in Neoplatonism, the religious outcome of this philosophical development, "the old Greek dualism of Form and Matter is deepened, and is transformed into that of God and the World, the Infinite and the Finite, Good and Evil."[2] In the Old Testament, there is no sign of this metaphysical, psychological, or ethical dualism; human nature is the created work of God, a unity of soul (spirit) and body. In the New Testament, the contrast of the inner and outer life has no metaphysical significance, nor does the antithesis of mind and body supply the ultimate key to moral problems. Thus the future life requires the resurrection of the body, or the fashioning of an equivalent "pneumatic" body, to reconstitute its unity of existence.

---

[1] Siebeck, *Geschichte der Psychologie*, i. pp. 139, 186 ; ii. p. 72.

[2] Kilpatrick in *DB*, iii. p. 851. Neoplatonism as a theory is Pantheistic, tracing all to a single principle ; but its anthropology works out dualistically (see further, § 3); cf. Zeller, *Grundriss der Geschichte der griechischen Philosophie*[9], p. 312 : "The dualistic spiritualism of the Platonic school is here combined with Stoic monism to create something new."

On the other hand, the characteristic Greek conception of future life is not that of the resurrection of the body, but that of the immortality of the soul (*infra*, § 2 (*d*)). (*c*) Greek psychology describes, in a quasi-modern spirit, the nature and activity of the faculties or elements constituting the inner life; Hebrew psychology still moves in the circle of psycho-physical animism. Whereas, too, the later Greek thought employs its doctrine of "spirit" (*pneuma*) mainly to connect mind with body, or the immaterial with the material,[1] Hebrew religion develops from the same primitive idea of the "wind" its characteristic emphasis on the Spirit of God, connecting man with Him. To the Greek, man is more or less self-contained; to the Hebrew, his higher nature is directly dependent on God. The most important aspect of this contrast is the Greek assumption of freedom and the Hebrew (including the Christian) of grace. "Few things in the history of speculation are more impressive than the fact that no Greek-speaking people has ever felt itself seriously perplexed by the great question of Free Will and Necessity."[2] The Greek interest in freedom first becomes noticeable in Socrates, who holds that, since all men will happiness, freedom is determined by the degree of knowledge of what true happiness is; with this Plato is in practical agreement, but Aristotle goes rather deeper by his recognition of personal character as the decisive factor in action. Whatever should be the logical consequence of the materialistic monism of the Stoics, their emphasis on self-reliance, their proclamation of the doctrine of personal responsibility, is unmistakable. As for Neoplatonism, Plotinus argues for freedom in the sense of the self-determination of reason,

---

[1] Siebeck, *op. cit.* ii. p. 141.   [2] Maine, *Ancient Law*[14], p. 354.

in its aim at the highest good.[1]   Hebrew psychology, on the other hand, whilst not excluding practical freedom, is concerned with motive rather than knowledge, and is characterized by its open door to divine influence; its doctrine of the Spirit of God, in relation to man and his activities, develops from the most primitive ideas up to the Pauline conception of the same divine Spirit operating through and personalized in Jesus Christ.   Christian life becomes life in and by the Spirit of God; not the nature of freedom, but the reality of grace is the centre of living interest.   (*d*) The Greek conception of moral evil is intellectualistic; the Hebrew is volitional. Greek ethical theory traces evil to ignorance (with Socrates), to want of harmony (with Plato), to deviation from the happy mean (with Aristotle, but cf. p. 154).[2] The Hebrew consciousness of sin regards it as the rebellion of the human will against the divine.

From the first emergence of the problems of human nature in the thought of the Christian Church, until that dissolution of the Church's outward unity in the Reformation, which closes the period of Western œcumenical dogma, we can recognize the presence of the conflicting factors here indicated as ultimately Greek and Hebrew. The opposing factors are naturally clearest in the earliest forms of the conflict, namely, in the struggle of the Church in the second century with the dualism of Greek Gnosticism (reinforced by the polytheism of Oriental syncretism), and in the Pelagian Controversy of the fifth century.   This last can be regarded essentially as the clash of Eastern (Greek) ideas of man with Western experiential religion in the

---

[1] Siebeck, *op. cit.* i. pp. 170, 235; ii. pp. 105, 253, 329.
[2] *Ibid.* i. pp. 170, 237; ii. p. 109.

person of Augustine, in whom we have the rebirth of Pauline (Hebrew) doctrine. The controversial literature of Semi-Pelagianism turns on the issue between man's partial freedom and the absoluteness of predestinating grace. Through the long mediaeval period, and beneath the subtle distinctions of Scholasticism, the fundamental question in anthropology remains the same. In the Reformation itself, we are concerned with the veiled yet unmistakable Semi-Pelagianism of Catholicism on the one hand, and the Augustinianism of Luther and Calvin on the other. The last topics to be embraced in our survey of dogmatic anthropology are the revival of Augustinianism, which is known as Jansenism, and the Semi-Pelagianism known as Arminianism, each in protest against what seemed a one-sided statement of human nature and its relation to God. From the central problem of the relation of freedom and grace spring all the great anthropological questions as to man's origin and destiny, his sin and his righteousness; beneath that central problem lies the ultimate question of all religion, the reality of any relation between man and God.

2. PATRISTIC THEORIES OF HUMAN NATURE.

(*a*) *Psychology.*—The influence of Greek thought on Patristic anthropology is nowhere more natural or more obvious than in the realm of psychology. The implicit psychology of the New Testament supplied indeed the basis for the fundamental Christian emphasis on the spirituality of human life; but the familiar terms—body, soul, and spirit—gave a point of departure rather than the outline of a scientific definition. This could only come from the established and accepted results of Greek psychology, which for centuries past had been a recognized department of inquiry. It is true that the transference, conscious or unconscious, of these results to Christian doctrine involved a change in their use which was of the greatest significance. The naturalistic standpoint of the Greek, which made the soul a product of the world it existed to know and to modify, gave place to the Christian theism which held the soul to be God's creature, and the world simply the appointed means to the realization of its divine destiny.[1] But, with all allowance for the important modifications in the use of Greek psychology which must result from the new standpoint, we may trace back the two principal types of Patristic psychology[2] to the two systems of Greek philosophy which had most influence upon the thought of the ancient Church, namely, Stoicism and Platonism.[3] Stoicism, the less widely influential of these, contributes the basis of the psychology of Tertullian; Platonism influences the psychology of the Alexandrian school, and with profound modifications that of Augustine himself. The Stoic psychology[4] regarded the soul as the finest differentiation in man of the divine fire which is the one ultimate principle of the universe; it is continued, like the body whose corporeality it shares, from parent to child by ordinary generation; its highest (rational and volitional) activity is centred in the heart;

---

[1] Cf. Siebeck, *op. cit.* ii. p. 359.

[2] A further type of Patristic psychology may be seen (cf. Nitzsch, *Dogmengeschichte*, p. 347) in the view of Irenæus that the highest element of the soul is found only in the complete man; the incomplete man consists of the (lower) soul and body (v. 6, § 1; 9, § 1; so Tatian, 7).

[3] Including, of course, Neoplatonism.

[4] Zeller, *Grundriss der Geschichte der griechischen Philosophie* (ed. 9), p. 233.

it is absorbed into its source, with all else, at the close of a world-epoch. Tertullian, whose psychology may be gathered from his treatise, *De Anima*, shews his Christian outlook by reference to the divine in-breathing (Gen. ii. 7) for the origin of the soul (*De Anima*, c. 3); but, in avowed agreement with the Stoics, he maintains its essential corporeality (c. 5). The divine breath passed into the interior of the human body, filling all its spaces and acquiring its shape, so that it can appear in vision and is even possessed of a certain tangibility (c. 9). The soul is a unity, with many functional activities, of which that of the *nous* is the highest (cc. 10 f.); the body is simply its instrument (c. 40). Tertullian is thus a "dichotomist." The controlling principle of the soul is seated in the heart (c. 15), and possesses the independent power of freedom (c. 21). The soul, separated from the body in death, is immortal in its own right (cc. 51 f.). Tertullian, moreover, derives his "Traducianism" (*infra*, p. 162) from the Stoics. His own summary view of personality may be quoted: "The soul, then, we define to be sprung from the breath of God, immortal, possessing body, having form, simple in its substance, intelligent in its own nature, developing its powers in various ways, free in its determinations, subject to growth by opportunity (*accidentiis obnoxiam*), in its faculties mutable, rational, supreme, endued with an instinct of presentiment, evolved out of one (original)."[1]

The psychology of Plato ascribed to the incorporeal soul, itself self-moved, the movements of the body; the soul is without beginning or end; from its prior history

---

[1] C. 22; cf. E.T. in "Ante-Nicene Christian Library", vol. ii. p. 462. (I have occasionally quoted from this series of translations, as well as from that of the "Post-Nicene Fathers", without further acknowledgment.) Further details of Tertullian's psychology may be found in Siebeck, *op. cit.* ii. pp. 371–374.

comes the possibility of its present knowledge through the memory of the world of Ideas once open to its vision; its present use of freedom will decide its future destiny; its nature consists in a (pre-existent) divine and immortal part, the *nous* or *logistikon*, and a mortal part, comprising the higher *thumoeides* (the "spirited" part) and the lower *epithumetikon* (desire); these three elements are seated respectively in the head, the breast, and the abdomen.[1] This triple division of the soul naturally appears in the Alexandrians, whose debt to Plato is so great. Clement (*Pæd.* iii. 1) writes: "The soul is threefold, having an intellectual part, which is called rational, and is the inner man ruling this visible man . . . ; the spirited part, allied to animal nature, is a near neighbour of frenzy; the third, that of desire, has more forms than Proteus."[2] Clement makes these two lower elements in the soul together intermediate in function between the higher "ruling faculty" and the body (*Strom.* vi. 16). A similar "trichotomy" of body, soul, and spirit (which the New Testament could plausibly be made to support) runs through the work of Origen;[3] his psychology is, however, closely bound up with his characteristic Platonic doctrine of Pre-existence (*infra*, p. 161). For the later developments of Alexandrian teaching, Gregory of Nyssa may be taken as a type. Here, also, we find the triple constitution of the soul (though in the Aristotelian form of vegetative, animal, and intellectual parts); but "the true and perfect soul is naturally one, the intellectual and immaterial,

[1] Zeller, *op. cit.* pp. 146–148; but Plato is by no means always consistent.

[2] For another example of contact with Plato, see *Strom.* vi. 12: "This is the nature of the soul, to move of itself."

[3] Harnack, *Dogmengeschichte*, i. 632; E.T. vol. ii. p. 363.

which mingles with our material nature by the agency of the senses" (*On the Making of Man*, c. 14; cf. c. 8). The lower elements of the soul are of the nature of accretions from without (*On the Soul and the Resurrection*, E.T. in "Post-Nicene Fathers", p. 441). Gregory rejects the Origenistic doctrine of pre-existence and pre-temporal fall (*Making of Man*, cc. 28, 29), but retains the Platonic view of the soul's essential independence of the body, though this is crossed with a different conception of the body as itself spiritual.[1]

The psychology of Augustine is of the first importance in this period, whether we regard it from the scientific standpoint or in the light of its historical influence. In him culminates the psychological emphasis of Western, as compared with Eastern, Patristic thought; he begins a new epoch, and has been with justice compared and contrasted with Aristotle.[2] He formally retains the "trichotomy" derived from Plato (*De Fide et Symbolo*, x. § 23; quoted in Nitzsch, *Dogmengeschichte*, p. 347) of spirit, soul, and body; but the two former are grouped together as a unity, over against the body. In this unity of different aspects and relations, the will is the central and characteristic feature: "Will indeed is in all; nay, rather, all are nothing else but wills" (*De Civitate Dei*, xiv. 6). This emphasis on the will and its inherent impulse towards self-realization is the new and epoch-making feature in the psychology of Augustine. The good will realizes itself in freedom through the love of God, which is inspired within it by grace; the evil will also realizes itself in freedom through the love of self, which is the

---

[1] Siebeck, *op. cit.* ii. p. 377.
[2] Harnack, *op. cit.* iii. p. 99; E.T. vol. v. p. 107.

characteristic of its fallen state (*infra*, § 4). In this
way Augustine "replaces the metaphysical dualism of
matter and spirit by the ethical and religious dualism of
sin and grace." [1]

(*b*) *The origin of the soul.*—It is characteristic of
Patristic psychology that it does not confine itself to the
explanation of states of consciousness; from these it
passes both backwards and forwards, to man's origin and
to his destiny. Three theories of the origin of the soul
divide the field amongst them, namely, those of Pre-existence, Traducianism, and Creationism. The first of these is
that of Origen, and forms one of the Platonic elements in
his system. God originally created a definite number of
rational spirits, all equal and alike, and gifted with the
inalienable attribute of moral freedom; according to the
varying conduct of these spirits in their prior existence is
their present varying fortune, as angels, men, demons,
with graded varieties in each class. This fortune is
partly seen in the differing quality of the material bodies
assigned. The varieties of human lot are therefore a
judgment on past conduct, the fallen soul being further
defiled through its union with a material body, though its
freedom still remains, to work out its salvation until the
final restoration of all (*De Principiis*, ii. 9. 1, i. 8. 2, ii. 1.
1 f.; *c. Cels.* vii. 50). This theory, it will be seen, supplies
a striking and logical solution to the problems of human
individuality, if its premise be granted; but, from its very
nature, it was peculiar to Alexandrian thinkers, and in
543 was condemned at Constantinople: "Let him be

[1] Siebeck, *op. cit.* ii. p. 397; in which context will also be found a
detailed discussion of Augustine's various contributions to psychology on the
more technical side, *e.g.* to epistemology, and to the inter-relation of faith
and knowledge.

anathema who asserts the fabulous pre-existence of the
soul and the rash restoration of all things."[1]   The second
theory, namely, Traducianism, has Tertullian for its chief,
though by no means its only, representative,[2] and goes
back to Stoicism, just as the first theory did to Platonism.
The name signifies the "handing on" of the soul from
human parent to child; *i.e.* the soul is begotten with and
like the body, through the sexual intercourse of the
parents.   Thus Adam is the one root from which comes
every propagating branch or "layer" (*tradux*).   Adam's
flesh was clay, and his soul was the breath of God; from
the one comes the seminal moisture of generation, from
the other its warmth (*De Anima*, c. 27).   These two
corporeal constituents of human nature develop *pari passu*
to adult age (*ibid.* c. 38).   To ourselves, under the influence
of modern biology and the doctrine of mental and
physical heredity, Traducianism presents itself as the only
approximation, amongst ancient theories, to those now
current amongst men of science.[3]   The dogmatic interest
of the theory, however, lay in the explanation it provided
for the solidarity of the race and the doctrine of its unity in
Adam.   The help thus afforded to the Augustinian theory
of the Fall and its consequences (*infra*, p. 189) is obvious;
indeed, Augustine's position, with its stress on a corrupt soul
as well as a corrupt body, seems logically to require it.[4]   But

[1] The first of the fifteen anathemas against Origenistic doctrine passed at
the Synod of Constantinople (Hefele, *Conciliengeschichte*, ii. p. 772).

[2] It was held, *e.g.*, by Gregory of Nyssa (*Making of Man*, c. 29).

[3] *i.e.* as far as the *development* of personality is concerned, and without
prejudice to the truth underlying Creationism; see iv. § 2 (*d*) and v. § 2 (*a*).

[4] Augustine saw clearly that on the theory of Creationism he must assume
the soul to be corrupted through its presence in a corrupted body, and in fact
his emphasis on *concupiscentia carnis* is in part a consequence of his open
mind to Creationism (cf. Loofs, *Dogmengeschichte*[4], p. 384).   The problem

as a matter of fact, Augustine was repelled by what seemed the underlying materialism of the theory, and attracted towards the third theory, that of Creationism, according to which each soul is directly created by God ; physical conception alone comes through human generation. Augustine's final attitude was one of "not proven" as to the issue between the two theories (*Ep. ad Hier.* 166). The first explicit statement of Creationism is that of Lactantius (late third century, A.D.), who argues that, whilst a body can be produced from a body, a soul cannot be produced from souls (*On the Workmanship of God*, c. 19). " God is daily making souls ", writes Jerome (*ad Pamm.* 22) ; and from his time onwards, Creationism became the dominant view. One of the chief objections to it seems to have been God's practical recognition of birth from adultery ; Jerome's sound reply is an appeal to natural law (*loc. cit.*).

(*c*) *Original and fallen state of man.*—The theories of origin already noticed have involved some reference to the Fall ; we have now to notice in what way this event, accepted as historic, became central in the anthropologies of Patristic writers. We have already noticed its comparatively unimportant place in the Old Testament and the limited use made of it in the New. In the Old Testament (cf. Chap. I. § 4 (*e*)), the narrative of the Fall is a fragment of the history of civilization and, however interpreted, a minor and negligible element in the literature and religion of Israel. But the sin of the first man presented an obvious point of departure for the theology of later Judaism,[1] whence it passed into the

meets us again in Aquinas, § 5 (*d*), and is seen in the dilemma that to explain the universality of sin we must make it necessary, yet that which is necessary cannot have the moral attribute of guilt ; see, however, Chap. V. § 4 (*t*).

[1] Bousset, *op. cit.* pp. 466 f.

Pauline anthropology (Chap. II. § 3(*b*)). It is, however, when we pass from the Bible to the Church that we note the great change of emphasis and proportion in the treat-ment of the Fall. With characteristic difference of inter-pretation in the East and in the West, it becomes, as an undisputed historic event, the principal datum for the interpretation of human nature ; it is a postulate, or rather an axiom, from which to work out the theorem of man's present state and the problem of his salvation and future destiny. It does not seem too much to say that the theory of the Fall occupied a place as central and unquestioned in the anthropology of the Church up to the modern era as the theory of evolution occupies in any discussion of human nature at the present day.

For the state of man prior to the Fall, a natural basis for discussion was found in the words of Gen. i. 26 f.: "Let us make man in our image, after our likeness ", etc.   The probable suggestion of the synonyms "image" and "likeness" is that man is given a dominion over other earthly creatures, like God's over all (so *e.g.* Holzinger), though it is possible to ascribe this dominion to the spiritual endowment (Dillmann) or self-conscious reason (Driver) which distinguishes man from lower animals.   It was natural, at any rate, for Patristic exegesis to emphasize man's *rationality* and *freedom* as the central constituents of his likeness to God.   Justin's statement of this position may be taken as typical and generally true for all Patristic writers: " In the beginning He made the human race with the power of thought and of choosing the truth and doing right, so that all men are without excuse before God ; for they have been born rational and contemplative " (*Apol.* i. 28; E.T. in ANCL, p. 31).   But, with this central agreement, there was room for much individual variety. Tertullian, for example, includes also physical likeness to God and immortality (*De Bapt.* 5); the Alexandrian theologians (*e.g.* Clement, *Strom.* ii. 19) explicitly reject the reference to the human form, as does Augustine, who writes: "We must find in the soul of man, *i.e.* the rational or intellectual soul, that image of the Creator which is immortally implanted in its immortality" (*De Trin.* xiv. 4). Some writers differentiate the synonymous "image" and "likeness" into the rational or natural endowment of man and the (Christian) moral character to be acquired. So Origen :—"The possibility of attaining to perfection being granted him at the beginning through the dignity of the divine image, and the perfect realization of the divine likeness being reached in the end by the fulfilment of the works" (*De Prin.* iii. 6. 1). Such differentiations are naturally coloured by the characteristic conceptions of individual writers; Irenæus, for example, assigns the "image" of God, in the sense of physical resemblance, to the imperfect or carnal man, whilst reserving the "likeness" for the man made perfect through the Spirit of God (v. 6. 1). Behind these differences there lies, of course, the problem of the human and divine contributions to the making of character ; [1] this central problem of grace and freedom will meet us most clearly in the Pelagian Controversy (*infra*, § 4 (*a*)).

The constructive use made of Adam's act of disobedience is markedly and characteristically different in the two lines of Eastern and Western writers. To the former, that act is the primary type of man's sin; to the latter, its fountain-head. On the one hand, Adam stands in the

[1] Cf. Harnack, *op. cit.* ii. pp. 133, 134 ; E.T. vol. iii. pp. 261, 262.

forefront of a long line of sinners like himself, for whom the chief consequence of his act lies in the universal mortality of the human race; on the other, Adam has once for all corrupted the human nature which flows from his loins, and has left it in helpless guilt before God. These, at any rate, are the ultimate issues of the two lines, logically and historically; it will be seen that the Western line of development implies a much deeper anthropological interest and supplies a much more impressive datum of thought.   The broad truth of this contrast may be illustrated from some of the great representatives of Greek and Latin theology.   The former may be said to begin with Justin.   In regard to the Fall, he says that men, "becoming like Adam and Eve, work out death for themselves . . . and shall be each by himself judged and condemned, like Adam and Eve" (*Dial.* 124); the human race as a whole "from Adam's time had fallen beneath death and the Serpent's deceit, each of them doing wickedly through his own fault" (*ibid.* 88).   Justin, apparently, does not even ascribe the universality of death to the Fall, but rather to its actual repetition in men.[1]   In the majority of Eastern writers, however, the emphasis falls on mortality as its primary result, as may be seen from the *De Incarnatione* of Athanasius, *e.g.* c. 5 : "Men, having rejected things eternal, and by counsel of the devil turned to the things of corruption, became the cause of their own corruption in death, being, as I said before, by nature corruptible, but destined by the grace following from partaking of the Word to have escaped their natural state, had they remained good. . . . But when this was

---

[1] This line of thought runs onwards to Theodore of Mopsuestia and the Pelagians (*infra*, § 4).

come to pass, men began to die, while corruption thence-
forward prevailed against them " (E.T. in PNF, p. 38).
The subjection to death and to the devil (or demons) was
matched by general deterioration in man's knowledge and
freedom, *e.g.*: " This departure from the good introduced
in its train every form of evil to match the good—as for
instance, on the defection of life there was brought in the
antagonism of death; on the deprivation of light darkness
supervened; . . . and against every form of good might
be reckoned a like number of opposite evils " (Gregory of
Nyssa, *The Great Catechism*, c. 8; E.T. p. 484). But it is
characteristic of the East that this general effect of the
Fall still leaves man free. This may be seen, *e.g.*, in
Origen's elaborate defence of freedom in the *De Principiis*,
iii. c. 1, notwithstanding the fact that he has raised the
Fall from the level of an historic event to the pre-mundane
explanation of the present order; this change is due to
Platonic influences, and involves the allegorical interpreta-
tion of the narrative in Genesis.

The Western interpretation of the Fall may be traced
back not only to its chief founder, Tertullian, but, in part
at least, to Irenæus, who stands at the parting of the ways
in this, as in other respects. Irenæus has, indeed, two
distinct lines of thought—one more in harmony with the
Eastern writers, which makes man's original state one of
incompleteness (*supra*, p. 165), so that the Fall becomes
an incident rather than a decisive factor in man's history;
the other that which is bound up with his doctrine of
"Recapitulation." In this doctrine we see the Pauline
conception of the first and second Adam worked out
along the lines of what may be called symbolic realism.[1]

[1] The term "mysticism" does not do justice to the thought of Irenæus,

Adam and Christ are both centres of racial solidarity;
but what Adam has done by his disobedience through the
tree, Christ undoes through His obedience on the tree
(iii. 21. 10, etc.).   The important element here is that of
the unity of the race, *in some sense*, in Adam ; but there
is no conception of an inheritance of corruption.   This
second element in Western anthropology is due to
Tertullian, and stands in closest relation to his Traducianism.   He accepts the rational element of the soul as its
proper and original nature : " But the irrational element
must be understood to be later, as that which happened
through the impulse of the serpent, though it was the
wrong of their own transgression ; after then, it took root
in the soul and grew up along with it, in the likeness now
of the natural, because it happened at once in the
beginning of nature " (*De Anima*, 16).[1]   But this corruption is not conceived by Tertullian as total : " Still there is
a portion of good in the soul, of that original, divine, and
genuine good which is its proper nature " (*ibid.* 41).   Nor
must we conceive the inheritance of a corrupted soul
through the line of Adam's descendants as the inheritance
of his guilt, which requires personal acts of sin for its
creation.   This third element, inherited guilt, is due to
Ambrose, who speaks of man as " having incurred guilt
in Adam " (*in illo culpæ obnoxium*), and writes in his
comment on Ps. xxxviii. 9 that man is bound over to
guilt by the very inheritance of a penal state.[2]   The

which seems genetically connected with the " symbolic magic " of primitive
peoples, according to which the performance of an act in one sphere is held
to accomplish something similar in another.

[1] Cf. *De test. An.* c. 3, where it is said that the whole human race is
tainted through its descent from Adam.

[2] Quoted by Nitzsch, *op. cit.* p. 359.   Migne, xiv. c. 1103.

general position of Ambrose is also that of Augustine in his earlier period (before 397), man being still conceived as capable of the voluntary reception of grace. The later position of Augustine will be considered in more detail in relation to Pelagianism.

(*d*) *Immortality and resurrection.*—We have seen above that the chief result traced back to the Fall by Eastern writers is man's universal mortality. In harmony with this conclusion, their chief conception of salvation was deliverance from this mortality, *i.e.* from all the perils to human destiny that gathered round the fact of physical death : for more ethical conceptions we have to turn to the Western development. But, in regard to the Church as a whole, there were two ways of conceiving immortality in relation to the Christian. A smaller group of writers conceive it as a gift to the soul; the rest conceive bare immortality as an inalienable and natural possession of the soul, capable of being either a curse or a blessing. To the former group belong the Apologists (Justin, Tatian, Theophilus), with Irenæus, Arnobius, and Lactantius.[1] Justin's remarks may serve to illustrate the general position of this group (*Dial.* 5, 6). " I do not say, indeed, that all souls die ; for that were truly a piece of good fortune to the evil. What then ? The souls of the pious remain in a better place, while those of the unjust and wicked are in a worse, waiting for the time of judgment. Thus some which have appeared worthy of God never die ; but others are punished so long as God wills them to exist and to be punished. . . . If it (the soul) lives, it lives not as being life, but as the partaker of life" (cf. Irenæus, ii.

---

[1] The proof of this statement will be found in Nitzsch, *op. cit.* pp. 352, 353.

34. 4 : " The soul herself is not life, but partakes in that life bestowed upon her by God "). To the majority of ecclesiastical thinkers, however, immortality is an inherent possession of the soul. Thus Tertullian, in his treatise on the soul, declares that it is not mortal (c. 14); " Death happens not by way of natural consequence to man, but owing to a fault and defect which is not natural " (c. 52). He maintains that souls after the death of the body are kept in Hades (c. 55), the good and bad separately (c. 56), until their resurrection in the body and final judgment (c. 58). This doctrine of resurrection, a common article of the Church's faith, shews the Hebrew parentage of the anthropology of the Church, just as the conception of immortality is largely due to Greek influences. Greek dualism could conceive the continuance of the essential personality without a body; but the stress of Hebrew thought, as we have seen in Paul, fell on the unity of soul and body. Thus Tertullian, in his treatise "On the Resurrection of the Flesh ", argues for the resurrection of the same body, since it would be absurd, unworthy, and unjust "for one substance to do the work and another to reap the reward " (c. 56); he is even at pains to find a heavenly use for bodily organs (c. 61). The chief deviation from this, the normal doctrine of the ancient Church, is found along the Alexandrian line of thinkers, who think of a spiritual body as the future partner of the soul. Origen, *e.g.*, who holds this view, defends it as teaching a true continuance of the physical body with changed substance; the body, dissolved into the dust from which it was once fashioned, " will be again raised from the earth, and shall after this, according to the merits of the indwelling soul, advance to the glory of a spiritual

body" (*De Prin.* iii. 6. 5). The Platonizing Origen is really committed to a purely spiritual continuance of the soul;[1] thus there is something artificial in his endeavour to find room for a conception that has come along a different line of thought and is due to the Hebrew psychology.

3. THE CONFLICT WITH DUALISM.

(*a*) *The problem of Sin.*—Every theory of human nature must, in one form or another, deal with the problem raised by the universal presence of Sin (*i.e.* of moral evil considered in its relation to the righteous God). Sooner or later the thought of the Church was bound to ask the twofold question—How does such evil come to be at all, and how does it come to be in all men? The general answer of the Church to the first part of the question was to trace evil to the free choice of man, for which God could not be held responsible; the difference between the Eastern and Western Church on this point was that the former saw this free choice continued from Adam onwards, and the latter was led to regard the freedom exercised by Adam as lost to his descendants by his act. This latter position carried with it the answer to the second part of the question; Adam's act became the explanation of the universality of sin in the race. The Greek Church, however, had no one dominant theory of this fact to offer, except so far as its emphasis on human mortality may be taken to carry with it the general conception of human weakness and accessibility to bodily temptation. There was a strong tendency to explain moral evil as sensuousness;

[1] Cf. Seeberg, *Dogmengeschichte*[2], i. p. 455.

it may be illustrated from the general movement towards asceticism as the higher morality, the growing insistence on clerical celibacy, the place given to fasting and physical penance, etc.   As a general example of the Eastern attitude, we may take the statement of it given at the end of the Patristic period by John of Damascus († 750): "Man, being rational, leads nature rather than nature him ; and so when he desires aught he has the power to curb his appetite or to indulge it as he pleases. . . . The assault of the wicked one, that is, the law of sin, settling in the members of our flesh, makes its assault upon us through it.   For by once voluntarily transgressing the law of God and receiving the assault of the wicked one, we give entrance to it, being sold by ourselves to sin.   Wherefore our body is readily impelled to it" (*Exp. of the Orthodox Faith*, ii. 27, iv. 22).   This recognition of at least a practical opposition of body and soul could obviously be carried further into metaphysical dualism, by making matter and spirit distinct and opposed in origin.   The rejection of this theory by the consciousness of the Church forms the prelude to the distinctly anthropological controversy of the fifth century ; it is seen in the conflict with Gnosticism in the second century, and with Manichæism in the fourth.

(*b*) *The Gnostic dualism.*—Here we are not concerned with the bewildering complexity of Gnostic cosmology, on the one hand, or the subtle problems of the origin of the Gnostic movement through religious syncretism on the other.   It is sufficient for our purpose to note that Gnosticism is essentially a dualistic "gnosis" or philosophy, applied to the moral problems of human life as a practical gospel; it is a serious and earnest attempt to explain the felt opposition of body and soul by relating them to opposing forces, and to save the soul by delivering it from the slavery of the body. "Redemption is the separation of spirit from matter; and matter is not to be transformed, but destroyed."[1] The dualism is more emphasized in some forms than in others, and in the Oriental forms more than in the Alexandrian;[2] but its presence is characteristic of Gnosticism, and underlies the principal Gnostic positions, namely, the separation of the highest God from the Creator of the world, who is identified with the God of the Old Testament; the separation of the true (Gnostic) Christ from the historical Jesus, so that, *e.g.*, the latter alone suffers physical death (docetism); the separation of men into different classes as spiritual and material (or psychical); the separation of spirit (soul) from body, with the practical consequences of asceticism and sometimes libertinism, and the denial of any bodily resurrection.[3] All these positions, except practical asceticism, were instinctively opposed by the Church,[4] which rightly felt that her historic faith could not be drawn into this dualistic circle without ceasing to be a Christian gospel. The peril was the greater because it threatened from within; Gnostic thinkers regarded themselves as

[1] Krüger, *Realencyklopädie*[3], vi. p. 736.

[2] The dualism of matter and spirit points to Greek influences, that of opposing deities to Oriental. We may perhaps say broadly of Gnosticism that the dualism latent in Greek thought was quickened into activity through Oriental influences. The Gnosticism which influences dogma is, in any case, predominantly Greek (Harnack, *DG*, i. p. 218; E.T. vol. i. p. 230).

[3] Krüger, *loc. cit.* ; see also Duchesne, *Histoire ancienne de l'Église*, vol. i. ch. xi. ; Gwatkin, *Early Church History*, ch. xv.

[4] The spiritual aristocracy of Gnosticism, with its insurmountable class barrier, is not to be confused with the Alexandrian distinction between faith and the knowledge which may crown it (cf. Clement, *Pæd.* i. 6).

Christians. The greatness of the peril is measured by the effect on the Church of the reaction against it; the consolidation of the Church, and its acceptance of the "apostolic" ministry, canon, and rule of faith, are historical monuments of the energy of protest against the movement which divorced body and soul into perpetual enmity. But the instinct of the Christian consciousness was sound, that what God had joined together, no man should put asunder; the ascetic practices of the Church can be regarded as a partial surrender to a false view of the body, but the rejection of avowed dualism was unmistakable.

(*c*) *The Manichæan dualism.* — The metaphysical principle of Gnosticism passed to the independent religion founded in the third century by Mani, on the basis of the old Persian dualism, though with Babylonian and other elements. Indeed, Manichæism has been described as the most developed and logical of all Gnostic systems, with one of the central forms of which (Ophitism) it seems historically connected.[1] As an independent religion, it represented religious dualism outside the Church, just as Gnosticism had represented it within. Mani had no desire to incorporate into his system the historical traditions of Christianity, as had been the aim of Gnosticism. His dualism took the form of opposing kingdoms of good and evil, light and darkness; the problems of life spring from the imprisonment of portions of light within the creations of darkness. The redemption will come by a "process of distillation"[2] of the light from the darkness, through the true "gnosis";

---

[1] Kessler, *RE*, xii. p. 198.
[2] Harnack, *DG*, i. p. 791 ; E.T. vol. iii. p. 325.

on the other hand, all bodies and the souls of the unredeemed belong to the realm of darkness. There was much to attract in such a resolution of evil into material substance, presented, as the religion of Mani was, with the accompaniment of earnest devotion and high ascetic morality; the best evidence of this was the loyalty of Augustine himself to this religion for nine years (374-383), in a position corresponding to that of a Christian catechumen.[1] But it was open to the fatal objections felt against its predecessor, besides being an avowed enemy of Christianity; in particular, it brought in a naturalistic basis for moral distinctions, since good and evil were presented by it as attributes of nature, not products of freedom.

(*d*) *The privative theory of evil.*—Augustine's escape from Manichæan dualism came philosophically through his Neoplatonism, as he makes clear in his "Confessions": "That evil, whose origin I was seeking, is not a substance; because, if it were a substance, it would be good. For either it would be an incorruptible substance, that is to say, a chief good, or a corruptible substance, which could not be corrupted unless it were good. And so I saw, and saw clearly, that all that Thou hast made is good; and there are no substances at all which Thou didst not make."[2] The argument of which

---

[1] Here may be named the mediaeval revival of Manichæism amongst the various sects (Paulicianists, Euchites, Albigenses, etc.) usually grouped as "Catharists." They flourished particularly in southern France and northern Italy, during the twelfth and thirteenth centuries, though they appear to be historically as well as speculatively linked to the earlier movement. We find amongst them the accompaniments of the dualistic theories indicated above, *e.g.* the division into those who observed a partial and a strict asceticism, and the rejection of the Old Testament.

[2] vii. 12; E.T. by Bigg.

this is a fragment and specimen reduces evil to the privation of good, and is known as the negative or privative view of evil. The good alone has reality; the evil is measured by the absence of the good, that is, by the absence of (metaphysical) reality. This philosophical conception of evil appears particularly in writers of the Alexandrian line, *e.g.* in Origen (*De Principiis*, ii. 9. 2): "To depart from good is nothing else than to be made bad. For it is certain that to want goodness is to be wicked. Whence it happens that, in proportion as one falls away from goodness, in the same proportion does he become involved in wickedness." This explanation of evil obviously relieves God of the creation of evil, but it is open to the serious criticism that it confuses the metaphysical with the moral aspect of evil and does not do justice to the positive character of evil in experience. In fact, as we shall see, Augustine virtually passes from the negative to a positive conception in his characteristic theory of the evil will.[1] The privative theory of evil represented by Neoplatonism goes back to the Platonic conception of matter as the unreal.[2] But if the unreal be given the power to check and modify the real—as it must when it is made the explanation of the world of experience—it virtually becomes a second principle, and the system practically dualistic. Clearly

---

[1] Müller, *The Christian Doctrine of Sin* (E.T.), i. p. 292.

[2] But Plotinus goes beyond Plato by his conception of matter as evil: "All evil is traced back by Plotinus to a defect, a non-being; from it springs all evil in the physical world, and from the body that in the soul" (Zeller, *Grundriss*, p. 318). Neoplatonism forms a parallel development to Gnosticism and the philosophy of Philo, but without the Oriental syncretism of the one and the Jewish monotheism of the other. Harnack (*DG*, iii. p. 204; E.T. vol. v. p. 219) ascribes to Manichæism Augustine's use of the Neoplatonist conception "non-being" as an evil principle.

the dualism is of a different order from those of Oriental origin noted above; they involved the active conflict of the two elements, matter being active as well as spirit. In Neoplatonism, on the other hand, matter is passive. In spite, however, of this difference, and of the fact that Neoplatonism and Manichæism are at opposite poles of metaphysical thought when viewed as complete systems, they are both in their several ways productive of a dualistic and ascetic anthropology. The privative theory of evil is as foreign to the Hebrew-Pauline conception of human nature as is the dualistic, and it is the Hebrew-Pauline conception that was destined to emerge in the consciousness of Augustine, in spite of the continued hold of Neoplatonic philosophy upon him.[1]

(*e*) *The will as the cause of sin.*—The result of the Church's conflict with dualism was to bring out with clear and definite emphasis the truth that sin must be traced back to the human will; anything short of this gave an inadequate conception of what sin is, and anything that went beyond this seemed to remove personal guilt by the substitution of naturalistic or deterministic causation. So far as the Greek Church was concerned, the characteristic emphasis on human freedom, as an attribute maintained notwithstanding Adam's fall, is clear evidence of this result. But this reference of sin to the opposition of the human will to the divine left

---

[1] Augustine throughout retained his negative (Neoplatonist) theory of sin (cf. the passages collected by Loofs, *DG*, p. 379); but his emphasis on the will practically makes his conception a positive one; cf. Müller, *op. cit.* i. p. 292: "Evil is indeed, according to Augustine, a negation, but in the same sense in which fire, for instance, is a negation, because it tends to destroy the material on which it feeds."

unexplained, because of its bare individualism, the universal presence of sin in the race; nor did Eastern volitional indeterminism do justice to the psychology of the will. It was reserved for Augustine, carrying forward the whole anthropological development of the Western Church and interpreting its resultant conceptions in the light of a religious experience comparable in intensity with that of Paul, to make the greatest contribution to Christian anthropology in the whole period before us (*supra*, p. 160). The contribution was made in the course of the Pelagian Controversy, with which we shall be next concerned, and in particular through the characteristic Augustinian emphasis on the grace of God. Its statement is, of course, bound up with the ecclesiastical theory of the Fall; but its value, as a renewal of the Hebrew and Pauline emphasis, should be estimated apart from that particular postulate of the age. In the light of Augustine's synthesis of the power and the love of God, " the ontological imperfection of creaturely being becomes the moral imperfection of godless willing."[1]   " I asked ", writes Augustine, as he describes his abandonment of dualism, " what wickedness was; and I found that it was no substance, but a perversity of will, which turns aside from Thee, O God, the supreme substance, to desire the lowest, flinging away its inner treasure and boasting itself an outcast " (*Confessions*, vii. 16).

4. THE PELAGIAN CONTROVERSY AND ITS SEQUEL.

(*a*) *The opposed interests: freedom and grace.*—The conflict with Gnostic and Manichæan theories, though

[1] Harnack, *DG*, iii. p. 110; E.T. vol. v. p. 118.

involving most important anthropological issues, raised these in a larger setting. It is not until we come to the beginning of the fifth century that anthropological controversy, in the particular and exclusive sense of the term, is found to occupy the centre of the arena. Theology and Christology had preceded anthropology, because the speculative activity of the Eastern Church was first on the field, and because, in any case, the objective elements in religion will usually arouse attention and interest before the subjective. But we have noticed the gradual emergence of the distinctively Western line of interest in reference to the doctrine of the Fall and the problem of sin. It might be foreseen that, sooner or later, the contrasted anthropological interests of the Eastern and the Western Church would be likely to clash, and that the contest would take place primarily in the West, with its characteristic attention to human nature and the problem of sin. The fulfilment of these anticipations is found in the Pelagian Controversy, in which the continued Eastern emphasis on human freedom comes into conflict with the developed Western emphasis on human sinfulness, and with the consequent emphasis on divine grace which characterizes Augustine. It is easy to collect from the Greek Patristic writers a long succession of illustrative passages, shewing, amid all varieties of doctrine, their recognition of man's essential freedom to accept or reject what God offered to him, to choose good or evil with their consequences of life or death. " Each man," as Justin says (*Apol.* ii. 7), "by free choice acts rightly or sins"; and this note recurs again and again through the teaching of the other Apologists, Irenæus (iv. 37), Clement of Alexandria (*Strom,* iv. 24), Origen (*c. Cel.* iii.

69), Cyril of Jerusalem (*Cat. Lectures*, iv. 19), Athanasius (*c. Gentes*, 4), the Cappadocians (*e.g.* Gregory of Nyssa, *The Great Catechism*, c. 30), etc. It belongs, indeed, as an essential element, to the Greek conception of Christianity. On the other hand, it must not be forgotten that the Western Fathers, through whom we trace the rise of "Augustinian" anthropology, still ascribe some measure of freedom to fallen man. Thus Tertullian speaks of God as calling, threatening, and exhorting man in His laws, "and this on no other ground than that man is free, with a will either for obedience or resistance" (*c. Marc.* ii. 5). Cyprian speaks of the law by which "a man left to his own liberty, and established in his own choice, himself desires for himself either death or salvation" (*Ep.* 59. 7). Even Ambrose,[1] and Augustine in his earlier period, make the acceptance or rejection of the divine grace, on which the otherwise helpless sinner depends, to turn on the sinner's initial freedom. Thus Augustine wrote, in 394: "That we believe belongs to ourselves; but that we work good belongs to Him who gives the Holy Spirit to those who believe in Him."[2] But this Western conception of freedom, as of grace, springs from a conception of personality different from the Eastern, and in the difference lies the key to the Pelagian Controversy. Here, as is so generally the case in earnest and disinterested controversy, the opponents do not mean the same thing, though they use the same terms.

The Greek conception of freedom, which finds expression in the Pelagian leaders, is the power of alternative choice; free will to them necessarily implies the concurrent

---

[1] Illustrative passages are given by Thomasius, *DG*, vol. i. p. 501.

[2] *ad Rom.* c. 60 (quoted by Nitzsch, *DG*, p. 360).

possibility of evil and of good. Thus Pelagius [1] says: "We have implanted in us by God a possibility (of action) in both directions" (*possibilitas utriusque partis*); Cælestius appeals to the words of Scripture: "I have set before thee life and good, and death and evil . . . ; therefore choose life, that thou mayest live" (Deut. xxx. 15, 19).[2] Julian gives the formal definition: "The freedom of will, wherein man is set free from God, lies in the possibility of committing sin or of abstaining from it . . . , since to be able to do good is the vestibule of virtue, and to be able to do evil is the evidence of liberty."[3] The conception of freedom which we find in Augustine, on the other hand, stands in marked contrast with this bare idea of double possibility. The freedom of the will for him lies in its spontaneous self-expression, the absence of external constraint; "No one", he agrees with Julian, "is forced by God's power unwillingly either into good or evil" (*c. duas Epp. Pel.* i. c. 18). The will's inherent power of self-determination is accordingly seen, whether the product be good or evil; it requires no alternatives of choice to constitute its freedom. The only time in the history of the race when such alternatives were open was in man's unfallen state; that probationary condition was mediated by the help of special grace (*infra*, p. 188 f.). Since the Fall and the withdrawal of that grace from man's now wholly corrupt will, it remains free in the single capacity to express its own evil nature (*ibid.* c. 2). But if divine grace renews this fallen will, it becomes free in the single capacity (so far as the renewal is complete) to express its new nature;

---

[1] As quoted by Augustine, *De gratia Christi*, i. 19.
[2] As quoted by Augustine, *De perfectione justitiæ hominis*, c. 19.
[3] As quoted by Augustine, *Opus imperfectum*, i. 78.

and this alone is freedom in the deepest and truest sense:
"Where the Spirit of the Lord is, there is liberty" (*De sp.
et lit.* c. 30). . . . "By the health of the soul liberty is
given to the will." It will be seen how impossible it was
for opponents to agree whose conceptions of "freedom"
were so different as these. By the Pelagian definition,
Augustine's view was nothing but sheer determinism, so
far as man's present condition was concerned; for
Augustine, the indeterminate will (*infra*, p. 187) is both
psychologically a fiction and ethically an evil.

Not less opposed were the Pelagian and Augustinian
conceptions of grace. In addition to the fundamental
difference that "freedom" is central in the Pelagian
scheme and "grace" in the Augustinian, the word
"grace" itself, like the word "freedom", had two
different connotations. For Pelagius, grace means the
natural gifts of creation, the possibility of choice itself
(*posse in natura*), the subsequent gift of instruction,
whether by the Law or by Christ, the forgiveness of sins
given in baptism;[1] grace, in short, is the external help
which makes easier the realization of the natural
possibility, together with the natural possibility itself.[2]
Julian's position is similar; there is no recognition of
grace as working within man.[3] Instead, the one aim in
all Pelagian references to grace seems to be to admit only
so much as leaves the will free in the isolated sense of the
Pelagian definition of freedom. The main positive con-

---

[1] As quoted by Augustine, *De gratia Christi*, i. §§ 5, 8, 43 ; it should be
noted that Pelagius comments on Rom. v. 17 : "Justitia donatur per
baptismum, non ex merito possidetur" (Zimmer, *Pelagius in Irland*, p. 297).

[2] *Ibid.* i. 30 : "Ut quod per liberum homines facere iubentur arbitrium,
facilius possint implere per gratiam."

[3] Bruckner, *Julian von Eclanum*, p. 164.

ception of grace is that of illumination, the communication
of knowledge; here again we discover the continuity of
the Pelagians with the general Greek line of interest
and emphasis. In clearest contrast stands Augustine's
definition of grace: "It is not by law and doctrine utter-
ing their lessons from without, but by a secret, wonderful,
and ineffable power operating within, that God works in
men's hearts not only revelations of the truth, but also
good dispositions of the will"[1] (*De gratia Christi*, c. 24).
It is, in short, the Hebrew stress on spiritual dynamic as
central in religion which here reappears in Augustine,
over against the Greek stress on knowledge.

The events of the Pelagian Controversy, briefly noted,
will bring out these essential issues; but with them are
entangled two ecclesiastical dogmas which claimed an
important place in the controversy. One of these—the
theory of the Fall—we have already noticed; the other
is Infant Baptism. As a standing practice of the Church
at this time, both parties accepted it, and it becomes
a pillar in Augustine's doctrine of original sin. The
Pelagians ought logically to have rejected it; but this
would have placed them too obviously in the wrong;
accordingly they were forced to invent a wholly artificial
explanation for it, as will be seen.

(*b*) *The history of the controversy.*—The course of
events through which the above contrasted principles
found explicit utterance is simple and straightforward,
and lies within narrow limits of time and place. Early
in the fifth century, a British monk named Pelagius, of
high character and earnest morality, came to Rome, where
an advocate named Cælestius became attached to him.

---

[1] Consequently *in singulis nostris actibus* (*De Gestis*, 31).

The laxity of Christian life around them led them to emphasize the need for virtuous effort. A well-known incident of this period brings the protagonists of the controversy into significant opposition. Augustine had written in his *Confessions* (**x.** 29) the prayer: "Give what Thou commandest, and command what Thou wilt"; and this characteristic expression of utter dependence on God is said to have provoked an angry contradiction from Pelagius, when quoted by a certain bishop in his presence; from the point of view of Pelagius, the words obscured the truth of human freedom and so weakened the very basis of Christian morality. The actual outbreak of hostilities belongs to the year 412, when Cælestius, seeking ordination as a presbyter at Carthage, was convicted of heresy on seven counts.[1] According to this decision, he had taught that Adam was mortal by nature, and did not transmit death or other injury to the race; that infants are born as he was before his fall, and have eternal life though unbaptized; that the Law can save as well as the Gospel; and that there were men without sin before the coming of Christ. Here we notice the prominence of the two cardinal dogmas noted above, namely, the Fall and Infant Baptism, together with the idea of grace as illumination. The second chapter of the controversy was enacted in Palestine, whither Pelagius had gone after leaving Cælestius at Carthage. Orosius brought the report of the African decision to John of Jerusalem and accused Pelagius; the ensuing debate

---

[1] They are preserved by Mercator, and will be found, *e.g.*, in Gieseler's *Ecclesiastical History* (E.T.), vol. i. p. 374. Evidence for almost ,all the statements of this subsection will be found in Bruckner's very convenient reprint of the chief Latin sources (*Quellen zur Geschichte des Pelagianischen Streites*).

turned on the possibility of human sinlessness. In the same year (415) Pelagius was accused before the Synod of Diospolis by two Westerns, themselves absent. Pelagius was acquitted on the ground of his adequate recognition of the co-operation of free will and grace in salvation ; the verdict aroused Augustine's suspicions of the adequacy of the inquiry. From a purely historical standpoint, the result illustrates the general sympathy of the East with the Pelagian position. The Western answer came in 416 from the Synods of Carthage and Mileve, and their condemnation of Pelagianism secured the approval of Innocent of Rome, when reported to him by Augustine and others. The Pelagian counter-move was the winning over of Zosimus, the successor of Innocent. Confessions of faith were submitted to him by both Cælestius and Pelagius. The former sought to maintain Infant Baptism, as " the rule of the universal Church ", whilst denying original sin. Pelagius declares that the baptism of infants should be celebrated with the same formula as that of adults. He takes his stand on Creationism in regard to the origin of souls. " We thus ", he says, " confess free will, as saying that we always need the help of God, and that they are equally wrong who say with Manichæus that man cannot avoid sin, and those who assert with Jovinian that man cannot sin; for both destroy freedom of will. But we say that man is able both to sin and not to sin, so as to confess that we always have free will." [1]   Africa responded vigorously to the Roman verdict (Zosimus) that Pelagius and Cælestius were men of sound faith, especially at the Council of Carthage (418), when upwards of two hundred bishops

---

[1] The whole confession of faith (preserved by Augustine and Jerome) will be found in Hahn's *Bibliothek der Symbole und Glaubensregeln*[3], § 209.

anathematized Pelagianism, in respect of its assertion of
Adam's natural mortality, its refusal to make Infant
Baptism necessary because of original sin and its ascription
of a modified salvation to the unbaptized, its failure to
recognize operative as distinct from merely illuminative
grace, and its attempt to explain away the full significance
of personal confession of sins (*e.g.* in the Lord's Prayer).
This decision was confirmed by imperial action (418),
including the banishment of Pelagius and Cælestius, and
Zosimus found it prudent to change sides.   His " Epistola
Tractoria " required the episcopal renunciation of Pelagianism and provoked the opposition of eighteen bishops,
headed by Julian of Eclanum, who now becomes the protag-
onist of Pelagianism, and is its most systematic exponent.
The edict of Honorius marks the practical suppression of
Pelagianism in the West.   The nominal condemnation of
the heresy in the East at the Council of Ephesus (431)
resulted from the personal relation of its supporters with
the Nestorians, and was based on no explicit dogmatic
grounds ; the East was too much in sympathy with the
basis of Pelagianism to be earnest in the condemnation
of its conclusions.   When the Pelagians took refuge in
the East, they were supported by Theodore of Mopsuestia,
the head of the school of Antiochene theology.   Their
emphasis on the moral nature of man was in full harmony
with his own tendencies, and he wrote a work, in 419,
" against those who say that men sin from nature and not
from free insight."   In the literary conflict between Julian
and Augustine, the contrasted principles of Pelagianism
and Augustinianism are made clear.   In particular,
Julian defended marriage against asceticism, and the
innocence of the sexual impulse against Augustine's view

that *concupiscentia* is the means of transmission of the *peccatum originale*. Mercator, a friend and scholar of Augustine, was prominent in the closing period of Pelagianism.

(*c*) *The anthropology of Augustine.*—The victory of Augustinianism, though secured, like many another ecclesiastical result, by policy and force, represents a clear and positive advance in the Christian doctrine of man. It constitutes an event of unique and supreme significance in the line of march from the first century to the sixteenth. The sympathy of a modern mind is sometimes aroused for Pelagius, not only as the defeated combatant, but as standing for the clear truth of moral responsibility against the oppressive and obscurantist dogma of original sin. Closer examination of the facts, however, corrects such a hasty impression. Pelagius, as we have seen, is the conservative reactionary, and Augustine the pioneer of a deeper conception of human nature. That the truth lay rather with the Pelagians in some points of exegesis,[1] in the recognition of the death of the organism as a natural incident, and in the refusal to admit the damnation of unbaptized infants, would be admitted by most modern minds. But their fundamental indeterminism of the human will is psychologically false; character and its problems, practical and theoretical, only emerge when we come to relate the nature of the will itself to its own activity, and leave behind us the thought of a number of isolated actions and of unmotived willing.[2] Over against this cardinal error we have Augustine's truer

[1] In regard to Rom. v. 12, Augustine was misled by the false translation *in quo*, as if referring to Adam.

[2] Cf. Harnack, *DG*, iii. p. 182 (E.T. vol. v. p. 196)!; Bruckner, *Julian von Eclanum*, p. 130 f.

conception of the will as itself possessing character, and of true liberty as found only when that character is good. In particular, his emphasis on the internal operation of grace, and on man's need of that grace in a profounder degree than the plausible yet superficial admissions of the Pelagians really allowed, corresponds to the vital claims of the deeper religious experience. Anthropology becomes through Augustine the vestibule of soteriology, and not its prison-wall. As for the dogma of original sin, whatever may be thought of its formal truth or falsehood, it at least gives full weight to the data of which the significance was so missed by the Pelagians, namely, the influence of heredity and environment, and the universality of sin as a fact of experience. The extension of Adam's guilt to the race was due to the survival of the primitive psychology of the " group " (corporate personality), with its imperfect sense of individuality. Yet it remains true that moral evil is a racial as well as an individual fact, and that there are elements in the nature of every man which make him member of a cosmic unity (see Chap. V. § 4 (*d, e*)).

The anthropology of Augustine centres around three main points, namely, the primal state of man, the first sin and its consequences for the race, and the energy of grace in the renewed will.[1] Adam was created in the image of God, with harmony of nature, knowledge of truth, and goodness of will. That he might be able to remain good, in spite of the limitations of created being, it was necessary that divine grace should aid his good will; even in this state

[1] Illustrative passages are conveniently brought together by Loofs, *DG*, pp. 381–393, to whom the following summary is considerably indebted ; the problems raised are clearly discussed by Shedd. *History of Christian Doctrine*, ii. pp. 50–91.

of original righteousness, Augustine would not ascribe to the finite will absolute efficiency for good. This divine assistance (*adjutorium*) was accordingly given to Adam, but only to the extent of causing him to realize the good which he might will, not of ensuring that he should will it. A potential righteousness (*posse non peccare*) thus belonged to man, and it carried with it, as its consequence, a potential immortality (*posse non mori*). The nature of the divine help thus afforded to Adam still left it open to him to turn from this double potentiality and to do evil, for which the finite will is causally efficient, since it is created out of nothing and can fall away from good to its own works; this constitutes evil, as the negation or privation of good (*supra*, § 3 (*d*)).[1] Consequently man in his primal state was so far free, even in the Pelagian sense, that he had the choice of alternatives; not because freedom implied this, but because probation required it. To this wholly unique and temporary condition an end was put by Adam's sin; his finite will fell away from good into self-love, and so became the (ultimate) cause of sin. His act was the abandonment of God; its inherent punishment was abandonment by God; for the finite will, deprived of the *adjutorium* of grace, was no longer capable of good, and the harmony of human nature was lost. The last result is particularly seen in *concupiscentia*, as is implied by the recorded sexual shame of the first pair. It is through this *concupiscentia* that subsequent men are born with corrupted natures (though Augustine did not commit himself to Traducianism)

---

[1] *De civitate Dei*, xiv. 11 : "Mala vero voluntas prima . . . defectus potius fuit quidam ab opere Dei ad sua opera, quam opus ullum . . . , vitium (est) . . . in ea (natura) quam creavit ex nihilo."

in body and (directly or indirectly) in soul. The fallen will of man can no longer produce anything but evil from a religious standpoint; it remains free to express its evil nature in acts of evil, and always does so; but prior to the commission of these free acts of sin for which it is guilty, it is guilty from birth through " original " sin, the sin that accrues to it from Adam, its origin. To the Pelagian objection that "original" sin is not sin at all, since it is involuntary in the individual, Augustine can reply that it was voluntary in Adam; and since we were all in Adam,[1] we all sinned voluntarily in him, and rightly share his guilt.[2] This is the present condition of the human race, which is unable to avoid sin and death, apart from the intervention of divine grace in the case of the elect, those whom God has predestinated for salvation. The reason why He selects just those from the common *massa perditionis* belongs to His hidden counsels; but it is not because He has foreseen their merit. The rest of the race He simply leaves to themselves; they deserve the (various degrees of) punishment they will receive. His grace towards the elect essentially consists in the impartation of energy for good, the " inspiration

---

[1] Harnack points out (*DG*, vol. iii. p. 200, n. 3; E.T. vol. v. p. 215, n. 1) the ultimate incongruity between his idea of the race as actually (seminally) contaminated through Adam's sin, mediated through the *concupiscentia* of all successive acts of generation, and the " mystical " conception connected with his exegesis of Rom. v. 12 (*in quo*). The latter is probably reinforced by his Platonizing " realism "; but it goes back ultimately, like many conceptions of theology and philosophy, to primitive psychology, *i.e.* in the present instance to the idea of "corporate personality" already indicated in Irenæus and Paul and Hebrew thought generally. Cf. Heb. vii. 9, 10.

[2] This is the point at which the modern mind is most out of touch with Augustinianism; our developed individualism makes it difficult for us even sympathetically to understand the corporate personality of primitive psychology, on which the doctrine of original sin ultimately rests.

of a good will "; they are justified by being made just, and the divine grace, which is so absolute in operation that it includes even the initial act of faith (at one time ascribed to man by Augustine), can be viewed in a three-fold light—as prevenient, operating, and co-operating—according to the stages of the process. The cardinal fact is that it is " irresistible " for the elect, to whom is given the *donum perseverantiæ*, the gift of endurance to the end. This absoluteness of predestinating grace forms the culminating point of Augustinianism and the point of departure for the immediately ensuing period of anthropological discussion. The criticism this doctrine provokes is obvious ; it does not leave room for human freedom, even in the Augustinian sense of self-expression. What moral continuity is there between the evil self that can only turn from God and the will whose new goodness flows wholly from what is imparted to it from an external source? This has been clearly put in another form by a writer in general sympathy with the Augustinian doctrine, namely, Thomasius : " The attempt at reconciliation (of freedom with absolute predestination) remains only a play on the word 'liberty.' Actually, Augustine denies the *liberum arbitrium* ; for he suffers the divine will of grace to operate only in the manner of the absolute will of power, and human freedom is nothing else but the form of this absolute manner of operation, the appearance which it has in our subjective consciousness " (DG, i. p. 538).[1]

(*d*) *The sequel in " Semi-Pelagianism."*—The victory

---

[1] Augustine, however, as Loofs (*DG*, p. 411) points out, is not a determinist ; psychologically, man is free within the realm of his capacity, and is indeed the efficient and ultimate cause of evil.

of Augustinianism, however complete as against Pelagianism, obviously provided the point of departure for
further controversy. The consciousness of the Western
Church had explicitly accepted Augustinian doctrine in
regard to such consequences of Adam's fall as were seen
in mortality, the necessity for the forgiveness of sin
(in baptism) even for infants, and the impossibility of a
perfectly sinless life ; it had been led by its deeper anthropology to recognize that saving grace must work as
energy within the human heart, and not only as illumination from without. But no synodal conclusions had
been reached as to the further elements of Augustine's
doctrine noticed above, namely, absolute predestination
and irresistible grace. To him these were the logical
consequence and safeguard of that supremacy of grace
which his religious experience demanded; but when the
chain of reasoning starts from them, it is difficult or
impossible to bridge the gulf that separates them from
any recognition of the reality of human freedom. Here,
then, was a point at which further controversy might
arise between those who followed Augustine the whole
way in his system and those who were equally decided,
to their own judgment, in rejecting Pelagianism, but
maintained that even fallen man retains some measure
of responsible efficiency for salvation, though its attainment is impossible apart from grace. The representatives
of this latter view were called "Semi-Pelagians" by a
much later age. The name finds historical justification
in the fact that their attempt to vindicate human freedom
continues the main interest of Pelagianism, and that
their prominent men were in actual touch with Eastern
thought; on the other hand, as Loofs has said (*DG.*

p. 438), we might with almost equal truth call them
"Semi-Augustinians", if only because of their recognition
of the direct work of grace within the human heart. This
sequel to the Pelagian Controversy covers a century,
instead of the quarter of one; and this fact itself indicates
that the opponents shared much more ground in common.

The new problems are first seen arising in the corre-
spondence between Augustine and some members of
the African monastery of Hadrumetum (426), which
reflects the obvious abuses of the doctrine of absolute
predestination when divorced from a vital experience of
religion. This was, however, the mere prelude to the
conflict which, from first to last, centred in Southern Gaul.
From this quarter the Augustinian Prosper called his
master into the field. The current impression of the
doctrine of predestination was that of a veiled fatalism;
it was accused of denying the universality of grace, of
making a man's salvation turn rather on his nature than
his merit, and of allowing no point of contact in the
human heart for the gospel appeal. It is clear that
absolute predestination was regarded by many thoughtful
men as a perilous novelty in doctrine.[1] The chief representative of the protest against it at this period is John
Cassian of Massilia, who argues against Augustine that
"free will always remains in man, which can either neglect
or love the grace of God . . . all who perish, perish in spite
of the will of God."[2] Cassian's standpoint is that of a
co-operation between man and God, in which the initial
impulse may come from either side; this assertion of

---

[1] The classical argument of Vincent of Lerinum (434) for the catholicity
of truth is indirectly aimed at the Augustinian extension of established
doctrine (Loofs, *op. cit.* p. 436).

[2] *Coll.* xiii. 12, and 7, quoted by Loofs, *op. cit.* p. 438.

13

man's potentiality naturally affects his view of the consequences of Adam's fall for the human will, which,
according to him, still retains within it the seeds of virtue.
On the other side, the attempts to defend the Augustinian
position are such as Prosper's distinction of the predestination of good and the simple prescience of evil, itself due
to the will of the creature; or that of the unknown author
of the *De vocatione gentium* between a general and a
special grace; neither of which goes to the heart of
the difficulty. The continued prevalence of "Semi-
Pelagianism" in Gaul is shewn by the attitude of the
Synods of Arles and Lyons in 475, and by the contemporary Faustus of Reji, who gives less place to the
inner energies of grace than did Cassian half a century
earlier. The close of the "Semi-Pelagian" opposition,
though by no means of the attitude it expressed, is
marked by the Synod of Orange in 529,[1] over which
Cæsarius of Arles presided. The decisions of this Synod
are Augustinian as far as they go, but its silences are
eloquent. It is emphatically recognized that man is
totally incapable of good without grace, and that no
element in him can be, so to speak, isolated from the
corruption of his fallen nature; on the other hand, there
is no declaration that grace cannot be resisted, and the
only reference to the companion doctrine of predestination
is in the form of an anathema on any who assert that
men are divinely predestined to evil. The statements
serve to remind us that the whole controversy, whose
formal epitaph they write, has bequeathed to the Christian

---

[1] The twenty-five "Canons" and the accompanying Confession of Faith
will be found in Hefele, *op. cit.* ii. pp. 704 f. ; Hahn, *Symbole u. Glaubensregeln*, pp. 220 f. ; or Bright's *Anti-Pelagian Treatises of St. Augustine*,
pp. 384 f.

consciousness the deeper recognition of both sin and grace, and of the impossibility of marking off any element in man as untouched by sin, or any good act of his as independent of grace. But the problem of the reconciliation of these deepest truths of experience into a formal system is not solved, not even yet attempted; it is bequeathed to the Church of the next thousand years, a legacy found to be as prolific in controversy and difference of attitude at the end as at the beginning of the dogmatic period. The Pelagian Controversy brought out the indispensability of inner grace; its sequel indicated the problems that remain, and perhaps must ever remain, when we try to reduce the relation of God and man to a formula. The long period prior to the Reformation, which we have next to pass in summary review, contributed nothing of primary importance to Christian anthropology —nothing, *e.g.*, comparable with Augustine's emphasis on the inner dependence of man on God for all that is good.

5. MEDIAEVAL AND SCHOLASTIC ANTHROPOLOGY.

(*a*) *The Mediaeval Church and the institution of Penance.* —The last three sections have dealt with the primary contributions to the Christian doctrine of man made by the thought of the Church, largely under or in relation to Greek influences, up to the fifth century. The present section deals with a period more than twice as long in mere duration, but marked by ecclesiastical activity rather than by creative thought. The Roman influences may now be said to succeed to the Greek; the authority, organization, and legislation of the Western Church form her chief interests and mark her inheritance from the

Western Empire.   Her thought is primarily an inheritance from Augustine; the mediaeval and scholastic anthropology can be stated naturally in terms of their agreement with or difference from Augustinianism.   But Augustine had made his own great contribution to the conception of the Church itself, as well as to the doctrine of the human nature for which the Church existed; the Donatist Controversy had left its mark as deeply as the Pelagian on Church doctrine.   Augustine's conception of the Church as the "City of God" is in some respects prophetic of the outward course of Western history for the next thousand years.   The Church, like her embodiment in some cathedral city, overshadowed men's activities as the divine institution for the administration of the grace of God, through the mediation of her supernatural sacraments.   Amongst these sacraments that which came to be of supreme importance for practical purposes was the slowly evolved sacrament of Penance.   "Just as the Lord's Supper removes venial sins, and Baptism the guilt of original sin, so is Penance appointed for doing away with mortal sins. . . . The whole religious life has its centre in the institution of Penance."[1]   The long story of its development from public sorrow to private confession, from evidences of a penitent heart to "satisfactions", from restoration by the brotherhood to Papal Indulgences, cannot here be traced.[2]   What must, however, be noticed is the effect of this long-continued dominant influence upon the interpretation, if not the

[1] Seeberg, *DG*[1], ii. pp. 117, 159; cf. Harnack, *DG*, iii. p. 521 (E.T. vol. vi. p. 243): "in practice the most important means of grace."

[2] English readers may be referred to Lindsay's sketch in *The Cambridge History of the Reformation*, pp. 123–128, or to his own book on the Reformation vol. i. pp. 216 f.

actual formulæ, of the doctrine of man. The formulæ, as we shall see, remained for the most part Augustinian; but the institution of Penance brought into prominence the very conceptions most alien to a religious experience such as Augustine's. The imperfect idea of repentance (*attritio*) which came practically to replace the genuine sorrow over sin (*contritio*), the ideas of merit attaching to the performance of "satisfactions", the spirit of calculation "which killed the nerve of morality and transformed penitence for sin into fear of punishment"[1]— these belong to the darker side of Mediaeval Christianity, even though the confessional[2] may often have deepened the genuine sense of sin. The issue—and sufficient comment on the whole result—of the sacrament of Penance is seen in the practice of Indulgences, against which, as all the world knows, that initial protest was directed which marks the close of Mediaeval Christianity and the beginning of a new epoch.

(*b*) *Mediaeval Augustinianism.*—That the anthropology of Augustine was the chief doctrinal inheritance into which the Mediaeval Church entered may be seen by glancing at the teaching of certain typical figures, prominent for one reason or another in the period between the sixth and the eleventh centuries. At the outset stands Gregory the Great (Bishop of Rome, 590–604), who is doubly significant. On the one hand, we see in him the advancing power and influence of the ecclesiastical and penitential system; on the other, the retention of Augustinian formulations of doctrine, but with such a

---

[1] Harnack, *DG*, iii. p. 250 ; E.T. vol. v. p. 271.
[2] Recommended in 813 at Châlons, and made obligatory in 1215 at the Fourth Lateran Council.

change of emphasis or interpretation as really involves an essential change of meaning. As to the former, he holds that "the Church possesses what Christ her Head acquired; she sacrifices for her members, and calls them to penitence; she is, in fact, through baptism, preaching, mass, penitential discipline, and the various branches of the care of souls, the institution of grace which mediates salvation."[1]

As to anthropology, "almost all in Gregory has its roots in Augustine, and hardly anything is really Augustinian."[2] Through Adam's sin, we are born into the weakness of sickness (*Moralia*, xviii. 45) rather than the utter incapacity of death, though we depend on prevenient and subsequent grace for all our good. Because of this prevenient grace, "we are said to free ourselves, who yield to God freeing us" (xxiv. 10). Gregory does not conceive grace as irresistible, any more than did the Synod of Orange; he accepts predestination, some being chosen and others left to their evil, but bases this on prescience (xviii. 29). Thus, there is room for human merit, because room for human co-operation with God, and consequently room for the whole penitential system and the connected order of ideas.

Such loose "Augustinianism" as this was only possible in the absence of rigorous and logical thought. The single landmark in anthropology between Gregory and Anselm is the Predestination Controversy of the ninth century, provoked by the attempt of Gottschalk (805–868) to make Augustinianism rigorous and logical. He approached the doctrine of Predestination in the theological rather than the anthropological interest. God is

---

[1] Loofs, *DG*, p. 452.   [2] Seeberg, *DG*, ii. p. 12.

without change, and therefore His purposes cannot be conceived to depend on the temporal course of events. Consequently, we must speak of a double predestination, both of the elect and of the reprobate; it must be in both cases of the person to the respective destiny, and of the destiny to the person; it must not be based on prescience, though what God predestinates He of course foreknows. All that God foreknows without predestinating is the actual evil, which, being the act of the evil person, makes his predestination to eternal death a merited one.[1] From God's point of view, all He predestinates is good, whether the benefit of grace or the judgment of justice.[2] Gottschalk was by no means the first to teach the predestination of the evil; Augustine himself had sometimes spoken in this way,[3] which was in any case only the making explicit of what was logically involved in any predestinating election of the good;[4] but Gottschalk's concentration on this theme gave it a new significance and aroused much controversy (from which his lifelong imprisonment withdrew him). His opponents, *e.g.* Rabanus, misrepresented his position as asserting that God makes men sin against their will. Hincmar, the most prominent amongst them, secured the recognition of his own Semi-Pelagianizing

---

[1] No solution is given of the problem suggested to a modern mind, namely, how there is room for moral personality in such a scheme.

[2] "Sicut electos omnes prædestinavit ad vitam per gratuitum solius gratiæ suæ beneficium . . . sic omnino et reprobos quosque ad æternæ mortis prædestinavit supplicium, per justissimum videlicet incommutabilis justitiæ suæ judicium" (*Migne*, cxxi., c. 365; the "Confessions" of Gottschalk will be found in the same context).

[3] *RE*, xv. p. 592: "Juste prædestinavit ad pœnam" is there quoted rom Opp. x. 909.

[4] Cf. Mozley, *Predestination*, p. 392: "There is no real distinction between abandoning men to a certain state, of which punishment will be the consequence, and ordaining them to that punishment."

views at the Synod of Quiercy in 853, which asserted a single predestination of the elect (*secundum præscientiam suam*) and an abandonment of the rest of the *massa perditionis* because of the divine foreknowledge that they would perish. The more definitely Augustinian views were, two years later, recognized at Valence by the assertion of a double predestination, in which, however, the mercy of God preceded good merit in the case of election, whilst evil merit preceded the justice of God in the case of rejection. The appeal to prescience in the latter case separates even the supporters of Gottschalk from himself; Gottschalk alone of his age shews himself a consistent Augustinian. Anselm (1033–1109) is important in the history of dogma by his soteriology, not by his anthropology, though the two are closely interwoven. His position is in general Augustinian (unlike that of his younger contemporary, Abelard); that is to say, he teaches the doctrines of original sin (passing to Adam's posterity), of the ascription of all human good to divine grace, and of divine predestination. But important modifications are visible when we examine his statements. Original sin is conceived negatively rather than positively;[1] it is the absence of the "original righteousness" of Adam, not the transmission of guilt through *concupiscentia*, that is primarily in view, both in Anselm's direct anthropological statements and in his theory of Atonement. The "original sin" of infants is wanting in the element of "will", which is essential to sin (however true it is that they have inherited the "necessitas" of sinning); nor "ought they to be punished for it, as

---

[1] Cf. *De conceptu virginali*, c. 27 (*justitiæ debitæ nuditatem*); in regard to infants, *ibid*. c. 22.

though they had individually sinned in person as Adam did." As for grace, it is indeed the one source of all man's good; the fallen will cannot of itself recover the "rectitude" that has been lost, and the gift of that rectitude through grace is a greater miracle than the restoration of the dead to life. But when grace has worked that miracle, the will has the power to keep what has been given, and thus to keep it merits additional grace. The contribution of man to the good act lies simply in the maintenance of what is given; his act could not be good without grace. As to predestination, this depends on prescience, and what is eternally predestined is temporally contingent. There is no conflict between predestination and freedom, because "God does not accomplish predestined acts by the compulsion or constraint of the will, but by leaving it to its own powers" (*De concordia præscientiæ*, ii. 3).[1]

(*c*) *Merit and grace in Scholasticism.*—With Anselm we have reached the Scholastic period of the Middle Ages, *i.e.* the period extending from the eleventh to the fourteenth or fifteenth centuries,[2] in which theological activity was chiefly concerned with the systematic formulation of existent material. In regard to anthropology, two lines of tendency are of primary importance ; the conflict of their respective interests gives to the Scholastic doctrine of man its characteristic features. The first of these tendencies was the emphasis on the merit of man's righteousness, an emphasis largely due to the cumulative effect of the ecclesiastical system and of

[1] References for the preceding statements will be found cited or quoted in the clear and concise account of Anselm's anthropology in Thomasius, *DG*, ii. pp. 152, 153, 163–165.

[2] Gabriel Biel (1495) is sometimes called " the last of the Scholastics."

the institution of penance (already regarded as a sacrament by Petrus Damiani in the eleventh century). But human merit logically implies human freedom in a sense for which the Augustinian doctrine of grace really left no room. The second main tendency was the interpretation of the Augustinian supremacy of grace through the Aristotelian doctrine of God as the "prime mover", the absolute and universal primary Principle. Augustine's metaphysic had been Neoplatonic; it is not until the thirteenth century that the full influence of the Aristotelian system reveals itself, as it does, for example, in the works of Alexander of Hales, Bonaventura, Albert the Great, and Thomas of Aquino.[1] Aristotle conceived God as the attractive goal of the world, not as its Creator and Administrator, as in the Christian scheme; hence his theism does not issue in determinism.[2] But in combination with the Augustinian doctrine of grace, it could be made to give a strongly deterministic view of human activity. "God", says Aquinas, "is the First Cause, setting in motion both natural and voluntary causes",[3] *i.e.* the operations of natural law and the volitions of the human agent. The particular conception of grace developed from this general philosophical basis is that of an energy or motion imparted to the soul,[4] a conception quite

---

[1] Cf. Loofs, *DG*, p. 529 ; Thomasius, *DG*, ii. p. 62, etc.

[2] Cf. Siebeck, *op. cit.* ii. p. 105, for the absence of determinism ; Zeller, *op. cit.* p. 186, for the absence of any idea of a divine will directed towards the world, or of creative activity.

[3] *Summa Theologica*, I. Q. lxxxiii. Art. i ; cf. the discussion in Mozley, *Predestination*, pp. 239 f.

[4] Thomas, *S.T.* I.b, Q. cix. 6. The substitution in the idea of grace of an impersonal energy from God, for personal communion with God in Christ (Paul), goes back to Augustine (Seeberg, *DG*, ii. p. 102 ; Harnack, *DG*, iii. p. 554 ; E.T. vol. vi. p. 279).

capable of being harmonized with that of the subsequent
acquisition of merit by the soul.   But this line of reasoning
met the problem of freedom and grace simply by thrusting
it into the background, where it still remains as that of the
relation of the primary to the subordinate cause.

The chief dialectical task of Scholastic anthropology,
in which these contrasted tendencies are at work, is to
reconcile the conception of the absolute grace of God
with that of the reality of human merit, implying human
freedom.   As thus stated, the task is an impossible one ;
even the appearance of a solution can only be found by
the use of subtle distinctions, which, at the lowest, are
purely verbal and, at the highest, conceal the concurrent
use of two levels of thought or points of view.   A
typical example of the Scholastic attitude towards the
two interests of divine grace and human freedom may
be found in Peter the Lombard :[1] " The will of man which
he has by nature is not capable of being stirred to the
effectual willing or actual completion of good, unless
liberated and aided by grace—liberated to will and aided
to perform."   " There is in the rational soul a natural will
by which it wills good by nature, although feebly and
remotely, unless grace assists ; this, when it comes, assists
it and stirs it to the effectual willing of good."   Those
who followed the Lombard, *e.g.* Alexander of Hales,
developed a more elaborate terminology with the same
general purpose ; this may be seen in Alexander's distinction of *meritum* as *de congruo* and *de condigno*.   Man is
required by God to prepare himself, so far as his fallen
state permits, for the reception of grace ; this preparation,

[1] *Sent. Lib.* II. Dist. xxv. 16 and xxiv. 5 ; Migne, cxcii., coll. 709 and
702 (quoted by Thomasius, *DG*, ii. p. 162).

though not merit in the full sense (*de condigno*), is yet the vestibule of merit, and in harmony (*de congruo*) with the consequent gift of grace, through which merit in the full sense can be acquired. But even this distinction is buttressed by another further back, between *gratia gratum faciens* (the grace just named) and *gratia gratis data*, conceived as underlying the preparation of the will itself. This last, however, can hardly be distinguished from "what God as Creator and Preserver gives and is to all men."[1]

(*d*) *The anthropology of Aquinas.*—The foremost of the Schoolmen, Thomas of Aquino (d. 1274), does not, like Alexander and Bonaventura, resolve the relation of grace and freedom into a virtual Semi-Pelagianism, concealed by subtle distinctions. His system proceeds from a full recognition of the absolute power of God, and, so far, re-produces the Augustinian anthropology as combined with Aristotelianism. That he can notwithstanding find room within the supremacy of grace for the ample recognition of human merit, is due rather to the interchange of his levels of thought than to any merely verbal adroitness. He does justice to both levels, according to the standpoint of his age ; but he cannot be said to have co-ordinated them, whilst *at the same time* retaining their characteristic values. His procedure is rather to give emphatic expression to the doctrine of predestinating grace, and then, when the ground is cleared by this recognition, to deal with the secondary causation of the human will as a sufficient basis for freedom and the resultant merit. Consequently we have psychological freedom combined

[1] Loofs, *DG*, p. 546, where may be found the passages from Alexander and his disciple Bonaventura, on which the above statements are based. For other distinctions, especially in regard to the existence of evil, see Mozley, *op. cit.* pp. 247 f.

with metaphysical determination,[1] and Aquinas can say,
" What is through free will is from predestination "
(*S.T.* I.a, Q. xxiii. 5).   He sees clearly that this predestination (which is quite independent of the prescience of
merit) involves the parallel reprobation, in the sense that
God permits some to fall short of eternal life (*ibid.* 3).   God
is not, however, the cause of sin, which is ascribed to the
human will, though He is the cause of the action (*actus*)
which is made formally sinful by voluntary departure from
God, according to the privative theory of evil (*supra*, § 3
(*d*)).   All evil which God permits is, however, overruled
to the ultimate good of the universe (I.b, Q. lxxix. 2, 4).
The fate of the sinner is no more to be a ground of
accusation against God than the wreck of the ship, when
no obligation lay on the steersman to control it, is a
ground against him (*ibid.* 1).   In general, we may say that
" the omnipotence of God becomes in the light of the
doctrine of freedom the mysterious background of all that
happens."[2]

According to Thomas, man was originally created in
the image of God, *i.e.* with " natural capacity to understand
and love God " (I.a, Q. xciii. 4).   His original possessions
were threefold, namely, his constituent nature and faculties,
an inclination towards virtue, and the superadded gift
of grace on which depended his original righteousness
(I.b, Q. lxxxv. 1).   Thus, even from the first, all merit
is made dependent on grace ; there is no temporal interval
between creation and the addition of this grace, from
which addition resulted man's " rectitudo ", *i.e.* the harmony

---

[1] Seeberg, in *RE*, xix. p. 712.
[2] Loofs, *DG*, p. 552.   Mozley (*op. cit.* ch. ix.) brings out clearly the
failure of the attempted explanation of evil in regard to divine omnipotence.

by which reason was subject to God, the lower powers to
reason, and the body to the soul (I.a, Q. xcv. 1). The
cause of all sin is the unrestrained love of self (*inordinatus
amor sui*, I.b, Q. lxxvii. 4) ; more particularly, the sin of
Adam is specified as pride (II.b, Q. clxiii. 1). The
immediate result of the Fall was the loss of man's original
righteousness, that is, of the harmonious inter-relation of
his nature, through the complete withdrawal of the gift
of grace and the decrease of his inclination to virtue
(I.b, Q. lxxxv. 1). The disorder of his nature, when
uncontrolled by grace, shews itself materially in *concupiscentia* and formally in the want of original righteousness
(I.b, Q. lxxxii. 3), these two elements constituting the
" original sin " which passed to Adam's descendants, with
the accompanying " guilt " (I.b, Q. lxxxi. 3). Amongst the
results of the Fall is death, for the divine gift that was lost
had controlled the body as well as the soul, and gave to
man a certain incorruptibility (I.b, Q. lxxxv. 5, 6). Thomas
is a Creationist in his view of the origin of the soul
(I.a, Q. xc. 2), and explicitly rejects the Traducianism
which would have most easily explained the transmission
of original sin (I.b, Q. lxxxi. 1). He holds indeed that
the human nature which passes seminally from Adam to
his descendants carries with it its corruption (*infectio*) ;
but the subject of sin is the soul, not the body
(I.b, Q. lxxxiii. 1). Thomas does not shew clearly how
the soul, created by God and placed in the generated
body, becomes corrupt ; his interest lies rather in shewing
that the guilt attaching to it is based, as all guilt must be,
on evil volition. The volition indeed is not that of the
individual descendant of Adam, but of Adam ; yet all
men are one, through the common nature they receive

from Adam. As in the individual the will moves the several members, so in the race the will of Adam moves those sprung from him (I.b, Q. lxxxi. 1). The salvation of the elect begins, continues, and ends with the grace of God : " Free will cannot be converted to God, unless God converts it to Himself" (I.b, Q. cix. 6). The grace of God is essentially the supernatural gift creating a new nature (I.b, Q. cx. 2, etc.) ; the new energy (*gratiæ infusio*) imparted to the soul is the primary element in justification, from which issue the other three elements, namely, the motion of the free will towards God and against sin, together with the remission of sins (I.b, Q. cxiii. 8). It is the grace of God, then, that moves man to meritorious good ; and this grace can be regarded as both " operative " and " co-operative " (I.b, Q. cxi. 2). At this point, therefore, when absolute becomes co-operating grace, the foundation is laid for the whole conception of human merit, as already indicated (I.b, Q. cxiv. 3).

(*e*) *The anthropology of Duns Scotus.*—In avowed contrast with Thomas, the Semi-Pelagianizing tendencies noticeable in Alexander of Hales and Bonaventura, and to some extent even in Anselm, were carried forward to more open statement in the work of Duns Scotus (d. 1308). From Thomas and Scotus sprang the rival schools of the Thomists and Scotists, their opposition being reinforced by the rivalry between the Dominican and Franciscan Orders, with which they were respectively connected. In their controversy we see again represented the conflicting interests of grace and freedom, which are the characteristic moments of dogmatic anthropology as a whole. The salient feature of the system of Duns Scouts is his emphasis on will, both in man and God.

But, in his anthropology, the absoluteness of the divine will falls into the unregarded background of the free activity of man, and predestination becomes a name rather than a reality.[1] In the individual man, "the will is the total and immediate cause in respect of its own volition";[2] no other cause is to be sought.

The only change wrought in human nature by the Fall was the loss of the supernatural gift which kept order in the otherwise rebellious constitution of man; original sin is therefore no more than the absence of the righteousness owed by man, which should have passed from Adam to his descendants, and is not conceived positively through a corrupted nature (II. Dist. xxxii. Q. unica, 7). As for "*concupiscentia*", it is properly a natural element in man, becoming sinful only as the will permits its excess. The Fall consequently becomes of relatively small account.[3] The attitude of Duns Scotus is similar in regard to the acknowledged necessity of grace to co-operate with the will (II. Dist. vii. Q. i. 15); the chief motive for the admission of such co-operation seems to be caution, lest the position approach Pelagianism (I. xvii. Q. iii. 29) by ascribing merit to the purely natural activity of man. But, though God is said to require the grace He inspires in man as the ground of merit, there is no intrinsic reason why human merit may not precede divine grace, as human freedom is avowed to do.[4]

[1] Loofs, *DG*, p. 595; cf. Harnack, *DG*, iii. p. 578 (E.T. vol. vi. p. 306 n.); Seeberg, *DG*, ii. p. 135.

[2] *Sent.* II. Dist. xxxvii. Q. ii.; this, together with sources for most of the following statements, is given by Gieseler, *Ecc. Hist.* (E.T.), iii. pp. 308-309.

[3] Harnack, *DG*, iii. p. 575; E.T. vol. vi. p. 302.

[4] Note the passages quoted in Harnack, *DG*, iii. p. 581 (E.T. vol. vi. p. 309); cf. also Loofs, *DG*, p. 597, and Seeberg, *DG*, ii. p. 143. It is significant that Duns Scotus treats justification in connection with the

6. TRIDENTINE ANTHROPOLOGY AND THE AUGUSTINIAN REACTION.

(*a*) *Original Sin and Justification at the Council of Trent.* — Before we consider the contribution to the Christian doctrine of man made by the Protestant Reformers, it is desirable for several reasons to study the formulation of anthropology made at the Council of Trent (1546-1547; Sessions V. and VI.). This properly follows the last section, as the Tridentine doctrines were based on the Scholastic, with most careful recognition of the scope of debate between the Thomist and Scotist schools. It is true that the dogmatic decisions reached at Trent presuppose Protestant anthropology; this is clearly seen in the fact that the doctrine of Justification, the central interest of the Reformers, is the chief Tridentine topic, to say nothing of the fact that twenty-nine out of the appended thirty-three anathemas are directly levelled against Protestantism.[1] But constructive interest itself requires that we pass from the less important formulation of older doctrine at Trent to the fresh factors which mark the beginning of a new period. Even from the standpoint of general history, this order would be justified, since the Council of Trent was in large measure the outcome of a genuine Catholic demand for reforma-

Sacrament of Penance. In the latest period of Scholasticism, Pelagianism is found in close relation to the Nominalist philosophy, which attached itself to the Scotist succession. But here, also, over against Occam (d. 1347), we have the Augustinian reaction of Bradwardine (d. 1349), with his complaint concerning his contemporaries that "almost the whole world has gone off into error after Pelagius."

[1] Ed. Tauchnitz, pp. 35-39; cf. Harnack, *DG*, iii. p. 645 (E.T. vol. vii. pp. 71, 72), where the most striking are quoted.

14

tion—if not so much in doctrine, yet most emphatically in the morals and organization of the Church.

The Tridentine anthropology may be generally described as the combination of a Thomist scheme of sin and grace with such modification of its statement as would allow a Scotist interpretation. The presence of both elements in the Council was the direct result of the history of the previous centuries. Whilst, on the one hand, the Augustinianism of Thomas had the greater professed reverence, on the other, the controlling influence of the Jesuit theologians, Lainez and Salmeron, was exerted on the side of Semi-Pelagianism. But behind and above these rival theological interests was the purpose to maintain the ecclesiastical system which stood or fell with the theory of the sacraments. Here lay the chief interest of the Council, and accordingly the doctrine of the sacraments is almost the only other doctrinal subject treated. To the doctrine of the sacraments the anthropology is subordinated—this being the inevitable outcome of the Scholastic development. Such a subordination implied, even in the case of an Augustinian Thomist, an anthropology different from that of Protestants; consequently the Council, however divided, theologically and politically, within its own ranks, could present a united and unmistakable front against Protestantism.

The doctrine of Original Sin, promulgated at the fifth Session of the Council, is apt to impress the casual reader as more or less consistently Augustinian. The five sections respectively declare that (1) the effects of the Fall are the loss of original righteousness, together with guilt, death, captivity to the devil, and change " for

the worse" in man's body and soul; (2) the consequences
of this sin affect all men ; (3) they are removable only by
Christ's merit through baptism; (4) this is necessary for
infants as well as adults; (5) the grace conferred in
baptism wholly removes original sin, the *concupiscentia*
remaining in the baptized not really being sin. But it
is sufficient to indicate three points in which room is left
for laxer views of Semi-Pelagian tendency. In the first
place, original righteousness is spoken of as that in which
Adam had been "constituted" (c. 1), this term having
been substituted for the originally drafted term "created."
The result of the change is that the question at issue
between the Thomist and the Scotist remains undecided ;
the former maintained that Adam received the supernatural gift of grace, on which his righteousness depended,
from his creation ; the latter, that Adam received it
subsequently, after congruent merit.[1] In the second
place, the Thomistic view of *concupiscentia* as the material
side of original sin is definitely rejected, whilst the Scotist
was free to assert his view of original sin as essentially
the simple absence of man's original righteousness. In
the third place, whilst the fifth Session declares that Adam
was wholly changed through the Fall, in body and soul,
"for the worse" (*in deterius*), the sixth Session definitely
states that the change does not imply the extinction of
free will, but simply its weakening and bias.[2] This is the
most explicit statement of Tridentine Semi-Pelagianism.

The doctrine of Justification is formulated much more
elaborately, and is perfectly definite in its rejection of

[1] Harnack, *DG*, iii. p. 574 ; E.T. vol. vi. pp. 301, 302.
[2] C. 1, at end : "Liberum arbitrium minime exstinctum . . . viribus lice.
attenuatum et inclinatum."

the Protestant doctrine of Justification by faith. The
Catholic doctrine, formally defined as essential to salvation
(c. 16), may be termed Justification by sanctification
through infused grace. The three problems of Justification here in view relate to the manner in which it is first
gained, then maintained, and finally regained when lost
through mortal sin. The virtual answers are that it is
gained through the sacrament of baptism, through which
is received "not only the remission of sins, but also the
sanctification and renewal of the inner man" (c. 7);
it is maintained through the performance of good works
(the keeping of the commandments of God and of the
Church), resulting in an increase of justification (c. 10);
it is regained by the sacrament of penance, and the
consequent "satisfactio" made by fasting, alms, prayers,
etc., the latter meeting the temporal (including purgatorial)
penalty of the sin, whilst the priestly absolution removes
the guilt and the eternal punishment (c. 14). It will
be seen that the emphasis falls throughout the three
divisions on the two sacraments and the merit of good
works;[1] nor is the significance of this emphasis annulled
by such statements as that human merits are really
divine gifts (c. 16) and due to the infusion of divine
grace. For against such statements must be set, not
only the recurrent references to human co-operation,[2]
but still more the initial discussion (cc. 1–6) of the
necessary "preparation" on man's part for the whole
process. This is indeed verbally safeguarded by the
reference to "prevenient grace"; but this grace is that

---

[1] As a natural consequence, there can be no "assurance" of salvation
(c. 9).

[2] *e.g.* "Per voluntariam susceptionem gratiæ et donorum" (c. 7).

of the divine call, requiring the free assent and co-operation of the human agent, who is able to reject what is offered to him (c. 5). In this preparation, faith is no more than assent to the divine revelation (c. 6) —on which definition the Canon (9) anathematizing "Justification by faith alone" might win even Protestant acceptance. It is in such testing differences that we are enabled to see how far the Tridentine, *i.e.* the mediaeval level of discussion, falls below that of the Reformers at their best.[1] The permanent significance of the Council of Trent lies in the official acceptance of this lower level, just as its immediate result was the sharp dogmatic differentiation of Catholicism from Protestantism.

(*b*) *Jansenism.*—Within Catholicism itself, as we have seen, there remained the differences in regard to which a compromise was verbally made at the Council of Trent. The subsequent revival of Augustinianism known as Jansenism is as eloquent in regard to the actual continuance of these differences as its fate is of the supremacy of Jesuit Semi-Pelagianism or Pelagianism. Jansenism was a genuine Catholic revival of the teaching of Augustine, by no means a product of Protestantism. Its direct dogmatic value is small, since it breaks no new ground; its history is, however, valuable, as shewing the explicit Catholic rejection of Augustine's cardinal teaching, which was implicitly abandoned in the decrees of the Council of Trent. A significant prelude to Jansenism and its fortunes is supplied by the appearance of Bajus (1513–1589), on the one side, and Molina (d. 1600), on the other. The former was condemned through Franciscan influence in 1567 for teaching a series of Augustinian

[1] Cf. Harnack, *DG*, iii. p. 635; E.T. vol. vii. p. 56.

propositions in regard to grace; the latter, who had published a work in 1588 in exposition of the Jesuit synergism, was assailed in vain by the Dominicans, and the lengthy commission which sat on his work (1598–1607) ended without result. In these events both the Jesuit supremacy and the whole trend of thought against which Jansenism protested may be clearly seen.

Jansenism derives its name from Jansen (d. 1638), Bishop of Ypres, whose *Augustinus*, published in 1640, was condemned in 1642 as continuing the heresy of Bajus. It is substantially a restatement of the teaching of Augustine in order to get behind the influence of Aristotle and the Jesuits, who were correlated by Jansen with the Arminians of his day. The influence of this book was chiefly seen in France, where it was the dogmatic basis of the school of Port-Royal. The first of this school was Saint-Cyran, a friend and fellow-student of Jansen; after the death of these two, the prominent names are those of Arnauld, Pascal, and, finally, Quesnel. A sufficient indication of the dogmatic trend of the movement may be gained from the five statements derived from the *Augustinus* and condemned by the Papal Bull "Cum Occasione" of 1653.[1] Their central features are two— the irresistibility of divine grace, and the compatibility of human " freedom " with the presence of divine " necessity ", though not "compulsion." We have in Jansenism, that is to say, simply the Augustinian conception of " freedom " (psychological); Pascal defends this vigorously in contrast with the Calvinistic doctrine of grace, which, he maintains,

---

[1] These will be found in Harnack, *DG*, iii. p. 665 (E.T. vol. vii. p. 94); Thomasius, *DG*, ii. p. 727 ; or Seeberg, *DG.*, ii. p. 445.

leaves no room for such freedom.[1] It is not necessary here to discuss the Jansenist attempts to evade the full force of this condemnation, or the events culminating in the destruction of Port-Royal in 1710 and the condemnation of Quesnel in 1713 by the Bull "Unigenitus." It is enough to emphasize what has already been said, that the exclusion of genuine Augustinianism from the Catholic anthropology was the inevitable outcome of the whole mediaeval development of sacrament and merit. The fortunes of Augustinianism, with which, in spite of all qualifications, the best interests of Christian anthropology are bound up, must now be followed in that more successful revival of it which goes by the name of the Protestant Reformation.

7. THE REFORMATION.

(*a*) *The preparation in mediaeval religion.*--In our survey of the anthropological development of the Middle Ages, it was convenient to confine our attention to the vast structure of thought elaborated by the great Schoolmen and culminating in the decisions of the Council of Trent. The salient feature of mediaeval religion is the ecclesiastical system, particularly the sacrament of penance. It presents a code of sacramental ethics, built up by Græco-Roman, especially Aristotelian, thought on an Augustinian basis. But the religion of Augustine was not crystallized into dogma without leaving an inheritance of mystical and devotional thought. It was this great inheritance which

---

[1] The important passages are collected and criticized by Mozley, *Predestination*, Note XXI. pp. 402–409. An interesting popular account of the whole movement is given in Marguerite Tollemache's *French Jansenists* (1893).

mediated to the Reformation that Hebrew spirit of religion which Augustine had renewed. Through the Middle Ages there runs an undercurrent of personal religion, awaiting only the fulness of the time for its independent strength to be manifested. Amongst the foremost representatives of this mystical piety may be named Bernard of Clairvaux and Francis of Assisi, in whom respectively it was the accompaniment of ecclesiastical statesmanship and of missionary devotion ; one of its chief Scholastic types is Thomas of Aquino. It is along this line of personal religion—always to some extent the corrective, where the supplement, of sacramentarianism— that we are to look for the emergence of the Reformation principles. " The real roots of the spiritual life of Luther, and of the other Reformers, ought to be sought for in the family and in the popular religious life of the times."[1] This positive line of development is more significant, for our purpose, than any negative criticism, through previous " Reformers ", of the ecclesiastical system, inasmuch as the Reformation itself is the establishment of a new principle rather than the mere rejection of old abuses. In Luther himself, both the positive and negative relations of the Reformation to mediaeval religion are clearly seen from the outset. On the one hand, his reaction from the abuse of Indulgences, and consequently from the whole doctrine of penance in which they were rooted, finds expression in the publication of the 95 Theses of 31st October 1517. On the other hand, his essential dependence on the personal piety of the generations before him may be exemplified by his publication and commendation of

---

[1] Lindsay, *History of the Reformation*, vol. i. p. 114 ; the positive religious tendencies of Luther's age are here sympathetically depicted.

the volume known as the *German Theology* (1516 and 1518), which is the direct outcome of the mystical religion at the heart of so many "brotherhoods" of the time.[1] The former act is really the outcome of the attitude represented by the latter, the expression of a religious individualism which instinctively condemns the prevalent system from the standpoint of inner experience. A new point of view is thus reached, yet one linked in historical continuity with the deepest religion of the preceding period. The doctrine of man expands into a doctrine of man's true relation to God, and as such becomes the central principle of the Reformation. " Behind this religious trust in the grace of God in Christ the whole field of ethics in the narrower sense fell back, as the conditioned behind the conditioning. The new element in Luther's Christianity was primarily this religious grasp of the Gospel."[2]

(*b*) *The central principle—Justification by Faith.*—We may best approach the definition of the doctrine of Justification by Faith—the doctrine cardinal to Protestantism—by remembering that for this doctrine " faith " does not mean intellectual assent, but personal trust. The Canons of the Council of Trent, as we have already seen, condemned the doctrine of justification by faith alone *in the former sense* (c. 9 f.), or at least in a sense involving much less than the surrender of the whole personality to God in Christ. But the primary emphasis of that mystical religion from which the principle of the Reformation sprang was precisely on that complete surrender ; as the

---

[1] An excellent popular account of these will be found in the recent volume by Rufus M. Jones, *Studies in Mystical Religion*, pp. 196 f.

[2] Loofs, *DG*, p. 714.

Theologia Germanica (c. 10) expresses it: "Where men are enlightened with the true light . . . they renounce all desire and choice, and commit and commend themselves and all things to the Eternal Goodness. Nevertheless, there remaineth in them a desire to go forward and get nearer to the Eternal Goodness; that is, to come to a clearer knowledge, and warmer love, and more comfortable assurance, and perfect obedience and subjection; so that every enlightened man could say: 'I would fain be to the Eternal Goodness what his own hand is to a man'" (Winkworth's trans. p. 31). These typical words are taken from the book of which Luther wrote in his preface to it: "Next to the Bible and St. Augustine, no book hath ever come into my hands whence I have learnt, or would wish to learn, more of what God and Christ, and man and all things are." This fact alone should remind us that by "faith" Luther meant a relation much fuller and richer in content than intellectual assent. He meant the initial act of that new relation to God in Christ which had ended the conflicts begun in the monastery; he meant a living experience which could not but find expression in a new life. So far, his conception of justification ultimately implies actual righteousness as necessarily as the Catholic doctrine of justification by infused grace. But the change of emphasis brings a change of meaning; the believer no longer waits to achieve justification by the process of holiness; he is brought by faith itself into a vital relation to God which needs nothing to complete its reality; like a good tree, it will henceforth bear good fruit. The doctrinal presuppositions of this new relation are chiefly two: on the one hand, man's original sin, revealed in the actual sins of each individual[1] and resulting, through the work of the law, in the consciousness of condemnation; on the other hand, the work of Christ for man, in suffering in man's stead the penalty due to man's sin. Both these presuppositions are derived from the previous doctrine of the Church, though necessarily modified by the new point of view given through the central principle of the Reformation. The three are brought together in such a passage as Luther's comment on Gal. ii. 16 (a classical statement of the doctrine, in opposition to that of Catholicism): "Faith, Christ, acceptation, or imputation must be joined together. Faith taketh hold of Christ and hath Him present, and holdeth Him inclosed as the ring doth the precious stone. And whosoever shall be found having this confidence in Christ apprehended in the heart, him will God account for righteous. This is the mean and this is the merit whereby we attain the remission of sins and righteousness. . . . God doth accept or account us as righteous, only for our faith in Christ" (fol. 62 of the Eng. trans. of 1575).

The doctrine of justification by faith, in its earliest, simplest, and most living form, can be best studied in two documents of 1520 and 1521 respectively, namely, in Luther's tract "On the Liberty of a Christian Man", and Melanchthon's article on "Justification and Faith" in the *Loci Communes*. The keynote of the former is the all-sufficiency of faith to the believer; as the author says in his accompanying letter to the Pope, "It is a little book

---

[1] Adam's sin is conceived generically, as it was by Augustine ; see above, § 4 (*c*). It is imputed to the race "not immediately", but "mediately", *i.e.* through the inherited corruption of the individual. "Immediate" imputation belongs to a later stage of Protestant theology ; cf. Müller, *op. cit.* ii. p. 334 ; Fisher, *History of Christian Doctrine*, p. 302 and Index, *s.v.* "imputation."

as far as paper goes; but if its meaning be understood the sum and substance of a Christian life is comprehended within it." Luther starts from man's double nature, as physical and spiritual, and urges that no outward thing can make the inner man pious; the only means is the Word of God concerning Christ, which at once proclaims our utter insufficiency and sets before us One who invites our trust and offers forgiveness and justification. Thus the believer becomes a true child of God; his soul is transformed by the Word as iron by fire. The divine commandments which worked despair are now fulfilled by faith, and from that faith flow love to and delight in God, with their corresponding "works", though these have nothing to do with justification. Thus is created the liberty of a Christian man, made a king and a priest unto God by his faith, yet by his faith bound to serve his fellows. It is essentially the same conception which we meet in the first edition of Melanchthon's work, praised in the highest terms by Luther. Much of the article in question (pp. 165–182 in Kolde's ed.) is taken up with the rejection of the *assensus* (the *frigida opinio* of Scholasticism) as a true conception of faith. Melanchthon's method is a study of Scripture examples of faith. Faith is defined as "nothing other than trust (*fiducia*) in the divine mercy promised in Christ . . . , first giving peace to the heart, then kindling those of us who are, as it were, ready to give thanks to God for His mercy, that we may keep the law willingly and cheerfully" (*ibid.* p. 168). The new relation to God shews Him not as a Judge, but as a Father (*ibid.* p. 169); and the new certainty is contrasted with the uncertainty of any justification by works (*ibid.* 178). The emphasis on the divine mercy is cardinal, and our inevitable dependence on it is the reason why we must be justified by faith (*ibid.* p. 184). To say that justification must be ascribed to faith is simply to say that it is ascribed to the mercy of God (*ibid.* p. 185). Melanchthon confesses his inability to unfold in words the nature and significance of faith (*ibid.* p. 186); and the acknowledgment is significant, for the relation of man's personality to God's can never be fully stated. The reality of this central doctrine is expressed not by a formula, but by an experience.

(*c*) *The formulation of Protestant anthropology.*—The principle of justification by faith, which forms the common centre of the doctrine of the various Reformers, could not fail to modify the whole body of anthropological belief and to lead to the systematization of Protestant doctrine along lines other than the Catholic. The conception of Christ as the only and direct way of access to God revealed sin as essentially a moral and spiritual barrier; its ecclesiastical aspect vanished. The conception of grace as the personal activity of God in Christ, and as man's one hope, gave new and vital content to the doctrine of predestination and destroyed all idea of man's merit. But within this broad circle of agreement there was, of course, room for the characteristic interests and emphases of the various leaders of the Reformation: from these, in conjunction with national differences and political factors, springs the systematic formulation of what was destined to become, in various types, Protestant orthodoxy. This formulation takes place along a double line in the first century of Reformation thought, namely, that of the "Lutheran" Church, in which Melanchthon is of primary importance, and that of the "Reformed" Church, represented by Zwingli in the first and by Calvin in the second generation. The development along the former line lies between the Augsburg Confession of 1530, shaped by Melanchthon, and the Formula of Concord of 1577, directed against Melanchthon's later development of "synergism", yet the outcome of a Protestant "Scholasticism" to which he had been one of the chief contributors. Within these fifty years lies a series of anthropological controversies, largely due to protest against Melanchthon's movement away from the Reformation determinism. Luther himself was deterministic in thought;[1] but his doctrine of predestination does not occupy the foreground of his interest, which lies in emphasizing the supremacy of grace in the personal experience of the believer. Melanchthon came to see three concurrent causes in conversion, namely, the Word of God, the Holy Spirit, and the assenting will of man.[2] It is against this position that the close of the second article of the "Epitome" of the Formula of Concord declares: "There are left, therefore, before man's conversion two efficient causes only (efficient for conversion), to wit, the Holy Spirit, and the Word of God which is the instrument of the Holy Spirit, by which He effects man's conversion." This explicit statement does not prevent the Formula of Concord, in the article on "Predestination" (xi. § 75), from ascribing to the ungodly as cause of their damnation a will that resists the Spirit of God. The final position reached by the Lutheran formulation of anthropology does not exclude a

---

[1] Seeberg, *DG*, ii. p. 227; Loofs, *DG*, pp. 755 f. Luther's attitude is seen in his controversy with Erasmus, who criticized him from the Semi-Pelagian standpoint; *e.g.* "Deus omnia in omnibus movet."

[2] In the 1559 edition of the *Loci Communes*, as quoted by Loofs, *DG*, p. 845, though the position was reached in the thirties.

Semi-Pelagianizing interpretation; unconditional election is not asserted.[1]

The development of Protestant anthropology along the "Reformed" line begins with Zwingli, and finds its most important expression in the *Institutes* of Calvin. Zwingli, though by no means wholly independent of Luther's influence, shews characteristic differences from him in respect of the doctrine of man. Luther held to the Augustinian doctrine of original sin as against the "Pelagianism" of the Scholastics; but Zwingli, whilst admitting the inheritance of a corrupted nature, developed a view of original sin (by 1526) which regarded it as not including the idea of guilt and as comparable with the state of slavery into which a man might be born without fault or crime of his own.[2] On the other hand, Zwingli emphasizes the sole causality of God, and gives to the doctrine of predestination that dominant place which it came to hold all along this "Reformed" line of anthropology.[3] The historical importance of this doctrine, as central in "Calvinism", justifies more detailed notice.

(*d*) *The doctrine of Predestination, and the Arminian reaction.*—Few doctrines lend themselves more easily to caricature, or more essentially demand from the modern mind a sympathetic approach through history, than the doctrine of Predestination. It is difficult for the ordinary Christian of to-day to be patient with such a statement as that of Jonathan Edwards: "When the saints in heaven shall look upon the damned in hell, it will serve to give them a greater sense of their own happiness . . .:

[1] Cf. Loofs, *DG*, pp. 925–927.
[2] Loofs, *DG*, p. 806 ; Thomasius, *DG*, ii. p. 416.
[3] Thomasius, *DG*, ii. p. 411.

with how much greater admiration and exultation of soul will they sing of the free and sovereign grace of God to them!"[1] Yet what seems a contradiction of Christian character is a logical inference from a doctrine rooted and grounded in the religious experience of the Reformers. We may see, for example, the experiential side of the doctrine, its personal genesis in the case of its most distinguished representative, by reading Calvin's auto-biographical preface to his *Commentary on the Psalms* (1557), in which he compares his life with that of David, and traces the series of divine overrulings which led him ultimately to his life-work, namely, the death of his father, the "sudden conversion" of 1533, the apparently accidental route through Geneva (in 1536) which brought him under Farel's influence. The exposition of pre-destination in the *Institutes* (bk. iii. cc. xxi.–xxiv.) begins from the observed facts of experience, that "the covenant of life is not preached amongst all men equally, nor does it find the same place amongst those to whom it is preached. . . . It is undoubted that this variety also serves the will of God's eternal election." The call of the Gospel is indeed universal, in respect of the external preaching of the Word ; but its efficacy lies in the special calling through which that Word abides in the heart.[2] The metaphysical basis for this distinction in human destinies is found in the conception of God as Will ; God's glory lies in His absolute sovereignty, and all that is—election and reprobation alike—manifests and

[1] Sermon on "The Wicked Useful in Their Destruction Only", pp. 213, 214, in *Practical Sermons* (Edinburgh, 1788).

[2] iii. ch. xxiv. 8. This contrast of the general and special call should be compared with Luther's contrast of the revealed and hidden will of God, which it replaces (cf. *RE*, xv. p. 601).

ministers to that glory. "Calvin was as pure, though
not as conscious and consistent, a Pantheist as Spinoza.
. . . Calvin may be said to have anticipated Spinoza in
his notion of God as *causa immanens*."[1] The logical
determinism of the system may be seen both in its
reprobationism and in its supra-lapsarianism. It is consistently recognized that election involves its opposite
(*ibid.* c. xxiii. 1); the passing by of those who are left to
the deserved fate of men, as all alike sinful and guilty,
really constitutes, with election, a double predestination
by God. It is also consistently asserted that "Adam fell
by His predestination" (*ibid.* 4); thus behind all human
sin without exception lies the will of God. The predestination of Adam's fall does not, however, prevent
Calvin from asserting that man fell "*suo vitio*" (*ibid.* 8),
and that we ought to look rather on this nearer (secondary)
cause, this "*propria malitia*", than seek for the "hidden
and wholly incomprehensible (primary) cause" in the
predestination of God. Calvin does not attempt to make
clear to us how the two are to be reconciled; here, as
elsewhere, in his reply to objections, the final answer
is the reference to the inscrutable will of God, whose
right there is none to dispute.[2] The most obvious
objection to the doctrine of predestination, then as now,
is the fatalistic consequence in spiritual destiny of its
exclusion of human freedom. Calvin's answer not only
emphasizes the earnest morality through which election
becomes visible, and of which election is the ultimate
ground, but retorts in effect that they who derive the

[1] Fairbairn, *The Place of Christ in Modern Theology*, pp. 164, 165.
[2] On this Scotist element in the Calvinistic doctrine of God, see Seeberg,
DG, p. 387.

15

libertinism of the fatalist from the doctrine simply shew
that they *are* reprobate (*ibid.* 12). The assurance of
salvation, representing one of the chief values of the
doctrine, is conceived in a way that ought to guard it
against abuse: "Since it is Christ into whose body the
Father appointed the incorporation of those whom He
willed to be His own from eternity, that He might have
for sons as many as He acknowledged among His
members, we have a sufficiently clear and firm testimony
that we are written in the Book of Life, if we have fellowship with Christ" (c. xxiv. 5). Calvin's emphasis on
predestination inevitably weakens the emphasis on the
"means of grace" which we find in Lutheranism.[1]   Still
more decidedly, it makes the Catholic emphasis on merit
impossible. Thus, in the antithesis of Calvinism and
Catholicism, there stood revealed the original inconsistency between Augustinian predestinationism and
Augustinian sacramentarianism.

The prominence of the doctrine of predestination
within the "Reformed" group of Protestant Churches[2] is
seen in the fact that dogmatic controversy, after the first
Protestant generation, centres round it alone.   The
doctrine is found in the moderate form of the Anglican
Articles (XVII.), and much more stringently in the
typical form of the Westminster Confession, where the
fundamental emphasis on the divine glory is clearly
brought out. The chief point of interest in the later
development of the doctrine lies in the Arminian reaction
from it—a reaction which significantly corresponds within

[1] Cf. *RE*, xv. p. 599.

[2] Loofs, *DG*, p. 933. The ground covered by these Churches may be
seen at a glance, from Lindsay's very useful map, or in Heussi's *Atlas zur
Kirchengeschichte*, Map X.

the Protestant Church to the Jansenist reaction within
the Catholic, though the positions are characteristically
reversed. Arminius, who has lent his name to this
assertion of universal and not irresistible grace, died in
1609. In the following year, the (five) Arminian Articles,[1]
or "Remonstrantia", urged the following points: (1)
God has eternally proposed to save those who through
(the help of) grace believe on Christ and persevere, and
to condemn the incorrigible and unbelieving; (2) Christ
died for all potentially, and for all believers actually;
(3) Man has saving faith, not of himself, but by new
birth through the Spirit; (4) All good in man comes
from this grace, though it is not irresistible; (5) This
grace is sufficient for the believer's victory; whether it
can be lost is a question which requires determination
from Scripture. In reply to these positions, the Synod of
Dort (1619), constituted by representatives of all the chief
"Reformed" Churches, emphasized the doctrine of unconditional and particular election, the particular reference
of the all-sufficient work of Christ, particular calling and
regeneration, and the inalienability of grace. Nothing
would be gained, for our purpose, by discussing the details
of this controversy. The contrast of Calvinism and
Arminianism leaves us indeed with a clearer view of the
problems inevitable for any definition of the respective
contributions of man and God to man's salvation; but
it cannot be said that they are solved by Protestantism,
any more than they were solved in Augustinianism. On
this characteristic antithesis, then, dogmatic anthropology

---

[1] They will be found, together with the Canons of Dort, in Schaff's *The
Creeds of the Evangelical Protestant Churches*, pp. 545-597; the points of
difference are summarized by Fairbairn, *op. cit.* pp. 169, 170 n.

ends. This controversy is the last that calls for our notice—not because no influences as profound as any of the past have shaped more recent Christian thought concerning man's nature, but because the contribution and opportunity of the Church in its corporate and united function here cease. Not only is the Church henceforth beyond even the fiction of representation by a single œcumenical council, with power to define doctrine, but the conception of the Church amongst the progressive nations becomes a different one. The exclusive declaration of authoritative truth passes out of her hands, and the other tribunals of the modern world claim a share in her intellectual and moral jurisdiction. This will be the distinctive feature of the third main phase of the evolution of Christian anthropology; the task of to-day is to formulate its results.[1]

[1] For a brief survey of Christian anthropology and of its modern issues, see the article "Soul (Christian)" in the *Encyclopædia of Religion and Ethics*, xi. pp. 733-7 (1920), by H. Wheeler Robinson.

CHAPTER IV.

THE CONTRIBUTIONS OF POST-REFORMATION SCIENCE AND THOUGHT.

1. THE LARGER HORIZON.

THE Reformation introduces a new period in the development of the Christian doctrine of man, not only because there now ceases to be a single ecclesiastical authority, creative of dogma, in the Western Church, but because the authority of any and every section of the Western Church is in process of profound modification, if not of dissolution. The Renaissance and the Reformation emancipated thought from ecclesiastical authority in principle, however slowly the emancipation was actually effected. A new method of studying the history of anthropological thought is consequently necessary. Even if it were possible to notice the long array of individual Christian thinkers, from the Reformation down to the present day, the results for our subject would have but a secondary value. In each generation we should be compelled to turn back to the movements of thought which shaped the systems of these successive individuals. This is, of course, true even of the period already studied; but the changed conditions justify a new manner of approach. Recognition of the intrinsic claims of truth will always imply the comparative subordination of its pioneer or exponent. Our modern attitude to conceptions of human nature is to be explained through general tendencies of thought rather than through the results reached by any single authoritative thinker, like those of Augustine or Aquinas in the previous period.

Two broad streams of modern thought, flowing through the Post-Reformation period, have their springs in the Renaissance, namely, the scientific and the philosophic. Their influences on Christian anthropology are clearly distinguishable, however much they have in common. During the last century, a third influence, that of sociology, has been making itself deeply felt in modern thought. The conditions and problems of modern industrialism have given it a present importance not less within its own sphere of application than that of the others. Science, philosophy, and sociology, in the broadest senses of these terms, have respectively enlarged our conception of human nature, in regard to the universe of which we are a part, the personality which constitutes our being, and the society on which we depend. We are here concerned simply to indicate in broadest outline these characteristic contributions on their positive side. From these elements the atmosphere of modern Christian thought is constituted; their presence explains its characteristic differences from that of the Bible or the authoritative Church. From the conceptions thus formed of the world, the self, and the social order, we can advance to that which is conditioned by them, and largely constituted through them—the conception of the relationship of man to God, in which lie the deepest problems and profoundest possibilities of our nature.

2. THE SCIENTIFIC CONTRIBUTION.

(*a*) *The birth of modern science.*—The modern man is so penetrated with the broad generalizations of science that it is difficult for him to do justice to those conceptions of human nature we have already traced, just because they lie in what must be called the pre-scientific period of human thought. Science, in the modern sense of the term, begins only with the Renaissance, of which it is one of the most characteristic productions. Its first great field of operation was astronomy; literally from the ends of the universe (as accessible to man's inquiry) have the problems and results of modern physics been brought to a focus on the earth. The characteristic feature of modern science is the appeal to experience by observation and experiment, and the mingled process of induction and deduction whose first and last standard is observed fact; in this appeal it is quantitative (mathematical) measurement which is decisive. The chief result for thought of the progress of science has been the mechanical conception of the universe, as governed by unvarying law and manifested in unbroken causal connections. To this conception, whose fruitfulness has so abundantly justified its truth within its own realm, the last century has added another, not less fruitful—that of the evolution of the solar system in general, and of man in particular. It may help us to realize how wide is the gulf that divides us from the thinkers of the early or mediaeval Church, if we glance at the characteristic contributions made by those foremost observers to whom these conceptions are chiefly due.

(*b*) *The founders of modern science.*—In the history of the exact observation of Nature four men claim a unique place by the influential and epoch-making character of their results; these are Copernicus, Galilei, Newton, and Darwin.[1]   Copernicus (1473–1543), as every one knows, rejected the dominant theory which made the earth the centre of many revolving spheres, and substituted for it the heliocentric theory.   He still conceived the universe to be bounded by the heaven of the fixed stars ; he had no explanation to offer of the motion of the planets, including the earth, round the sun—a motion he understood to be circular.   But he swept away by his simpler idea the burdensome complexity of the Ptolemaic astronomy, with its spheres and epicycles ; and he shewed the adequacy of his simpler idea to explain the observed phenomena.   Galileo Galilei (1564–1642) has been called the father of nature study, and of the scientific view of the world.   The laws of motion associated with his name are, in a sense, the charter of mechanical inquiry ; his confirmation of Copernicanism by the telescopic discovery of the satellites of Jupiter illustrates the nature of the final appeal in the world of science.   Like his contemporary Kepler (who had substituted the ellipse for the false circles of the planetary orbits), he emphasized the mathematical conception of Nature, the quantitative as the basis of qualitative distinctions.   The crown to this conception was given by Newton (1642–1727), whose theory of gravitation linked up the universe and supplied what was previously wanting in the mechanical view of it. " The great philosophic importance of Newton's discovery of gravitation consists, before all else, in the verification

---

[1] For fuller details, see Höffding's *History of Modern Philosophy*, which is characterized by the breadth of its survey. See also Windelband, *Die Geschichte der neueren Philosophie*.

of the fact that the physical laws which hold good on the surface of the earth are valid throughout the universe, as far as we can know anything of it."[1] The *Principia* appeared in 1687, and it is not until 1859, the year of the publication of Darwin's *The Origin of Species*, that we shall find a comparable landmark of progress, in spite of advance along so many lines. It was not, of course, that Darwin invented the very ancient idea of development, but that he brought home to the world the significance of that idea in application to living organisms, and with special reference to their relationship. His characteristic principle of " Natural Selection " is defined by him as follows : " If variations useful to any organic being ever do occur, assuredly individuals thus characterized will have the best chance of being preserved in the struggle for life; and from the strong principle of inheritance, these will tend to produce offspring similarly characterized."[2] The significance of Darwin's work is independent of the validity or sufficiency of this principle to account for evolution ; the important fact is the inclusion of the human organism, as an evolved product, in the evolved and evolving universe already portrayed by Laplace.

(*c*) *Resultant conceptions.*—The influence on the conception of human life exercised by these centuries of scientific progress cannot but be profound. The universe in which man lives has withdrawn its roof and walls to an unimaginable distance at the magic touch of astronomy ; a not less bewildering perspective of man's origin is opened up by the combined labours of geology and biology ; the old supernaturalism has lost the right to speak until it has fully reckoned with the laws of the

[1] Höffding, *op. cit.* i. p. 408.　　[2] *The Origin of Species* (ed. 1902), p. 160.

physical universe. We are concerned here not so much with the false claims made on the basis of the new knowledge, to the prejudice of Christian doctrine, as with the positive contribution to the interpretation of that doctrine which all germane knowledge must necessarily bring. Three principal conceptions, at least, must be noticed, namely, those of (1) the larger universe; (2) the process of evolution; and (3) natural law—the last especially in relation to the principle of the conservation of energy.

(1) The first of these is of indirect rather than direct concern; after all, its appeal is more to our imagination than our reason. It is undoubtedly true that the representatives of the Church, both Catholic and Protestant, felt that Copernicus had introduced a pernicious error in robbing the earth, and therefore man, of the central place. But neither this change, nor the suggested possibility of other inhabitants on other planets, really affects the issues of man's life, or the spiritual values in which it essentially consists. Unreflective imagination may be oppressed by the magnitude of the universe, beside which man and all his works shrivel into practical invisibility; anthropomorphic ideas of religion, as yet unconscious of their essential limitation, may find difficulty in the thought that heaven is farther off than the child conceives it to be ; but both imagination and religion are really enriched by emancipation from the provincialism of the horizon of earth.[1] We are not bound to suppose that the stellar universe exists only for discovery by the telescopes of the inhabitants of one obscure planet; inhabited or uninhabited, it can fulfil the divine purposes, without derogation from human dignity. It has been argued that the

[1] Cf. the eloquent passage in Martineau's *Seat of Authority*[2], p. 17.

earth alone presents habitable conditions;[1] whether this be admitted or not seems of small account. The real question for man is—does a larger universe affect the reality or worth of his spiritual life? and the answer must be emphatically no. On the other hand, the greater glory of God which the heavens of this larger universe declare must ultimately confer new dignity on man, of whom He is mindful, if the testimony of spiritual life be true.

(2) The process of evolution as conceived by science raises much deeper problems. The central emphasis here falls on the *immanence*, within the organism or its environment, of energies adequate to explain its development. This may be seen from two typical definitions of evolution. "The doctrine of evolution may be defined as the teaching which holds that creation has been and is accomplished by the agency of the energies which are intrinsic in the evolving matter, and without the interference of agencies which are external to it. . . . The science of evolution is the science of creation" (Cope, *Primary Factors of Organic Evolution*, p. 1). "Evolution is (1) continuous *progressive change*, (2) *according to certain laws*, (3) and by means of *resident forces*" (Le Conte, *Evolution*, p. 8). If we were here concerned with the bearing of evolution on the idea of God and of the universe, several elements in such definitions would call for examination—*e.g.* the fact that they posit the matter to be evolved and the laws of operation of the various agencies.[2] But our positive interest is not in the assumed adequacy of "Nature" to account for man,

---

[1] *e.g.* by A. R. Wallace in *Man's Place in the Universe*.

[2] Reference may be made to Underhill's essay, in *Personal Idealism*, on " The Limits of Evolution."

but in the prejudice that has often arisen, explicitly or implicitly, from the close connection of man with the lowest forms of life, and even with the inorganic realm. It is not sufficient, in combating this prejudice, to emphasize the fact that the evolution of man is not yet shewn to be continuous. Science, it is true, has no evidence to offer of the transition from the inorganic to the organic, even if we accept the transition from life to consciousness as conceivable. But what is here to be said would be unaffected by proved continuity along the whole line of man's development from inorganic Nature. The fundamental issue is that values are not to be prejudiced by origins, that the conscious life of man, with all its wealth of intellectual, moral, and spiritual activity, offers most important data to be considered in themselves, however much science has compelled us to modify our ideas of their development. Not only so, but these data themselves challenge a purely mechanical or biological view of the process of evolution. The significance of a series lies not less, but more, in its highest term than in its lowest. If it be true that immanent energies alone have produced these highest values we know, they must be adequate to the product ; if, as we may rationally claim, mechanics and biology cannot explain the mind which has created these very sciences, we can urge that rational or teleological factors have been present from the earliest forms of matter. Such factors are those posited, *e.g.*, by Ward, and termed self - conservation and subjective selection,[1] with the inference that " wherever a material system is organized

---

[1] *Naturalism and Agnosticism*, i. p. 290. This book is the ablest and most convincing modern criticism of the mechanical view of Nature.

for self-maintenance, growth, and reproduction, as an individual in touch with an environment, that system has a psychical as well as a material aspect."[1] The truth is that each of the sciences must necessarily abstract from life in its concrete reality ; physics, chemistry, biology, and psychology all deal with certain aspects of life only, and no single one of them can give an adequate explanation of its experienced wealth as a whole. The conclusion is that evolution itself depends on factors implying the very qualities and realities it has been supposed to discredit. We always find life associated with an organism, but the organism cannot explain the life in its entirety, however much it may condition its activity and manifestation. If this important limitation of the conception of evolution be grasped, we are free to accept the conception as one of the greatest value for the Christian doctrine of man. Some of its consequences will be indicated in the next subsection ; it is sufficient in this place to point out that the essential problem of evolution for our subject is already contained in the history of the individual. We have no need to look down the long road travelled by biological, geological, chemical, and astronomical speculation to face it ; the problem lies in the microscopic cell, the one hundred and twenty-fifth of an inch in diameter, in whose fertilization the life of the organism began. The channels of the child's inheritance are said to be the twenty-four rod-shaped bodies known as chromosomes, to which an equal number is contributed by the spermatozoon and the ovum ; [2] here, then,

---

[1] *Ibid.* p. 285. For the above argument it does not matter whether the psychical (teleological) factor be internal or external to the organism.

[2] J. A. Thomson, *Heredity*, pp. 46, 58.

are drawn the limits of possibility, in interaction with the future environment, for all the achievements of the individual life. Yet the emergent personality cannot be reduced to its chromosomes without leaving a remainder, and that remainder is vital in the deepest sense. It is not otherwise when the organism has passed through its maturity to decay and dissolution; death is as natural an event as birth, though possibly of much less significance for personality; but the chemical analysis of a corrupting corpse surely belongs to a different level of reality from that of the personal values which gave the living body all its meaning. How we are to conceive those personal values belongs to another range of inquiry; what ought to be clear to one who admits them at all is their ultimate transcendence of the physical side of birth and death.

(3) Finally, modern science has given us the conception of a reign of law as the inner aspect of the larger universe, and as the controlling principle of its evolution. The great scientific service of this conception, so abundantly verified in so many distinct branches of natural science, need not be emphasized; but it is not less influential for the idea of man's life and of God's government of the world. Primitive animism was at the mercy of a mob of spiritual tyrants, who had to be individually propitiated; pre-scientific supernaturalism, so far as it subordinated the events of Nature to the control of God, glorified divine wilfulness and human self-importance; natural science has banished the superstitions that attach to a piecemeal and erratic world, and has inspired the confidence that springs from the idea of an orderly universe. This progress in our conception of Nature from incomprehensible happenings to methodic

and regular administration is as great in its own realm as that from "customary" morality to the Kantian idea of absolute moral law. But we should pay too great a price for this great gain if we were compelled to extend the idea of an orderly universe into that of a rigid and impenetrable mechanical system. This is a quite illegitimate inference from the idea of "law." We have always to recognize that the term "law" is itself in this connection a metaphor, so soon as we have considered it apart from a lawgiver. A law of Nature states what is, not what must be; it is not some independent entity, prescribing modes of behaviour to physical facts, but the interpretation of a particular group of experienced data. In other words, it expresses not originative causality, but connection of content, and points beyond itself for its explanation. We may admit the objective validity of the law as a statement of the order displayed in Nature—an order which is the revelation of that greater Mind with which, through Nature, our minds have to do. But the order is rational, not mechanical; it is included within, not hostile to, the moral purpose of the Mind to which it is due. We have not, therefore, to look through Nature to God as across prison bars; we are rather to think of natural law as an essential part of the education of God's children, which the grace of His Fatherhood has chosen for us.

The prejudice that has often arisen from the illegitimate use of the metaphor "law" is frequently focused into an appeal to the particular "law of the conservation of energy" (cf., for example, Haeckel). If energy, though variable in form, is invariable in quantity, the mechanical conception of the universe seems to be established, and no scope remains for the activity of Mind, finite or infinite.

Would not efficient causality imply alteration of the sum of energy? The law of the conservation of energy is unquestionably of great importance. With that other law which it is frequently assumed to include—the conservation of mass—it links together the various transformations of energy, just as Newton's law of gravitation linked together the solar system. But if we take any careful statement of the law, such as Clerk-Maxwell's,[1] we shall see that it does not warrant any inference to the prejudice of mind. "The total energy of any material system is a quantity which can neither be increased nor diminished by any action between the parts of the system, though it may be transformed into any of the forms of which energy is susceptible." It relates to the material; there is no sufficient ground for extending it to the mental. It belongs to the inorganic realm; if we trace its action through the material chain of processes that an organism exhibits, we are not entitled, without a proof by experiment that is hardly conceivable, to extend it to life, still less to mind. Further, the law relates to a closed system, an isolated group of phenomena which we isolate for our quantitative measurement; we have no warrant for applying it to the universe, as though this could be assumed to be a finite system, capable of being weighed in a balance. As applied to the universe, moreover, the law assumes that the quantity of matter, as well as of energy, remains constant. But the newer views of matter held by physicists make such an assumption somewhat perilous. The electrical theory of matter, for example, resolves it into "knots or twists or vortices, or some sort of either static or kinetic modification, of the

---

[1] *Matter and Motion*, p. 60 (Art. lxxiv.).

ether of space . . . the destruction and the creation of matter are well within the range of scientific conception, and may be within the realm of experimental possibility." [1] There is, indeed, a growing recognition of the limits and ultimate problems of physics, perhaps destined to give the *coup de grâce* to scientific determinism. Modern speculations as to the nature of matter and energy pass far beyond the region of possible experimental inquiry ; [2] their units are purely theoretical, and the supposed " fixity " of ultimate scientific conceptions is the survival of a discredited materialism. The net result of such criticisms is to leave us with the principle of the conservation of energy in all its validity within the realm of experimental science, but to rid us of those illegitimate extensions of its application to other fields where it does not apply. We are then free to appeal to the fact of personal activity, as something to be studied and evaluated in its own right, without prejudice from this particular physical "law." How the concomitance is to be explained, how the two realms are to be correlated, lies beyond the reach of science proper. For our present purpose, it is sufficient to leave the physical and the psychical side by side, each with its own characteristics. [3] Whatever be the statement of their ultimate correlation, the fact remains that the physical cannot swallow up the psychical

[1] Lodge, *Life and Matter* (ed. 4), pp. 32, 33.

[2] Cf. the acute article by More, in the *Hibbert Journal* for July 1910, on " The Metaphysical Tendencies of Modern Physics."

[3] Lodge (*op. cit.* p. 158) suggests that we should regard life as directive of energy rather than a form of it, so that material energy is controlled, without alteration of its quantity. But, besides the doubtful separation of " direction " from " energy ", this proposal leaves us where Descartes' pineal gland left us, with the problem of relating the psychical and the physical. Some deeper unity than that of directive control is required. The hypothesis seems a needless concession to the principle of the conservation of energy, in a realm where it cannot be shewn to apply.

16

or dismiss it as a mere by-product. Science as such can-not prejudice the testimony of experience to spontaneous activity and free personality, however much it may affect our statement of the manner of operation of that freedom.

(*d*) *Evolution in relation to Christian anthropology.* —Amongst the various contributions of modern science to our subject, a central place belongs to that theory of man's racial origin which holds him to be the product of organic evolution. When this theory is disentangled from all materialistic and agnostic prejudices, *i.e.* when it is a purely scientific theory, it relates simply to the method of man's creation, the precise way in which he came to be what he is. The ultimate problems of his origin and nature will still remain, but it cannot be denied that our acceptance of the theory will affect in important ways their statement and precise form. (1) Evolution gives us an enlarged conception of racial providence, and pro-vides a richer perspective of man's history than any theory of special creation could do. When we consider the cosmic purpose which, at such æonian cost, has culminated in man, may not the religious mind give a new turn to the words that pierced Zinzendorf's heart, and hear God say, " This have I done for thee ; what dost thou for Me ? " The pious Israelite (Deut. xxvi. 5) was bidden to look back, from his basket of fruit brought to the altar, to Jacob, that wandering Aramæan who was his father, and to thank God who had brought him to present prosperity from such a humble beginning. Our backward look to the dim beginnings of life provides a longer view, but the principle still holds good that thanksgiving ought to be deepened by the vision of lowly origins. (2) In spite of much asseveration to the contrary, we may gain a nobler conception of man and his destiny when we view him as the evolutionary crown of Nature. In him the process has so far issued; whatever purpose belongs to the process belongs to him in whom and through whom, so far as we can see, its future realization lies. Nor is there any finality in the evolution we know that limits our hopes as to what we do not yet know. In the past, whenever the resources of one level have been exhausted, those of a yet higher level seem to have been appropriated to the "one increasing purpose." Why may we not see in the past the promise, if not the whole potency, of a higher spiritual destiny for man? The inference is only strengthened by the fact that the Christian will construe that destiny through the Person of Christ, not through the apotheosis of lower levels in the form of a "superman." (3) The growth of the sense of social solidarity (which receives fuller notice in the following section) is certainly in part indebted to this new and impressive vision of our common origin. We have deeper roots than were planted in the Garden of Eden; the travail of Nature has come to mean more to many men than that of Eve could ever have done. The personification of Nature may indeed lead us astray into anthropomorphic interpretations of her processes; but if we are to speak of Nature's egoism, we must speak not less of her altruism. Nature has risen by bearing her cross, and making one bear it for others, even though subjection to it was as unwilling as was his of Cyrene. (4) Both the birth and the death of man are illuminated by the evolutionary theory of the individual organism, as subject to natural law. That organism is seen to have a natural history from birth to death, whatever mysteries of its spiritual history rise above the reach of natural science. In the constitution of the cell, which forms the biological unit, the possibilities of life are already outlined, though its actualities are contingent. Ancient speculations as to the origin of the soul (Chap. III. § 2 (*b*)) are replaced by what we know of the interplay of heredity and environment. We have no evidence for the supposition that spiritual personality is thrust ready-made into the material organism at any one point in its development. On any spiritual interpretation of Nature that is not hopelessly dualistic, we may believe in the gradual creation of spiritual personality in and through the natural processes —a creation conditioned and mediated by racial past and social present, continued through life and consummated beyond death. As for that last " cloak'd shadow ", whatever meaning it may gather for spiritual beings, the incident of death in the history of the individual organism is not a penalty for sin, but a purely natural event that springs from the very constitution and nature of the organism itself. (5) Finally, the statement of the Christian doctrine of sin will be profoundly affected. The Adamic theory of racial sin is simply set aside—a removal the less to be regretted because it was not able to solve the problems of sin. Over against the theories of corporate personality or imputation, we have a new view of social solidarity, and of individual and social heredity, though it must not hastily be assumed that the new theory will buttress up the old doctrine when the history of Adam has become allegory.[1] We shall have

---

[1] A recent attempt to superadd the doctrine of the XXXIX. Articles on an acceptance of evolution (*Evolution and the Fall*, by Prof. F. J. Hall) will serve to illustrate the necessary failure of such compromises.

to ask in the proper place how far the theory of evolution is sufficient to explain the consciousness of sin; we must not expect too much from it, unless we believe it is sufficient to explain personality. In any case, there will remain the problem of the place and meaning of moral evil in a progressive order under the guidance of God.

3. THE PHILOSOPHIC CONTRIBUTION.

(a) *Influence of the old Scholasticism and the new Science.*—The period of modern philosophy (which began with Descartes, gained its most outstanding figure in Kant, and has not yet found its natural historical limit) is often characterized as the emancipation of thought from its Scholastic subordination to the authority of the Church. True as this is, the break with the subordinative attitude of Scholasticism did not involve an equal break with the ideal of an absolute system. The classic systems of philosophy of the seventeenth century are in one sense the related successors to the Scholasticism they repudiate; like it, they conceive it possible to grasp the whole of things in an ordered unity of thought, in which man's nature and place shall be defined as rigorously as under the influence of Augustine and Aristotle. What distinguishes them from their predecessors is rather the source and character of their data than their constructive ideal. Their content is supplied from the rich material made accessible by the Renaissance in its manifold activities, and in particular from the new science. Indeed, it is not too much to say that the new science itself replaced the authority recognized by the old Scholasticism;[1]

---

[1] We must not, of course, forget the great progress involved in the replacement of extrinsic by intrinsic authority.

the mechanical interpretation of the universe created an absolutism not less rigorous than that of the dethroned Church. The systems of Descartes and Spinoza in the seventeenth century are the reflection in philosophy of the mathematical principles indicated in the previous section; Leibniz accepts them, though he penetrates through them; these three great systems have lost the fluidity of thought of that typical Renaissance thinker, Bruno, in gaining the clearer enunciation of formal statement. We shall not find a corresponding capacity for the creation of systems until we come to Kant and the post-Kantian Idealism of Fichte, Schelling, and Hegel; in our own day, we have yet to await the full working out of the impetus given to thought by the science of the nineteenth century, though Spencer again illustrates both the impetus and influence of its new data.[1] An estimate of the results (for our subject) of so complex a development must of necessity be largely subjective and impressionist; its aim is simply to shew the philosophic recognition of human personality and its values, against Naturalism below and Absolute Idealism above.[2]

(*b*) *The metaphysical reality of spirit.*—Perhaps the most striking general impression to be gained from a review of philosophy in the modern period is the failure of materialism to secure any permanent place in philosophic (as distinct from popular) thought. Not only has materialism at the present time no philosopher to call its own, but the past three centuries shew its inadequacy to satisfy any thinker of first-rate importance other than

---

[1] Cf. also the recent work of Bergson, *L'Évolution Créatrice* (1908).

[2] Cf. the preface to *Personal Idealism*, p. vi. : "Naturalism and Absolutism, antagonistic as they seem to be, combine in assuring us that personality is an illusion."

Hobbes.[1] Spiritualistic systems display a bewildering variety of method and result; but they are one in this, if in nothing else, that they posit the reality of spirit. Whatever man is, in origin, nature, and destiny, the philosophic tradition established by three centuries of emancipated thought points to an explanation from within rather than from without. This recognition of the metaphysical reality of spirit meets us at the outset, in the great systems of the seventeenth century. Descartes gives the fullest scope to a mechanical explanation of the world; but over against matter he places spirit, and it is spirit which is immediate in his method. Spinoza sees in thought and extension parallel forms of ultimate Reality; but that Reality is spiritualistically, not materialistically, conceived. Leibniz, by his resolution of Reality into the monads, found nothing but spirit to be real, and introduces the striking succession of idealistic thinkers. The most important challenge to this recognition came from English empiricism. But the history of the Associationist analysis of mind demonstrates its own inadequacy. The psychology of Locke and Berkeley culminated in Hume's reduction of all ideas to impressions, and the consequent abandonment of the idea of a spiritual substance (as well as of a material); by introspection, it is said, the self assumed to exist is never found, but only particular states of consciousness. Such of our beliefs as do not rest directly on sensational experience are due to the tendency of our ideas to be associated together in various ways. This doctrine of Association, as a full and complete explanation of

[1] Hume (see p. 249) belongs strictly to Agnosticism, though, historically, his influence has operated through the naturalistic school.

consciousness, found its classical expression in James Mill's *Analysis of the Phenomena of the Human Mind* (1829), which formed the original basis of his son's thought. But the synthesizing factors themselves could not have come from experience, as a chemistry of sensations. From John Stuart Mill himself comes the most remarkable evidence of the inability of psychology to explain states of a self without positing a self to experience them. In his *Examination of Sir William Hamilton's Philosophy*, published in 1865, he writes: "If, therefore, we speak of the Mind as a series of feelings, we are obliged to complete the statement by calling it a series of feelings which is aware of itself as past and future; and we are reduced to the alternative of believing that the Mind, or Ego, is something different from any series of feelings or possibilities of them, or of accepting the paradox that something which *ex hypothesi* is but a series of feelings can be aware of itself as a series " (p. 248, ed. 6). The admission is the more striking since the writer still believed matter to be explained adequately as the "permanent possibility of sensation." Hume's dissolution of mind into its products, however, was overthrown from without as well as from within the school. The significance of Kant and his Idealistic successors lies (for our present purpose) in their recognition of the activity of mind, and the central or even exclusive place given to it. The emphasis of Kant, as the result of his critical analysis of mind, fell on its constructive activity in the shaping of experience. The raw material of sensation is already, as such, received under the purely subjective forms of space and time. To these forms of perception the mind further contributes, as " Understanding ", the various categories, such as causality,

through which experience is interpreted—or rather constituted. Still further, the mind as "Reason" posits the
"Ideas" of God, freedom, and immortality as its highest
concepts, though these are not "constitutive", but merely
"regulative." Kant did not allow the synthetic activity
of mind, which weaves the texture of experience, to have
any possible application to the unknown realm of ultimate
Reality. Contact with this realm was to be found only
through the categorical imperative of the Practical as
opposed to the Pure Reason. But Kant's work was so
fundamental that it opened a new chapter in philosophy
and initiated a second period of system-building on the
grand scale. With Fichte the emphasis fell on the activity
of the finite ego in moral experience; with Schelling on
the duality of subject and object within the Absolute;
with Hegel on the ultimate identity of thought and being,
so that his system is the very apotheosis of mind. We
shall notice (p. 250 f.) what seems, to a growing number of
present-day thinkers, the deficient recognition of individuality and personal freedom characterizing Absolute
Idealism; this must not hide from us the significance
of its testimony to spirit as the ultimate key to Reality,
and to the supreme worth of man's inner life. The
opposing movement of Naturalism sprang, as we have
seen, from the positive scientific progress of the nineteenth
century; its frequent accompaniment of Agnosticism
was related, in this country, through Huxley to Hume.
Naturalism would give but a subordinate, and almost
accidental, place to mind, as the emergent by-product of
a particular phase of the development of matter. But
the tide of Naturalism which passed over English thought
within the last generation has ebbed, or is ebbing; the

representative criticisms of T. H. Green and James Ward may be taken as typical of the lines on which a spiritualistic philosophy has again been victorious. Green in his *Prolegomena to Ethics* (1883), approaching the issue from the standpoint of the intellect, successfully argued that science presupposes more than the facts with which it can deal ; Ward, more recently, in his *Naturalism and Agnosticism* (1899), from the standpoint of the will, has not less successfully upheld the teleological as opposed to the mechanical view of the universe. Their difference within the common ground of a spiritualistic philosophy will serve to raise the further question of the significance of the individual. Is the emphasis to fall on the value of the individual for himself, or is he to be regarded as simply part of some larger whole?

(*c*) *The individuality of spiritual life.*—The conception of man fundamental to the Absolute Idealism of the Neo-Hegelians (Green and the brothers Caird) may be fairly suggested by the following quotations from the *Prolegomena to Ethics*: " In the growth of our experience, in the process of our learning to know the world, an animal organism, which has its history in time, gradually becomes the vehicle of an eternally complete consciousness " (p. 72);—" a certain reproduction of itself on the part of the eternal self-conscious subject of the world— a reproduction of itself to which it makes the processes of animal life organic " (p. 102). On the other hand, Ward asks (*Naturalism and Agnosticism*, vol. ii. p. 280): " May we not regard each individual subject, everything that is anything for itself and in itself, as a living law, or, if you will, as an active essence or character, inter- acting in its own peculiar manner with other subjects equally determinate?" to which the comment is added, "This lets contingency into the very heart of things." The issue between these two positions is perfectly definite, though the problem raised may prove one of those ultimates we cannot solve. The issue is as to the emphasis we decide to place on individuality in human nature; the problem is its metaphysical explanation. In the modern period of philosophy, two thinkers of foremost position have given this emphasis a central or prominent place in their systems—Leibniz and Lotze. When we consider how salient a fact of common experience the individuality and uniqueness of personality is, the paucity of its philosophic representatives may surprise us, until we remember the overpressure of the ideal of unification which frequently mars both philosophic and scientific explanation. Leibniz (*Monadologie*, 1714) is the classical representative of the position. His system of Reality is pluralistic, though the "monads" or simple beings which constitute it are ultimately derived from God. Their individuality is their salient quality—"for there are never two beings in nature perfectly alike" (*Mon.* 9)—and this individuality lies in their varying degrees of perception, which Leibniz compares to the different views of the same city, to be gained from different quarters (*ibid.* 57). The result is that "each is a living and perpetual mirror of the universe" (*ibid.* 56). Leibniz employs the sub-conscious elements of psychical experience as a basis of inference to the nature of monads other than the soul, and thus his system becomes wholly idealistic. Each monad is wholly self-contained, and there is no interaction; the harmony of the world of experience is due to the divine pre-adjustment. "The

Monads have no windows through which anything can enter or go forth" (*ibid. 7*). It is at this point that the individual reals of Lotze (1817–1881) differ from those of Leibniz;[1] in the later system, there is reciprocal interaction, and, indeed, it is from this interaction that Lotze develops his proof of the necessary existence of God. The apparently self-less material world really shares in the self-existence belonging to the individual minds God has created. The positive freedom of these individual spirits is unmistakably asserted; its mystery belongs to its very nature.[2] Religious faith, as Lotze says,[3] rejects the mechanical theory of the world as a complete statement: "It assumes that the freedom of finite beings introduces into the cosmic course new beginnings of action which, having once come into being, proceed according to the universal laws of that course, but have not in the past any compelling cause of their appearance." Lotze's closing review of his *Microcosmus* puts the strongest emphasis on the individuality of spiritual life: "It seemed to us that everywhere the universal was inferior as compared with the particular, the class as compared with the individual, any state of things insignificant as compared with the good arising from its enjoyment. For the universal, the class, and the state of things belong to the mechanism into which the Supreme articulates itself; the true reality that is and ought to be, is not matter and is still less Idea, but is the living personal Spirit of God and the world of

---

[1] Cf. Pfleiderer, *Philosophy of Religion* (E.T.), vol. ii. p. 299.

[2] Cf. Upton, *Hibbert Lectures*, p. 290, where also a vigorous criticism of Absolute Idealism will be found, in relation to this cardinal point of human individuality.

[3] *Microcosmus* (E.T.), vol. ii. p. 708.

personal spirits which He has created" (vol. ii. p. 728). At the present day, the fuller recognition of the individual is being urged from within and without the Idealistic school of thinkers;[1] there seems to be a growing consciousness that with the acknowledgment of God's immanence in man's spiritual life there must be fuller scope than philosophy has in general allowed for activity, indeterminate freedom, and the values of individual personality. It is in the demand for this that the chief present value of the movement known as Pragmatism may be found. It asks us to construe the world as "a social scheme of co-operative work genuinely to be done . . each several agent [doing] its own level best."[2]

(*d*) *The values of personality.*—The modern emphasis on the "values" of personality belongs to the second half of the modern period—that more subjective phase of thought which the Critical Philosophy of Kant inaugurated. His fundamental distinction between the Pure and the Practical Reason, *i.e.* between intellect and conscience, issued in the result that our moral experience becomes the basis of certain postulates—freedom, immortality, and God—which the intellect in its pure rationality cannot establish, because they lie outside the realm of phenomenal experience. In this way arose the important distinction between judgments of truth and judgments of value, with which we are only so far concerned as to notice that philosophy began to recognize a new group of data —in this case the data of moral experience. Amongst modern thinkers, Lotze has given the most striking place

---

[1] *e.g.* by Galloway, *The Principles of Religious Development*, and by Bergson, *L'Évolution Créatrice*.

[2] James, *Pragmatism*, p. 290.

to the moral values and their metaphysical significance. He draws a line beyond which theoretical deduction as to God is unable to proceed, and says: " Henceforth, we can only determine *a priori* and without going to experience what concrete qualities belong to the supreme principle, by consulting the needs and claims of the affections and of the heart."[1]   The argument, of course, rests on the assumption that the world would be irrational if the highest range of value our human life possesses were not represented effectually in God as well as in man:[2] " If this eternal sacredness and supreme worth of Love were not at the foundation of the world, and if in such a case there could be a world of which we could think and speak, this world, it seems to me, would, whatever it were, be left without truth and order."[3]   Here, again, we are concerned less with the metaphysical argument than with the recognition, as its starting-point, of the transcendent meaning of human life on its moral side.   To this recognition of personal values by Kant and Lotze must be added the central place given to religious experience by Schleiermacher, who in this respect initiated that epoch of thought to which we ourselves belong.   He found the characteristic element of that experience in feeling, or rather in the dawn of conscious surrender to God, itself prior to all analysis of the experience into feeling and intuition.   Religion is thus " the immediate consciousness of the Deity, as we find Him both in ourselves and in the world " (*Reden*, ii. *ad fin.*).   Schleiermacher thus offered a new basis of

---

[1] *Outlines of a Philosophy of Religion* (E.T. by Conybeare), p. 122.

[2] Cf. Ormond, *Foundations of Knowledge*, p. 354.

[3] Lotze, *Microcosmus* (E.T.), ii. p. 724.

construction for theological thought—a basis important not only for Ritschlian thinkers, but also, in varying degrees, for those of practically every modern school. His emphasis on feeling was partly due to reaction from the Kantian emphasis on morality, and the subjectivity of his position is an obvious weakness; but these and other criticisms ought not to hide the importance of his recognition of the deep things of personal life. From such sources, then, as Kant, Lotze, and Schleiermacher, has flowed the stream of modern thought which seems to bear the greatest promise of life to the fields which philosophers cultivate to-day. As illustration of the truth of this statement, it will be sufficient to quote a single sentence from one of the foremost living historians of philosophy. Windelband, in concluding a recent course of lectures, says: "We seek less, and expect from philosophy less—what she was obliged to offer earlier—a theoretical plan of the world, to be gathered from the results of the separate sciences, or fashioned from them on its own lines, harmoniously self-contained; what we to-day expect from philosophy is the consciousness of the abiding values which, beyond the changing interests of the day, are grounded in a higher spiritual reality." [1] Such a transference of emphasis as this is of more importance for the Christian doctrine of man than any particular result of any particular philosopher; it ought to herald the dawn of a revival of spiritual interest and of religious life throughout the world. The range of values to which metaphysics must give heed is naturally wider than the circle of those with which the Christian doctrine of man is directly concerned; it includes, of course,

---

[1] *Die Philosophie im deutschen Geistesleben des xix. Jahrhunderts*, p. 119.

the æsthetic and intellectual interests of human life. But it is characteristic of the Christian consciousness, from Jesus onwards, to emphasize the moral and spiritual as supreme in quality and jurisdiction, however true it may ultimately prove to be that the Good, the True, and the Beautiful form a synthesis of perfect order and harmony.[1]

(*e*) *The philosophic recognition of Christian data.*—The general results of modern philosophy go to form the atmosphere in which Christian thought has its being, not the authority by which it is to be rejected or accepted. The philosophy 'of every age is more subtly interwoven with its theology than is often recognized, for every theology is an implicit philosophy, not forgetting that theology which is most alien to all "metaphysics." It is, then, of great significance for the Christian doctrine of man that personality has claimed a central place in philosophic thought. The emphasis corresponds with that of the Gospel itself, and it is one to which the Gospel has materially contributed. The growing emphasis can be traced, as we have seen, from the recognition of the primacy of mind in the seventeenth century through that of the mind's constructive activity in Kant; its most striking phase at present is the remarkable interest taken in the psychological side of religion. With all this, and as a development of it, there is the increasing recognition of the moral and spiritual values of personality and of the intrinsic worth of man. This is seen both in the victory of the teleological over the mechanical view of the universe and in the conception of the immanence of God in man; there is also the claim that between the two relationships, that to Nature and that to God, room must be

[1] See p. 282 f., Chap. V. §2 (*c*).

found for the individuality of man and his own consciousness of a unique experience. At the present time there is perhaps no single philosophic theory with the right to be called specifically " Christian", in contradistinction from the rest. Certainly, there is none that seems able to win general acceptance by its inclusion of the many-sided life of man in its conception of ultimate Reality without some sacrifice of either philosophic unity or the reality of individual experience. We gain nothing by trying to exploit this fact as the " failure " of philosophy, supposed to clear the ground for the acceptance of Christian thought. But if it be true that no system has yet adequately related the finite to the Infinite, and that all monisms are compelled to resort to different " levels " of thought for man and for God, there is nothing that is unphilosophic in the appeal of Christian faith to history, as interpreted by the " levels " of thought implied in Father and son, King and subject, Saviour and sinner.

4. THE SOCIOLOGICAL CONTRIBUTION.

(*a*) *The transition from an individual to a social emphasis.*—In our rapid survey of the factors influencing modern thought about human nature since the Reformation, we have noticed the contributions made by science on the one hand and by philosophy on the other, resulting respectively in a new conception of man's physical nature and relation to the phenomenal world, and in a new emphasis on human personality and its significance for ultimate thought. We have now to glance at those influences which have led to a new interpretation of man's social relationships.

17

Broadly regarded, the centuries lying between the Reformation and the present day shew a double swing of the pendulum. The Reformation, as we have seen, was essentially individualistic, both in its positive conception of faith and its negative criticism of the great sacramental society of Catholicism. The new individualistic emphasis, on its religious side, was itself a particular application of the intellectual forces of the Renaissance. But in other realms, notably the economic, the principle of individualism worked itself out more slowly. "Western Europe was still organized on a system of which the basis was, virtually, a surviving feudalism . . . it was a world still mainly mediaeval in political, in economic, and in social relations."[1] The disintegration of this system was due to two primary factors, namely, the growth of modern Industrialism and the rise of social democracy. For the latter, the accepted landmark is the French Revolution, which stimulated so many movements of political consequence and revealed so many currents of social tendency; for the former, we have the not less significant "Industrial Revolution" since 1750. Here England becomes of foremost importance; mechanical inventions (cf. James Watt, 1736–1819) and the resultant massing of labour at particular centres have vitally altered the nature of economic problems. The reconstitution of society has served to emphasize the social rather than the individual claims of life; the tendency has been reinforced by the theory of evolution, as applied to society, and by the consciousness of a new science of "sociology" (a term first used by Comte in 1838). The recognition of corporate and social responsibility has profoundly affected, and is

[1] Webb, *Fabian Essays* (ed. 1908), pp. 35, 37.

still affecting, our political and social life. But the newness of many of the practical problems must not obscure
the fact that earlier phases of history offer instructive
parallels to the general course of this modern development—a development from mediaeval society through
intellectual and religious, political and economic individualism to a new social emphasis. We may think of the
process by which the primitive member of a social group
passed from the pressure of its accepted customs and its
social solidarity to the exercise of an independent moral
consciousness, and thence into the national life of the
ancient world. Similarly, we have seen that an essential
feature in the development of the Hebrew religion was
the differentiation of Israel's relation to God into that of
individual Israelites, whilst the spiritual individualism of
the New Testament was again merged into the corporate
and institutional life of the Catholic Church. Throughout
all such movements, from the individual to the social
emphasis, there is the unity of a common principle; man
is constituted what he is by his fellowship in a society,
and the two terms in the relation are constantly acting
and reacting on each other, to the enrichment of both.
The characteristic feature, therefore, of the most recent
example of this recurrent movement is simply the new
field, the broader arena in which it takes place, together
with the deeper consciousness of what is involved.

(*b*) *Some typical theories of society.*—Amongst the various
theories of social history there are at least five clearly
defined types belonging to modern times, namely, those of
Rousseau, the English Utilitarians, Spencer, Marx (with
recent Socialism), and Tolstoi. The first of these is
intimately connected with the French Revolution, of which

it constituted the underlying philosophy. Rousseau, whose *Social Contract* appeared in 1762, worked on the basis of Hobbes and Locke. His pronounced individualism finds expression in the alleged "Rights of Man." The original goodness of man had issued in the corruption of the contemporary world just because the free play of individualism had been checked by governmental control. The remedy for social evils lay in a return to the natural sovereignty of the people, who must recover their lost liberty and themselves govern. This doctrine of "Natural Rights" issued, significantly enough, in the anarchy of the Revolution and the autocracy of Napoleonism. Individualism of a type quite distinct from this is afforded by the English Utilitarians. Bentham had no sympathy with Rousseau's "Rights of Man"; he started from individual self-interest, and conceived the ideal society to exist as producing the greatest happiness of the greatest number. The latter principle became therefore the standard of right and wrong; it was correlated with the self-interest of the individual by the assumption that enlightened self-interest would harmonize with general happiness. James Mill applied this theory to the practical problems of government, emphasizing the need for individual security in the product of labour. John Stuart Mill was a foremost upholder of the value of individual liberty, to be restrained only where injurious to the liberty of others. A third type of individualism is that of Herbert Spencer, though it is open to dispute whether this is consistent with his general philosophy. Society is here conceived to be an organism, and the use of the term is explicitly urged as signifying more than a mere analogy or metaphor (*Social Statics*, p. 262).

Society is to be conceived "as having a natural structure in which all its institutions, governmental religious, industrial, commercial, etc., are interdependently bound—a structure which is in a sense organic" (*ibid.* p. 365). From this point of view, Spencer criticizes Bentham's assertion that government creates rights: "Clearly the conception of 'natural rights' originates in recognition of the truth that if life is justifiable there must be a justification for the performance of acts essential to its preservation, and therefore for those liberties and claims which make such acts possible" (*ibid.* p. 390).

In complete contrast with the individualism of these theories stands the Socialism of Karl Marx, though his interpretation of society is, like Spencer's, evolutionary. The doctrine of evolution, as learnt from Hegel, is directly applied to the economic problems. The salient feature of society becomes the economic struggle or class-war between capital and labour—a struggle forming a parallel to that of the Darwinian theory of existence. Labour is the one standard of value; since the labourer, in the hands of the capitalist, is reduced to a bare subsistence wage, the surplus-value of his labour goes to increase capital. The consequent injustice must culminate in a catastrophic reorganization of society; the means of production will be socialized, and the labour-product equitably distributed. This theory is avowedly based on materialistic premises; its clear-cut formulation and classic statement in Marx's work *Capital* (vol. i. 1867) make it a convenient type for brief statement, but many of its details and assumptions, other than the general principle of Collectivism in the means of production, would be criticized by present-day Socialists. Apart from particular forms of economic theory and method, the Socialist movement itself might be sympathetically defined as an attempt to give material expression to the formal principle of Kant—"Be a person, and treat others as persons." The essential meaning of personality in the Socialist movement is citizenship. From one point of view, this contrast may be expressed by saying that whilst Kant emphasized the inner life in its individuality, in order to establish a kingdom of God, Socialism emphasizes the outer life in its social relations, in order to establish a perfect social order.

Perhaps the nearest approach to the Christian position (in its New Testament expression) is what may be called philosophic anarchy, the outstanding exponent of which is Tolstoi, so far, at least, as its practical application is concerned. His appeal is to the influences of love working through the individual, and not to force, whether applied by State Socialism or in any other way. "The abolition of governments will merely rid us of an unnecessary organization which we have inherited from the past—an organization for the commission of violence and for its justification." [1] "I understand now that true welfare is possible for me only on condition that I recognize my fellowship with the whole world. I believe this, and the belief has changed my estimate of what is right and wrong, important and despicable." [2] "If people would but understand that they are not the sons of some fatherland or other, nor of governments, but are sons of God, and can therefore neither be slaves nor enemies one to another —those insane, unnecessary, worn-out, pernicious organiza-

---

[1] *Patriotism and Government*, ch. viii. (E.T. in *World's Classics*, p. 258).
[2] *My Religion*, p. 256 (E.T. by H. Smith, 1889).

tions called governments, and all the sufferings, violence, humiliations, and crimes which they occasion, would cease."[1] If we are tempted to dismiss Tolstoi's attitude as literalistic and hopelessly impracticable, we are at least bound to admit our present failure to apply Christian ideals in the realm of social and international relationships, as is so constantly emphasized in his writings.

The criticism of these and similar theories in their direct economic or political application lies beyond our limits. In regard to the underlying principles themselves, the original theory of the "Natural Rights" of the individual is now seen to be as pure a fiction as that of the "Social Contract"; the evolutionary study of human society has displaced both from serious consideration. Utilitarianism broke down in the hands of J. S. Mill; the recognition of a qualitative difference in pleasures is a no less fatal breach in the system than the failure to pass from the actual self-interest of the individual (by which he must be controlled) to the interest of the community. In regard to the general theory of evolution as applied to society, a modern mind necessarily recognizes the truth of the principle of development in this as well as in the individual life. The peril lies in allowing too much to be read into the comparison of the social aggregate with the single biological organism.[2] We may easily fall into such a one-sided statement as that of Kidd: "Progress everywhere from the beginning of life has been effected in the same way, and it is possible in no other way. It is the result of selection and rejection."[3] To such a view we

---

[1] *Patriotism and Government*, p. 261.

[2] Cf. Bosanquet, *The Philosophical Theory of the State*, pp. 21–27.

[3] *Social Evolution* (ed. 1895), p. 36.

can assent only when we are prepared to disregard those spiritual values of personality which lie at the heart of the Christian doctrine of man and are emphasized by Tolstoi. No valid ethics, and therefore no real religion, can be distilled from the " organism " metaphor rigorously applied as a theory. With a recent philosophic writer it seems necessary to say that " the form of evolution which is the constant unfolding of an idea potential in the beginning, and strictly fixed in all its stages, cannot be shewn on the evidence to apply to historical development . . . historical development in virtue of its individual aspect will always have a contingent element whose operation is real, if subordinate." [1]

(*c*) *The rise of social democracy.*—Throughout the period to which the above theories of society belong, there has been steady progress in the extension of political power on a democratic basis. The relation of social theory and political practice is more or less close, as may be seen from the influence of Rousseau on the French Revolution. In the case of England, there have been three important extensions of the franchise in the last century, namely: (1) that of the Reform Bill of 1832, which served to admit the middle classes to political power by a £10 household voting qualification in boroughs and one of £50 for owners and occupiers in the counties ; (2) that of 1867, extending the franchise to all borough householders ; and (3) that of 1884, extending the same rights to county householders.[2] Political power, thus placed in the hands of the community, is more and more likely to be used for the good of the community rather than for that of the

---

[1] Galloway, *Principles of Religious Development*, pp. 21, 26.
[2] Cf. Courtney, *The Working Constitution of the United Kingdom*, p. 13.

State or official governing body. How far this new emphasis is reflected in social measures at home and in international relations of peace will ultimately depend on education in the largest sense of the word. But, other conditions equal, the weight of social democracy will certainly tell against the cost of modern warfare, and therefore in favour of peace ; this tendency is reinforced by the inter-dependence of trade and the growth of the facilities of transit and travel. In home affairs, social democracy has found a more or less successful voluntary expression in the Co-operative Movement on the one hand and in Trades' Unions on the other. Beneath all these movements, whether political or social, we can recognize the unity of a common tendency from the more individualistic to the more social emphasis. In their several ways, and notwithstanding their limited range from the standpoint of the religious thinker, they call attention to those social factors of modern life which must necessarily be incorporated in our thinking; on the practical side, they serve to bring home to the individual the practical aspects of his responsibility for others. In this respect, a broad-based suffrage and an efficient local government have an educative moral and social influence, which the Christian doctrine of man cannot afford to neglect.

(*d*) *The socialization of Christian anthropology.*—When we attempt to count the chief gains for Christian thought from these various social tendencies, we must not forget that they owe their value to that individualistic development which preceded them, from which they are a necessary reaction. The problems and possibilities, the hopes and fears of modern social reconstruction largely spring from the richness of the individual life as developed since the Reformation. Here lies, indeed, the first contribution—the recognition of the value of man as man; the great mediaeval societies have been broken up, we may say, just in order that the value of the individual lives, their worth for themselves and for others, might be more fully realized. Whatever be the ultimate category of their reincorporation, whether it be primarily ecclesiastical, political, or economic, the gain in the recognition of this value is a positive advance, to be welcomed by all who are loyal to the emphasis placed by Christ on the infinite worth of human personality. The advance may be expressed, in one of its aspects, by saying that social justice is more than charity.

A second element enriching Christian thought is the broader basis of values—broader, that is, than the Church has usually claimed as her own, though her direct contribution to social life has been much greater than is usually supposed. Life has been deepened by the fuller recognition of the social side of personality; it is more clearly seen, and more keenly felt, that the quality and value of personality is essentially expressed in the range and intensity of its relations to other persons. The principle goes back to the New Testament, and beyond it; but a principle is always enriched when a new field for its application is discovered. Perhaps never before in history was there a keener sense of social responsibility than is felt to-day—a sense which in many is the substitute for, or the nearest approach to, a definite religion. The Church is faced with the question of her relation to the kingdom of God.

Finally, and in close relation with this larger conception of life, we have the direct interpretation of Christian morality in social righteousness. This does not mean that the Christian is committed to any of the social and economic theories illustrated above. The Christian attitude towards Socialism, for example, is conditioned by two factors, which should be clearly distinguished. If a man is convinced, after proper inquiry, that the abolition of Capitalism in favour of the collective ownership of the means of production is the best remedy for the admitted evils of competition, the inequality of opportunity, the pauperism and unemployment of to-day, his duty as a citizen, especially as a Christian citizen, is to be a Socialist. If, on the other hand, he thinks (with the present writer) that even worse evils would attend any such limitation of individual development, his Christian duty is to oppose the economic theory of Collectivism. But in regard to the moral attitude, as distinct from the economic theory, there can be no difference of opinion. That attitude must be one of admitted individual responsibility for the social conditions of our life and of individual duty, conditioned by individual opportunity, towards all the persons who constitute the society.

CHAPTER V.

THE CHRISTIAN DOCTRINE OF MAN IN RELATION TO CURRENT THOUGHT

1. INTRODUCTION.

(a) *The relation of historical to systematic statement.*— "If", says a contemporary writer, "we can hope everything from a son who loves his parents, we must not despair of an age that loves history."[1] This general characteristic of our time has a particular bearing on Christian doctrine. In this, as in so many other studies, there is an increasing emphasis on genetic growth, a conviction that the best and truest way of stating what an idea is will be found by tracing its continuous development from century to century. It may be due in part to inevitable reaction from what have seemed the excessive claims of systematic theology to the knowledge of the mystery of God. But modern interest in the history of dogma in preference to its reconstruction involves much more than this. There is a logic of the race as well as of the individual; Newman's "Securus judicat orbis terrarum"[2] is capable of critical as well as of uncritical application. Amid the pageantry of successive generations, the permanent and essential features of cardinal

[1] Sabatier, *Vie de S. François d'Assise*, Intro. p. iii.
[2] *Apologia* (ed. 1900), p. 116.

truths are revealed by a dialectic to which the span of a single life cannot attain. At the bar of history, judgment often goes by default; what is arbitrary and untrue is condemned by its simple failure to survive. It is, indeed, by this silent process that the pressure of the great problems is usually relieved. The formal problem finds no categorical solution, but the attainment of another point of view disposes of many of the old questions, whilst setting new. For example, the doctrine of original sin became a principle of cosmic injustice if individual responsibility for Adam's transgression were not proved; yet how was it to be proved? Modern views of the Bible and of the origin of the race remove Adam's transgression from the data of the problem; yet we shall see that the acceptance of the evolutionary theory still leaves us with the essential problems of sin, though the approach to them is different.

The study of the idea in the past does not, however, set us free from the attempt to evaluate it in the present; even our interpretation of the past is already the silent manifestation of a present reconstruction. One of the perils of historical study is to forget that the mere sum of previous stages of thought does not exhaust the idea that is being studied. The record of past thought is the record of many imperfect stages in the grasp of a reality which lies beyond our perfect definition. The Christian doctrine of man cannot be completely stated, not only because of the new data to be contributed by generations yet to come and by nations yet to become Christian, but because the idea we strive to seize has its goal in the unsearchable thought of God as well as its cradle in the amœba. Finality of statement is not to be realized; all that can be attempted is service to present need and fidelity to the truth of the past which is entrusted to us for the future. If the survey which has been given of that past is justified, we have already before us the lines on which a present statement of Christian anthropology must proceed. It has been necessary to draw a wide circle, though one of varying circumference. The doctrine of man and sin constantly presupposed one of God and salvation. But at the centre of the circle we have found a group of three closely inter-related topics, namely, personality, sin, and the experiential side of salvation. In regard to each, Christian doctrine is historically committed to a definite position. Human personality is a spiritual fact, incapable of any naturalistic interpretation or limitation. The sin of man springs ultimately from the freedom which is an essential element in spiritual personality. Salvation from sin is in the hand of God, and for it man must depend on God. To these three principal topics a fourth may be added in view of the present tendencies of our thought, namely, the social relationships of man, which form the conditioning environment for the other three.

(*b*) *The Biblical data of Christian experience.*—Our survey of the history has revealed three primary periods in the development of the Christian doctrine of man, each making its own characteristic contributions to the idea, *i.e.* the Biblical, the ecclesiastical, and the "modern" (the last covering the science and philosophy of the last three centuries). The period covered by the Old and New Testaments is of primary importance, because to it belongs the birth of Christian experience in some of its simplest yet profoundest forms. Apart from all questions of "authority", there is an intensity, a fragrance, a heroic passion in the earliest Christian generations that would alone suffice to make their experiences fundamental data for our subject and classical standards for the Christian conception of man.   The value of their contribution is the greater, because it is made for the most part unconsciously, with the naïve simplicity of childlike candour.   Its characteristic features are (1) the high worth of human nature (sonship to God); (2) the dynamic of the new relation to God (doctrine of the Spirit); (3) the new ideal of character, seen partly in the principle of the Cross (victory through defeat), partly in what is another aspect of that principle, the social realization of morality. All these distinctive doctrines of the New Testament are closely related to the Old; their characteristic form comes to them through Christ.   The Christian Church has always rightly refused to separate the Old Testament from the New, notwithstanding the fact that there are many elements in the Old Testament which must be condemned by Christian principles.   Christian anthropology is rooted and grounded in the Hebrew conceptions of human personality, character, and relationship to God.   Further, we have seen that throughout both Testaments the emphasis repeatedly falls upon the dependence of man on God for the realization of his destiny.   Man is dependent in origin (creation), fortune (Providence), the need for forgiveness (the Gospel), character (the Holy Spirit), and life beyond death (resurrection).   This dependence underlies each of the distinctive features of New Testament anthropology indicated above.   It is clearly fundamental for any statement of anthropological doctrine which can claim to be Christian in the historical sense.

(*c*) *The ecclesiastical development of the problems.*—The characteristic contribution of the Church, from the second to the seventeenth century, lies not in any new range of experience comparable in originality and intensity with that of the first century, but in the growing consciousness of the problems which spring from the Christian life. We find here a striking evidence of continuity in the fact that the primary interest of Christian anthropology throughout more than a thousand years was the practical antithesis of freedom and grace.[1] We have seen that behind that antithesis there was the contrast of national interests, the Greek and the Hebrew. It is useful to think of the modern parallel in the contrast between the scientific and religious temper. Science, as we know, can become deterministic, and religion, too, as we know, can forget its dependence on supernatural grace; but it is broadly true that the claims of freedom and of grace are those of two temperaments, attitudes, lines of activity—the rational and the religious. Whatever we may think of their ultimate reconciliation, it is at least beyond question that the Church tried in vain, through her thousand years of unchallenged authority in the West, to find a formula that could satisfy both interests. Within this primary problem lay that of sin —the sin which needed freedom to explain it and grace to save from it. Indeed, the poles of thought for some of the foremost Christian thinkers are sin and grace rather than freedom and grace. That is certainly true of Paul, Augustine, and Luther—the three men who

---

[1] It is, of course, not implied here or elsewhere that these are in direct or logical antagonism, but simply that they are alternatives of primary interest, and that the choice between them as such characterizes the dogmatic anthropologies.

stand respectively at the three partings of the ways of civilization—when the Empire was at its best, when it broke up in the West, and when its great successor, the Western Church, in turn was rent asunder. Is it not a fair inference from the history of the Church and of its anthropological doctrine that when the next great epoch, comparable with the Reformation, shall come, its foremost religious thinker will be not less conscious that sin and grace are his cardinal problems?

(*d*) *Lines of modern approach.*—The chief general characteristic of the Christian consciousness in modern times has been the recognition of a wider horizon of facts than either Bible or Church affords. Science has opened up fields of knowledge as to which the Bible, and pre-Reformation thinkers in general, shew no concern and no cognizance; the new knowledge cannot but affect our statement of the Christian doctrine, even though it leave the central verities untouched. Philosophy has ceased to be bound by dogmatic premises, at least by such as are not of her own creation; she claims, and so far justifiably, to include theology. The Christian doctrine of man cannot be isolated from the whole world-view we hold. The Christian doctrine of man is that philosophy of man which maintains that his Christian experiences are the most vital part of his history and furnish the key to the fullest interpretation of his nature. Thus, a modern statement of Christian doctrine is committed to the acceptance of scientific data and philosophic criteria, since the arena of discussion is no longer the palaestra of the Church. But this larger horizon inevitably raises the important question of "authority." What is to be our ultimate court of appeal? The alternative to

18

the Church seems to be the Bible, as the Reformers, for their immediate purpose, rightly held. But the problem is not so simple. The canonical Scriptures of the New Testament are the largely unconscious deposit and instinctive selection made by the consciousness of the Early Church; the authority they properly exercise over our thinking is itself derivative from the inspiration of those who wrote them; the revelation is historically mediated through the Christian experience created in them by the Spirit of God. The potential authority of the Scriptures becomes actual over us only through the continuity of this experience within us, as mediated by the historic society. This reference to the consciousness of the believer is characteristic of modern theology since Schleiermacher; not simply the believer, but the harmony between him and what Scripture records becomes the proper starting-point of inquiry. This unity of the historical and individual consciousness goes back at last to the Spirit of God, on whom both depend. This is the religious expression of what is more than a pragmatic appeal to consciousness; we may put it philosophically by saying that the only rational appeal to authority is ultimately an appeal to intrinsic truth. We appeal to the intrinsic truth, the self-evidencing credibility of the experience which runs through Bible, and Church, and the life of the Christian man to-day. " Was not our heart burning within us, while He spake to us in the way, while He opened to us the Scriptures ? "

2. HUMAN PERSONALITY.

(a) *Personality and evolution.*—We have already seen, in estimating the respective contributions of philosophy and science to the Christian doctrine of man, that the central emphasis of the former in modern times falls on the conception of human personality, and of the latter, on the theory of evolution. Clearly, there is no initial question of greater consequence than the co-ordination of these contributions. In some quarters there is still the lingering fear that they cannot be co-ordinated, and that the recognition of man's place in the more or less continuous series of natural evolution means the surrender of that spiritual personality which Christian doctrine demands. The prejudice can be met only by patient thought on the essential attributes of personality; these afford no ground for fears and suspicions of such a kind. It would be generally admitted, by all to whom the concept of personality represents a reality, that its salient aspect is that of self-consciousness, with the included notion of permanence or identity; that personality is further characterized by some measure of individuality within and of activity without; most thinkers would doubtless agree that the value or worth of this self-conscious and active individual is essentially manifested through his power of ethical self-determination. If these attributes of personality be taken as essential and as a sufficient *philosophic* basis for the Christian doctrine of man,[1] then

[1] The distinctive features of the doctrine itself have been indicated above, § 1 (*b*). The following discussion of its modern problems of course assumes that these features are kept in mind throughout, as a summary of the permanent New Testament contribution to any constructive statement. This section

we can categorically deny that personality in any way suffers when we see it thrown up against the perspective of organic evolution. Consciousness is seen to be conditioned by a particular nervous organization, itself the product of natural selection ; more rudimentary forms of consciousness may accompany lower forms of organization; but there is absolutely no scientific ground for the assertion that consciousness is a mere function of brain and a by-product of nerve-tissue. It is sufficient to repeat, what ought to be a truism, that no completion of our knowledge of the physiology of the brain, still so scanty, can be conceived as bridging the gulf between matter and mind ; so far as their phenomenal activities go, they are disparate. On the other hand, the whole process of natural evolution is unintelligible, except in terms of mind; it cannot explain away that which is needed to explain it ; the very knowledge of evolution implies evolution and something more. What is true of the process of evolution is true of its purpose: "The whole evolution of the cosmos through infinite time is a gestative process for the birth of spirit—a divine method of the creation of spirits."[1] Self-consciousness gains a new dignity when we see the cost at which it has been produced or manifested. In regard to human individuality and activity, all that we are here concerned to maintain is that man contributes a real element to the evolution of which he is part, and, as a spiritual being, is not to be wholly included under any naturalistic generalization. History ceases to be history when it is interpreted

and the next (§§ 2, 3) are partly of the nature of philosophical prolegomena ; the more specifically Christian position is given in § 4 ; a brief indication of its social application in § 5.

[1] Le Conte, *Evolution and its Relation to Religious Thought* (ed. 2), p. 329.

by mechanical or even biological categories.[1] The individuality and activity of selfhood emerge in human personality just because it belongs to a higher plane than that of organic evolution. Whatever spirit *is* in ultimate essence, it must have this power of assimilating the products of a lower plane into its own unique selfhood, and of projecting itself efficiently into the phenomena of that lower plane under the conditions of their normal working; for this is the ultimate fact (for us) of the relation between mind and body. To conceive this may be difficult; it is certainly no less difficult to conceive how the observed sequences of a lower level of experience can disprove it. Further, personality is bound up with the Christian sense of ethical worth; that worth must be found in the individual, and man must be an end in himself. No subordination of the individual to the race is reconcilable with personality which does not provide a permanent place for the ethical worth of the individual. The race will apparently come to an end, whatever progress it may make;[2] it is in the individual that the ultimate meaning of the whole development must be found, even though we have to conceive the individual as incorporated in a new society beyond our present range of experience. Evolution can and must approve this spiritual individuality, if it be applied to the whole conception of life as characterized by progress—for what other goal can human life have? If, on the other hand, evolution be confined to the realm of the organism, what can it say against the higher destiny of the supra-organic human personality? It will be seen that these and similar con-

---

[1] See the excellent discussion of this theme in Galloway, *op. cit.* ch. i.
[2] Cf. Siebeck, *Religionsphilosophie*, p. 413; *infra*, p. 285.

siderations are all more or less due to the fundamental
unlikeness of the phenomena of the organism and of self-
consciousness; we are unable to resolve one into the
other, though every minute we live affords evidence that
the connection between them is of the closest. But the
supremacy of personality over the facts of the temporal
and spatial order points to some higher realm for its own
explanation. It is at this point, then, that the Christian
religion presents itself as the sufficient answer to the
problems of our thought and the demands of our life. It
seeks to relate our human personality to an eternal order,
in which the individual is an end in himself; it presents
an effective motive, by which spiritual personality may
escape the oppressive or destructive influences of the
plane beneath it. The Christian religion has itself been a
primary factor in the development of the conception and
reality of personality; the truths it declares concerning
the unseen world point to a fuller realization of that
personality. The Christian doctrine of the relation of
personality to the eternal order of reality, the spiritual
world, is both illustrated and constituted through the
Founder of Christianity.

(*b*) *Human nature as interpreted by Christ's Person.*—If
the argument just outlined has made its intention clear, it
will throw light on our conception of the relation of Jesus
Christ to the whole course of evolution. For, whilst all
personality is dependent on evolution for the clay of its
physical manifestation, all personality must transcend the
course of such physical evolution by the inbreathed breath
of spiritual life, though that breath of God go back to the
very beginnings of life. This implies that evolution
presents us with a problem which it cannot solve; we

meet that problem in acuter form when we recognize the presence of Jesus Christ, the Son of God, in the field of history. We may emphasize as we may, and ought, the closeness of His relation to the ideals of Israel, the intimate interweaving of His thought as well as His life with all the tendencies of His time; we may recognize the limitations to His power in the defeat of His hopes for Israel, and the limitations to His knowledge, as in the eschatological outlook of some at least of the discourses ascribed to Him in the Synoptic Gospels; the fact remains that there is a uniqueness in His own consciousness of Himself, in the historic presentation of His personality in the New Testament, and in His influence on the subsequent centuries of human life, that forbids us to regard Him as simply one of ourselves. Our gaze is turned on the central feature of that uniqueness in its human aspect when we speak of the sinlessness of Jesus. It is in the moral realm, the realm of character, that we seem to be in presence of an absolute type, and not merely of one link in the chain of evolutionary process. It is not enough to believe "that one transcendent soul was lifted clear above the common infirmity, and lived from the first in undisturbed communion with God."[1] If we admit historical transcendence, and at the same time look on history as the working out of a divine purpose, we are bound to carry our thoughts back along some such lines as those of the Prologue to the Fourth Gospel and relate this unique Person uniquely to God. Emphasis is there laid on the double relation of the Logos-Son to the race. Through Him it has come to be, together with all that is; He became flesh to complete His work in the spiritual children of God. From such conceptions it is

[1] Drummond, *Studies in Christian Doctrine*, p. 313.

not far to the recognition of all human personality as the partial manifestation of the pre-existent Son of God; *i.e.* the supra-naturalistic element we have recognized in all personality is spiritually akin to its one transcendent manifestation in Jesus Christ. The possibility of the Incarnation in any case requires admission of the kinship of man and God as recognized in modern doctrines of immanence. "The affinities of the natures may be said to be the common principle of our higher philosophies." [1] If it be asked how such an Incarnation be conceivable in connection with the acceptance of evolution, the answer is not an appeal to supernatural birth (*necessary* to Augustinianism only), but to the presence of personality in and amid the working of natural law in the case of every man. We know this without being able fully to explain it; so we may know the presence of Him who forms a new beginning. His coming "introduced a new species into the world—a Divine man transcending past humanity, as humanity transcended the rest of the animal creation, and communicating His vital energy by a spiritual process to subsequent generations of men." [2]   With these words of a theologian may be compared those of a scientist: "The Christ, the ideal man, may be only the goal and completion of human evolution, and yet is he also a birth into a new and higher plane—*the Divine*." [3]   If this be true, the cardinal appeal to history can find no higher norm, no more ultimate standard for the knowledge of what man's nature is than the Person of Christ. In His personality we have the concentration of His teaching and its authoriza-

---

[1] Fairbairn, *The Place of Christ in Modern Theology*[2], p. 472.

[2] Illingworth, in *Lux Mundi* (ed. 1904), p. 152.

[3] Le Conte, *op. cit.* p. 361.

tion. What then are the primary realities of human nature revealed by the *personal* attitude of Jesus Christ to the seen and unseen worlds? The answer is, chiefly, three, namely, the fellowship of God and man, the identification of the individual with human society, and the absolute and eternal worth of moral achievement. It is not necessary to develop the illustration of these in detail; to do so would be to write the life of Jesus. We have only to think of the personal attitude that lies behind some of the great, familiar words: "I am not alone, because the Father is with Me"; "Go, and do thou likewise"; "My meat is to do the will of Him that sent Me." These make the values of human life as Jesus lived it; and as to them, and all the infinity of application they cover, He makes clear the conditions of attainment. Such values are individual in their origin, though universal in their possibility; the call comes to men one by one, and their opportunity waits them at their own turn of the road. Such values are spiritual in their essence, creating a kingdom of God within the soul, and attached to the external accompaniment of ritual and profession no more permanently than is the personality of man to his physical organism. Such values are immortal in their destiny, so that He whose they are in their fulness can say, "I am the Resurrection and the Life." In these things lies the Christian doctrine of man, and they elude our formal statement by their subtle simplicity—in these alone, if we put aside for the moment that which had no place in the Person of the Saviour, the fact of sin and the need for divine pardon. Because of their fulness, they open to our vision the goal of humanity, the principle and purpose of the whole process of evolution, the perfection of human character.

We see that the possibility of that perfection lies in the reality of the kinship of God and man—a kinship which every Christology must assume. If we wish to raise the question why the result should have been manifested when the evolution is still in process, the simple answer must be that Christ is the means by which the destiny of His brethren shall be realized, as well as the end to which their journeys point.

(c) *The eternal values and their independence of death.* —The values thrown into prominence by the attitude of Jesus are, as has been indicated, personal values. Indeed, personality and value come to be interchangeable terms : " In our experience personal beings appear in existence as centres of value, by which I mean as the living central points in which value can be felt and acknowledged. It is personality which in the world of our experience invests all other things with value."[1] This basal principle throws light both on the Christian values themselves and on the Christian faith[2] in their survival of bodily death. Fellowship with God, like all the relationships that are the sacraments of life, love, duty, home, church, involves the intercourse of persons. The common worship of God is the expression of personal penitence and thanksgiving, thought and aspiration, under conditions which make His invisible presence more real to us. We approach Him through the greater personalities who in life and literature become the priests of humanity ; we acknowledge this vicarious personal approach in every

[1] Höffding, *Philosophy of Religion* (E.T.), p. 279

[2] " Faith . . . always contains an element of risk, of venture ; and we are impelled to make the venture by the affinity and attraction which we feel in ourselves . . . to those eternal principles which in the world around us appear to be only struggling for supremacy " (Inge, *Faith*, p. 53).

Christian prayer offered in the name of our great High Priest. The hours which register our furthest advance in the knowledge of God are those which are subtly inter-woven with the deeper personal experiences of life—the hours when the youth flings himself down in the long grass in utter shame of defeat and the strong man stands helpless by the bed of the sufferer whose agonies he cannot lighten. The chief significance of such experiences is this, that they reveal the little things in their littleness and the great things in their greatness. Those great things are all seen to cluster round the relation of man to men and to God—the relation of personalities, human and divine. The specific Christian conception of fellowship with God gains its content from the double emphasis placed by Jesus on personal ministry and personal moral achieve-ment; for He makes these the conditions and tests of all religion worthy the name. The particular quality, indeed, of the personality of Jesus springs from the intimate blending of obedience to the will of God with practical helpfulness to men. "It is easy", says Emerson, "in the world to live after the world's opinion; it is easy in solitude to live after our own; but the great man is he who in the midst of the crowd keeps with perfect sweet-ness the independence of solitude." Both these qualities, then, are essentially bound up in personal relationships, so that all the values of the Christian doctrine of man lift us into the realm of personality, and all the problems of those values are problems of personality. To grasp this point, simple as it is, is to gain at a step the power to distinguish between the relevant and the irrelevant, the essential and the accidental in human nature and destiny.

The objection may be raised that the Christian values,

as stated above, are limited to the Good and neglect, if they do not exclude, the True and the Beautiful, though these also breathe the spirit, not of time, but of eternity. It is indeed true that, if we agree to take the attitude of Jesus as our highest norm of what is Christian, purely intellectual and æsthetic values are at least subordinated to the moral and treated as negligible in regard to them.[1] But the intrinsic nature of the moral values relates them most closely to that dependence on God which characterizes religion. The Christian religion belongs to a higher realm than that of the self-dependence of thought or the egoism of æsthetic enjoyment. Grant the Christian values at all, and you grant their supremacy, and their supremacy is all that is needed to explain this aspect of the Incarnation. Had Jesus come to Athens instead of to Jerusalem, Greek art and Greek thought might have been as conspicuous in the beginnings of Christianity as they were in its development. But, in the Providence of God, the Light of the World shone forth from the line of history for which religion was supreme, and for which religion was morality, shallow or deep, Pharisaic or prophetic; that is why He turns from the visible glory of the Temple, which His disciples would have Him praise, and bids them rather praise the deed of the woman who sacrificed her pitiful all to its ends. This does not mean, of course, that art and knowledge have no place but on sufferance in Christian life. They, like morality, are personal values, "three distinct ways of appreciating our fellow-men."[2] But it does mean that there is a scale of

---

[1] The references of Jesus to the birds and the flowers, the whitening fields and the ruddy sky shew a religious rather than an æsthetic interest in Nature.

[2] Sturt, in *Personal Idealism* ("Art and Personality"), p. 312.

values for the Christian, and that in that scale the highest is membership in the family of those who do the will of God, whether or not they have attained also to feel the beauty of His handiwork and to think His thoughts after Him.[1]

These values must meet the challenge of death. Clearly, the one question is as to the continuance of personality after the dissolution of the physical organism, with which it is now associated ; all else in the Christian outlook towards the future is dependent on this. The eschatological background of the New Testament is for us replaced by the inevitable issues of cosmic evolution on its physical side ; the lurid physical catastrophe of Jewish apocalypse has yielded to the more sober, yet more awe-inspiring vision, afforded by modern science, of the degradation of energy and the cessation of life on a planet that has fulfilled its purpose. But both these conceptions are no more than scenic background ; the vital issue is the permanent vitality of personality. Here the Christian answer is unmistakable. The Chorus in *Antigone*, after enumerating the triumphs of human achievement, sorrow-fully admits that from Hades man finds no escape. The Christian apostle sees the greatest triumph of all in the present conviction of victory over the grave and its sting. We do but supplement his argument in a minor detail when we link to it the evolutionary conception of death

---

[1] A problem arises in relation to these wider values of art and intellect, which attaches, however, rather to Christology than anthropology. Their realization in humanity must be part of the divine idea of man, which therefore is wider than its particular historical manifestation in Jesus Christ. But this sacrifice of other values to concentration on the moral and spiritual is to be explained by the doctrine of κένωσις, and by the necessity for the supremacy of the latter to be fully revealed.

as the natural fate of the physical organism; Paul might well have welcomed that conception as part of his hope of deliverance from this dead body. But we need to see that his argument itself involves the essential permanence of the Christian values; for him, faith, hope, love *abide* into the eternal world to which they belong. This intrinsic claim of the higher life to be eternal is but a special form of that argument already indicated in regard to personality in general. Here is to be found the ultimate argument for immortality—the self-evidencing character of the spiritual. We catch a glimpse of what this means whenever we read the classical autobiographies of the spiritual life, such as St. Teresa's *Interior Castle*, or Bunyan's *Grace Abounding*. What is apt to strike us most is the intense reality of spiritual experience to these its pioneers. The outer world pales and loses its brilliance, that the inner world may be seen in its eternity; whereas the ordinary man is constantly feeling the contrast between the unreality of what the minister says and the reality of that world into which he steps as he passes out of the church door. It is such intenser spiritual experience that can say, without any shallow idea of "compensation", "if in this life only we have hoped in Christ, we are of all men most pitiable." Here, then, the weight of the Christian argument for immortality must rest; values of life are values for a personality, and those persons who have them in their Christian form are least likely to question their intrinsic eternity.

The term "immortality" is preferable to "resurrection", because our whole line of thought points to the immortality of the soul and its values rather than to the resurrection of the body. On this point Greek thought contributes more than the Hebrew, unless we follow up the attractive and suggestive speculation of Paul, that a new spiritual body, of which the germ is already planted in the natural, will serve the needs of the spirit in the spiritual life. But the manner of continuance is of little importance; we do better to think of the continuance of all the personal values in the intercourse of the risen Lord with His disciples than to speculate as to the nature of His resurrection body. The only vital questions in regard to the future life, other than the eternal aspect of the personal values and personality itself, spring from the fact of sin, and will be noticed farther on. But we may here insist on the individuality of the concept of personality, and on the inability of the Christian doctrine to sacrifice one iota of all that such individuality means. We cannot give to the values of fellowship with God, social service by the individual, and moral achievement their Christian sense, unless we conceive them to be retained in their individual aspect in the life continued beyond physical death. This proviso is to be maintained when we seek to carry the implicates of our Christian faith concerning man up into the comprehensive vision of a world-view. The Christian faith, it has been already urged, implies a philosophy; that philosophy must leave abundant room for the individual aspects of personality. If, for example, we are convinced that a monism of the Neo-Hegelian type (Green and the Cairds) does not do this, then that philosophy is so far unchristian, in spite of the noble types of Christian character which have found their thought-home within it. But, on the other hand, we cannot be content with an ultimate philosophy which does not carry up all these values and personality itself into

God as their home and source and hope. In claiming
that man's nature is something higher and greater than
its present setting, we do not send it forth on perilous
adventure through the universe, like the dove of the
Deluge story; we hold that it is higher and greater,
because it derives from God and rests in Him; we believe,
as Christians, that He who called man into being and
gave him that measure of independence from which moral
responsibility springs, can still sustain man in continued
fellowship with Himself under the changed conditions of
the spiritual world beyond death, without sacrificing one
single element of all we count dear and worthy in the
individuality of our present life and relationships.

3. FREEDOM AND MORAL EVIL.

(*a*) *The reality and problems of freedom.*—The personal
values already indicated have implied the reality of one of
the most important aspects of personality, namely, freedom.
The free activity of the individual self is the underlying
condition of moral worth, of genuine social interaction,
and of fellowship with God. Moral worth implies moral
achievement, and this requires the presence to the self of
real alternatives,[1] of which the higher is preferred to the
lower. The prayerful submission of Jesus and the
traitorous kiss of Judas in Gethsemane maintain moral
qualities from our belief that they might have done
otherwise than they did, and that their respective actions
were not absolutely determined by surrounding circum-

---

[1] This implies that individual destiny is at stake, but not the destiny of
the universe; Christian faith admits of no doubt as to the ultimate triumph of
the divine purpose. See § 4 (*g*).

stances or past conduct. Men normally act under a sense
of freedom, with the conviction that they might do otherwise than they are doing; they judge their actions in the
retrospect as morally good and bad, as well as by
standards of utility. For various reasons, the significance
of this self-judgment comes out most clearly in that attitude
of a man to his own evil deed which we call remorse, itself,
as has well been said, "only a darker name for man's
conviction of his own free-will."[1] There is a quality in
such an attitude quite different from that which attaches to
the perception of a blunder or the memory of a breach of
good taste. Nor can this quality be explained away on
evolutionary lines as due to the reaction of social utilities
on the individual, transmitted by descent until they have
become personal self-judgments of praise or blame. The
fatal flaw in all such utilitarian explanation is the difference
of quality between the useful and the morally good. The
testimony of consciousness must not be unduly pressed
into the service of any particular theory of freedom; but
it is valid so far as it shews moral action to be bound up
with either the reality or the illusion of moral freedom;
the latter alternative is clearly inadmissible on a Christian
view of God and the world. Further, the whole effective
interaction of society and the individual is realized in
ordinary life on the presupposition of moral responsibility,
i.e. responsibility for action notwithstanding environmental
conditions. In practice, we treat each other as free; the
vocabulary of morals and the ethics of law are built on
moral responsibility. It is true that a plausible argument
for the retention of moral and legal categories might be
drawn simply from their admitted influence as encourage-

---

[1] Illingworth, *Personality, Human and Divine*, p. 35.

19

ments and deterrents ; *i.e.* it would be useful to society
to continue to build on the moral fiction of individual
responsibility. But to admit this is by no means to admit
that society could have arisen or could permanently
continue on a moral basis unless the very condition of
morality, namely, moral freedom, were the possession of the
individual. Indeed, this view of the influence of environment allows the existence of freedom, since it admits that
conduct can be modified, and since freedom is not unmotived
willing. Finally, the essential Christian conception of
fellowship with God as open to man must imply some
measure of freedom on man's part as well as on God's, if
it is to have any moral value. If man is worth to God
all that Jesus claimed, it cannot be because his ways are
perfect like those of a planet, but because there is a
voluntary, *i.e.*, personal, quality attaching to his longing
after God and enjoyment of Him, which is incomparably
superior to the perfection of a mere machine. All this is
recognized in the Gospel invitation, in the continuance of
fellowship with God by means of Church and sacraments,
and in the " pressing forward " of such a Christian as Paul,
in order to enjoy the fellowship with God through Christ
into which he has been called. Thus for each of the
values of personality lying at the heart of the Christian
experience freedom is cardinal, and freedom in the sense
of real alternatives, introducing an element of contingency
and risk into individual destiny. This seems to be presupposed in the continued emphasis of Scripture and of
the Church on probation as an inevitable aspect of human
life in this world. It is probable that the common view
which makes death the end of that probation is a fore-
shortening of the true perspective, comparable with that

involved in the eschatological outlook of primitive Christianity. Indeed, it is difficult to do justice to the conception of probation at all, in view of our larger historical horizon, if we confine it to the opportunities of this life. However this may be, and whatever other problems may present themselves in regard to a liberty involving real alternatives, we seem justified in claiming this as vital to the Christian conception of personality. There is, of course, no inconsistency between such a claim and the recognition that Christianity also points to liberty in a fuller and much more perfect form—the liberty of entire moral harmony with the will of God, when all hesitation, conflict, uncertainty as to the issue is banished through the perfection of character. Freedom in the first sense is the present stage of development to liberty in the second and fuller sense—the sense emphasized by Augustine.

This, then, is the reality of freedom we must claim for the Christian idea of personality, whilst admitting that grave problems attach to its further definition and explanation—problems, indeed, that seem to pass beyond our grasp; perhaps this is inevitable, for we are dealing with the attribute of what is for us an ultimate, namely, personality. We need not consider among such problems those which spring from the side of a materialistic determinism, or of a dissolution of consciousness in the sense of Hume's analysis of it. Such difficulties have been met already in maintaining the reality of personality itself amid its evolutionary and transient setting; they spring from the ultimate denial of personality in any adequate sense. But there is a real psychological problem which we shall find passing into a metaphysical one.

The central psychological problem is raised by the apparently closed circle in which we move when we try to analyse volition. Behind the act of will there is a motive, which we may define as the idea of an end in relation to the self; behind the motive we find attention of the self to the end constituting the efficiency of the motive; behind attention we find interest springing from the specific character of the agent; but character is given by the quality of the will with the act of which we started. Begin where we may in this circle, we are brought round to the same point; the agent might have done other than he did, but only in case his character, interests, attention, motives had been other than they were—a conclusion which does not yield the freedom for the reality of which we have contended above. That freedom is not gained by acceptance of the circle and identification of the self of the agent with the character; self-determination in Green's sense does not yield the real alternatives of Christian freedom.[1] There is no one point at which the self may enter the circle of character as efficient agent; yet the self loses all intelligibility if it stands outside this circle in unmotived willing. Here, then, is our problem. On the level of psychological analysis, freedom seems impossible; on the level of moral personality, freedom is essential. Does not this point to the only kind of solution such a problem admits? The closed circle of psychological analysis lies *as a whole* within the reality of personality. The self (which is always more than its previously formed character) is not

---

[1] Cf. his *Works*, vol. ii. p. 318: "The determination of the will might be different [in any given set of circumstances], but only through the man's being different."

present at any single point of the circle because it is present at all—will, motive, attention, interest. Not one, but every element in the consciousness of volition involves more than a quasi-mechanical " causation "; the motive is a motive for self, the attention that of an interested self, the interest that of the character in which the self is so far revealed. In this way the psychological problem becomes a metaphysical one. We lift it into the higher category of personality to which freedom belongs. What remained inexplicable through a purely scientific psychology becomes sufficiently conceivable as the attribute of that personality which naturalistic hypotheses cannot explain.[1] Such a position as this in regard to the problem of freedom is paralleled both below and above its particular level of reality. When we pass from the inorganic to the organic realm, we find the lower transformed by its comprehension in the higher, and biology transcending the issues of chemistry. It is not otherwise with the theistic conception of the relation of God to the world; the reality of His providence presents a parallel to the reality of human freedom, and raises similar problems. A modern view of divine action does not conceive God as interposing His "free" activity in some chink in the system of "natural law." The natural order must be so within His spiritual purposes that it is subordinate to them; the higher plane of reality transforms the lower into a providential order, as finite personality can transform the psychological sequence into freedom. The Christian thinker should insist the more on the higher

---

[1] Cf. W. R. Boyce Gibson, in *Personal Idealism*, p. 169; he desiderates a psychology of "first causes" in order to recognize this independence of the subject.

level of personality as he remembers how vital to his faith is the doctrine of grace and of the moral energy which flows into the believer. Personality must be conceived by him, however imperfect and inadequate his imagery for the conception, as related to God not less closely than to the physical organism on which it at present depends. The problems and possibilities of human life must ultimately spring from this subtle poise of the human spirit between the higher and lower terms of reality. The discovery of a formula for individual freedom in both relationships—freedom to control the body, and freedom to surrender that control to its Creator—is less important than the recognition that Christian experience implies both. The ideal self, which is character not as made, but as in the making, is already outlined in those conditions of heredity and environment which belong to its evolution in time. But within those prescribed limits, so far assigning its place in the divine purpose, its destiny is in its own hands. The development of human personality cannot be made a foregone conclusion. But just as the Christian doctrine of sin requires freedom in this real sense, so the Christian doctrine of grace requires the interpenetration of the self by God to the fullest conceivable extent, yet without the coercion which would destroy personality.

(*b*) *Moral evil in relation to freedom.*—The approach to the Christian doctrine of sin [1] from the side of personal freedom already implies in large measure what that

---

[1] In what follows, moral evil is considered apart from its religious aspect as sin discussed in the next section. For a clear statement of the distinctions between " sin ", " evil ", " vice ", and " crime ", see Fairbairn's *Christ in Modern Theology*, pp. 452 f.

doctrine is here conceived to be. No further ground can be sought for the moral evil ot the world than the ultimate choice of persons able to do good or evil; the essential source of evil is the evil will, sin being, in Scriptural language, rebellion against God. God is responsible for the presence of sin in the world only in the sense that He created persons able to sin, sin itself being no necessary or inevitable element in their development; for God's purpose, the moral value of free personal agency could be secured only by liability to sin. No statement of the doctrine of sin which falls short of these requirements does justice to the Christian consciousness, whether we seek its testimony in Scripture, the thought of the Church, or in ourselves. If this be true, some of the typical explanations of sin are put out of court at once; we cannot listen to Spinoza when he resolves it into the illusion belonging to the finite and temporal standpoint, or to Leibniz when he traces it to the necessary imperfection of the finite. We cannot regard as adequate Schleiermacher's conception of the reality of sin as consisting in our consciousness of it, or Hegel's of its relativity as a necessary stage in moral development.[1] It is the last of these solutions which seems to present most attraction at the present day to those who have abandoned the ecclesiastical theory; the conception of relativity is, however, frequently linked with biological rather than with metaphysical ideas of evolution. We have to ask how far the evolutionary view of man, to

---

[1] No attempt is here made to discuss these and other modern theories, partly because of the limits of space, and partly because all that could be given is already provided in Tennant's *The Origin and Propagation of Sin* and Orchard's *Modern Theories of Sin*. See also Kirn's excellent article, "Sünde", in RE^3.

which we are committed, is adequate to explain the problem of evil.

It would, no doubt, be generally accepted that moral evil, viewed under the category of development, is the survival of the natural into a stage of growth at which it has become unnatural. The history of ethics supplies frequent examples of the virtue of one age becoming the vice of the next. This is corroborated by careful observation of the moral development of children. There is little in the child to suggest a corrupted nature seeking an outlet for its expression; on the other hand, there is as little suggestion of an Adamic state of idyllic righteousness. What we actually find in the normal child is "the will to live", the biological "thrust" of the animal to maintain itself, gradually passing into the new forms imposed by self-consciousness. The characteristic vices of the child—selfishness, cruelty, and lying—are different manifestations of its life-energy, maintaining the ego against the pressure of society, asserting power over others, reacting in fear from particular consequences. Perhaps every fault may be traced to the perversion of some natural instinct. Later on, in the period of adolescence, we have still more striking examples of the same principle; the new powers of the nature tend to assert themselves, regardless of the limits of rational self-consciousness and social obligation. External observation along these lines is fully corroborated by introspective thought. So far as a man can recall the misdeeds of childhood, he is likely to find them consisting in the continuance of "natural" habits, against which there seemed often to be nothing but a certain uneasiness more or less due to external influences. The strong moral condemnation with which a man may come · to view the faults of his childhood is largely the product of later growth, as in Augustine's retrospect. There is usually no distinct experience of which the Fall story can be made a true allegory—unless that experience has been unconsciously moulded on Biblical teaching. Personality awakens to the consciousness of a more or less continuous development, in which the momentum of habitual act and thought is opposed by a tardier but normally increasing sense of moral self-blame. At first sight, then, we seem to have a simple explanation of the genesis of moral evil. It springs from the circumstances, more or less inevitable, of our natural development and the precedence of the " natural " over the " spiritual." All men are sinners because all men must pass through such a stage. Moreover, we can understand from this point of view the practical dualism of the ascetic or of common speech ; the life of the body is always tending to assert itself against the higher nature of the spirit, and in this conflict the whole course of evolution is recapitulated. But true as this explanation seems to be on its own plane, as a psychology of moral evil, it fails to give us the relation with personal freedom which a Christian view of sin requires. From it alone we might infer that evil was itself part of the whole process of development, just as from the Hegelian dialectic. For this evolutionary theory " universal sinfulness " becomes " simply the general failure to effect on all occasions the moralization of inevitable impulses and to choose the end of higher worth rather than that which, of lower value, appeals with the more clamorous intensity."[1] It is true that, as suggested

[1] Tennant, *op. cit.* (ed. 1), p. 107. Orchard's criticism of this statement

already, much objective " evil " is done with the minimum of evil intention—evil in the sense of the evil will; the profound pathos of human tragedy often lies just in the cry of Mildred in Browning's "A Blot in the 'Scutcheon"—

> " I was so young, I loved him so, I had
> No mother, God forgot me, and I fell."

But the experience which yields this testimony as to the lower end of the scale also requires us to acknowledge at the higher end the full ethical quality based on the consciousness of personality and freedom. However impalpable and gradual the beginnings of moral evil may appear, there can be no hesitation in its absolute condemnation by the healthy Christian consciousness, and its condemnation in just that aspect which is given by tracing it to the free choice of personality. We have thus another form of the problem which we encountered in considering the general relation of personality to evolution; the end implies much more than the beginning, and there is in the later position a quality—that which we call ethical or moral in the full sense—which cannot be elicited from the earlier, *considered alone*. We shall not solve it by asking at what point responsibility supervenes on the category of development, for that would be simply to ignore the fact that development applies to the moral as to the natural realm. On the other hand, the recognition of responsibility as itself developing in and through the natural conditions does not in any way deny its reality when developed. The essence of the category of development is that features

---

as a "reduction" of sin (*op. cit.* p. 98) seems justified, though Orchard's own subsequent "reduction" of guilt (p. 136) is much more serious.

arise in its course continuous with the past, yet presenting new qualities. In this case the new quality is that of moral responsibility. It does not conflict with the relativity of the lower order, because it gathers up the data of that lower order into a new presentation, just as we have seen to be the case with the psychological problem of freedom. From this standpoint, we sacrifice neither the general truth of development nor the ascription of evil to the freedom of personality. So far, then, as our study has gone, the central fact about personality seems to be that it is always more than our explanation of it. It reveals itself as something higher than each group of phenomena—physiological, psychological, ethical —which we strive to relate to it; it refuses to be comprehended within them, but it comprehends them within itself. Perhaps this is no more than we might expect, in view of the far-reaching claims for personality made by the Christian faith. Whatever be the explanation, it will certainly be found in relation to what is higher, not what is lower. The values of personality which have been indicated supply the positive element in the conception of what personality really is, and give us a clear basis for the mystery of its various activities. The infinite demand of the moral ideal, the universal fact of obligation, point forwards and upwards to God as the goal of personal life. We begin to enter into the reality of what personality is only when we pass on from the fact of moral defeat below to the obligation of moral achievement above; that is only another way of saying that in deep and wonderful ways the personality we know is but personality in the making.[1]

[1] If the argument of the above section in some points suggests the Kantian

4. SIN AND SALVATION.

(*a*) *Man's worth to God.*—Moral evil is considered in its religious aspect as " sin " when it is thrown up against the cosmic background of man's history, destiny, and worth to God.   To state what that worth is, to select its essential elements from the bewildering varieties of human character and civilization, might well seem an impossible and unprofitable task, were we not approaching it from the Christian standpoint, with its definite and unmistakable assumptions in regard to man.   The question flung out to the starry sky by the Hebrew poet-thinker, " What is man that Thou art mindful of him ? " was answered by Him on whom also " with shining eyes the Syrian stars looked down ", by Him who in Gethsemane turned not to the starry sky above, but to the moral law within.   The sacrificial prayer of Christ, " Not as I will, but as Thou wilt ", brings to a focus those personal values which His whole life expresses.   These, as we have seen, are fellowship with God, the absoluteness of moral obedience, and the realization of morality through social service.   But the essential and inherent claim of these " values " is that they have worth to God as well as to man.   Religion is a tragic illusion if man, seeking fellowship with God, be not in reality sought after by God Himself.   The one thing man can give to God in his absolute right is his freedom ; but the fragrance of this alabaster vase of precious ointment has been wasted in Gethsemane and

dualism of the intelligible and empirical self, it also offers an explanation of their relation in terms of evolution and comprehends the natural process within spiritual reality.   The responsible choice of evil is made within the process, not extra-temporally.   The ideal self is conceived to be the realization of the Christian values within the concrete human life.

countless times over, if the worth of moral achievement be not as real to God as is its cost to men. The social order is not simply the condition for the specific realization of duty, which would be meaningless *in vacuo*; it has always derived its most powerful sanctions to service from the clearer or dimmer consciousness that human destiny is divine purpose, and that the service of society is co-operation with God. These values, then, become the Christian measure of the worth of man to God. They indicate his significance within the double perspective of space and time; they form the ideal background on which moral evil throws the dark shadow of sin; the conviction that God intends their realization becomes the hope of salvation.

(*b*) *The nature and universality of sin.*—The approach to sin as the negation of man's worth to God should not in any way obscure the truth that sin must be positively explained as the product of personal freedom, *i.e.* as rebellion against God, and that the fact of its presence rests ultimately on the reality of human personality itself. Sin can be defined as selfishness, because it always involves the acceptance by the self of a motive constituted by the character of the self in its lower relations, without regard to the motive of higher worth which ought to spring from the relation of the self to God. Its actual content is explicable in terms of the category of development, as we have seen in the discussion of moral evil; the past survives into the present, whether it be the past of the individual self, or of his direct ancestry, or of the society which constitutes his environment. But because man is a person, endowed with some measure of freedom to choose between real alternatives, these powerful influences of the past and present, entrenched in the lines of habit, are not enough to account for his actual sinning or for the practical universality of sin within the race. They explain the form of the actual sins men commit, but not, in the full sense, why they commit them ; any such attempt to give an absolute and universal cause for sin would be to abandon the higher category of personality which constitutes man what he is. Evolution, therefore, may be said to prescribe the conditions of man's probation and discipline ; it still leaves us, as indeed the Bible does, with an unsolved mystery of iniquity, which throws us back on personal freedom. The ultimate individual choice is manifested in and through the natural conditions; its presence is necessary to make intelligible and rational the personal self-blame in which the consciousness of sin centres. The evil tendencies and influences of individual nature and social environment become motives, constituting temptation, only as they enter the consciousness of the agent to find welcome. But even as motives to the agent they do not necessitate sin, for the self is not exhausted by the sum of its motives, nor does it wholly lose the sense of being more than they. In the retrospect of its own act, it may indeed seem to have been drawn into a network of evolutionary causality by the analysis of motive. But the analysis leaves out the self which makes the motive, just as analysis of the dead organism leaves out the life which lifted the chemical elements to a new plane. The testimony to ultimate and original freedom of the self (limited by the conditions, but within those limits rising above them) lies in the surviving consciousness of guilt. Probably the chief objection likely to be felt against this presentation of the case will arise from the universality of sin—a fact of experience which it is no object of the present discussion to minimize. Does not this universality point back to some common centre, some sufficient cause, such as was supplied by the ecclesiastical doctrine of Adam's fall? In the first place, we must clearly distinguish between the dogmatic and the practical assertion of the universality of sin. We have seen that the Scriptural teaching on this point is intensely practical and includes nothing that really amounts to the Augustinian dogma of total depravity. When, for example, Paul says that "the scripture hath shut up all things under sin" (Gal. iii. 22), he has in view that practical dominion of sin which he accepts as a datum of experience and has elaborated in the early chapters of the Epistle to the Romans. We have further to notice that this datum of experience is not to be taken as meaning that all are equal in the degree of actual sin; on the contrary, our experience of life shews a practically infinite gradation of evil, from the most hardened and pestilent blackguard up to the noblest type of Christian saintliness. It is legitimate to appeal even to the sinlessness of Jesus, for this must be the product of moral freedom if we take His humanity seriously; no necessity of sinfulness can attach to human nature, so far as He genuinely shared in it. The practical universality of sin must not then be treated as a single fact, capable of explanation by some single dogmatic hypothesis; it is a collection of facts covering the widest range. At the bottom of the scale, it includes the grossest evil, wilfully committed, of which the penalty is often obvious to all; in the middle, it covers multitudes of easy-going lives, with no more than an occasional uneasiness to rebuke their respectability; at the top, the acute self-condemnation of the Christian saint, itself the

testimony to the height of his ideal. In the second place—
and this is the crucial point—the Christian consciousness
of sin, which acknowledges the infinite obligation of
personality, is not less the evidence of responsibility, that
is, of personal freedom. In other words, it is the very
repudiation of necessity in every form. How, then, whilst
we are true to that consciousness, can we expect to find
any cause for the universality of sin more ultimate than
personal freedom? Predisposing influences, *i.e.* all that
we usually include under temptation, we do find ; but just
as soon as we advance to a universal cause of the universality of sin, we have made moral evil a necessary element
in human personality as we know it, and robbed it therefore of its moral quality and religious condemnation.
When we say " personality ", we mean that which cannot
be reduced to the purely natural sequence of cause and
effect, that in which new beginnings are made. That in
various degrees all the human personality we know
witnesses to moral failure is a fact of experience which
forms an all-important datum for our thought ; but, as such,
it is to be accepted rather than explained. The search for
explanation, other than freedom, springs from an inadequate
view of personality. We see this in the Augustinian
theory. Over against the Pelagian assertion of personal
responsibility, vitiated by an impossible psychology of the
will, the Augustinian doctrine of total corruption sacrificed
freedom in the sense of real present alternatives of good
and evil. It is true that Augustine attributed a certain
freedom to Adam ; but, on this view, " there has never
been more than one solitary hour of real probation for the
human race " ;[1] the unity of the race with Adam in the

[1] Martineau, *Types of Ethical Theory*, i. p. 18.

sense required is no longer possible with our modern conception of individual personality. But, even if it were possible, the theory defeats its own end. For when we have said that the river of life runs corrupt, because the single fountain of humanity was morally poisoned, we have either maintained a necessary actual sinning on the part of all, which contradicts the Christian consciousness of responsibility, or else we have left an unbridged gulf between the corruption of nature which is inherited, as the disposition or tendency to actual sin, and the actual sin itself, which must require the free choice of the will to be sin in the full Christian sense. The former position is the weakness of Augustinianism; the latter that even of theories far removed from Augustinianism, which refer to heredity as the explanation of the universality of sin.[1] It is, of course, a fallacy to suppose that we escape the ultimate problems by simply substituting an evolutionary theory for Augustinianism. Heredity is an important conception in regard to the continuity in the race of tendencies to evil;[2] and this applies to what may be called " social " as well as " direct " or organic heredity. Modern social emphasis has made us see more clearly the whole influence of the environment on the child and the man we owe to Schleiermacher and Ritschl the fuller recogni-

---

[1] Even writers who recognize the essential place of the will in sin often refer to heredity in terms that at least obscure the problem before us ; cf. James Drummond, *Studies in Christian Doctrine*, p. 231 : " The immediate source of sinful choice is the inherited discord of our nature " ; W. N. Clarke, *An Outline of Christian Theology* (ed. 11), p. 242 : " When sin has once taken hold of the race, the natural reproduction of life becomes reproduction of life morally injured and faulty."

[2] The appeal to direct heredity must be made with caution ; biology does not, in its present phase, allow us to assert dogmatically the inheritance of acquired characteristics (cf. J. A. Thomson, *Heredity*, 1908).

20

tion of the solidarity of the race in evil.   All this helps us
to understand the grip which moral evil has on human
life; tendencies within and influences without, which
heredity, in the twofold sense, makes continuous, provide
abundant occasions for the evil act and explain the
particular forms it assumes.   But not all of them together
explain one such act wholly, so long as we agree that sin
must go back to personal freedom.   Heredity, personal or
social, can explain moral evil fully only to a determinist.
Personal causation is something higher than all the
natural phenomena which it controls, nor does it admit of
the classification and explanation which applies to them.
We may make the probabilities as strong as we like that
any one man will "fall", or that all men at some time will
"fall", but a great gulf is fixed between probability and
necessity.   The only "proof" of the universality of evil is
the appeal to our actual experience of life; apart from this
experience, every human personality is a new venture, not
to be generalized into a conscious machine, or forced into
the circle of scientific explanation so as to lose its vital
initiative.   The general conclusion is that whilst we may
speak of the whole mass of evil tendencies in the race,
transmitted from one generation to another by heredity,
organic and social, as alien to the divine purpose for man,
we must not call it sin in the full sense, since, apart from
personal freedom appropriating it, it lacks the essential
element of guilt.   Here the explanation differs from the
Augustinian theory, which called this mass "original sin",
ascribed guilt to it, and based this guilt on the responsibility
of the race for Adam's act.   The explanation differs from
both the Augustinian and the evolutionary theory of sin
in repudiating any *necessary* connection between inherited

qualities of human nature and any act that can be called sinful in the full sense. When personality awakens into self-consciousness (which may be the hour of its creation), it finds itself already entangled in a causal sequence of "natural" tendency; yet its very nature refuses to allow that its swaddling clothes are the permanent denial of its freedom. Admittedly, this view of the facts leaves unexplained the universality of sin; yet if there be such a thing as real personal freedom, how can we ever go behind it, without denying its reality?

(*c*) *The consequences of sin.*—There is no more solemn confirmation of the dignity and worth of human life than the series of closely interlinked consequences which can be seen to follow from the individual act of sin. They begin in the mystery of personal freedom ; they issue in the mystery of man's power to defy God's character and frustrate God's purpose. They directly concern the individual, under the aspects of guilt and penalty; they increase the social influences alien to God's purpose, which operate through heredity and environment; they are recorded in a cosmic history which no human penitence can efface. This estimate of their nature does not depend on any ecclesiastical theory of sin; it follows from the intrinsic nature of sin, as the wilful refusal to realize those personal values which God has put within the range of each man's power to realize. Sin regarded as a personal attitude necessarily implies guilt; the individual is responsible for the attitude he has chosen to take to the true worth of life, and, having shewn himself unworthy, is the proper subject of moral condemnation to all who recognize the obligation to realize that worth. Sin as an act opposing the moral government of God has arrayed against it whatever forces uphold that government; it suffers, therefore, not only the loss of those values it has rejected, but also from the active opposition to itself of all that is good. Similarly, because it is rebellion against God, it joins what may be called the insurgent forces of the cosmos operating in and through other lives; and because it constitutes the actual, if temporary, defeat of the divine purpose in the creation and conservation of man, it is lifted from the temporal to the eternal plane, and cannot be considered as a transient phase of individual development. All these consequences follow logically from the initial acceptance of the Christian conception of man's worth to God. But we may also look for their confirmation in the course of our experience, so far as they lie within our present horizon—always remembering that such confirmation may be temporarily obscured or absent through the very prevalence of evil within the world.

The consciousness of guilt is the clearest and most specific testimony we have, both to personal responsibility and freedom, and to the solemn character of sin. History and literature, as well as religious autobiography, preserve some of its most impressive records; the dying words of Wolsey and the haunting dreams of Lady Macbeth are in their way evidence as good as Augustine's memory of a boyish theft. Guilt properly belongs to every unworthy volition; the Christian sense of guilt owes its peculiar intensity and quality to the specific values emphasized by the Christian religion. Are we then justified in saying that the consciousness of guilt is universal? Yes, if we remember that such consciousness in evil men can be weakened or even perhaps destroyed by the obscuration of the worth on which it depends, and that, on the other hand, there is an endless variety in the individuality of personal life. The consciousness of guilt may range from the faint uneasiness reflected apparently from conventional morality up to the spiritual penitence of one awakened to the claims of the holiness of Christ. The consciousness of guilt is conditioned as to its intensity by many factors; it varies with the manner of development, the different presentation or emphasis of Christian doctrine, even with the period of life. All men are not equally guilty; nor do all men discover their guilt in the same way or at the same time. Indeed, it is truer to say that the Christian consciousness of guilt springs from the Christian values than that it ought to precede their realization. As Martineau says of the acts of worship, "the profound sense of sinful imperfection is not ready on the surface of even the humblest mind";[1] Newman expresses the same thought when he pictures the soul brought into the presence of Christ—

> "The shame of self at thought of seeing Him
> Will be thy veriest, sharpest Purgatory."[2]

There is thus a profound truth in the familiar paradox that the acutest consciousness of guilt is felt by the holiest saints. This points to the true metaphysic of guilt. It is explicable only from our relation to higher reality, which carries with it the deepening consciousness of unbounded obligation. Particular acts of sin bring home

[1] *Life and Letters of James Martineau,* vol. i. p. 383.
[2] *The Dream of Gerontius.* Cf. the question proposed by Newman to T. Mozley: "What does Scripture present to us as the ruling motive and that most contributing to form the Christian character and life—the sense of sin, or τὸ καλόν, the beauty of holiness and high moral aims?" (*Reminiscences,* i. 212).

to the sinner the fact of his guilt; but the consciousness of that fact depends on our consciousness of God. Thus guilt points backward to personal responsibility for sin, and forward to the possibility of salvation from it; guilt carries the metaphysical demands of human freedom and divine immanence.

The penalties of sin are not less closely bound up with its nature. The juristic imagery which the word "penalty" suggests may tend to separate the idea from that of guilt as of something artificially superadded, something externally adjusted to the offence. A deeper and more spiritual view of penalty sees in it primarily an experience of what sin is—the necessary outcome of wilful opposition to the divine government of the world. The penalty of rejecting the fellowship God seeks and offers is, in the first place, exclusion from that fellowship; disloyalty to the higher motive means the loss of the higher character; whilst to save one's life in selfish isolation from others is but to lose it. But, beyond the penalties which consist in the degradation of character, there are those which spring from the relation of the individual to other persons and to the cosmos. If the universe is God's, and the administration of its history is in His hands, then, sooner or later, opposition to His purposes means unavailing struggle against the forces of the universe, and therefore suffering. Suffering, as the Book of Job has taught us, does not necessarily imply sin; but sin must necessarily imply suffering. The imperfect or corrupt state of society may in any given case ward off that suffering for a time from the sinner; the methods of divine government, natural and spiritual, may leave a certain scope for the maturation of sin; but simply because the universe is God's, the world cannot finally uphold and reward sin. In this connection we do not need to draw a hard and fast line between suffering as retribution and as discipline; it can be both in this world, and may continue to be both in another. Which of the two it is depends not on the suffering, but on the sufferer; it must continue to be retribution until it becomes discipline.

There are, further, social and cosmic consequences *of* as well as *for* sin. Hitherto we have looked at sin wholly in its relation to the individual; but the life of men is social, and no man lives to himself. The personal values which Christian faith upholds depend on social relationship for their realization; not less, the sins which Christianity condemns are committed at the cost of society, as well as of the individual. Perhaps there is no sin which a man can commit which does not, directly or indirectly, affect his fellows; the sin of which the secret is locked in the chambers of a man's heart will yet affect his relationship to others in many subtle and far-reaching ways. To realize this is to know that sin is no merely private affair between a man and his Maker, nor one hereafter only at the judgment-seat of Christ to be revealed. It is already registered in its consequences for other men's lives, and committed to tablets which the corruption of death cannot touch. It has already passed beyond individual control, unchanged for ever by the remorse or penitence of him who was responsible for it. These social consequences are visible to all when they consist of disgrace or penury for a man's family, the legacy of disease or vicious tendency to his children, the ruin of those who pay the price of his greed or ambition. The sufferings of others

entailed by sin are often the only effectual means of
bringing home to the sinner what sin is. But the conception gained is very inadequate until the less obvious
consequences also are seen, and, in particular, until the
wrong done to other men is recognized as a wrong done
to God. Here the Christian emphasis falls with all its
weight; it amounts to saying that we *are* dealing with
God in dealing with our fellows. A new and lurid light
is cast on sin, when the sunlight of God is reflected back
to us from the agonized eyes of those we have made to
suffer; in such a case the quality of self-reproach is quite
other than that which would spring from the blunder or
inadvertence causing similar pain to them. But there is
more than this. Beyond and above the suffering which
sin begets, it is the prolific incentive and inducement to
its repetition in other men. A man may refuse to beget
children because of some taint in his blood; he cannot
help some sort of spiritual paternity for good or evil in
other lives. To measure the consequences for which each
is responsible is of course far beyond our powers. But it
is clear that, in a very real sense, by example and influence, by silent attitude or spoken word, every one of us
contributes to the mass of social influences which oppose
God and beset man for evil. We refund by our own
voluntary act the evil influences that have helped us
to sin; we have a partnership in racial corruption. Instead, therefore, of regarding sin as the *necessary* consequence of racial corruption, we should regard the present
condition of the race, the moral disorder of the heart
within and of the life of family, Church, and State without,
as the monument erected by successive generations to
record their opposition to the kingly rule of God.

(*d*) *The cosmic significance of sin.*—We have seen that the necessary consequences of an act of sin are guilt, penalty, and social corruption; we have now to form some conception of what sin must be to God, if it means all this to man. We cannot conceive of sin as being in itself other than evil, both to Him and to us. The stepping-stones by which men rise to higher things are their dead selves, not the sin that killed the self. To ask men to believe that they will one day come to look on their past sins as so many blundering steps upward, is to ask them to wrong the consciousness of guilt which is a capacity of natural manhood. It is perfectly true that the consequences of sin which have been indicated can be transformed into sources of blessing by the subtle alchemy of God. But sin itself remains a positive evil in its two principal aspects. As the quality of the evil will expressed in particular acts of sin, it is ultimately enmity to God, a challenge to His character, purposes, and authority, which continues until the evil will becomes the good will. The technical name for this change is "regeneration"; for Christian faith, it is due to what may be called the dynamic action of grace (*infra*, p. 321 f.). But if we imagine that penitence entirely disposes of sin in relation to God, we are open to Anselm's trenchant criticism: "Thou hast not yet pondered how great is the significance of sin" (*Cur Deus Homo*, i. 21). There is a quality in the act of sin which he expressed by saying that a single look contrary to the will of God would purchase too dearly a universe of worlds. The act of sin passes into an unalterable past—unalterable, at least, in the sense that not even God Himself can make it not to have been.

The penitent sinner can sometimes do a little to modify the social consequences of his sin; what he cannot touch is the fact that he has sinned. What must this fact mean to God, or, rather, this series of facts, as He surveys the whole cosmic process in the light of His purpose for man? Even if it be true of the goal that He shall see of the travail of His soul and be satisfied, what of the process? If sin were to God, as some have held, no more than a phase of human development, necessitated by the evolutionary process, clearly there would be no difficulty here; the process of spiritual development would be as natural to God as any organic process. But this would make our consciousness of guilt an illusion, and for that reason has already been rejected. The Christian conscience condemns sin as that which ought not to have been; the condemnation derives its very character from the belief that it is an echo from the tribunal of God. Here, then, is the double problem set to grace by sin. The sinful will must be won from itself into filial obedience to God; the sinful past must be so transformed that it shall no longer be a blot on God's universe. In the former case, the task of grace is primarily individual, because the will is individual, and secondarily social, because the ordinary path to the individual lies through the social environment which shapes him into what he is; in the latter case, the task of grace is primarily social, because the past of each man is for ever merging into the past of the race, the unceasing cosmic process which lies spread before God, and secondarily individual, because atonement for that past for which each shares responsibility is the need of each.

(*e*) *Grace as cosmic atonement.*[1]—Christian confidence
in the sufficiency of the atonement has from the
beginning held that "God was in Christ reconciling the
world unto Himself"; the atonement for the wrong done
to God, though wrought in and through the values of
human personality, is ultimately an act done by God.
The wrong done to God belongs to the eternal realm
on whose frontiers human personality has its being; the
grace of God alone can deal with that which has passed
beyond man's power to alter. The necessary condition of
the work of grace in the visible and temporal order was
the suffering which culminated in the Cross; no sinless
realization of the values of personality in a sinful world
is conceivable apart from suffering. No one formula, of
course, exhausts the meaning of the Cross; but we can
see that, whilst it dominates the world as the highest
spiritual achievement, it also shews the cost of entrance
into a world of sin, the price God was willing to pay to
achieve His purpose, the measure in time of His eternal
grace as well as a manifestation of the magnitude of sin.

The Cross of Christ, considered as the culmination
of the life which gives it significance, is a unique
realization of the values of human personality,[2] because
Christ stands in a unique relation to the Father. It
thus becomes not simply part of a particular instance of
the realization of human personality, but the realization
within history of the divine self-sacrifice. The fact of

[1] The subject technically belongs to a different department of Christian
doctrine, that of soteriology. But the doctrine of sin would be a torso without some brief indication of the connected doctrine of grace. Further, the
statement here outlined specially emphasizes the close relation between
"justification" and "sanctification."

[2] See *The Cross of Job* (1916), *The Cross of Jeremiah* (1925), and *The
Cross of the Servant* (1927), by H. Wheeler Robinson.

sin has called forth the greater fact of the divine purpose, manifested in Christ, to conquer both the past record and the present activity of sin. If we try to think of the world without Christ, we must think of its sinful history as the defeat of God. But the Christian consciousness of salvation in Christ implies that the world is transformed in God's eyes by the presence within it of Christ. The grace of the Cross is triumphant in cosmic significance over the dishonour of sin to God. Where sin abounded, grace does much more abound. There could have been Incarnation apart from the need for atonement; but the grace of *this* Incarnation in a sinful world is greater than anything we can conceive God to have done apart from that need. Sin is not effaced by the atonement in the sense of being made to vanish from the cosmic record, nor is it merely outweighed by a greater quantity of virtue; we have rather to think of the introduction of a new "value" of *divine* personality into history, even through man's sin—the "value" of sacrificial love. This is God's victory; sin is overruled for good in the whole world-order, as it is in individual Christian experience;[1] through the Cross history, though with sin, is made a nobler and more glorious thing to God than it could have been without sin. This cosmic transformation is the work of Christ. The dark wave of sin, dashed on this "Rock of Ages", is made to flash beauty from its myriad elements in the sunlight of divine grace.

---

[1] In the microcosm, as in the macrocosm, reconciliation to God does not alter the fact of past sin; but all the consequences of sin are transformed by the new relation to God. The consciousness of guilt is interpenetrated by that of divine forgiveness; the penalties of sin, so far as they remain, become elements of discipline; the social results of sin, though never overtaken, form a constant stimulus to Christian service.

If the atoning work of Christ thus consists essentially in lifting the whole cosmic process to a new level, it must benefit the whole race. There is atonement for the sin of every individual, whatever his contribution to all the sins of the race. The only conceivable exclusion from its benefit will spring from persistence in sin, which is by definition wilful rebellion against the divine purpose for man. Even God cannot coerce such an evil will into willing acceptance of His grace. On the other hand, our penitent faith in Christ brings a spiritual union with Him which has a double result. The fellowship in the new society He has created carries with it the consciousness of reconciliation with God, the conviction that sin is forgiven, the trust in divine atonement for sin, here formulated as the vision of a cosmic history transformed through Christ. But this fellowship is also the family of those who do the will of God; union with Christ involves experience of the new dynamic of regeneration. The purpose of God must be realized in us as well as for us. The "subjective" aspect of atonement, as it is technically called, is needed to complete the "objective." In this intimate and inseparable relation of Christ's work for us and Christ's work in us, the essential unity of Christian experience is revealed.

We may see this more clearly by thinking of the worth of *Christian* personality to God and the significance of what may be called its "complementary cross-bearing." In the glory of the original act of grace by which God in Christ prevails over sin, no man can share. But any interpretation of the Cross which emphasizes its intrinsic rather than its transactional worth, *i.e.* its positive contribution to cosmic history, must also recognize the

presence of its spiritual principle in the world both before
and after its historic manifestation.   There have been
many partial realizations of the values of human personality, both within and without Christianity; perhaps all
of them have met with their meed of suffering in conflict
with an alien environment.   We can think of them all
as either anticipations or consequences of the coming of
Christ, and as having a real, though subordinate, part
in what has been the divine aim throughout—the spiritual
up-lift of the cosmic process.   Is it too much to say
that there must be no page of history telling of a godless
world triumphant over God?   Perhaps there is more
than Scholastic fancy in the demand made by Anselm
that there shall be elect of God in every generation.
Not only are we able to recognize the spiritual kinship
of men to Christ, and their own individual contribution
to the cosmic realization of the divine purpose which is
supreme in Him, but Christian doctrine demands that we
do recognize it.   The teaching of Christ lays an emphasis on
cross-bearing, of which the significance is only seen when
we remember that for Him its meaning is not the petty
annoyances caused by our own follies, but the burdens
necessarily accepted in the path of definite obedience.
Paul's consciousness of being crucified with Christ, which
must mean so much more than loyal discipleship or
mystical union, points to a fellowship in cross-bearing,
which becomes explicit where he says: " I rejoice in my
sufferings for your sake and fill up on my part that
which is lacking of the afflictions of Christ in my flesh
for His body's sake, which is the Church."   We do not
need to shrink from this large view of complementary
cross-bearing because it links Christ too closely with

man; it is the false isolation of the Cross from life that tends to rob it of reality; the Cross reveals its glory the more to us as we interpret it in the light of the noblest records of man's suffering for others. Vicarious suffering in its widest aspect becomes indeed a partial solution of the great mystery of pain; it helps us to explain that residuum of suffering which is not penalty and not discipline, but something which grace has made its own for the salvation of the world. Perhaps there is no innocent suffering that does not carry in its heart of sorrow the possibility of a service like that to which the prologue to the Book of Job testifies—the answer to the challenge of man's worth to God.

We have here, then, a conception of cosmic atonement which recognizes the unique and central place of Jesus Christ, whilst uniting to Him in social solidarity all whom His spirit inspires. Their contribution to the realization of God's purpose is ultimately His, as we shall see in looking at that other aspect of grace known as regeneration.[1] The victory of grace over sin is continually being won in and through them. Yet their own peace does not rest on their own achievements, which flow from the new relation in which they stand to God through Christ. It rests on their conviction of the worth to the Father

---

[1] We approach in this way the historical issue between Catholic and Protestant anthropology; are we to regard sanctification as the ultimate condition of justification, or justification as the fountain-head of sanctification? The answer implied above is that justification and sanctification ought not to be so contrasted, since they both spring from the relation of the believer to Christ. Salvation is not of merit, but of grace; yet the grace of Christ is the gift of both energy and peace. The Protestant emphasis comes nearer to the truth, notwithstanding the scholasticism of its original statement; the attitude of faith in justification implies the implicit energy of sanctification.

of the Son's life and death, and their conscious fellowship in the new social order which centres in the Son. For just as the consequences of sin must be social, man being what he is, so the consequences of the work of Christ must be felt through all who are in social relationship with Him. The ultimate unity of that which we have analysed into cosmic and regenerative grace is shewn by the fact that they are inseparable in operation; the new relation of the believer in Christ to God is one of membership in a redeemed cosmic order and of participation in an individually regenerative principle. Thus we recover that unity of "subjective" and "objective" interpretations of the atonement, which characterizes the Pauline presentation and springs from the unity of the Christian life itself. The advantage which may attach to this way of interpreting the reality of the atonement lies in the attempt to put into modern terms and conceptions that which older "objective" theories expressed by metaphors and figures to many minds no longer satisfactory. Instead of an animal sacrifice, or a commercial payment, or the infliction of a penalty, or the public recognition of authority in the interests of government, it is the category of development to which our thoughts are lifted—a category which has become the "second nature" of so much of our thinking at the present time. We raise no standard external to God, to which He must be expected to conform, but we recognize that His holy purpose for man must be realized, and that the sin of man must be not only forgiven but conquered, and conquered on the arena of history as well as in the heart of the individual. The statement does not deny the truth variously expressed by the metaphors of sacrificial ritual, private debt, penal suffering, public expediency—it insists on "objective" atonement as necessitated by the nature of sin; but it expresses that truth through another metaphor, more congenial to our present thought —the metaphor that can be drawn from the flower in the crannied wall, the metaphor of growth applied to the long perspective of cosmic history. The briar is transformed by the ingrafted rose.

(*f*) *The Spirit of God in the Christian life.*—The work of divine grace in cosmic atonement is integrally united with its dynamic regenerative activity in the individual life; the two are but different aspects of the unity of God's purpose to save men from sin, and of the accomplishment of that purpose through Jesus Christ. He has shewn us the nature and goal of human personality; He has atoned for our sinful failure to realize that nature and reach that goal; He has become the principle and centre of the fullest development of human personality yet known to us. What Christ has to do for us, in this last respect, is to bring to realization the possibilities of our nature interrupted or defeated by the sinful will. Sin is the intruder, not Christ; His work is essentially the true development of that which personality has in it to be, apart from sin. Clearly this way of conceiving the Christian life carries with it certain large assumptions; it assumes the universal relation of man to God and the universal possibility of higher development on the one hand; on the other, the spirituality of human life, its membership in or kinship with a spiritual order which makes possible effective response to the influences of that order. Both

21

assumptions underlie the Gospel as proclaimed by Jesus and His apostles; both have been sufficiently emphasized in the preceding statement.

There is general agreement in the testimony of religious experience, Christian or non-Christian, to the fact of dependence on higher life for the true realization of the lower; indeed, this is one of the central elements in any attempt to define religion. In the history of the Christian Church we have seen the abiding conviction that there was no salvation for man without grace. When other truths, such as human freedom, were thrown into conflict with the truth of grace, the Church was more ready to sacrifice the truth of freedom than the truth of grace as the source of the higher life. Indeed, there is much in the most profoundly religious experience to warrant the sacrifice, so long as we remain in the realm of religious feeling;[1] man has and can have no thought of his own strength when he really stands in the presence of God. A man who is converted in the New Testament sense is one who has surrendered to forces immeasurably greater than anything he has of himself; one who has awakened to the overwhelming consciousness of a spiritual world brought to a focus before him in the Person of Christ; one who finds the little bay of his individual life, with all its little pebbles, and little shells, and little weeds, flooded by the tide of a great deep, over which the very Spirit of God broods. It would be to repeat more

---

[1] A typical modern attitude to the problem here raised is expressed in Harnack's comment (*Dogmengeschichte*[3], iii. p. 229 n. (E.T. vol. v. p. 249); cf. Loofs, *Dogmengeschichte*[4], p. 438): "Semi-Pelagianism is no 'half-way-house', but wholly right as a theory, if a theory has to be formulated, whilst wholly wrong as an expression of self-judgment in the presence of God."

grossly the folly and impertinence of Canute's courtiers
for a man to measure himself with that measureless
sea. In the realms of spirit, as of nature, we rule by
obedience; the world seems made for each of us,
through the pressure of God's hand in outward
Providence and the mystic breath of God's Spirit in
the most sacred hours of life; we depend on God, and
even the most grudging recognition of our independence
seems out of place. The apparently antithetic line of
human freedom is reached from different data. Yet,
however great be the difficulty of the metaphysical
correlation of spiritual dependence and moral independence, it is certain that no practical difficulty arises
for religious experience. Its orthodox formulæ have
usually emphasized the divine influences, and rightly,
though sometimes to the point of denying the human
contribution; but in the experience itself there is the
intimate blending of human and divine personality in
subtle ways defying our analysis; man, in fact, becomes
deeply conscious of his moral responsibility when most
fully aware of his absolute dependence on God. To
the metaphysical problem we shall return. In regard to
the religious experience, it is enough to note that
temporal and spatial figures are inadequate and
mechanical suggestions are misleading; the activities of
man and God are both present, not intermittently, but
throughout the whole extent of religion that is moral.

The dependence of the Christian life on God for its
realization is expressed in Christian doctrine by the
characteristic conception of the Spirit of God. We
have traced the development of this conception through
the Old Testament and into the New, where it gains

a new and overwhelming significance through its application to Christ. The historic facts of the life, death, and resurrection of Jesus are made by Paul the vital points of connection between man and God—points through which the Spirit of God acts, or with which God's Spirit is identified. The essential thing, in summary statement, is that in relation to Christ men have to do with God, and may experience in themselves the energies of God. We have as much of God as we get through Christ; we think of God as the God and Father of our Lord Jesus Christ. The Spirit of God, whose presence in the believer's heart makes the new life of sonship, is the Spirit of Christ, or is Christ Himself, for the Spirit is God present with us, and we find Him present in and through Christ. Here, then, we have the dynamic of the Christian life, the power of God unto salvation; the life of faith is essentially the life of dependence on Him who dwells in the heart by its faith. There is here, obviously, an element of intelligent knowledge concerning Christ, and faith must have its preachers; but the chief and central thing is the new dynamic, the whole resources of the Spirit of God, through which not only Christ is raised from death, but every one also who is crucified with Him in spirit.

There are doubtless many problems here for Christian thought, but there are none that need obscure the possibility of the continuance of this New Testament experience. The chief problem is that of the relation of history to experience, the dependence of faith on a series of historic events in the remote past. This crucial question cannot, of course, be discussed here; it must be sufficient to point out the spiritual view of all history which our discussion implies. If history be subordinated to a divine purpose, and can issue in no irrational blind alley, then the central place Christ has attained will be maintained. But a central place in the time-order implies a corresponding place in the eternal; history is somehow the underside of spiritual reality, and the flow of phenomenal events is controlled, with all its contingencies, to a spiritual purpose. The eternal is manifested in the temporal; without the eternal there would be no temporal. We are compelled to deal with the eternal through the temporal, for only in this manifestation is it known to us. It is this blending of the temporal and the eternal which makes the central mystery of personality. We come to love wife, child, parent, with an infinity of trivial circumstance interwoven with the course of our love, but not less with a wealth of universal meaning in that love, which we never need to unlearn. There may be much in the circumstances of the Incarnation that is of little significance for the spiritual destinies of man. But in our relation to the historic Person made known to us in and through all these circumstances, we find ourselves in a relation to God which is its own highest evidence. Faith projects itself into the unseen realm after the risen Lord, and finds Him there, and, in finding Him, finds God through Him. However true it may be that God has many channels for His Spirit, and many ways of leading human personality to the realization of His purpose, the path that takes us farthest is that which the risen Lord makes for man in the trackless realms of the Spirit. The personal relation to Him may be the simplest and most human, as it was during His earthly life; but it rises into a relation to God in which the historical manifestation becomes the channel of energies creative of a new life.

Since this new life is the unanalysable offspring of the marriage of the human spirit to the divine, we may look at it either from above or below with characteristic differences of aspect. Regarded from above, it is initiated by what is usually called "regeneration", a descriptive term borrowed from the New Testament metaphor of a new "birth." Regarded from below, the entrance into this new life is known as " conversion ", a term figuratively suggesting change of moral attitude. In regard to regeneration, the metaphor itself suggests that an introduction into a new level of existence, with characteristic qualities, is intended; that is to say, we have something analogous to the transition from chemistry to biology, and again from biology to psychology. In each case we note the entrance of new factors which cannot be explained wholly in terms of what went before on the lower plane, though all that is true of the lower plane remains true when lower elements are incorporated into the higher. The Christian life which can claim any historic continuity with the experiences described in the New Testament is life on a higher plane of being than that of human personality in general, though it gathers up into itself all that belongs to the lower planes, natural and spiritual. We may have many individual cases on or near the boundary line we choose to draw, just as we have crystals that simulate life, and animal psychology that may puzzle us to distinguish it from self-consciousness. But there can be no doubt that Christian life as a whole has usually claimed for itself a distinctive character and source, the character being manifested in conduct, and the source being the Spirit of God in Jesus Christ. For those who do not challenge that claim, the chief problem is the relation of this second birth to the first. The broad answer here intended has been implied above. If all men by virtue of their human personality stand in some sort of spiritual relation to God, and if regeneration be entrance into the life of conscious sonship to God, we must regard regeneration as the normal and "natural" completion of what was begun in the first birth. This view, of course, implies nothing to make regeneration less wonderful, less an introduction into a new order of life, for we have already urged that personality itself lies above the level of naturalistic development. The reality of personality is simply lifted by the Spirit of God to a new level in order to carry its promise and possibilities to completion. This is in direct opposition to the view of regeneration required by any theory approaching the Augustinian, which assumes the total corruption of the will and presents regeneration in sharp antithesis to what has preceded. But such a theory as the Augustinian is not required to explain the fact that regeneration implies conversion or moral change. The new life is the life of a new morality higher than the old, as the character and life of Jesus are higher than that of other men; the newness is not destroyed by recognition of the fact that there are many moral levels in the life of men prior to regeneration. The metaphor itself becomes misleading so soon as we forget this. In this connection we must notice the existence of those who have been called the "once-born "[1] in distinction from the "twice-born." There are

---

[1] Cf. James, *The Varieties of Religious Experience*, pp. 80 f.

men of undoubted religion who pass into the filial relation
to God by what seems a continuous natural development,
without the travail-pangs of the second birth. This
simply illustrates the individuality of the whole experience and the incompleteness of the metaphor of
"birth" to express all we mean. If the Spirit of God
brings a man into the realization of the Christian
values apart from the normal Christian experience, we
must simply enlarge our conception of what Christian
experience is.

The psychology of conversion brings home to us the
intense individuality of the Christian life. Apparent
similarity of experience may spring from a common type
of doctrine or the traditions of a particular religious community. Unconscious suggestion and imitation play
their part here as elsewhere. But underneath all this
there is the incommunicable inner self, usually inarticu-
late, yet always unique. Conversion is the conscious
surrender of this inner self to the energies of the Spirit of
God; Christian conversion implies that they are, in one
way or another, mediated through Christ. The variety of
conversion-experiences, when the external pressure of
conformity to type is allowed for, reflects the variety of
the individual self and of the angle of its vision of God in
Christ. The broad distinction between "subjective" and
"objective" views of salvation introduces us to one of the
most prolific sources of variety; conversion may be
primarily moralistic by its conception of Christ as an
example and attractive influence, or "religious" in its
conception of Him as a fulcrum of divine grace. The
contrast between what are called "instantaneous" and
"gradual" conversions may be largely explained by

psychological differences of temperament.   Modern psychology has here rendered an important service to the doctrine of conversion by its theory of sub-consciousness.   There is much in our psychical experience which seems to spring from what lies just outside the circle of consciousness, in some sense of it, but not in it.   This dim realm forms a sort of storehouse for the human spirit, and the storekeeper may forget or remain unconscious for a long time of what is there.   In this sub-conscious laboratory of the soul, all sorts of operations may conceivably go on in waking life, just as we know they often do in sleeping life.   Here may be deposited the raw material of convictions of which the activity at some crisis is always startling and dramatic—convictions of which the substance has been built up, like some coral reef, beneath the visible ebb and flow of the great deep.   In this way the subconsciousness may serve to bridge over many apparent gaps in the life of the conscious self.   What distinguishes an "instantaneous" from a "gradual" conversion may be simply the "possession of a large region in which mental work can go on subliminally, and from which invasive experiences . . . may come."[1]   In all this, the constant relation of the natural to the spiritual is illustrated in striking ways, as is the case also when we turn to the connection between adolescence and conversion, which modern inquiry has emphasized.   Statistics prove that

[1] James, *op. cit.* p. 237.   What is said above does not raise the further question, whether " the 'more', with which in religious experience we feel ourselves connected, is on its *hither* side the subconscious continuation of our conscious life " (*ibid.* p. 512).   Certainly this is not a complete statement of the spiritual relation of man to God, as implied by the Christian doctrine of the Holy Spirit.   But, acknowledged as partial, it may help us retain the " open window " to wider reality, which characterizes ancient rather than much of our modern psychology.

the majority of conversions belong to the years of adolescence—the years from about thirteen to seventeen,[1] when the physical basis of life is so radically affected and the claims and calls of the larger life are so deeply felt. Many of the experiences that have figured so largely in narratives of conversion—deep melancholy, anxious doubt, emotional abandonment, expanding ambition—are most intimately linked to the new consciousness of sex and the expansion of the physical, intellectual, and moral life which accompanies this consciousness.   There is, of course, no reason why the Spirit of God should not brood over the waters of this deep as over any other; indeed, there is every reason why the higher possibilities of life should be thus brought home to the young man or woman at the threshold of wider relationships.   "It is only in that freshness of our time that the choice is possible which gives unity to life, and makes the memory a temple where all relics and all votive offerings, all worship and all grateful joy, are an unbroken history sanctified by one religion."[2]

The most universally recognized elements of Christian conversion are repentance and faith; "they are the natural and only suitable acts for one who wishes to turn from sin to God and goodness."[3]   They present no particular problems from the standpoint of the present discussion; they are the acts of a morally responsible person brought into relation with Jesus Christ, and so under the influence of the Spirit of God.   They are not independent acts done prior to the reception of that influence, neither are

---

[1] Cf. Pratt, *The Psychology of Religious Belief*, pp. 218, 219.
[2] George Eliot, in *Felix Holt*, p. 385 (of a moral decision in youth).
[3] Clarke, *An Outline of Christian Theology*[11], p. 401.

they experiences of the Spirit's activity in which human personality is purely passive—an impossibility in the case of any act which is truly moral. The presence of the higher life as revealed in Jesus Christ means the moral condemnation of the lower and the purpose to renounce it; this is the attitude of penitence, which runs from conversion onwards through the Christian life. Side by side with it, and giving vitality and actuality to it, there is the attitude of Christian faith. It is the response of the whole personality to the appeal of the larger life of God in Christ; it is the personal trust which goes out to find that larger life; it is the primary condition of all Christian experience, for it is the upward thrust of the new life towards the light and air and warmth it needs. Psychologically, it involves elements that are intellectual and emotional and volitional; the variety of the self will display itself here as elsewhere in the proportion of emphasis on these elements. Ultimately, it rests on a "value-judgment" of the infinite worth of all that God in Christ is to the soul—a value-judgment as rational, though as undemonstrable, as those which underlie the assumptions of science and ethics.[1]

The technical name for the process of development into which Christian repentance and faith form the natural entrance is "sanctification."[2] Christian conversion is the initiation into the fuller realization of the specific Christian "values" of personality. Christian salvation lies essentially in fellowship with God, and this is morally and socially conditioned. The social conditions will form the subject of the next section; the most striking of

[1] Cf. W. Adams Brown, *Christian Theology in Outline*, p. 382.
[2] For the companion conception of "justification", see pp. 319 f.

the moral characteristics can all be developed from the example of the Cross of Christ.   Here we have the heroic element, the venture of faith, which must enter into every life of high endeavour; the sacrifice of self which is the genuine discovery of life; the confidence in victory through defeat which marks the whole ministry of Jesus, onwards from His acceptance of the laws of the Spirit in the desert of temptation.   Christian sanctification is defined in terms of Christ's Person and life; in Him we have the goal of Christian development.   Here, again, we meet with the variety of individual development, found in conversion and illustrated in all phases of Christian experience.   There is no one mould of saintliness; there is no one specific means by which the highest saintliness can be attained.   What is common to all is dependence on the Spirit of God, whose presence is felt in so many ways and through so many agencies.   All that is developed in Christian character is defined for the Christian as "the fruit of the Spirit"; there can be no division of the product into "natural" and "spiritual" virtues, because there is no such division of the man; he is compact of both.   From this union of "nature" and "spirit" spring the conditions of the process, its slow and partial realization, its frequent interruption, the task left undone at death.   But over against the task that seems illimitable must be set the consciousness of un- limited resources that accompanies the highest range of spiritual life.   Amid the broken vow and the frequent fall, there can still be an ultimate fidelity of spirit to the vision of conversion.   It has well been said that the importance of conversion is constituted by its power to shew to a human being, though transiently, " what the

high-water mark of his spiritual capacity is."[1]   That
capacity is found by the Christian in his relation to God
in Christ—a relation expressed by the doctrine of the
Spirit of God.   Instead of speaking, as has been done, of
the Spirit of God in the Christian life, it would be truer
to speak of the Christian life in the Spirit of God; for
throughout that life we find the expansive sense of entrance
into a larger experience.   This, then, is what a metaphysic
must find room for, if it is to be called Christian, and
what our theological formulæ must not obscure in their
desire to escape heresy—a personality which is able to
realize its own will in the freedom of moral choice
between alternatives, yet to find its true realization and
freedom only in surrender to God, where its individuality
is maintained in and through moral and spiritual union
with Him.

   (g) *The relation of the human will to the divine.*—
Throughout both the historical review and the constructive statement, we have been repeatedly thrown
back on the ultimate fact of human personality and
the culminating problem of its relation to the divine.
Here we have found the centre from which the many
problems of sin and grace all radiate; our interpretation
of them has been in terms of this relation.   The relation
itself we cannot possibly reduce to a formula; but the
experience of its practical meaning is open to every
Christian life.   There is an intrinsic quality in such life
which we express by calling it eternal, and we mean that
the values of personality so realized are due to the
immanence of God in human life and belong already to
the unseen world.   That world we cannot hope to express

---

[1] James, *op. cit.* p. 257.

adequately in terms of what is visible; we can do no more than reverently tell to one another what we see as in a mirror darkly, knowing how much is left for the direct vision which higher life may possess.

The general assumptions of Christian theism are that God is "omnipotent", unless it be thought that He limits Himself by the creation of finite personality, possessing moral freedom; that His cosmic purpose is gracious towards all men, all having some subordinate part to play and being in some real sense His children; that His activity is ever directed towards the achievement of that purpose, subject to the conditions He has chosen. The cardinal assumption of the Christian doctrine of man we have seen to be the reality of his moral freedom, within the definite limits of his inherited nature and social environment; ordinary experience of life shews us the very varied use made of this freedom by men, though all have sinned and come short of the glory of God; Christian experience finds itself dependent on fellowship with God in Christ for the noblest and fullest realization of this freedom. If we try to conceive the relation of man to God in the interests of the possibilities of freedom alone, we find how easy it is to slip into quasi-Deistic statements, and to isolate man from God; if we think only of what salvation means, we are apt to make human experience the finite and partial aspect of the God-consciousness and to accept a quasi-Pantheistic metaphysic. The only path between this Scylla and Charybdis seems to be recognition of divine self-limitation; God has called into being, through the whole cosmic process, persons so far akin to Himself that they can enter into real fellowship with Him, yet so far able by

their constitution to choose good or evil that the fellowship into which He invites them is always moral.   The
evil they may choose cannot be in Him ; it can be at all
only through the permissive aspect of His self-limitation ;
He suffers this, in order that from its possibility He may
reap His cosmic harvest of moral fellowship.

From such a statement, it follows that the only dualism
Christian thought can allow is that of opposing wills
—the human and the divine.   There is, indeed, much
in our experience that seems at first sight to point to
a profounder dualism, such as that of rival world-rulers,
or matter and spirit, or rival kingdoms of light and
darkness.   In that intensity of moral conflict which most
earnest Christian lives experience, sin is naturally regarded
as having objective existence, as being an external enemy.
This may be embodied in a doctrine of evil spirits, which
beset man, as God does, behind and before.   All we can say
of man's opposition to God is that it need not be ultimate,
and that experience hardly requires such speculations to
explain it.   The natural tendencies and instincts, which
have no moral quality till taken up into moral consciousness, are so constantly brought into the service of the
evil will that the conception of the sensuous as essentially
evil is bound to arise.   Again, the social expression of
the evil will is so tenacious and continuous that the world
can be presented (cf. the Johannine doctrine) as a rival and
enemy of God.   But natural and inevitable as such forms
of expression are, the only enemy of God our Christian
thought can recognize is neither the nature He made nor
the world He made for it, but the finite will to which
God permits, in our present experience, the exercise of
its freedom.   The mystery of pain, as of death, is partly

explicable from the conditions of human development; but the mystery of moral evil finds no solution, save in the will of rebellious man.

It goes without saying that, from the standpoint of the present discussion, the doctrine of predestination in its stricter sense has no place in Christian doctrine. In the broad and general sense of a divine purpose which is to be realized—a goal to which all things shall ultimately contribute—it is, of course, essential to our conception of the relation of the divine will to the human. The reason for rejecting the Augustinian or Calvinistic form of predestination is simply its ultimate inability to account for moral responsibility. The same objection cannot lie against divine prescience, however difficult it be for us to state. Christian faith in the divine providence cannot rest in the thought that God is ignorant of our destiny until we realize it, or that He takes no thought of that morrow as to which our anxiety is wrong. The Providence of God must, indeed, be such as leaves room for the contingency which is a mark of human action. The divine foreknowledge is, accordingly, sometimes presented as a foreknowledge of alternatives; different paths lie before us, but God stands at the end of each and allows for the possibility of this particular choice, like a skilful chess-player. This explanation is certainly inadequate; it conceives God too Deistically, and leaves us without Him in the crucial hour of our choice. Appeal can, however, be made to the analogy of human foresight. In the large majority of cases, we know what a familiar friend will do; yet our prevision does not affect his freedom. It can be urged that God's prevision, entirely accurate though it is from His perfect knowledge of the self and its circumstances, similarly leaves human freedom intact. So far as this argument simply appeals to the distinction between human prevision as discursive (moving from point to point) and divine as intuitive, it hardly meets the chief popular difficulty—that divine foreknowledge of any kind implies fatalism. But those who feel this difficulty forget that the divine foreknowledge is in no case accessible to us. Our decisions are made in absolute ignorance of it, and it cannot therefore fetter our choice. Thus there is full scope for human contingency; for divine foreknowledge does not enter as an operative factor into our volitional activity. In this way, divine foreknowledge appears to be not irreconcilable with that freedom which is demanded by the Christian doctrine of sin, whilst it is certainly not more difficult to conceive than the interpenetration of human life by the divine which is demanded by the Christian doctrine of grace.

It is in regard to our conception of the final issues of human destiny that the relation of the human and divine wills becomes our acutest problem. We have set aside the doctrine of election, in the sense of any exclusive choice to salvation, whilst maintaining an election to service as an essential element in all salvation. But the problems men once felt under the ecclesiastical forms of this doctrine are not banished by its modification. There remains too much diversity in the moral attitude and conduct of men for any easy dogma of universal salvation. Within the limits of our experience, we see not only the surrendered will of the Christian passing into the harmony of moral union with God, but the will surrendered to a servitude of sin, which points to an increasing degradation, if not destruction, of personality. The moral tragedies of our

22

experience are too many for the confident assertion that there can be no final tragedy of human destiny, no will of man unwilling to turn to God. We cannot, indeed, be satisfied with the thought of everlasting rebellion against God and the punishment it must involve, for God is not victorious whilst there is one recalcitrant will. But we cannot be satisfied, either, with any theory of conditional immortality which hides God's failure rather than avoids it. The only sure footing for our thought seems to be in the confidence of a divine victory that will be unbroken by unconquered soul or unredeemed human failure. The will of man cannot, indeed, be subjugated from without. To be won at all, it must be won through spiritual relationship, since God is Spirit. But the infinite resources of grace forbid us to think that God has not means of bringing every self He has created into His home, though the paths be as varied as the lives. If freedom has issued in the practical universality of sin, we may at least hope that it will issue, through the divine grace, in the universality of salvation, though in both cases the very nature of freedom forbids dogmatism. The compasses of death draw but a narrow horizon, after all, around our point of birth ; a land of far distances lies beyond, and its resources may well be vast enough for every life to which personality can be attributed. As for the King of that land, clouds and darkness are round His face, but righteousness and justice are the visible pillars of His throne.

5. MAN IN SOCIETY.

(a) *Individual development socially conditioned.*—The Christian doctrine of man is primarily concerned with the individual life. Jesus dealt with men one by one, as they will hereafter stand before Him at the judgment-seat. He brings home to men their individual sin; He calls them into an individual relationship with God; He teaches that each life projects its individual qualities into the next world. The same emphasis recurs in the Pauline doctrine of sin and grace, and in its ecclesiastical developments. We have found the mystery of evil to be ultimately the offspring of individual freedom, though its actual form and extension are socially mediated. The experience of salvation is initiated by the individual attitude of faith. The harvest of life, with which the fields of time are white, is one of personal values, garnered into the individual soul and carried through the lonely valley of death into the eternal realm. These values, indeed, suggest their own continuance and expansion in more perfect forms of society beyond death; but it is through individual lives, not social forms, that the visible world is linked to the invisible. This marked emphasis on individuality is characteristic of Christian doctrine.

All this in no way denies or neglects the truth that progress in social order is a part of the divine purpose for man, and that the service of man is co-operation with God. The lower order does not lose its intrinsic value because it prepares for the higher. The magnitude and detail of Nature must have their own meaning for God as well as their ministry in the evolution of man. In like manner, we cannot think of Him as indifferent to the progress of man himself in all that belongs to his social welfare. But neither can we be satisfied with the far-off goal of a perfect social order on earth, to reach which numberless individuals have been sacrificed. In their spiritual passion they may forget themselves and desire only to contribute to the ideal future of their fellows; we cannot think that God forgets them or throws away the individuality He has been at such pains to create. In comparison with His higher purpose, as Christian faith interprets it, all social conditions must be regarded as simply a higher stage in the development of individual personality, just as biological conditions formed a lower. The peril of any corporate identification of Christianity with particular forms of social theory—a peril very real at the present day—is one of false emphasis. The lesson of history is that there has been a continuous development of Christian life amid constantly changing social forms; slavery, serfdom, and modern labour are but different planes on which the same spiritual issues have been encountered. It is with these spiritual issues that the Christian gospel is directly concerned. It seeks the betterment of society primarily that its message may be the better heard.

Whilst Christian doctrine thus unmistakably emphasizes the individuality of any true development of human personality, it not less clearly recognizes that such development is possible only in and through the various social relationships of life. The Christian ideal of character can become real only in the various forms of human intercourse. Each widening circle of social relationship makes or can make its peculiar contribution. In the home the child may learn obedient trust and the parent the larger life of love. In the fellowship of the Church we realize our own needs and possibilities the more clearly in finding that they are shared by

others. Our dependence on others is usually brought
home to us by the daily work; our responsibility for
others finds opportunity in the larger life of the
community. These, of course, are commonplaces; but
we are apt to forget that it is Christianity which has made
them common in Western civilization.

(*b*) *The basis of Christian brotherhood.*—Whatever be
the actual forms of human society, Christian faith is committed to their interpretation in the light of the Christian
idea of man. That idea carries at its centre the conviction of the infinite worth of human personality to God.
The consciousness of a common humanity, the natural
and instinctive sympathy of an unspoiled heart with the
life of others, the patience begotten through long experience
of human frailty, are all properly enlisted in the scope of
Christian love for others. But the claims of that love are
so great, so far beyond the natural reach of the majority
of men, that it can only thrive as something more than a
name when its highest principle has been grasped and
loyally accepted. Jesus deliberately connects Himself
with the lowliest of His brethren, and bids us see Him
in them; He claims of us, in our spiritual attitude to the
germ of possibility in our brother, what would be natura
in us only towards its noblest development. If it
be said that this claim is explicit in relation to the
Christian society only, it is implicit in the Cross in relation
to all men. The ultimate basis of Christian brotherhood
is the grace of atonement and regeneration, universal in
its offer, whatever be ultimately true of its acceptance.
Jesus died for man's sake; for His sake man has a new
value in Christian eyes. This, the Christian is bound to
say, was my brother worth to God, whether or not my

brother has yet been drawn by the Cross into the new society through which the life-blood of Jesus pulsates. We meet no man whose potential membership of that society we can deny. At man's worst, he is still one of the race to which Christ belongs by His human nature; at his best, he is a member of the spiritual society, the family of God, *i.e.* those who do the will of their Father. Man enjoys fellowship with God only so far as he is taught by Christ to think and act towards other men, in his own finite measure, as God thinks and acts towards them. Few thoughts are more humbling, because more capable of revealing the half-heartedness of our faith in Christ, than our shrinking from this claim. It was this that sent Francis back to kiss the leprous flesh; it is this that often tests our Christian manhood in less romantic ways. How many men would dare to say that they had lived a single day under the mastery of this vision of the ideal manhood of each person they had met? Yet the sentiment of brotherhood goes but a little way without the principle, and the principle will be inoperative without the faith on which it rests. We cut the nerve of Christian character when we allow the demand for that faith to be put aside in our inmost heart. The Christian doctrine of man requires that we strive to think habitually of all with whom we have practical relations as natural or spiritual children of the one Father, themselves conscious or unconscious of their position, loyal or disloyal to their spiritual relationship. The limits of "my neighbour" in the parable are marked by the road on which I journey, not by my likes and dislikes. The example of Christ is sufficient on this point. He applies His principle according as each successive day offers occasion. He takes life as it comes, and allows it to prescribe the opportunities, because it is in the hands of God.

(*c*) *The inter-relation of human and divine fellowship.*— The specific application of this principle to the different spheres of human fellowship naturally lies beyond the limits of this discussion. In the normal life, home and Church and State form the successive circles of growth, and that which lies nearest is most sacred. It is from the home that Jesus has drawn His most significant metaphor to describe the relation of God to man, and it is the home which can contribute most to make that metaphor a spiritual reality. But we must not think of the values of human fellowship as merely illustrative of the relation in which we stand to God. They are both educative and constitutive. As educative, they are seen to depend on such intrinsic principles and qualities as redeem them from all provinciality. The astronomer never expects to find some corner of the universe in which Newton's law of gravitation does not apply; the prophet does not hesitate to believe that his own heart can be a true revelation of God's. There can be no human friendship that is not potentially a preparation for fellowship with God; if we have not loved the brother whom we have seen, we have lost our chance of training in the love of the unseen God. But there is a deeper aspect of human fellowship than this. The social relationship constitutes in a real sense within its own range our fellowship with God. The Christian doctrine of the Spirit requires our conception of God's presence in every life; the metaphysic of personality requires that life be in Him and He in it. There is a simple truth, devoid of all pulpit rhetoric, in the assertion that face to face with our fellowman, in the ordinary ways of daily life, we are face to face with God. Here God meets us, using man, the highest product of the evolutionary order, for the vehicle of His manifestation. Our duty, so conceived, becomes a trust and a test; and the recognition of our duty is the measure of our ultimate faith. That God seeks us in the disguise of humanity is perhaps the necessary condition for any love of the highest for its own sake. It can be no ground of complaint that Mordecai comes to call us to our opportunity clad in sackcloth and ashes; that is the principle of the Incarnation in its wider aspect. Even the mystic, with his immediacy of experience, cannot afford to forget that human personality is our closest approximation to the divine.

6. Conclusion.

(*a*) *Historical continuity of the Christian idea of man.* —The aim of the present chapter has been to state in modern terms the essential features of Christian anthropology. These have been found to be its emphasis on the worth of man to God as spiritual personality, its practical recognition of an individual self, possessing moral freedom and responsibility, its condemnation of sin as that which ought not to be, its assertion of human dependence on divine aid for the realization of spiritual possibilities, its definition of personal development in terms of social relationship. These elements in the idea have been presented as mutually consistent, though passing beyond our powers of complete statement; nothing in modern science necessarily conflicts with them, whilst much of the higher thought of to-day is in harmony with them. Yet they are not the product of modern thought; they themselves have largely helped

to produce it. They are so involved in the commonplaces
of our Western civilization that we may easily take them
for granted and forget the claims of their ancient and
noble lineage. But how impressive is their history in its
unbroken continuity! In the Providence of God, through
the dim travail of desert tribes, a nation was born that
they might be, and, as a nation, was crucified that its ideas
might become Christian. Within that nation arose a Man
unique in all the generations, who taught these truths
and gave them the simplicity of His lowly life, the
dignity of His arresting death, the prophecy of His
victorious resurrection. From Him, and through Him,
they became the foundation of the Gospel proclaimed by
an ambassador great in thought as in deed—a Gospel
of which Paul was not ashamed, because it proved itself
the power of God unto salvation. The Church received
them, learnt in weary controversy their unsuspected
problems and in moral failure their high demands;
she interpreted them through the categories of Greek
philosophy and Roman law, enlarging their application
or debasing their content through the light and shade
of many centuries. At length the unity of the
Church was rudely broken, that the unity of spiritual
truth might have free course to prevail; these elements
of the truth as to man's nature ceased to be the pre-
rogative of the Church that they might the better
penetrate the higher thought and life of men. They
often fulfil their mission to-day through other sacraments
than those of the Church; they are the secret sanction
of uncovenanted codes of honour, and provoke prayer
to God by altars that have known no human con-
secration. In the crucible of modern thought, they

have been purged from the dross of centuries, and shine more brightly freed from antiquated psychology and faulty exegesis. Next to their intrinsic truth, their continuity with the New Testament and the Old gives them an authority which is reinforced by the racial progress they have largely inspired. They come to us with an historical momentum that can hardly be exaggerated ; the study of their development yields not only insight into their inherent depth of meaning, but confidence in their essential vitality and permanent authority.

(*b*) *Some rival conceptions of human nature.*—From the other great religions no rival anthropology comes that has any promise of successful appeal to the progressive nations of the West. Buddhism is of the East eastern; it may attract the weary Western here and there by its very denial of the individuality with which his whole life pulsates, but Eastern life and ideas must conquer Western before Buddhism can be a world religion; on the other hand, the Christian idea has amply shewn in history its inherent and adaptive universalism and the truth of its claim to be the faith of both East and West. From the thought of the West have come many challenges noble and ignoble. Few have had more majesty of outline, more statuesque dignity of form than Spinoza's resolution of human life into the transient expression of the eternal Substance; but the altar of intellectualism claims too great a sacrifice when we are asked to confess our life one long illusion. Materialism, such as Haeckel's, is plausible to those only who ignore the most important data of human nature, and it can enlist no first-rate thinker of to-day in its defence. At the present time, two movements or tendencies supply conceptions of human nature in practical competition with the Christian doctrine of man. The first of these is the naturalistic. In the more rigid form of scientific determinism, this tendency has probably spent its force; the earlier dogmatism is breaking or has broken up, especially through the newer conceptions of matter and energy. But there remains the general influence of the theory of evolution, as supplying a sufficient hope of progress for those optimistically inclined. The attitude is more or less vague, but in the opinion of a competent observer it forms "a new sort of religion of Nature, which has entirely displaced Christianity from the thought of a large part of our generation."[1] The obvious criticism of this conception is to ask what lies at the end of cosmic evolution, what is its purpose and its goal—a question which necessarily raises the very problems which the Christian conception of man seeks to answer. But besides this vague hope of betterment, there is an acuter form of present-day naturalism, which may be said to have found its most brilliant exponent in Nietzsche. Here a one-sided view of natural law supplies the idea of Nature as essentially egoistic, and a justification for sheer individualism. In actual life this conception underlies much of "the gospel of success." In Nietzsche's expression of it we have the direct antithesis to the Christian idea of morality, which he regards as the protective device of the weak against the strong. He therefore dismisses this "slave-morality" of meekness and self-sacrifice, in favour of aggressive self-assertion.[2]

---

[1] James, *The Varieties of Religious Experience*, p. 91.

[2] For a clear statement and criticism of the Nietzsche-naturalistic position, see Dewey and Tufts, *Ethics*, pp. 368–375.

In criticism of this attitude, it may be said that Nature is social as well as individualistic, altruistic as well as egoistic; that it is quite inadequate to consider human nature from the biological standpoint alone; and that the corrective of the attitude lies in a larger spiritual culture, which does justice to those characteristics of human nature which exalt it above the nature of the mere animal. Ultimately, of course, the movement represents that deification of the " natural " man, against which the Christian conception of man has always had to contend ; obviously weak as a theory, it finds its strength in the tendencies behind it, which are represented in every one of us.

The second movement to be noticed is so protean in its varieties that it is not easy to reduce it to a single formula. It includes Buddhistic theosophy of the Blavatsky type, " Spiritualism " in the popular sense of the term, and " Christian Science." Any detailed criticism of the various cults which belong to this group would be out of place here; they may be all regarded as more or less misguided protests against materialistic conceptions of man. As a religious movement, " Christian Science" doubtless attracts by the directness of its message and the reality of the success of " Mind-cure " within a limited range of cases; these contrast favourably with the unreality in much Christian worship, caused by the gulf between actual experience and devotional vocabulary. The very vagueness in the pantheistic background of " Mind-cure ", which condemns it in the eyes of the thinker, probably makes it attractive to those who are repelled by what seems the over-precision of Christian " dogma." In regard to Spiritualism, we have to reckon with the desire for verification, the appeal to " fact "

that may make the future life credible.[1] The Christian
answer to this demand is that the ultimate evidence of
moral truth must be itself moral, and that instances of
spirit-return, even if verified, could not form the proper
basis for a moral and spiritual faith. In regard to the
whole group of tendencies here in view, the great corrective
for many who are influenced by them would be a deeper
knowledge of history. This would display both the
vitality of Christian ideas in their long development and
the earlier rejection of similar superstitions. The chief
practical lessons Christian teachers may learn from the
popularity of these cults is the need for so stating the
Christian conception of man as to supply a real moral
and spiritual dynamic, and a clear answer to the hopes
and fears of man as to his nature and destiny. The
writer has heard the prevalent tone of Protestant Churches
to-day described as that of a "coarse mysticism", *i.e.*
an intermittent surrender to pietistic conceptions and
spiritual ideas, which in no way interferes with the
materialism of the ordinary life. So far as this is true,
it explains the rise of these spiritistic cults, which are, at
any rate, in earnest, and it points to the deeper sincerity
by which they may be successfully met.

To the two main tendencies alien to the Christian
doctrine of man which have been indicated, two others

---

[1] This is well represented by F. W. H. Myers, whose pilgrimage through
Hellenism, Christianity, and Agnosticism to the goal of Spiritualism is so
clearly told in his *Fragments of Prose and Poetry*. Elsewhere, he tells us
that he was compelled to abandon the Christian faith by its want of evidence
for the Resurrection of Christ; of his final position, he says: "This fresh
evidence—while raising that great historic incident of the Resurrection into
new credibility—has also filled me with a sense of insight and of thankful-
ness such as even my first ardent Christianity did not bestow" (*Human
Personality*, vol. ii. p. 295).

might perhaps be added, on a somewhat wider review, which deserve at least to be named here. One is the whole tendency of the coarser sacramentarianism (as, *e.g.,* in crude Catholicism), which, although within the Christian Church, is obviously as alien to that conception of Christian doctrine which has been presented in these pages as any of the explicit rivals. The other is the whole movement of modern humanitarianism, when it becomes, as for some men it does, a species of religion. Here the practical agreement with much of Christian ethics goes with a refusal to accept Christian doctrine. But the logic of humanitarianism points forward, as in Comte, to a religion ; its morality really involves the creed of the worth of human nature, the possibility of its redemption from evil, the confidence in winning a cosmic victory. But where shall we find the guarantee of such a victory save in God ? and where a "plan of salvation" nobler than the Christian faith hallowed by many centuries of endeavour ? The nobler the morality of social life, the less can it dispense with Christ to maintain its purity and sustain its effort.

(*c*) *The adequacy of the Christian idea of man.*—One further question must be faced, which perhaps involves a more subtle peril to the Christian idea than any of its avowed rivals. Is that idea, the history of which has been outlined in these pages, adequate to cover the realities of human life? or is it simply an important contribution to modern civilization, of which the absolute claims fell with the theory of the absolute authority of the Church ? Granting that the Christian idea expresses adequately enough the worth of the Good, and that it can be reconciled with the True, what of the Beautiful, which is to many a religion, though it has little place in the creed of the Gospels? What shall we say, again, as to the practicability of Christian ideals in modern society?

The answers to these questions would require a philosophy of art on the one hand, and a philosophy of society on the other. But, as criticisms of Christianity, they spring from judgment on the stages of a process as though they were its final goal. It is true enough that the unity of thought and feeling and will in personality points forward to the ultimate unity of their full satisfaction, the ultimate harmony and kinship of the True, the Beautiful, and the Good. But neither the historical conditions of the Incarnation nor the practical exigencies of concentration in conflict for the Good have allowed the full unity to be reached. Puritanism, even of the iconoclastic sort, has its justification. If it be granted, as it must be, that the moral life claims intrinsically supremacy within the cosmic process over both intellectual and artistic culture, then it may be the condition of the recognition of that supremacy that the legitimate if subordinate claims of other sides of personality temporarily suffer. The perils of what is called the artistic temperament are a sufficient comment on this. In regard to the larger problem of modern civilization, it is true that the Christian idea of man finds realization to-day in individual men rather than in societies. But is not this what we should expect from the necessarily individualistic appeal of the Gospel? Does not the hope of the kingdom lie in the working of the leaven? However difficult it may be for us to conceive the full application of Christian ideals to social and international relations—*e.g.* non-resistance and the absolute condemnation of war—we must not be guilty of the fallacy of denying its possibility *when the conditions of society are changed.*[1]   It is the Christian faith that these conditions will change, and that the Christian conception of man will be the most powerful instrument in effecting that change.   It may be that, within the earthly horizon, the Christian conception of man will always be an ideal unrealized ; even so, the steady progress towards it will be the best school of personality.   Such thoughts carry us forward, as does so much else in our experience, to a larger life beyond death for the completion of what we are.   " Beloved, now are we children of God, and it is not yet made manifest what we shall be.   We know that, if He shall be manifested, we shall be like Him, for we shall see Him even as He is."

[1] This important limitation of our estimate of what is possible is well stated, though in another realm, by W. Reason, in *Mansfield College Essays* pp. 133–148 (" The Constant and the Contingent in Economics ").

APPENDIX

———◆———

RECENT THOUGHT ON THE DOCTRINE OF SIN

THERE would be general agreement that no one had
written on this subject in recent times with more acute-
ness and distinction than Dr. F. R. Tennant. His
Hulsean Lectures of 1902 had dealt with *The Origin
and Propagation of Sin*, whilst the larger book of 1903,
*The Sources of the Doctrines of the Fall and Original
Sin*, gave historical support and elucidation to his main
contention—the separation of actual sin from " original
sin," and the explanation of the former by evolutionary
science. The chief criticism of this position was that
any " explanation " of the universality of sin by reference
to man's animal origin seemed to make actual sin just
as inevitable as did the doctrine of original sin—a result
which is felt to contradict both Scripture and conscience,
for sin is not sin if it is inevitable. In 1912, Dr. Tennant
met this criticism by his book, *The Concept of Sin*, an
exceedingly able and closely reasoned essay in definition
which avoided some of the less guarded statements in
the earlier work, and clearly asserted man's full moral
responsibility. Thus he writes (p. 78) that sin " can
never be a *necessity* for man at any stage of his development," whilst (p. 234) " Characters are not made evil in

23

the strictly moral sense by environment or by disposition." The special value of this book is that it challenges all who work at this subject to clear thought and exact definition of what they really mean by " sin." Dr Tennant's own definition is " moral imperfection for which an agent is, in God's sight, accountable " (p. 245). This, of course, rules out the term " original sin " as a misnomer, and sharply distinguishes the historical fact of moral imperfection in the race from the individual volition which essentially constitutes sin. The standard of judgment is relative to man's knowledge of God's requirements ; the wrong act consists in the choice of a lower end when a higher is consciously present. The material or occasion for the sin is supplied by the natural impulses, which in themselves are not sinful or morally evil. There is no sin in the fact of temptation, and there is no guilt where there is no moral accountability

Mr. S. A. McDowall's *Evolution and the Need of Atonement* (1912, 1914) dealt with sin on similar lines of evolutionary science. It is maintained that " in all life there is something of freedom, even in response to environment " (p. 50). Man's inturning of consciousness upon itself introduces a larger degree of indetermination, as compared with that at lower levels, so that man can choose whether he will identify himself with what Bergson called the *élan vital*, or whether he will sin by " enlisting his will on the side of the downward forces that rule matter " (p. 68). Sin is conscious opposition to the Divine purpose as revealed in the vital impulse (pp. 122, 132). Sin is thus not merely negative as being failure to moralize the natural, but positive, as the conscious misuse of experience (p. 82). The consequences of sin, whilst continuing to be consequences for the race, become punishments for the individual (p. 137). There is no race-sin because there is no race-indetermination (p. 143). "We cannot say that the sin is hereditary —that it will reappear in the next generation, and the work of Weismann forbids us to build anything on the inheritance of acquired characters, such as the tendency to misuse freedom (p. 146) . ." "sin, or rather the tendency to sin, becomes hereditary in the race, not by the inheritance of acquired characters, but by the creation of an environment which acts, on a community of self-conscious beings, towards the cessation of selection of those with the higher instincts " (p. 150). Another way of putting this is to say that in human as distinct from animal society, individuals committing anti-social acts (and all sins are of this character) are not so rigorously eliminated, so that racial evil tends to increase.

This recognition of the social tradition of moral evil is a conspicuous feature of the modern doctrine of sin. "Social heredity, as taught by Ritschl, is a wiser assertion than brutal or Adamic heredity, not simply because it lies within a truly moral region, but because it points to a combination of corporate wrongdoing with individual guilt " (R. Mackintosh, *Christianity and Sin*, 1913, p. 162). But this particular reference to " corporate wrongdoing" may illustrate Dr. Tennant's criticism of the use of terms, as does the companion statement on the previous page, " inheritance, if it does not exclude real guilt, at least seriously lessens responsibility." The issue can hardly be left in that hesitating fashion, after Dr. Tennant's incisive discussion. The

modern doctrine of sin must face the issues as boldly as
did the Augustinian, and not shrink from the consequences of its own logic. The natural is not to be confused with the moral. Canon Lacey, in his brief but
illuminating study of the Augustinian position (*Nature,
Miracle, and Sin,* 1916), refers to the persistent delusion
by which " we are led to discover evil in nature. .
Because it would be an evil thing for me to lay waste
fenced cities into ruinous heaps, therefore I infer that
pestilence and earthquake are evil ; because I know that
it is wrong for me to be like horse or mule, whose mouths
must be held with bit or bridle, therefore the qualities
to the likeness of which I have sunk seem to me evil in
themselves " (p. 142). This author argues that the
Augustinian scheme is coherent in its assertion that the
world is good, sin only excepted.

In 1917 there appeared two important books of opposite tendencies which indirectly concern us, and may
remind us that the doctrine of sin can never be adequately
studied apart from the doctrines of grace and of God.
These two books were Principal Oman's *Grace and
Personality*, and Professors Otto's *Das Heilige* (Eng.
tr. by Harvey in 1923, as *The Idea of the Holy*). The
moral emphasis of the former leaves no room for anything but the moral relation of the individual, as actual
sinner, to God. The consequences of sin remain after
penitence, but their meaning is transformed. " To be
justified, then, is not to have the consequences of sin con-
doned or even obliterated, but so to be reconciled to God
in spite of sin that we can face all evil with confident
assurance of final victory over it, and by God's succour
transform all its consequences, whether the evil be

natural or moral, the outcome of our own sin, or from our necessary fellowship with others in His family" (p. 221, 2nd ed.). On the other hand, Otto's well-known and widely influential book urges that we cannot reduce either our idea of God or our reaction to that idea to a purely moral or rational content. The conception of the wrath of God—say in the ninetieth psalm—illustrates this overplus in the idea of the holy. There is a hidden depth in God—" the numinous "—which cannot be rationalized or moralized by us. This provokes in man such confessions as those of Isaiah and Peter (" Woe is me! for I am undone. . . Depart from me, for I am a sinful man, O Lord ") : " these outbursts of feeling are not simply, and probably at first not at all, *moral* depreciations, but belong to a quite special category of valuation and appraisement . . . the feeling of absolute ' profaneness ' " (Eng. tr., p. 53). In God there is "the positive *numinous* value or worth, and to it corresponds, on the side of the creature, a numinous *disvalue* or ' unworth ' " (*ib.* p. 53). It is this aspect or element that gives the peculiar religious quality to sin. " Mere ' unlawfulness ' only becomes ' sin,' ' impiety,' ' sacrilege,' when the character of *numinous unworthiness* or *disvalue* goes on to be transferred to and centred in *moral* delinquency " (p. 54 f.). The guilt of a bad action is to be clearly distinguished from its moral pollution. This religious element can be neither moralized nor conceptualized, a fact which condemns all quasi-mathematical theories of atonement. The whole chapter (viii.) on " Sin and Atonement " should not be overlooked by the student of the doctrine of sin. It offers a sort of religious parallel to Dr. Tennant's moral differen-

tiation of sin and " original sin." Dr. Tennant argues
that sin is not sin unless and until it is moralized ; Dr.
Otto, that sin is not sin unless and until it is *numinous*.
The fuller recognition of the *numinous* in the doctrine
of God might have important consequences for the
doctrines of sin and atonement It would leave room
for both the lower sub-ethical and the higher " mystical "
element, as well as for the central content of morality,
and would thus remind us of the mystery of personality,
human and divine, the invisible rays beyond the visible
spectrum.　Negatively, it would exclude both the
rationalization of the Atonement and the attempted
" explanation " of that abuse of freedom we call sin.
Moreover, the weakening of the sense of God's majesty,
and of the reality of the " wrath " of God, has proceeded
side by side with the decay in the consciousness of sin ;
a recovery along one line would assuredly encourage a
recovery along the other.

The 1920 volume of the *Encyclopædia of Religion
and Ethics* contained a representative and judicial
article on " Sin (Christian) " by Professor H. R. Mackintosh, comparable in quality with the excellent article
by Kirn in the *Realencyklopädie für protestantische
Theologie*, which was on an ampler scale (xix. 132–148).
The criticism of Dr. Tennant's position made by Dr.
Mackintosh may be quoted : " Penetrating and illuminative as Tennant's work is, it may be doubted whether
his ' logically perfect ' concept of sin will be approved
by those who hold with St. Paul and Augustine, not to
speak of numerous modern students of society, that men
are ethically as well as physically involved in the unity
of the race, and that we desert experience if we ignore

either aspect of sin, the voluntary or the constitutional."
In the same article the irrationality of sin is clearly
stated : " To refer moral evil to the free activity of will
is less an explanation in the proper sense (all true explanation being teleological) than an implicit admission
that sin is radically unintelligible—the one thing in the
universe rightly to be called ' irrational,' as not merely
an irreducible fact, but the negation of all rationality.'

The best recent attempt to rehabilitate the ecclesiastical doctrine of sin is that of Mr. E. J. Bicknell (*The
Christian Idea of Sin and Original Sin*, 1922), though it
must be admitted that the doctrine suffers a " sea change "
in the process. He fully recognizes that the present
position of biology allows of no dogmatism on the inheritance of acquired characteristics, but says, " We are
content to maintain that whatever be the issue of the
debate, the inheritance of evil tendencies can be maintained independently of physical transmission " (p. 40).
He argues that " original sin may be inherited through
our social environment " (*ib.*), in the sense of " the
movement of the race away from God's purpose "
(p. 42). That this movement is a fact would be admitted
by most Christians ; the point is whether, especially in
view of Dr. Tennant's cogent criticism of the use of
theological terms, this racial evil ought to be called by a
name which denotes something very different from social
heredity. Nor can it be held that the social environment
replaces heredity as an explanation of the universality
of sin, such as the doctrine of original sin did supply.
The moral evil of my social environment is no doubt the
occasion of my temptation, but it cannot be made the
cause of my sinful volition without being open to the same

criticism as the doctrine of original sin itself—that it demoralizes sin. "Original sin" ought to denote at least sin that springs from origin rather than from social environment, and the term did denote this in the Augustinian theory, which is the classical form of the doctrine. It is perilous to use the term in a sense so different from that for which it was framed, and the peril is illustrated by a footnote on p. 118 of Mr. Bicknell's book, where he says, "This is not the place to discuss how such freedom from original sin was possible in one who was truly man," with apparent reference to the Virgin Birth, rather than to the social setting of the Incarnation. A not less perilous tendency to confuse the natural with the moral is seen on p. 111, where the statement is quoted with approval that "it is the malignity of the struggle that has produced the venom of so many reptiles." Surely such a statement projects a moral meaning into the term "malignity" which is quite out of place in the evolutionary struggle for existence ; it would be as reasonable to say that it is "selfishness" that makes an infant suck. As a matter of fact, Mr. Bicknell elsewhere agrees with Dr. Tennant that "this material, the instincts and impulses that we inherit, is non-moral " (p. 100). We may, however, sympathize with Mr. Bicknell's insistence on the moral disorder of human society as a problem to be faced on its own account, and with his protest against the easy-going optimism as to the progress of the race—a protest made not less by Dr. Tennant (*The Concept of Sin*, p. 278). But the way to deal with this further problem of racial evil is not to entangle it with that of individual sin, but to view it from without as a fact of history. However responsible

I am for my individual contribution to the moral disorder of the world, and to whatever degree that disorder is the occasion of my temptation, the world's wrongdoing cannot be represented as an individual volition, as it could when Adam was conceived either as the historic head or the corporate representative of the race.

In the same year (1922), there appeared a more ambitious book on *The Doctrine of Sin*, by Mr. R. S. Moxon, which usefully traces the history of the doctrine from the New Testament times onwards, down to and including modern theories. The final chapter, professedly constructive, and entitled " The Psychological View of Sin," is unsatisfactory It seems not simply dangerous, but also untrue to say, " We must think, then, of sin as something inseparably connected with personality " (p. 246), or that " The sense of sin takes the same place in the spiritual development of man as is taken by the vital impulse in the physical " (p. 228). Much is said about the sublimation of instincts, in terms of psycho-analysis, but little that contributes to the real problems of the doctrine " Original sin " is defined (p. 246) as " the universal tendency in man, inherited by him from his animal ancestry, to gratify the natural instincts and passions and to use them for selfish ends " —a definition which raises more questions than it answers.

A convenient and competent approach to the doctrine of sin from the standpoint of modern psychology and the comparative study of religion may be found in the chapter devoted to " Sin and Repentance " in Principal Selbie's book, *The Psychology of Religion* (1924). The consciousness of sin has developed from that of a breach of custom and taboo into a genuine moral and spiritual attitude, and (in this broad sense) " the history of religion justifies us in regarding it as universal " (p. 228). On psychological grounds we may say that " at the root of every sinful act or disposition lies an ultimate choice of the lower and an inhibition of the higher springs of action " (p. 242). Psychologically, this volition is " largely a question of attention " (p. 235), which we can at least previously control, affected by the content of the subconsciousness, for which we are ultimately responsible (p. 236). It does not seem possible to explain volition without resort to a self or personality (p. 231), whilst conscience is itself, as moral consciousness, the expresssion of that personality as a whole (p. 234). In regard to original sin, our rejection or modification of the theory must not blind us to the existence of facts which it professed to explain ; but original sin cannot mean original guilt, and we should speak of inheriting, not sins, but only a tendency to sin (p. 241). Attention is called to the fact that psychotherapy distinguishes moral disease from sin as that condition in which morbid complexes give rise to uncontrollable impulses (p. 229). Dr. Selbie, of course, recognizes that there are definite limits to the contribution of psychology to the doctrine of sin, *e.g.* " the question of freedom can never be adequately dealt with on psychological grounds alone " (p. 232).

Finally, we may open Dr. Garvie's recent book, *The Christian Doctrine of the Godhead* (1925), in order to learn how the problem of sin presents itself to a modern theologian within his general constructive statement. Whilst he criticises Dr. Tennant's use of a human (subjective) standard of judgment for the definition of sin, he agrees that "sin is a conscious, voluntary act, even although a man's own conscience is not the final measure of it" (p. 299). "We may dismiss from consideration the possibility of the transmission of moral depravity or corruption by physical heredity" (p. 307), but there is a social inheritance of moral evil, which justifies us in speaking of mankind as a sinful race (p. 311) and in saying that each child enters the world under a handicap (p. 309). Actual sin is an intrusion into God's world (p. 312), but though there is risk for the individual there is none for the universe (p. 313); God's final victory is certain, though it must be won by moral and spiritual means in order to be worthy of Him (p. 314).

As we review the course of thought on the doctrine of sin for the last dozen years, we may feel some disappointment that no contribution has been made of equal calibre with that of Dr. Tennant. The relatively small attention given to the doctrine, as compared with that given, say, to immortality, may be partly traced to the admitted decline in the general consciousness of sin, from which theologians themselves may not be exempt. There seems to be the same lack in German theology ; at least, I have found no constructive works (other than monographs on special points) which call for notice here.[1] Thus there is real need and opportunity for a book that would face the problem of "racial sin" in all its implications, with the same firm grasp and keen insight that marked Dr. Tennant's study of individual sin. The present review appears to warrant certain conclusions:

[1] A possible exception is R. Seeberg's *Christliche Dogmatik*, vol. ii. pp. 1–126 (1925).

1. The sciences of biology, psychology, and sociology have made, and may yet make, important contributions to the natural history of sin. They help us to disprove some theories of it which are erroneous or inadequate. But these sciences cannot of themselves give an adequate basis for the doctrine. The raw material with which they deal is taken up into human personality, where the issues become philosophical and theological. We must not be misled, for example, by the important contributions of psycho-analysis to psychotherapy into thinking that these are vital contributions to a *doctrine* of sin. In particular, we must beware of offering an " explanation " of the " universality " of sin from the mere existence of this raw material in the individual or the race. This is clearly said by Dr. Tennant : " The ' material of sin ' by no means suffices in itself wholly to explain or account for sin, and indeed is to be sharply distinguished from sin " (p. 140) ; yet in another place (p. 259) he writes of these propensities : " Their presence in every human being, making the inducement to sin common to all men, is the sufficient explanation of the fact that few, if any, of mankind, who possess a moral code embracing the many departments and complex relations of human life, go through this world without contracting some stain of sin." The apparent inconsistency may be no more than verbal, but most students of theology will feel that the practical universality of sin does raise questions of its own that call for a more complete answer —if only the conclusion that the freedom of personality by its very nature excludes the deterministic category of causation, and that a scientific explanation of sin is as impossible as a scientific declaration of the ultimate

destiny of the individual. Here a remark from Mr. C. C. J. Webb's *God and Personality* seems worth quoting : " The *possibility* of Sin is after all involved in freedom to choose the good ; and it would seem meaningless to find a new problem in the *reality* of what is already understood to be in a true sense *possible* " (p. 190).

2. On the other hand, the fact and nature of racial evil ought to be studied without prejudice from the historical theories known as " original sin " and " the Fall." We cannot put new wine into these old wine-skins without the inevitable result. Our social solidarity for evil is a fact of experience—but so is our social solidarity for good. We can comprehend that one evil will operating freely in a human society propagates itself by example and multiplies incentives to evil conduct beyond all human power to reckon. The sin of one will affect all ; though there are many grades of sinning, which the mouth-filling word " universality " tends to obscure. But, on the other hand, the believer in the Incarnation must maintain that the influence of a sinless will is also at work in the race, and that the victory will be with the good. Environment can save as well as destroy—so far as environment ought to be said to do either. Individual experience is endlessly repeating the story of Gen. iii., and we may speak with a certain truth of an individual " fall," though even this use of the term can easily be misleading. But the race, *with Christ in it*, is moving upwards—not automatically, and not catastrophically, but by the immanent operation of God through Christ. We should speak not of the fall of the race from some level previously possessed, but only of

the failure of the race (through the actual sin of its individual members) to attain to the level of God's purpose.

3. The theologian of to-day finds it impossible to draw the boundaries of doctrines as sharply as his predecessors, or to draw them over the old lines. In his endeavour to construct a dynamic rather than a dogmatic theology, he discovers the close inter-relation and ultimate unity of " doctrines " that are often handled in isolation. His central concern is with the relation of human personality to the Divine, in all its aspects, and any doctrine of sin divorced from a doctrine of grace or of God is an abstraction.[1] Now one of the most important aspects or attributes of personality is its power of transformation. At each level we can see something becoming something else within the realm of personality, something that gains new attributes without loss of the old by being taken up to the new level. Thus neural activity is transformed into sensation, and sensation into perception, and perception into conception, within the realm of psychology. So within the ethical realm, there is the lifting up of the whole closed circle of the volitional consciousness—will, motive, attention, interest—into an experience of freedom ; again, there is something more in the complex result than the sum or mechanical composition of the constituents. It is the same, also, on the still higher level of religious experience, where we first encounter sin in the strict sense, though its material content has met us as " crime " or " vice " at other levels. The new fact of sin raises two problems, or sets

---

[1] A very able study of sin and guilt in this, its true setting, will be found in H. R. Mackintosh's forthcoming book, *The Christian Experience of Forgiveness*, ch. iii.

of problems, which ought to be distinguished. There is the need for personal forgiveness, opening into the whole of the new relation of the individual to God, and including the taking up of the sinner's sin into the Divine holiness, where it is transformed into suffering—the eternal Cross of God. (The *spiritual* suffering of the saint through the sin of others is the human analogy to this.) The suffering is voluntary, but not arbitrary ; holiness cannot include sin within itself save as transformed into suffering.[1] The temporal consequences of moral evil remain, but whether they remain as penalties, or as discipline, or as opportunities, will depend on the attitude of human personality towards them ; they themselves are transformed. All this concerns the individual in relation to God ; the other set of problems arises from man's racial history, that history which is not a fiction and foregone conclusion, but a reality This must mean that racial evil is a new fact for God to face. Apart from the guilt of actual individual sin, there is the fact of the objective failure of the race, measured by the Divine standard, a failure that cannot be ignored by God. He must not only, for His honour's sake, win a final victory within the race, but He must make that racial history as a whole into a new glory of God. This is the supreme transformation being wrought by personality—that where sin abounded, grace shall yet more abound. " In fact, a sinful world redeemed by the agony of Love's complete self-sacrifice is a better world, by the only standards of excellence we have, than a world that has never sinned " (W Temple, *Mens Creatrix*, p. 286).

[1] *Op. cit.* ch. viii.

GENERAL INDEX

The numerals refer to the pages. More important references are preceded by an asterisk.

Abelard, 200.
Achan, 29 f.
Adam, *59, 73, 116, *118 f., *165 f., 184, *188 f., 198, 205 f., 211, 225.
Agnosticism, 249.
Alexander of Hales, 203 f.
Ambrose, 168, 180.
Ancestor-worship, 39.
Animism, 6 f., 152 n.
Anselm, *200 f., 313, 318.
Anthropology :
  Augustinian, 187 f.
  Biblical, *68 f., 75, 148 f., 270 f.
  Mediaeval, 197 f.
  Patristic, 156 f.
  Primitive, 5 f.
  Protestant, 221 f.
  Scholastic, 203 f.
  Tridentine, 210 f.
Aristotle, Aristotelianism, 152 f., 159, *202, 204, 214.
Arles, Synod of, 194.
Arminianism, 227.
Arnobius, 169.
Articles, Anglican, 226, 244 n.
Asceticism, 81, 172, 173 f.
Athanasius, 166 f., 180.
Atonement, 39, 122 f., *315 f.
Attritio, 197.
Augsburg Confession, 222.
Augustine, Augustinianism, 157, *160 f., 162 f., 169, *175 f., 177 n., 178, 180, 181, 183, *187 f., 192 f., 196, 215, 304 f., 327.

Bajus, 213.
Baptism, 124 f., 212.
  of infants, 183, 185, 187.
Belly, 26, 106 n.
Bentham, 260.
Bernard of Clairvaux, 216.
Blood, 13, 15, 28.
Body, 12 f., 17, 26, 72, 103, 105 *129 f., 153, 237 f., 243 f., 276.
Bonaventura, 204.
Bones, 25.
Bowels, 23, 105 n.
Bradwardine, 209 n.
Brotherhood, 87 f., 134 f., 341 f.
Buddhism, 11, 346.

Cælestius, 181, 183 f.
Cæsarius of Arles, 194.
Calvin, Calvinism, 224 f.
Carthage, Council of, 185.
Catharists, 175 n.
Catholicism, 195 f., 209 f., 258, 259, 350.
Celibacy, 135, 172.
Christ. *See* " Incarnation," " Jesus," " Logos."
Christian Science, 348 f.
Church, 32, 90, 135, 150, 155, 195 f., 226, 228, 266, 272 f., 340, 345, 350.
Clement of Alexandria, 159, 165, 173 n., 179.
" Complementary cross - bearing," 317 f.
Comte, 258, 350.

Concupiscentia, 162 n., 187, 189, 190 n., 206, 208, 211.
Confession, 196, 197 n.
Conscience, 105 f.
Conservation of Energy, 239 f.
Contritio, 197.
Conversion, 98, 124, 142, 222, 326, *328 f.
Copernicus, 232.
Creation of man, 14, 61, 242 f.
Creationism, *163, 185, 206.
Cross of Christ, 315 f.
Culture, æsthetic and intellectual, 148, 256, 284, 351.
Custom and morality, 47 f.
Cyprian, 180.
Cyril of Jerusalem, 180.

Darwin, 233.
Death, 17, 25, 39 f., 60, 67, 70 f., 100 f., 112 f., 121, 146, 166 f., 169 f., 244, 282, *285 f.
Descartes, 246, 247.
Destiny, final, 133, 337 f.
Development of doctrine, 2, 75 f., 148 f., 268 f., 345.
Diospolis, Synod of, 185.
Docetism, 173.
Donatist Controversy, 196.
Dort, Synod of, 227.
Dualism, 20 f., 25, 69 f., 74, 81, 96, 104, 115, 143 f., 161, 170, 172 f., *335.
Duns Scotus, 207 f.

Edwards, Jonathan, 223 f.
Election, 63, 132 f., 191, 225, 337.
Embryo, 13, 14.
Ephesus, Council of, 186.
"Epistola Tractoria," 186.
Eschatology, *39 f., *70 f., *79 f., 96 n., 99 f., 134, 146, 285.
"Eternal Life," 102, 103 n., 144 f. ; cf. 286.
Evil, moral, 155, 294 f. ; cf. "Sin."
as privation, 175 f.
Evolution, 164, 231, *235 f., *242 f., 263 f., 269, 347.
Exile, influence on Israel, 34, 50.

Faith, 40, 66, 84, 124, 141 f., 191, 213, *218 f., 282 n., 331.

Fall, 58 f., 73, *118 f., *163 f., 181, 183, 206, 208, 211, 296 f., 303, 306.
"Family" of God, 78, 79, 85 f., 89.
Fatherhood, divine, 65 f., 78 f., 83 f., 96 f., 143.
Faustus of Reji, 194.
Fetishism, 9.
Fichte, 249.
Flesh, *24 f., 105, *113 f., 116, 143, 144.
Formula of Concord, 222.
Francis of Assisi, 216.
Freedom, 73 f., 98 n., 132 f., 167, *179 f., 189 f., *191, 288 f., *291 f., *334 f.
and Grace, 134, 154, 156, 165, 194 f., *322 f.

Galilei, 232.
Gehenna, 102 f.
"German Theology," 217, 218.
Gnosticism, 172 f.
Gottschalk, 198 f.
Grace, 55, 66 f., 82 f., 96 f., 132, 182 f., 192 f., 201 f., 207, 208, 211 f., 214, 220 f., 224 f., 227, *314 f., *322 f. *See* "Freedom."
Greek and Hebrew thought contrasted, 152 f.
Greek influences, 104, 151 f.
Green, T. H., 250, 287, 292.
Gregory the Great, 197 f.
Gregory of Nyssa, 159 f., 162 n., 167, 180.
Guilt, 43 f., 48, 53, 55, 95, 118 f., 190, 200, 206, 225, 302, *308 f.

Hades, 170, 285.
Hadrumetum, 193.
Hammurabi, Code of, 29.
Heart, 21, *22, 78 n., 105, 106.
Hegel, 249, 295.
Heredity, 119, 237 f., 244, 305 f.
Hincmar, 199.
Historical basis of Gospel, 76 f., 324 f.
Hobbes, 247.
Human nature, unity of, 1.
value to God, 80 f., 300 f. *See also* "Personality."
Humanitarianism, 350.
Hume, 247.

24

Idealism, Absolute, 250.
Ideals, Christian, 351 f.
"Image of God," *164 f., 188 f.,
205.
Immortality, 40 f., 67, 70 f., 72,
78 n., 102 f., 169 f., *286 f.
conditional, 338.
Imputation, 219 n.
Incarnation, 79, 280, 284, 351.
Individual and society, 27 f., 134,
148, 258 f., 277, 338 f.
Individuality, 11, 27 f., 66, 72 f.,
*251 f., 264, 287.
Indulgences, 196, 197, 216.
Industrialism, 258.
Infant Baptism. *See* "Baptism."
Irenæus, 157 n., 167, 169, 179.

Jansen, Jansenism, 213 f.
Jerome, 163.
Jesus :
central place of, 2, 75, 97, 345.
and evolution, 278 f.
and the Old Testament, 77 f.
personal attitude of, 281.
as prophet, 76 f.
as Saviour, 91 f.
Johannine problem, 136.
John Cassian, 193 f.
John of Damascus, 172.
Judgment, 76, 101 f., 128, 130 n.,
140, 147 ; cf. 307 f., 338.
Julian of Eclanum, 181, 182, 186.
Justification, 122 f., 128 f., 132, 207,
208 n., 209, 211 f., *217 f., 319 n.
Justin, 164, 166, 169, 179.

Kant, 246, 248, 299 n.
Kepler, 232.
Kidneys, 23.
Kingdom of God, 66, 81 n., *83 f.,
89, 100, 262.
Kingship, divine, 65 f., 78, 83.
"Knowledge" of God, 52, 145.
Kosmos, 138 n.

Lactantius, 163, 169.
Laplace, 233.
Leibniz, 246, 247, 251 f., 295.
"Liberty of a Christian Man," 219.
"Likeness of God." *See* "Image."
Liver, 23.
"Loci Communes," 219.
Lodge, Sir Oliver, 241 n.

Logos, 136 n., 148, *279.
Lotze, 252, 254.
Luther, 156, *216 f., 272.
Lutheran Church, 221 f.
Lyons, Synod of, 194.

Man. *See* "Table of Contents."
Manichæism, 174 f.
Marx, 261.
Massa perditionis, 190, 200.
Materialism, 246, 346.
Matter, modern theories of, 240 f.
Mechanical conception of the universe,
231, 239.
Mediaevalism, 195 f.
Melanchthon, 220 f., 222.
Mercator, 187.
Merit, 53, 98, 128 f., 201, 207, 208,
226.
Mill, James, 248, 260.
John Stuart, 248, 260.
Miracle in Old Testament, 63.
Molina, 213 f.
Monism, 287.
Moral responsibility, 267, 289 f.
Morality, its union with religion,
49 f., 51, 89, 249, 267, 347, 349,
350.
Mummy, 9, 10.
Myers, F. W. H., 349 n.
Mysticism, 216.

Natural law, 238 f.
"Natural Selection," 233.
Naturalism, 249.
Nature, Hebrew ideas of, 62 f.
Neoplatonism, 153, 154, 161, 175 f.
202.
Nephesh, 15 n., *16 f., 20, 26 f., 78 n.,
100, 105.
Neshāmāh, 15 f.
New birth, 142, 326 f. ;
Newton, 232 f.
Nietzsche, 347 f.
Nous, 105 f.

Occam, 209 n.
Omnipotence, divine, 63 f., 205,
*334 f.
"Once-born," 327 f.
Orange, Synod of, 194.
Orchard, 297 n.
Origen, 161, 165, 167, 170 f., 176,
179.

Original state of man, 164 f., 188 f., 200, 205, 211.
Orosius, 184.

Parousia, 109 n., **147.**
Pascal, 214 f.
Pelagian Controversy, 178 f.
Pelagius, 181 f., 209 n.
Penance, 196 f., 202, 212, 215.
Perseverantiæ, donum, 191.
Personality :
  Christian ideas of, 3, 148, 149, 270, 271.
  corporate, 8, 27 f., 46, 121, 188, 190 n., 244.
  defined, 275.
  and evolution, *275 f.
  Hebrew ideas of, 26 f.
  modern emphasis on, 253 f.
Peter the Lombard, 203.
Philo, 151 n.
Physiology, Hebrew, 7, 11 f., 22.
Plotinus, 176 n.
Pneuma, 78 n., 105, *109 f., 154; cf. " Ruach."
Politics and religion, 90.
Port-Royal, 214 f.
Pragmatism, 253.
Predestination, 64, 133 f., 192, 198 f., 205, 222 f., 336.
Pre-existence of souls, 14, 72, 161.
Prescience, divine, 199 f., *336 f.
Prosper, 193.
Providence, 63 f., 84.
Psuche, 78 n., 105, 108 f.
Psuchikos, 105, 108 f.
Psychology :
  ancient, 6 f.
  of Aristotle, 153.
  Associationist, 247 f.
  Australian, 8 f.
  of Clement (Alex.), 159.
  Egyptian, 9 f., 20 n.
  Greek, 10, 12, 154, 157.
  of Gregory of Nyssa, 159 f.
  Hebrew, 11 f.
  Indian, 10.
  of Jesus, 81.
  Judaistic, 71 f.
  of Origen, 159, 161.
  Patristic, 156 f.
  Pauline, 104 f.
  of Plato, 158 f.
  Semitic, 10 f.

Psychology :
  Synoptic, 78 n.
  of Tertullian, 158.
  West African, 9.
Puritanism, 351.

Quesnel, 215.
Quiercy, Synod of, 200.

Rabanus, 199.
" Recapitulation," 167.
Reformation, 156, 215 f., 229, 258.
" Reformed " Churches, 223, 226 f.
Regeneration, 313, 321 f., 326.
Renaissance, 229 f., 245.
Repentance, 34, 55, 97 f., 307, 330 f.
Resurrection, 41 f., 72, 101, 130 n., 131, 146 f., 170, 173, *286 f.
Retribution, 33 f., 41, 72. *See also* " Judgment."
" Righteous remnant," 31.
Ritschlianism, 255, 256.
Rousseau, 259 f.
Ruach, *18 f., 26 f., *64 f., 105 ; cf. " Pneuma."

Sacramentarianism, 215 f., 226, 350.
Sacraments, 124 f., 196, 210.
Salvation, 67, 91 f., 122 f., 144 f., 149, 188, *315 f., 337, 339. *See also* " Grace."
Sanctification, 122, 319 n., 331 f.
Satan, 96, 117, 118 n., 140, 172 335.
Schelling, 249.
Schleiermacher, 254 f., 274, 295.
Scholasticism, 156, *201 f., 245.
Scripture, authority of, 4 f., 270 l., *274.
Semi-Pelagianism, 156, *191 f., 210, 222 n., 322 n.
Sheol, 39 f., 71.
Sin :
  consequences of, 307 f. ; cf. 316 n.
  and death, 58 f., 121, 146, 169.
  defined, *301 ; cf. 45, 51, 94, 120, 139.
  evolutionary view of, *296 f., 302.
  and grace, 42, 70, 272, 314. *See also* " Grace."
  New Testament ideas of, *92 f., 99, 116 f., 138 f.
  Old Testament ideas of, *43 f., 49, 51 f., 67.

Sin:
  origin of, 57, 58, 95 f., 113 f., 140,
    165 f., 171, 177 f., 189, 206, 208,
    225 ; cf. "Sin defined."
  "original," 58 f., 73 n., *190, 200,
    210 f., 223, 244, 269, 306.
  and suffering, 35 f., 95, 139 n.,
    310 f.
  universality of, 56, 92 f., 112 f.,
    140, 171, *303 f.
Slavery, 135, 340.
Social democracy, 264 f.
  responsibility, 90, 258 f., 266 f.
Socialism, 261, 267, 340.
Sociology, 230, 258, 259 f.
Soul, 15, 16, 17 n. *See* "*Nephesh*"
  and "*Psuche.*"
Spencer, Herbert, 246, 260 f.
Spinoza, 225, 246, 247, 295, 346.
Spirit. *See* "*Ruach*" and "*Pneuma.*"
  of God, 7, 10, 25, 27, *64 f., 70,
    74, 111, 123, *125 f., 131, 136,
    137, 144. 154 f., *323 f. *See*
  "*Ruach*" and "*Pneuma.*"
  reality of, 246 f., 286.
Spiritualism, 348 f.
State, individual relation to, 90, 135,
    260 f., 264 f., 343.
Stoicism, 151, 154, 157, 162.
Subconsciousness, 329.
Suneidesis, 105 f.
Symbolic magic, 168 n.
Synergism, 222.

Tatian, 157 n., 169.
Tennant, 73 n., 295 n., 297.
Tertullian, 157 f., 162, 165, 168, 170,
    180.

Theodore of Mopsuestia, 186.
Theophilus, 169.
Thomas of Aquino, 202, *204 f.,
    216.
Thomists and Scotists, 207.
Tolstoi, 262 f.
Totemism, 9.
Traducianism, 158, 162, 189, 206.
Trent, Council of, 209 f.
"Trichotomy," 108, 159, 160.

Universal Fatherhood, 82.
Universalism, 337 f.
Universe, man's place in, 61, 234 f.
Utilitarians, 260.

Valence, Synod of, 200.
"Values":
  æsthetic and intellectual, 148, 256,
    284.
  permanency of spiritual, 134, 254,
    282.
  of personality, 253 f., 281 f., 300 .
    339.
  social, 343 f.
Vincent of Lerinum, 193 n.

Ward, James, 250.
Westminster Confession, 226.
Will, *160, 177 f., 187, 208, *292 f.,
    *333 f. *See also* "Freedom."
"Works," 128. *See also* "Merit."
"World" (Johannine), 136 f.

Yezer hara, 74 n., 120.

Zosimus, 185.
Zwingli, 223.

INDEX OF TEXTS

In a few cases, the Hebrew verse-enumeration is followed where it differs slightly from the English.

GENESIS.

		PAGE
i.–ii. 4a	. .	61
i. 2	. .	64
i. 26, 27	. .	62
ii. 4b f.	. .	61
ii. 7	.	14, 19
ii. 17	. .	60
ii. 23	.	24, 26
ii. 24	2	114 n.
iii.	. .	59
iii. 13	. .	116
iii. 19	. .	25
iii. 22 f.	. .	60
iv. 7	6c	116 n.
vi. 1–4	. .	60
vii. 22	. .	18
viii. 21	.	57, 58
ix. 4	. .	15
xii. 5	. .	17
xv. 15	. .	39
xx. 5	. .	22
xxii.	. .	29
xxiii. 8	. .	16
xxv. 10	. .	44
xxvi. 35	.	18, 18 n.
xxvii. 45	. .	18
xxix. 14	. .	26
xxx. 2	. .	14
xxxi. 36	. .	44
xxxiv. 7	. .	47
xxxv. 18	. .	17
xli. 8	. .	18 n.
xli. 38	. .	64
xlii. 21	. .	17
xlii. 28	. .	22
xlii. 37	. .	29

GENESIS—*continued*.

		PAGE
xliii. 9	. .	44
xlv. 27	.	18, 19
xlix. 6	. .	23
l. 17	. .	44

EXODUS.

vii. 23	. .	22
ix. 14	. .	22
x. 13	. .	19
xii. 49	. .	47
xv. 8	18, 18 n.,	19
xx. 5	. .	29
xx. 22–xxiii. 19	.	53
xx. 24	. .	53
xxii. 8	. .	44
xxv. 2	. .	27
xxviii. 3	.	22, 65
xxxii. 8	. .	44
xxxv. 21	. .	27

LEVITICUS.

iv. 1 f.	. .	53
iv. 13	. .	44
v. 14–16	. .	53
v. 17	.	53 n.
v. 19	. .	44
xi. 43	. .	17
xiv. 19	. .	53
xvi. 3	. .	53
xvii. 11	. .	15
xvii. 14	. .	15

NUMBERS.

		PAGE
v. 2	. .	17
v. 6	. .	45
v. 7	. .	44
v. 12, 27	. .	45
xiv. 9	. .	45
xv. 27	.	53
xv. 32–36	. .	54
xxi. 5	. .	17
xxiv. 2	. .	64

DEUTERONOMY.

i. 16	. .	46
ii. 30	. .	27
iv. 9	. .	22
vi. 5	.	26, 108
vi. 13, 16	. .	77
vii. 17	. .	22
viii. 3	. .	77
x. 19	. .	46
xi. 10–12	. .	63
xii. 6, 17	. .	53
xii. 23	. .	15
xiv. 21	. .	46
xv. 9	. .	24
xxi. 14	. .	17
xxi. 18, 20	. .	45
xxii. 21	. .	48
xxiv. 16	. .	31
xxiv. 17	. .	46
xxv. 1–3	. .	48
xxv. 2	. .	44
xxv. 5	. .	29
xxv. 8–10	. .	48

DEUTERONOMY—*contd*.

	PAGE
xxvi. 5	242
xxvii. 19	46
xxviii. 54, 56	24
xxx. 15, 19	181
xxxii. 6	66
xxxiv. 9	65

JOSHUA.

	PAGE
vii. 24–26	29
xi. 11	16

JUDGES.

	PAGE
v.	46
vi. 34	64
viii. 3	18, 19
xi. 29 f.	29
xiv. 6	19, 64
xv. 19	18, 19
xvi. 30	17
xviii. 20	22
xix 30	47
xx. 16	43

I SAMUEL.

	PAGE
i. 8	22
ii. 12	145 n.
ii. 25	44
ii. 35	22
iv. 13	22
vi. 3, 4, 8, 12, 17	44
x. 5, 6	19
xii. 17	45
xiv. 24–27, 37	49
xiv. 33	45
xv. 3	28, 46
xv. 22	46
xvi. 7	22
xvi. 14	19, 64
xix. 20 ı	64
xx. 1	44
xxiv. 5	108
xxv. 31	108
xxv. 36	22
xxv. 39	48
xxvi. 19	30
xxvi. 21	44
xxviii. 14	39
xxx. 12	18, 19

2 SAMUEL.

	PAGE
vii. 14	66
xiii. 12	47
xiv. 1	22
xiv. 7	28
xix. 35	59
xix. 37	39
xxi. 1–14	28
xxii. 16	16, 18, 19
xxiv.	48
xxiv. 10	108

I KINGS.

	PAGE
iii. 9	22
viii. 46	56
x. 5	18, 19
xii. 19	44
xvii. 17	16
xvii. 21	17
xix. 10	16
xxii. 49	35 n.

2 KINGS.

	PAGE
i. 1	44
iii. 5, 7	44
iv. 34	24
viii. 20, 22	44
ix. 26	29
xiii. 21	25
xviii. 7	45

2 CHRONICLES.

	PAGE
vi. 36	56
xx. 35–37	35 n.

NEHEMIAH.

	PAGE
ix. 30	65

JOB.

	PAGE
ii. 5	24
iv. 9	16, 18, 19
iv. 14, 15, 17–19	25
vi. 12	24
x. 4	25
xiii. 23	44
xiv. 4	57
xiv. 13–15	40
xiv. 22	25

JOB—*continued*.

	PAGE
xv. 13	20
xix. 25–27	40
xix. 27	23
xx. 15, 20, 23	26
xxi. 6	25
xxii. 29	24
xxv. 4	58
xxv. 4–6	25
xxv. 5, 6	25
xxvi. 4	16
xxvii. 3	16, 18, 19, 19 n.
xxvii. 6	108
xxix. 11	23
xxx. 17	25
xxx. 23	40
xxx. 30	25
xxxi.	37
xxxi. 1	23
xxxi. 15	14
xxxii. 8	16
xxxii. 18	12
xxxiii. 8–12, 17, 26, 27	37
xxxiv. 11	37
xxxiv. 15	25
xxxiv. 31–33	37
xxxiv. 37	45
xxxv. 11	37
xxxvi. 16, 22	37
xxxvii. 10	16
xxxviii. 4 f.	62
xlii. 7	37

PSALMS.

	PAGE
ii. 7	66
vii. 6	23
viii. 3 f.	62
xv.	55
xvi.	41 n.
xvi. 7, 9	23
xvi. 9	25
xvii.	41 n.
xviii. 16	16, 18, 19
xix. 1	62
xix. 7	17
xix. 10	52
xix. 12	54
xxii. 1	77
xxii. 10	58
xxiv.	55
xxxi. 5	77

PSALMS—*continued.*

		PAGE
xxxi. 10 .	.	. 26
xxxii. .	.	. 55
xxxii. 4, 5	.	. 55
xxxv. 4 .	.	. 16
xxxv. 10	.	. 25
xxxviii. 9	.	. 168
xl. 6–8 .	.	. 55
xl. 9	.	. 23
xliv. 26 .	.	. 26
xlvii. 2 .	.	. 66
xlix.	.	41 n.
l. 16	.	. 55
li. .	.	. 55
li. 5	.	57, 58
li. 11	.	. 65
lvi. 5	.	. 25
lviii. 3	.	. 57
lix. 5	.	. 44
lxiii. 2	.	. 25
lxv. 3	.	. 55
lxv. 9 f.	.	. 62
lxvi. 18, 19	.	. 55
lxviii. 5	.	. 66
lxix. 5	.	. 55
lxix. 30, 31	.	. 55
lxxi. 6	.	. 58
lxxiii.	.	41, 41 n.
lxxiii. 21	.	. 23
lxxiii. 23 f.	.	. 35
lxxiii. 25, 26	.	. 103
lxxvii. 4	.	. 27
lxxviii. 39	.	. 62
lxxxiv. 3	.	. 25
lxxxviii. 5	.	. 39
lxxxviii. 39	.	. 25
lxxxix. 27	.	. 66
xc. 5	.	. 62
xcv. 10	.	. 27
cii. 4	.	. 25
ciii. 13	.	. 66
ciii. 14	.	. 25
ciii. 15	.	. 62
civ. 4	.	. 63
civ. 14 f.	.	. 62
civ. 29	.	19, 62
cvii.	.	. 55
cvii. 25	.	. 62
cxix. 73	.	. 14
cxix. 120	.	. 25
cxxx. 3	.	. 55
cxxxi. 1	.	. 24
cxxxix. 4, 5	.	. 63

PSALMS—*continued.*

		PAGE
cxxxix. 7, 8 .	.	40 n.
cxxxix. 13, 15, 16	.	14
cxliii. 2 .	.	55, 56

PROVERBS.

ii. 10	.	. 16
vii. 23 .	.	. 23
viii. 22–31	.	. 62
xi. 4	.	. 54
xiv. 9	.	. 44
xiv. 30	.	. 25
xvi. 1	.	. 63
xvi. 4	.	. 64
xviii. 8	.	. 26
xx. 9	.	. 56
xx. 27	.	16, 26
xx. 30	.	. 26
xxiii. 6	.	. 24
xxiii. 16 .	.	. 23
xxvi. 22 .	.	. 26
xxvii. 20	.	. 23
xxviii. 22	.	. 24
xxx. 17 .	.	. 23
xxx. 19	.	. 13

ECCLESIASTES.

ii. 3	.	. 25
ii. 10	.	. 23
ii. 14	.	. 36
iii. 17	.	. 36
iii. 19–21	.	. 40
v. 5	.	. 25
vii. 15	.	. 36
vii. 15, 20	.	. 56
viii. 10, 12, 13, 14	.	36
ix. 2	.	. 36
ix. 4	.	. 40
ix. 11	.	. 36
x. 4	.	. 20
xi. 5	.	. 13
xi. 10	.	. 24
xii. 7	.	. 19
xii. 12	.	. 25
xii. 14	.	. 36

SONG OF SONGS.

v. 4	.	. 23
v. 6	.	. 17

ISAIAH.

		PAGE
i. 2	.	. 45
i. 5 f.	.	. 94
i. 24–31 .	.	. 31
ii. 22	.	. 62
iv. 3	.	. 32
vi. 5	.	. 58
vi. 13	.	. 31
vii. 3	.	. 32
vii. 9	.	. 52
vii. 15–16	.	. 59
viii. 16 .	.	. 32
x. 20	.	. 31
xi. 4	.	110 n.
xiii. 18	.	. 24
xiv. 10	.	. 39
xvi. 11	.	. 23
xxvi.	.	41 f.
xxvi. 9	.	20, 27
xxix. 24 .	.	. 27
xxx. 28 .	.	18 n., 19
xxx. 33 .	.	. 16
xxxi. 3 .	.	. 25
xxxii. 15	.	. 65
xxxv.	.	. 62
xl. 6	.	25, 62
xl. 26	.	. 63
xlii. 5	.	19, 61
xliii. 27	.	. 44
xliv. 3	.	. 65
xlviii. 8	.	. 57
lviii. 1	.	. 44
lix. 19	.	. 19
lix. 21	.	. 65
lxi. 1 f.	.	. 65
lxi. 1, 2 .	.	. 77
lxiii. 15 .	.	‹ 23
lxiii. 16 .	.	. 66
lxv. 2	.	. 45

JEREMIAH.

i. 4–10	.	. 32
i. 5	.	. 14
iv. 19	.	. 23
vi. 29	.	. 32
xv. 17	.	. 32
xv. 20	.	. 32
xvii. 5	.	. 25
xvii. 8	.	. 32
xviii. 2	.	. 33
xviii. 6	.	. 63
xviii. 7 f.	.	. 64

JEREMIAH—*continued*.

	PAGE
xxiii. 9 . . .	25
xxxi. 20 . . .	23
xxxi. 29, 30 .	33
xxxi. 31 f. . .	32
li. 5 . . .	44

LAMENTATIONS.

?. 13 . . .	25
i. 20 . . .	23
ii. 11 . . .	23
iv. 20 . . .	18
v. 7 . . .	33

EZEKIEL.

ii. 2 . . .	64
iv. 14 . . .	17
ix. 4 . . .	33
xi. 19 . . .	24
xviii. . .	33
xviii. 4 , . .	33
xviii. 6 . .	53
xviii. 21 . .	33
xx. 38 . .	33
xxiv. 16 . .	23
xxv. 12 . .	44
xxxii. 22 f. .	39
xxxiii. 12 f. .	33
xxxiv. 6 . .	44
xxxvi. 26 . .	24
xxxvii. . .	13
xxxvii. 5, 6, 8	19

DANIEL.

ii. 3 . .	18 n.
xii. . .	41
xii. 2 . .	42

HOSEA.

ii. 20 . .	145 n.
vi. 6 . 51, 52, 77, 88	
xi. 1 f. . .	52
xi. 1–3 . .	66

JOEL.

ii. 28 f. . .	65

AMOS.

	PAGE
iii. 2 . .	30, 51
iii. 8 . .	52
iv. 6 f. . .	52
iv. 13 . .	61
ix. 7 . .	30

JONAH.

i. 9 f. . .	62
ii. 8 . .	27

MICAH.

ii. 7 . .	18 n.
iv. 11 . .	23
vi. 8 . .	51, 88

HABAKKUK.

i. 13 . .	24
iii. 16 . .	26

HAGGAI.

i. 14 . .	18

ZECHARIAH.

vii. 12 . .	65
xii. 1 . .	19
xii. 10 . .	65

MALACHI.

i. 14 . .	66

4 EZRA (2 ESDRAS).

iii. 7 . .	119
iii. 26 . .	120
vii. 116–118 .	120
vii. 118 . .	119
vii. 118, 119 .	73 n.

WISDOM.

ii. 23 . .	72
ii. 24 . .	73
iii. 1 . .	72
iv. 7 f. . .	72
viii. 19, 20 .	72
ix. 15 . .	74
xvii. 11 . .	107 n.

ECCLESIASTICUS.

	PAGE
xi. 28 . .	38 n.
xv. 11 . .	73
xxv. 24 . .	73

1 MACCABEES.

iv. 46 . .	74

APOC. BARUCH.

xlviii. 42, 43 . 73 n., 120	
xlix.–li. . .	72
liv. 19 . 73, 116 n.	

ENOCH.

xxii. . .	71

JUBILEES.

xxiii. 31 . .	71

TEST. LEVI.

xviii. . .	74

MATTHEW.

ii. 20 . .	78 n.
iv. 1 . .	96
iv. 4, 7, 10 .	77
v. 3 . .	78 n.
v. 9 . .	82
v. 12 . .	98 n.
v. 21–37 . .	94
v. 22–24 .	88 n.
v. 23, 24 .	88
v. 26 . .	102 n.
v. 28 . .	78 n.
v. 29 . .	103
v. 30 . .	103
v. 38, 39 .	86
v. 43 f. . .	88, 89
v. 44 . .	88
v. 45 . .	82, 88
v. 47 . .	87
vi. 10 . .	100
vi. 12 . .	92, 94
vi. 15 . .	87

MATTHEW—*continued.*

		PAGE
vi. 25 f.		84
vi. 33		85
vii. 3–5		88 n., 93
vii. 7–11		84
vii. 12		89
vii. 14		145
vii. 16		94
vii. 21 f.		84, 101
vii. 23		94
viii. 12		103
viii. 19, 20, 21, 22		86
viii. 29		103
ix. 13		77
ix. 37		93
x. 16 f.		84
x. 28		100 n., 103
x. 30		84
x. 31		81
x. 32, 33		97
x. 37 f.		85
x. 39		100 n.
x. 42		89
xi. 19		81
xi. 20–24		95
xi. 27		91
xi. 27–30		97
xii. 7		77, 88
xii. 12		81
xii. 28		100
xii. 31, 32		99
xii. 32		102 n.
xii. 35		94
xii. 40		78 n.
xii. 49, 50		87
xiii. 19		96
xiii. 38		96
xiii. 39		96
xiii. 41		94
xv. 19, 20		94
xvi. 16		76
xvi. 18		90
xviii. 2 f.		93
xviii. 7		96
xviii. 14		82, 96
xviii. 17		90 n
xviii. 21–35		89, 93
xviii. 23 f.		94
xix. 13, 14		93
xix. 16 f.		86
xix. 29		98 n.
xxi. 11		76
xxi. 28–32		94

MATTHEW—*continued.*

		PAGE
xxii. 34 f.		86
xxiii.		92
xxiii. 8, 9		87
xxiii. 23		88
xxiii. 25, 26		95
xxiii. 28		94
xxiii. 37		96
xxiv. 12		94
xxiv. 34		100
xxv. 31 f.		101
xxv. 40		88 n., 89
xxvi. 24		92
xxvi. 28		77
xxvi. 41		78 n.
xxvii. 46		77
xxvii. 50		78 n.
xxviii. 10		88 n.

MARK.

		PAGE
i. 15		92, 96
ii. 1 f.		95 n.
ii. 6		78 n., 89
ii. 6 f.		92
ii. 8		78 n.
ii. 10		89
ii. 17		92, 93, 94
ii. 27		81
iii. 28–30		99
iii. 29		92
iii. 31–35		85
iii. 34, 35		87
iv. 26–32		100
vii. 9–13		85
vii. 10–13		89
vii. 14–23		82
vii. 21		78 n.
viii. 12		78 n.
viii. 14 f.		81
viii. 15		90
viii. 35		103
viii. 35, 36, 37		100 n.
viii. 36, 37		81
ix. 23		84
ix. 36, 37		93
ix. 43		145
ix. 43, 45		102, 103
ix. 43–47		81
x. 2–12		89
x. 14		93
x. 15		93, 99

MARK—*continued.*

		PAGE
x. 17 f.		86
x. 17–22		99
x. 30		88 n., 102
xii. 17		90
xii. 26		102
xii. 28 f.		86
xii. 33, 34		88
xiii. 11		84
xiv. 21		92
xiv. 34		78 n.
xiv. 38		78 n., 81, 96

LUKE.

		PAGE
i. 47, 80		78 n.
iv. 17–19		77
iv. 19		96
vi. 23		98 n.
vi. 35		82, 87
vi. 41, 42		88 n.
vii. 36 f.		97
vii. 41 f.		94
vii. 47		97
viii. 4 f.		81 n.
viii. 21		87
viii. 55		78 n.
ix. 24		100 n.
ix. 46 f.		93
ix. 57, 58		86
ix. 59–62		86
x. 2		93
x. 22		91
x. 25 f.		86
x. 29		47
x. 30 f.		93
x. 38–42		81
xi. 18		96
xi. 27, 28		86
xii. 7		81, 84
xii. 10		99
xii. 11, 12		84
xii. 15		145
xii. 20		101
xii. 32		100
xii. 47, 48		95, 102 n.
xiii. 1–5		95 n.
xiii. 3		93
xiii. 18 f.		82 n.
xiv. 14		102
xiv. 26		85
xiv. 27 f.		86

LUKE—*continued.*			JOHN—*continued.*			ROMANS.		
		PAGE			PAGE			PAGE
xv..	•	82	vii. 17	•	141, 145	i. 3	•	114 n.
xv. 7	•	93	vii. 37	•	145	i. 5	•	129
xv. 10	•	92	viii. 12	•	137	i. 9	•	110
xv. 11–32	•	97	viii. 15	•	144	i. 16	•	126
xv. 32	•	87	viii. 23	•	137, 139	i. 20	•	107
xvi. 9	•	98 n.	viii. 24	•	139, 141	i. 21	•	106
xvi. 19 f.	•	101	viii. 32, 34	•	139	i. 28	•	107
xvii. 3	•	88 n.	viii. 42	•	142	i. 28 f.	•	115
xvii. 6	•	84	viii. 44	•	140	ii. 5	•	106
xvii. 21	•	81	viii. 51	•	146	ii. 5–11	•	128
xviii. 13	•	92, 98	ix. 2, 3	•	139 n.	ii. 15	•	107, 112
xviii. 16, 17	•	93	ix. 5	•	137	ii. 28	•	114 n.
xviii. 18 f.	•	86	ix. 41	•	138	ii. 29	•	127
xix. 1 f.	•	97	x. 10	•	144	iii. 9	•	112
xix. 10	•	97	x. 15, 27	•	142	iii. 19	•	112
xx. 1–16	•	98	x. 36	•	137	iii. 20	•	112, 114 n.
xx. 35, 36	•	102	xi. 25	•	144, 147	iii. 22	•	124
xxi. 14 f.	•	84	xi. 26	•	147	iii. 25	•	123
xxi. 19	•	100 n.	xi. 40	•	141	iv. 1	•	114 n.
xxii. 32	•	88 n.	xi. 52	•	142	iv. 15	•	112
xxiii. 43	•	97	xii. 31	•	140	iv. 20	•	124
xxiii. 46	•	78 n.	xii. 35	•	137	iv. 24, 25	•	124
xxiv. 32	•	78 n.	xii. 36	•	141	v. 2	•	124
xxiv. 47	•	98	xii. 44	•	141	v. 5	•	128
			xii. 46	•	137	v. 12 f.	113, 118, 120, 121	
JOHN.			xii. 50	•	145	v. 14	•	112
			xiii. 2	•	140	v. 19	•	121
i. 5	•	142	xiii. 20	•	141	v. 21	•	117
i. 9–10	•	148	xiii. 35	•	145	vi. 1–11	•	124
i. 12	•	141, 142	xiv. 3	•	148	vi. 6	•	129
i. 13	•	142, 144	xiv. 6	•	144	vi. 6, 17.	•	117
i. 14	•	142, 143	xiv. 19	•	137	vi. 12 f.	•	129
i. 29	•	138	xiv. 26	•	137	vi. 12, 14	•	117
iii. 3	•	142, 146	xiv. 30	•	140	vi. 16–19	•	128
iii. 5	•	146	xv. 12	•	145	vi. 18	•	117
iii. 6	•	144	xv. 22	•	139	vi. 19	•	114 n.
iii. 16	•	137	xvi. 9	•	138, 141	vi. 22	•	117
iii. 19	•	138, 140	xvi. 11	•	140	vi. 23	•	112, 117
iii. 20	•	138	xvi. 14	•	137	vii.	118 n., 120	
iii. 36	•	146	xvi. 33	•	140	vii. 5	•	114
iv. 24	•	144	xvii. 2	•	144	vii. 6	•	127
v. 22	•	140	xvii. 3	•	145	vii. 7–25	•	115 f.
v. 28, 29	•	147	xvii. 6	•	142	vii. 12	•	112
v. 40	•	138	xvii. 25	•	138	vii. 23	107, 116, 117	
v. 43	•	141	xviii. 36	•	146	vii. 25	•	107
vi. 40	•	146	xviii. 37	•	139, 142	viii. 1–14	•	127
vi. 44	•	142	xx. 29	•	141	viii. 2	•	117
vi. 48	•	145	xxi. 22	•	147	viii. 3	•	131
vi. 51	•	146				viii. 4, 5, 6, 7, 8, 9 .		114
vi. 63	•	144	**ACTS.**			viii. 9, 10	•	126
vi. 68	•	144	ii. 16	•	65, 75	viii. 10	•	110
vii. 7	•	138				viii. 11	•	131